Selected Writings of

THE
AMERICAN
TRANSCENDENTALISTS

Selected Writings of

THE

AMERICAN

TRANSCENDENTALISTS

SECOND EDITION

*Edited, with an Introduction
by* GEORGE HOCHFIELD

YALE UNIVERSITY PRESS NEW HAVEN & LONDON

For Mayflower

First published as a Signet Classic in 1966
Second Edition published by Yale University Press in 2004

Printed in the United States of America.

Library of Congress Control Number: 2004106606

ISBN 0-300-10281-X (pbk.)

A catalogue record for this book is available from the British Library.

10 9 8 7 6 5 4 3 2 1

CONTENTS

III. THE VOICE OF THE DIAL

INTRODUCTION

I

Like those of all movements in intellectual history, the outlines of American Transcendentalism are indistinct. Its beginnings merge with the liberal tendencies of Boston Unitarianism; its endings are a confused record of unforeseeable careers, ephemeral publications, and a historical influence that still affects the intellectual life of contemporary America. Despite this vagueness at the edges, however, Transcendentalism was a real and significant event, a somewhat provincial and peculiar manifestation of the more general phenomenon of Romanticism. During its heyday—roughly the decade 1836–1846—it exerted a fascination over most of the active literary minds of the country, whether in sympathy or repulsion. It flowered brilliantly in the masterpieces of Emerson, Thoreau, and Whitman; the problems it raised concerning knowledge, freedom, nature, art, democracy obsessed the minds of Poe, Hawthorne, and Melville. And possibly of equal importance with its strictly literary manifestations, Transcendentalism made a lasting impression on the American character. It gave shape and meaning to a certain inchoate American idealism. The portrait of the self-reliant man, the follower of his conscience, the divinely inspired democratic individual, which is passionately delineated in the writings of the whole Transcendentalist group, helped to create and identify an American type that seems to have become a permanent element of the national life. It is hard to imagine the forms American rebellion might have taken during the past one hundred and twenty years if Brook Farm had not existed, *The Dial* had not been published, and works like "Civil Disobedience" had not been written.

Transcendentalism was, of course, as much a product of its time and place as an influence upon them. I have called it a manifestation of Romanticism, and its debt to certain key ideas that swept Europe in the early nineteenth century is unmistakable. The divinity of nature, the glory of human aspiration and freedom, the power of intuition as opposed to reason, the creative energy of the poetic imagination—these are some of the themes imported into America by writers like Hedge, Brownson, Ripley, and Fuller, as well as Emerson. Indeed, Transcendentalism, as a radical and innovating movement, invented the typical American avant-garde strategy of allying itself with European masters as both an offensive and a defensive measure against conservative resistance at home. Some of the most important acts of self-assertion by members of the group took the form of an exposition of foreign ideas or a tribute to a foreign hero. By such means the names and the thought of a whole range of writers, from Kant and Goethe to Cousin, Wordsworth, Coleridge, and Carlyle, entered into the discussion of American issues and broadened the scope of American literary culture.

But foreign influences did not create Transcendentalism; they would have been quite meaningless if they had not responded to a prior need stemming from an immediate cultural and intellectual predicament. This predicament, which may be defined as the impoverishment of religion and the mechanization of consciousness as a result of eighteenth-century rationalism and empiricism, was one, of course, which Europe shared. But in America, against the background of a successful democratic revolution and the subsequent release of enormous physical energy, it was a predicament which came to be felt with special acuteness as involving anomalies and limitations of thought intolerable in the light of social realities. What the young men who came of age in the 1820's and 1830's—the first intellectual generation born after the completion of the revolutionary struggle and the founding of the nation—what these young men felt most deeply was that a radically new world was taking shape around them, requiring for its comprehension and its fulfillment a new vision of man. It was the need for such a vision, and the literary means of defining it, that caused them to turn to the great European Romantics for inspiration; it was this need, more fundamentally, which called Transcendentalism into being and gave it its distinctive American character.

For in its essence Transcendentalism was an attempt to complete in the world of thought what the American revolution had begun in the world of action. If one may attribute, for the sake of definition, a single overriding motive to the Transcendentalist group, it was no less than the creation of a new literature, the literature, in a word, of democracy. Democracy had already taken political shape in America, and the democratic ideals of equality and liberty were already deeply implanted in the American spirit, but the inmost meaning of democracy—its new conception of the nature of man, his place in the world, and his relation to the divine—had hardly been thought about as yet and never adequately expressed. For the Transcendentalists, whether they understood themselves in these terms or not, the immediate duty and the prospective glory of literature was to bring into consciousness this inmost meaning which the life of society was already shadowing forth. This is not to suggest that they had a common program, nor that their concern with the meaning of democracy was only a variety of literary nationalism. Although they sometimes wrote of America as though its destiny was to be a messiah among the nations, the main tendency of their thought was universal, toward a new humanism that embraced all mankind and obliterated the petty distinctions of nationality. America, having found the path of democracy, might lead the way to millennium, but millennium was the age-old dream of the emancipation and unity of man.

II

The first distinguishable signs of what came to be called Transcendentalism appeared as expressions of dissatisfaction with the philosophic underpinnings of the reigning New England churches, both "orthodox" (i. e., Calvinist) and Unitarian. The theme of this dissatisfaction was the churches' reliance upon Lockian empiricism (what the Transcendentalist critics called "sensualism") as a way of explaining the origin and formation of ideas in the mind, including ideas about religion. But the real meaning of the attack on Locke, at first only hinted at but soon frankly asserted, was an impatience with the sterility and complacence of the churches, their failure to make religion a vital part of the lives of their communicants. The complaint, at bottom, was that New England piety was dying, and that a false philosophy was killing it. The churches had lost their power to inspire an active faith; they were absorbed in arid theological wrangling and hair-splitting, or they were simply, as Emerson said of Boston Unitarianism, "corpse-cold."

Locke was vulnerable to attack because his immensely influential theory of knowledge—which had become part of New England Calvinism through the agency of Jonathan Edwards, and which was the cornerstone of Unitarian apologetics—had become increasingly identified during the course of the eighteenth century with purely natural and rationalistic ways of thinking. Locke conceived of the mind as a blank page on which ideas of the external world were inscribed through the senses, or as a kind of mechanical organizer of sensations which were fed to it by "experience." This view appeared very well suited to explain the processes of scientific classification and experiment or the formation of common-sense judgments on practical matters, but it tended to create the assumptions that only the physical, the tangible, the measurable were real, and that consciousness was a prisoner of the senses. Locke had no intention of casting doubt on religion; he thought that religion could be defended by the means of common sense; but his epistemology proved to be a potent weapon of religious skepticism. The history of eighteenth-century religious thought shows the impossibility of making Christianity meet the standards of common sense. It is a history of steady drift, through all the forms of rational or "natural" religion, away from the ancient sanctions of revelation and dogma toward the open seas of mechanism or pantheism, idealism, materialism, antinomianism, or outright atheism.

The Romantic movement was, in one of its major aspects, a violent reaction against the assumptions created by Lockian epistemology. Stimulated by Kant and his followers in Germany, and by the revival of various forms of Platonism and intuitionism, the Romantics sought to free consciousness from the tyranny of sensation and to restore it as an active, generative force in the achievement of knowledge. By this means they hoped to reestablish communication with a realm of truth from which science and common sense had seemed fatally to divide man: the realm of inward illumination and spiritual insight, of value and meaning not given directly to the senses. Romanticism was not necessarily linked to a revival of orthodox Christianity —the Enlightenment had done its work too well for that— but it brought a fresh awareness of the spiritual possibilities in man that reawakened religious instincts all over Europe.

It encouraged the emergence of a new kind of religious individualism, and it set in motion currents of renovation that troubled the peace of those churches especially which had most fully come to terms with the Age of Reason.

Such a church was the Unitarianism of Boston and eastern Massachusetts in the first third of the nineteenth century. Unitarianism was probably at the farthest limit to which Christianity, in an organized form, could go in the direction of liberal, rationalized religion. Even before his conversion to Catholicism, Orestes Brownson referred to it as "the jumping-off place from the church to absolute infidelity." During its evolution in the eighteenth century from Calvinist origins, Unitarianism had gradually stripped itself of traditional dogma and ritual: the sovereign and potent God of the Puritans was transformed into a benevolent Father whose creation followed strict rules of cause and effect; the iron law of predestination was repealed in favor of a thoroughgoing Arminianism; Christ became a type of human perfection, a teacher and exemplar of the ideal life, no longer a person of the Trinity. The motive behind these changes was the same that shaped deism and all the other forms of rational religion in that period. Human reason grounded in natural experience had become the arbiter of truth; human dignity was no longer compatible with submission to a dogmatic, irrational faith. Yet the Unitarians insisted that they were faithful Christians. All they had done was remove the last vestiges of obscurantism and superstition clinging to the simple teachings of Christ. But they never meant to question the divine authority of these teachings—which they understood to refer primarily to conduct—or the right of Christ to speak on God's behalf. Not only was his character perfect and his message intrinsically beautiful, but his ministry was plainly vouched for by the miracles he had performed which were recorded in sacred Scripture.

The miracles of Christ had been a matter of considerable debate throughout the eighteenth century. Skeptics like Hume had dismissed them as incredible deviations from the observable order of experience, while a long line of Anglican apologists tried to defend them as consistent with the fundamental rationality of Christian belief. To the latter, this argument acquired a painful importance because miracles increasingly seemed to mark the dividing line between a faith that was specifically Christian and a merely natural religion, or no religion at all. At stake, so it appeared, was the validity of the Scriptural claim to divine revelation, the claim of Christianity to be something more than natural religion. The miracles of Christ stood as the one unmistakable body of evidence that the Author of nature was also the Author of the Christian religion.

The Unitarians of New England were deeply committed to this compromise position, as it may be considered. To free the religion of Christ from the toils of Calvinist theology, to refine and purify it so that the word of God became transparent in the light of human reason—that was one thing. But to give up the last remaining assurance that reason could ultimately rely on divine authority was quite another. Even the most liberal of Christians had their limits! As the eighteenth-century debates had shown, however, this compromise was far from secure. Once reason and experience were acknowledged to be the standards of Scriptural interpretation, it was well-nigh impossible to set a limit to their application. Why should miracles be sacrosanct? The Unitarians gave much thought to working out a line of defense on this question that would not betray them into either dogmatism or skepticism. Their chief mentor was William Paley, whose "inestimable work" (as William Ellery Channing called it), *Evidences of the Christian Religion,* was used as a textbook at Harvard. Channing's own Dudleian Lecture on the miracles is an able exposition of the viewpoint derived from Paley; its mild, thoughtful, firm tone is partly Channing's own, but in part it also reflects the confidence of Unitarian leaders that they had hit upon an ideal form of Christianity. Scripture and common sense were sweetly reconciled; the drift away from barbarous superstition was halted at just the right point: they felt themselves very nearly impregnable.

III

What they did not expect, and were wholly unprepared for, was rebellion within the ranks. The young men who eventually came to be called, and to call themselves, Transcendentalists, almost all grew up within the Unitarian communion. Many of them went to Harvard College and the Harvard Divinity School, which were solidly Unitarian institutions, and many of them served as Unitarian ministers for part or all of their careers. And when they began to complain that Unitarianism was cold and lifeless, that it did not satisfy their idea of Christianity at all, then the Unitarian church faced a threat it did not know how to resist, and its careful compromise started to break down.

For it was precisely the compromise itself that the young rebels denounced and not merely the arguments that upheld it. In seeking to define their position, they were drawn to the question of miracles because it illustrated for them the fatal incompatibility of the elements which Unitarianism had tried to bind together. To rest the authority of Christ on miracles, while appealing to the natural reason as the only arbiter of the credibility of miracles, was not to solve the problem of religion but to render it insoluble. Reason educated by the senses could never admit the certainty of miracles. The Unitarians thought they had circumscribed reason, but instead they had been trapped by it. No wonder their faith had lost its warmth and piety its zeal. To the budding Transcendentalists the issue was clear: choose Locke and the sensual reason or choose the religion of Christ—you cannot have both!

The restoration of religion, then, was the immediate purpose of the "new school" among the Unitarian clergy. To accomplish this purpose, they began to exploit a new idea —or an old one in new form—that seemed to them so effective and so much what the occasion demanded, that they fell in love with it. The idea was that consciousness itself is a reliable source of spiritual insight, that in man's mind, by virtue of its native, inherent capacities, the fundamental truths of religion can be found. Man possesses a faculty or a power—following Coleridge, they usually called it Reason—which can give him immediate access to supersensual knowledge. Thus the testimony of miracles can be dispensed with as misleading and irrelevant; men have a touchstone within themselves by which to judge the truth of Christ's ministry. "The divine message of the Gospel," said George Ripley, "corresponds to the divine instincts of the soul." Thus, too, Locke's analysis of the human understanding could be relegated to its own proper sphere, that in which mental experience was indeed conditioned by the senses (the sphere of the Understanding). The strategy of the Transcendentalists did not require the complete overthrow of Locke; they merely wished to redraw his map of the mind with greatly extended boundaries, so as to include much, in effect, of what he had excluded when he denied the existence of innate ideas.

The conception of a super-sensual Reason as the Transcendentalists understood it was derived in simplified form from Coleridge—in Brownson's case, from Cousin—who had derived it, with suitable modifications, from Kant and his successors in German philosophy. Inevitably there were gross changes and distortions along this line of descent, but what is most interesting from our perspective is not the history of the idea but the use to which it was put in the American context. Kant had been primarily concerned with the epistemological problems raised by British empiricism; Coleridge was looking for a means of reviving confidence in the certainty of spiritual truth within a framework of Anglican orthodoxy. But the Transcendentalists, having become interested in the epistemological question for immediate reasons very similar to Coleridge's, quickly went on to an affirmation that was uniquely their own, namely that Reason was the very essence of the democratic idea. It was Reason that created the peculiar value of human nature, and the value of human nature was the justification of democracy.

In thus discovering the link between Reason and democracy the Transcendentalists discovered their mission, which was to elaborate the meaning of democracy as a new unfolding of the human spirit. In this context, it should be observed, the word "democracy" takes on a far broader and vaguer significance than it usually has. The Transcendentalists were not especially interested in concrete political systems. More than anything else, democracy meant for them an ideal of human perfection which was implicit in the nature of man and in American society and institutions. The democracy so far achieved in America, however, was no more than a tentative groping toward the ideal, a very partial realization of what men were capable of. For this reason their writings are obsessed by the theme of freedom. Freedom was the key to progress toward the ideal; it was the means and the end of Reason's vision; it was the quintessence of paradise to be regained! In the history of American thought Transcendentalism is the nearest thing we have to an absolutism of freedom. Once they had seized upon this theme the Transcendentalists were carried a long way beyond their initial goal of revitalizing the New England churches.

Reason was not the only motive of the Transcendentalist quest for freedom. One other idea, intimately related to the theme of freedom, was at work in Transcendentalist thought almost without the awareness of the thinkers. This was what has been called the "organic metaphor," the tendency to conceive of reality in terms suitable to living things, to interpret the world by means of analogies with plant and animal life. Among the salient characteristics of such life are growth and change, potentiality and ripeness, creativity, and the interconnection of parts within a complex unity. Thus in Emerson's eyes—he was the most deliberate and subtle of American writers in exploiting this metaphor—nature was not a vast machine but a marvelously integrated diversity, a growing, dynamic, harmonious union of all beings in a single living Body. The Transcendentalists absorbed the organic metaphor from their German and English sources and used it with varying degrees of perspicuity, but its most important meaning for them was in the view it gave of human development. Human beings, to be sure, are living creatures, but, as we have seen, it had not been customary to think of human intelligence as an organic growth. Locke discussed the operations of the mind in essentially mechanical terms; it was with a shock of delight, therefore, that the Transcendentalists realized that the mind *grew*. As Sampson Reed put it, "The mind of the infant contains within itself the first rudiments of all that will be hereafter and needs nothing but expansion, as the leaves and branches and fruit of a tree are said to exist in the seed from which it springs." Later writers, with greater sophistication, substituted the word "Reason" for "the first rudiments of all that will be hereafter," and thus arrived at the formula which linked together the two basic elements of the Transcendentalist theory of consciousness, Reason and organic growth. The combination was to prove explosive.

IV

It was explosive because it both divinized man and endowed him with a dynamic and expansive energy. The attribution of Reason was not a mere change in epistemological theory; it was a new definition of human nature, the implications of which grew irresistibly. Once they had decided that men were capable of ascertaining divine truth by an examination of their own minds, the Transcendentalists saw that this capacity must be of the same nature as divinity itself. Men knew God because in some fashion God was within them—how else could the phenomenon of Reason be explained? Furthermore, this innate divinity, the "divine instincts" in Ripley's phrase, was an organic power, something that grew as men found ways of revealing it to themselves, something that pressed against all artificial constraints and demanded acknowledgment in the world. If men were divine, why should they everywhere be in chains?

Taken all in all, and despite some failings on the side of acerbity (Brownson) or self-righteousness (Parker), the Transcendentalists were a mild-mannered and kindly tempered set of revolutionaries. But revolutionaries they were, though it seems to have been a more or less inadvertent development from their premises. What happened was that the fusion of Reason with the organic metaphor generated a certain spontaneous millenarianism that gradually became the atmosphere of their thinking. The most striking evidence for this state of mind can be found in the conclusion of Brownson's *New Views*, which is an excited vision of redeemed society glimpsed by the eye of Reason. As they fastened their attention more and more on the latent possibilities of man's nature, and their conviction grew that "God look[s] out from human eyes," they became dazzled by the enormous opportunity that awaited mankind to remake its world from God's viewpoint. And not unnaturally, they were progressively disillusioned with the world as they found it. From a somewhat academic band of ecclesiastical rebels, the Transcendentalists were thus metamorphosed into the most thoroughgoing critics of society that had yet appeared on the American scene.

It is worth examining this process more closely. In criticizing the miracles of Unitarian theology, the Transcendentalists had begun by appealing to man's innate certainty of religious truth. Christianity was verified for them not by displays of magical power (which might very well have actually taken place), but by its "correspondence," as Ripley said, "with the divine spirit in man." It was true because men instinctively believed it; its evidence was in its own perfection, not in visible signs. The spirit of man, therefore, which they called Reason when they wanted to think of it as an instrument of knowledge, was or could be an infallible guide to eternal wisdom. At this point the question could not help but pose itself as to what eternal wisdom consisted of. What did men actually find in their consciousness with respect to Christianity or religious truth generally?

The Transcendentalists, for the most part, were in agreement that Christianity must be a divine revelation, but since Reason was the ground of their belief, they had necessarily to deny the right of any church or sect, however liberal, to impose a doctrinal formulation on the Christian message. Christ had spoken directly to what was godlike in every man and his words were very simple—he was the master, as Alcott said, of the art of conversation. Hence religious truth was contained in the plain sense of Christ's own words, which did not require the elucidations of Andrews Norton, or Calvin, or St. Thomas Aquinas, or even St. Paul. Men recognized by the blaze of their hearts in response that the Sermon on the Mount was an oracle. Churches and doctrines had only created obscurity and dissension in twisting the simple message to their own ends. Hence the Transcendentalists found themselves at war with what they persisted in calling "historical Christianity"—an expression that irritated their more orthodox opponents no end.

By "historical Christianity" they meant all the forms with which the pure, essential truth of Christ had been clothed ever since its original pronouncement. By these forms, without exception, the pristine Word had been adulterated, confused, betrayed. The history of Christianity was a history of the struggle to liberate the Word from the forms which imprisoned it. And Reason was obviously the force designed to accomplish this liberation once and for all. The Transcendentalists thus placed themselves at the vanguard of a new and final purification of religion; it was the first step on the path of iconoclasm to which they had set their feet.

This thesis concerning history, and the end of history, was the subject of many of the most important and notorious Transcendentalist declarations. Best known, of course, is Emerson's "Divinity School Address," which brought down upon him the unexpected violence of Boston's disapproval. But even earlier Ripley had preached his sermon "Jesus Christ, the Same Yesterday, Today, and Forever"; Brownson had published his outrageous *New Views,* which perhaps were too new to stimulate much of a response; and as late as 1841 Theodore Parker raised a storm with his "Discourse of the Transient and Permanent in Christianity." All of these pieces illustrate two significant points about Transcendentalism which are often overlooked and are worth dwelling upon for

a moment. First of all, it was a movement distinctly Protestant in character, with roots that went deep into the Puritan
soil of New England. Indeed, one might well regard Transcendentalism, as Brownson did after his conversion, as the
ultimate form of Protestant dissent. It had the passion for
simplification, for going back to the primitive origins of religion, that repeatedly has marked Protestant history. It
longed for a naked confrontation with the divine; it demanded that religion consume the soul, alter the affections,
change men's lives from top to bottom. It conceived of faith
as a thoroughgoing, heartfelt *piety*, in the manner of the
Augustinian fathers of New England, and its millenarian
spirit was an echo of the Puritan dream of a church of
visible saints.

At the same time, it is true, however paradoxical it may
appear, that the Transcendentalists were heirs of the
eighteenth-century Enlightenment. The content they gave to
religion did not differ in any marked respect from the natural
religion of the previous century. Since they relied on universal Reason as their guide to truth, they were not encouraged
to deduce complex systems of belief. On the contrary, so
far as articles of faith were concerned, Reason led to pretty
much the same conclusions as the despised reason of the
Unitarians. That there was a perfect God; that He created
the universe out of love and governed it benevolently; that
He endowed men with immortal souls; and that morality was
the essential substance of religion: these were the certainties
the Transcendentalists found ingrained in human consciousness. Of course, the intuitional basis of certainty produced
an element of mysticism, and, unlike the Unitarians, the
Transcendentalists welcomed enthusiasm as a sign of the
genuineness of faith. But these and other differences do
not obscure the fact that they continued a tradition with
which they were in large measure at odds. Since it was a
tradition incompatible with the kind of piety they wished to
promote, it may well have been a contributing factor in the
rather rapid decline of the movement.

In the beginning, however, the Protestant impulse combined
with natural religion and backed by Reason all pointed together to the churches, to "historical Christianity," as the
great obstacle standing in the way of Christ's reign on earth.
The widening of the issue from miracles to historical Christianity marked a decisive change in the character of the
Transcendentalist movement. Not only did it directly affect

the lives of a number of people—Emerson and Ripley resigned from the Unitarian ministry; Brownson moved away (temporarily) to his own post-Unitarian church, "The Society for Christian Union"; and Parker came as near being excommunicated as was possible among Unitarians—but it impelled them to examine the relations between church and society and gradually to extend the scope of their criticism beyond what any of them had originally foreseen.

V

At bottom, the Transcendentalist position which pitted the "divine spirit in man" against "historical Christianity" was not merely a criticism of the churches but a total rejection of them. It is a testimony rather to the millenarian temper of the movement than to its intellectual discipline. But the inner dynamic of this position was very hard to resist. Once they had defined Reason as the source of religious truth, and equated it with the truth of Christ, there was nothing for the Transcendentalists to do but assert the absolute incompatibility of Christ and Reason on one side and Christianity on the other.

They did so, as we might expect, in the name of democracy in religion. The churches, they came to see, by denying man's power to derive religious truth from his own consciousness, were really anti-democratic institutions. When Andrews Norton defended the miraculous evidence of Christianity on the basis of Lockian psychology, he was only falling back on the age-old view of man's fallibility, his depravity, his need of priestly guidance into the mysteries. The real meaning of the struggle between old and new in the Boston churches, then, was the question of whether man was to be trusted or not, whether he was to be *free*. Consistency with the principle of democracy required that the churches submit to the same process that was already under way in American political life. Out of unfettered human nature, not out of the priest's manipulation of evidence, would come the sanctification of human life on earth. From the Unitarian point of view, this was democracy with a vengeance!

But the Transcendentalists were by no means ready to stop at this point. Many of them, in fact, realized fairly soon that the democratization of the churches was after all only a peripheral issue for them. It was the democratization of society as a whole, a true reign of sanctity, that they were compelled to seek. Having committed themselves to a redemptive mission, there was no drawing a line between church and society. To confine themselves within the churches would, perhaps, have meant the salvation of a few souls at best, but, as Ripley saw it, "The purpose of Christianity . . . is to redeem society as well as the individual from all sin." It is no coincidence that this remark concerning the purpose of Christianity comes from a letter addressed by Ripley to his parishioners explaining the reasons for his resignation from the ministry.

To redeem society from all sin: this can well be taken as the ultimate expression of Transcendentalist motives. Not that they supposed it could be accomplished overnight, but their fondness for the expression, "It is the mission of the age . . ." gives a measure of the confidence they felt that their hopes were practicable and within reach. And why not? It was an age of confidence, of hope and progress. The powerful tide of democracy seemed to be releasing fresh energies every day, and it was already a habit in America to anticipate the emergence of a new man in whom the splendor of human nature would at last be vindicated. The Transcendentalists were perhaps the first to enshrine this democratic Adam in their temple, but it was not necessary to be a Transcendentalist in 1838 to share the sentiments expressed by Orestes Brownson:

> . . . here is virgin soil, an open field, a new people, full of the future, with unbounded faith in ideas, and the most ample freedom. Here, if anywhere on earth, may the philosopher experiment on human nature and demonstrate what man has it in him to be when and where he has the freedom and the means to be himself.

Language like this shows how close Transcendentalism was to a native American vision. Indeed, it was the fullest, most radical, rashest expression of that vision we have had: the "American dream" at its moment of greatest intensity and innocence.

What were the experiments which these philosophers proposed to try on human nature? How did they expect to redeem society and free man to be himself? We may briefly examine, for the sake of illustration, two of their answers to these questions under separate heads.

Education. It is quite possible that the most lasting influence of Transcendentalism has been exercised upon the theory and practice of American education. This subject rose to the surface of Transcendentalist social criticism very quickly, forced up, we may suppose, by the pressure of conflicting assumptions about human nature. We can see the outlines of a new theory emerging in that fascinating proto-Transcendentalist work, Sampson Reed's "Observations on the Growth of the Mind," but the major prophet in this field was undeniably Bronson Alcott. Whatever reservations his colleagues may have had about Alcott, and however flatulent his soaring prose may strike the modern reader, he was a man profoundly in tune with his age, and his educational writings as well as his practical experiments reveal the inner meaning of Transcendentalism as surely as anything else written or done during the period.

Alcott's basic idea was very simple, and he discovered it for himself long before he knew Emerson or became a member of the Transcendental Club. It was that education is a calling forth and cultivation of the divinity within man, not an imposition of external forms upon a passive intellect. "The province of the instructor," he wrote in his journal in 1828, "should be . . . awakening, invigorating, directing, rather than the forcing of the child's faculties upon prescribed and exclusive courses of thought. He should look to the child to see what is to be done, rather than to his book or his system. The Child is the Book. The operations of his mind are the true system." From this kernel grew Alcott's more fully developed theory in "Human Culture" and his experiments like the one at Temple School, as revolutionary an undertaking in its way as Brook Farm.

Alcott's method of teaching forms a striking complement to the quite independent body of ideas being hammered out by Brownson and Ripley during the very years of the Temple School's operation. Brownson's excitement over Cousin came from the fact that Cousin made psychology ("an exact classification of the mental phenomena") the "first part, the foundation" of philosophy. From such a beginning Cousin could go on to define the nature of Universal Reason and show how it "reveals to us God and the world on precisely the same authority as our own existence." Alcott would not have felt much sympathy with Brownson's enthusiasm—his own genius spoke to him in less complex language—but he too was basing his work on psychology, a direct approach

to mental phenomena. Instead of teaching, he probed the
contents of his pupils' minds (for the most part, very sen-
sitively), confident that by this means he could strengthen
and purify the light of Reason innate in them. His lessons
may now seem to us loaded with preconceptions and more
forcibly controlled than he was aware, but the evidence suggests that by treating young minds as though they were
capable of growth and not simply accumulation, he found
a way of making learning an active pleasure. It was an accomplishment valuable enough to entitle him to his place
as the patron saint of American progressive education.

Labor. But the redemption of American society posed a
far more difficult problem than the reform of the schools.
At the heart of the matter, the Transcendentalists came
slowly but inevitably to realize, was the question of property
and the relations between those who had little of it and
those who had much. None of them was equipped to deal
with this subject professionally, of course; they were ministers whose training and interests were primarily literary. But
they were drawn to it by what has come to seem a characteristic necessity of modern intellectual life: the necessity
to make some relation between the sphere of value derived
from religion and literature and the sphere of economic organization. Their sensitivity to the widening gap between
these two spheres is one of the measures of their relevance
to the history of American thought. They belonged to an
age of burgeoning industrialism, and they were among the
first Americans to see that this new social fact cast a
problematic and threatening light on the hope for democratic
fulfillment.

Although the Transcendentalists frequently brought to their
discussion of economics a rhetoric of Christian idealism
that cannot help but seem vague and sentimental in that
context, their thinking was informed by certain hard insights.
Most crucially, they saw that the private ownership of property, especially the means of capitalist production, was incompatible with the democratic ideal of individual freedom.
Private property tended to destroy the social equality on
which freedom was based; it seemed to be creating a new
class system and new forms of dependency in which masses
of men were the helpless victims of economic power controlled by a few. The factory system, which was hardly a
widespread phenomenon in the America of the 1830's, was
thus early recognized, particularly by Brownson, who was

the most prescient in these matters of the Transcendentalist group, as the most ominous fact of American life. Brownson did not think it absurd to compare the conditions of factory labor in the North with slave labor in the South and to give the advantage to slavery. His grim pages on this subject, and on the gulf between factory owner and factory worker, in "The Laboring Classes" are among the earliest signs of awareness in the United States that a dangerous contradiction was evolving out of the unexamined assumptions of American democracy.

Two other aspects of nascent capitalism disturbed the Transcendentalists: the competitive spirit which it encouraged, and its use of machinery. Although competition had not yet become an article of faith in a full-fledged business ideology, the Transcendentalists felt its presence as a cause of anxiety and insecurity; it threatened, in their eyes, to revive a state of primitive warfare in the midst of civilized society. Toward machinery they were generally hostile, but not without ambivalence, as Theodore Parker's "Thoughts on Labor" illustrates. On the one hand, they felt that machine labor disrupted the "natural" character of work, while its only social purposes seemed to be the increase of profits for a small minority of owners and the stimulation of trivial forms of consumption among the working class. But on the other hand, machines promised an eventual release from drudgery for the mass of mankind, and unprecedented leisure for "study, social improvement, the pursuit of a favorite art." These tentative attitudes have since, of course, become the stuff of cliches, but in the 1830's and 1840's they were, especially insofar as they expressed reservations about the tendency of American development, the heterodoxies of an intellectual vanguard.

In their responses to the problem of labor, the Transcendentalists again foreshadowed the solutions which would be proposed by later generations of American radicals. Two conflicting views emerged in their work: one essentially political, aimed at reforming the structure of society; the other Utopian, aimed at changing the quality of life. The first of these views was held in somewhat desperate isolation by Brownson, whose talent for pushing things to their logical conclusion often led him to brilliant diagnoses and utterly impractical remedies. Brownson saw more clearly than any of his contemporaries that money had become the only real source of power in the world, and that the only social distinction of importance was between those who possessed money and those who did not. He deduced that class warfare was in the offing, the object of which would be a redistribution of wealth, and so he made his perfectly rational proposal that hereditary property be abolished. It was rational because it followed "from the admitted premises of the American people."

> Hereditary property is either a privilege or it is not. If it is not, if it confer no social advantage on him who inherits it over him who does not, then there can be no harm in seeking to abolish it, for what we propose to abolish is declared to be valueless. . . . But hereditary property, unless the amount inherited by each individual could be rendered equal, is unquestionably a privilege. It gives, and always must give, to one portion of the community an advantage over the rest to which they are entitled by no natural superiority of intellect or of virtue. Will the public conscience, then, of the American people tolerate it?

This suggestion seems to have been offered, at least on second thought, as an alternative to bloodshed, but Brownson knew that any serious attempt to carry it out would involve violence, and he came dangerously close to justifying the necessity of violence in the cause of a more perfect democracy. Despite this passing ideological fury, however, Brownson's zeal never became detached from its original source. It is an idea of Man that sustains his passion, not a system of power; it is the longing "to prove what man may be, when and where he has free and full scope to act out the almightiness that slumbers within him." In "The Laboring Classes," then, Transcendentalism showed itself capable of producing some quite tough-minded social analysis and contemplating, if need be, extreme operations on the existing body politic.

Although Brook Farm has the look of an even more radical approach to social experiment, it was in fact animated by a different, less political spirit than Brownson's. Only at the end, when it converted itself into a Fourierist phalanstery, did it adopt an aggressive tone with respect to the society around it. Up till then, if we may judge by George Ripley's public and private statements, Brook Farm turned its attention inward upon the perfection of a style of life that would solve in miniature the problems of the world at large and thus provide a model for the rest of mankind. Ripley's main concern was to find a natural balance and harmony between intellectual and physical labor. He had in mind an ideal of wholeness like that propounded in Emerson's "American Scholar," in which action and thought did not exclude one another but formed a unity presided over by Nature. This, or something like it, was what lay behind the striking remark concerning Brook Farm in one of his letters: "We are striving to establish a mode of life which shall combine the enchantments of poetry with the facts of daily experience." Nothing could sound less subversive, but all the radical hopes of Transcendentalism are summed up in these mild words, and they conceal just as strong an impulse for change as Brownson's demand for the emancipation of the "proletaries."

Ripley's description of Brook Farm, which of course is deeply colored by his anticipation of the results it would achieve, is probably as close as we may come to a concrete vision of the sort of world dreamed of by Transcendentalist idealism. The interesting thing to note about this world is its fluidity and formlessness. There are no roles into which men must fit; they are to be equally at home in the field and in the study; and social distinctions of every sort vanish before the human dignity elicited by a way of life in which soul and body are equally satisfied. It is a perfect democracy, where washerwomen may walk with philosophers—indeed, where washerwomen may *be* philosophers, and philosophers do the laundry. This is what Ripley meant by combining "the enchantments of poetry with the facts of daily experience." It is so complete an integration of the physical with the spiritual that all actions are holy and all men divine. It is no wonder that Ripley could not resist thinking of Brook Farm, albeit in quotation marks, as a "city of God."

VI

The genuine Transcendentalist note is one of intense, almost limitless optimism, a feeling that arises out of the sense of living on the threshold of profound and glorious change. For the generation of Emerson, Ripley, Parker, and Brownson the American and French revolutions were still sending shock waves through the frame of society, and the inspiration of European Romanticism was fresh and tonic. When the optimism faded, Transcendentalism began to die; it was alive only so long as it could believe in its vision of a new man and a redeemed society.

Transcendentalism was, in its way, an attempt to solve the most acute and troubling problems of its century. Like other greater, though equally perishable, systems of nineteenth-century thought, it aimed at a synthesis of the rapidly fragmenting mind of its age. In the idea of Reason the Transcendentalists believed they had found the key to such a synthesis. It reconciled for them science and religion and made the resuscitation of Christianity in a new and viable form seem possible; it healed the split between mind and matter and restored the intellectual to a place in the world of action; it provided the basis for a new social order in which human dignity and freedom might triumph over the power of money and machines. The faith of the Transcendentalists in their premises and their prospects was certainly naive, almost incredibly so; and their vision of a future America, in which "the almightiness that slumbers within" man was to awake in a new age of liberty and brotherhood, can only be contemplated with the most generously ironic indulgence. But despite all their limitations, they wrote an irreplaceable chapter of American history. They were among the first of a breed which has played a decisive role in our culture: the unattached, committed intellectual who confronts the problems of society as a literary free agent. For this reason as well as the others that have been mentioned, they remain one of the important sources of our intellectual tradition. Both their example and their dreams continue to haunt us.

GEORGE HOCHFIELD
State University of New York, Buffalo

A NOTE ON THE TEXT

I have tried, in the following selections, to illustrate the major concerns—philosophic, social, artistic—of the Transcendentalist writers. My primary criterion, however, has been the intrinsic interest of the work itself, and no consciously predetermined plan or thesis has guided my selections. Furthermore, I have arranged the material in a roughly chronological order so that it gives some indication of the movement's history as well as its variety.

Of course, no view of Transcendentalism is complete which omits Emerson and Thoreau. But the object of the present volume—with some small exceptions, the unfamiliarity of which I hope will justify them—is precisely to omit Emerson and Thoreau. Their work is so well known and so readily available that it has almost come to be identified with Transcendentalism. I hope this book will help to rectify that impression, as well as throw light, for readers who are unfamiliar with the lesser Transcendentalists, on what the greater ones were talking about.

My decision to include the work of William Ellery Channing and Andrews Norton may require a word of justification. Parts of three essays by Channing are here because they offer the reader an extremely useful starting point for the study of Transcendentalism. Channing is a lucid expositor of the Unitarian point of view against which the Transcendentalists rebelled. At the same time, he reveals that strain in Unitarianism which blossomed into Transcendentalism. When we read his "Likeness to God," we cannot help but feel Emerson and Ripley immanent in it. On the other hand, Norton's "Discourse on the Latest Form of Infidelity" is the most famous and bitter of the Unitarian attacks on Transcendentalist heresy. It should remind the reader that Transcendentalism had its enemies—indeed, most re-

spectable men thought it a ludicrous or dangerous aberration—
and that it was almost always involved in more or less violent
polemics.

Anyone who compiles a selection of Transcendentalist writings owes an immense debt to the work of Perry Miller, whose
anthology of 1950 provides an invaluable guide to the source
material. My choices differ from his in certain ways, but they
could not have been made without a knowledge of his.

This reissue of *Selected Writings of the American Transcendentalists* by Yale University Press contains all the textual material
included in the original edition, plus one new selection. A
number of readers pointed out to me that the absence of any
commentary by Transcendentalist writers on the subject of
slavery was a grave omission. The Transcendentalists were
generally active campaigners in the abolitionist cause, the most
important reform movement of their day. I agreed with the
criticism and have added excerpts from Theodore Parker's "A
Sermon of Slavery," one of the earliest and most vigorous
denunciations of slavery from a distinctly Transcendentalist
perspective.

1

THE VANGUARD

William Ellery Channing

UNITARIAN CHRISTIANITY*
(1819)

[INTERPRETING THE SCRIPTURES]

We regard the Scriptures as the records of God's successive revelations to mankind, and particularly of the last and most perfect revelation of His will by Jesus Christ. Whatever doctrines seem to us to be clearly taught in the Scriptures, we receive without reserve or exception. We do not, however, attach equal importance to all the books in this collection. Our religion, we believe, lies chiefly in the New Testament. The dispensation of Moses, compared with that of Jesus, we consider as adapted to the childhood of the human race, a preparation for a nobler system, and chiefly useful now as serving to confirm and illustrate the Christian Scriptures. Jesus Christ is the only master of Christians, and whatever he taught, either during his personal ministry or by his inspired apostles, we regard as of divine authority, and profess to make the rule of our lives.

This authority which we give to the Scriptures is a reason, we conceive, for studying them with peculiar care, and for inquiring anxiously into the principles of interpretation by which their true meaning may be ascertained. The principles adopted by the class of Christians in whose name I speak need to be explained, because they are often misunderstood. We are particularly accused of making an unwarrantable use of reason in the interpretation of Scripture. We are said to exalt reason above revelation, to prefer our own wisdom to God's. Loose and undefined charges of this kind are circulated so freely, that we think it due to our-

---

* Discourse at the Ordination of the Rev. Jared Sparks, Baltimore, 1819.

selves, and to the cause of truth, to express our views with some particularity.

Our leading principle in interpreting Scripture is this, that the Bible is a book written for men, in the language of men, and that its meaning is to be sought in the same manner as that of other books. We believe that God, when He speaks to the human race, conforms, if we may so say, to the established rules of speaking and writing. How else would the Scriptures avail us more than if communicated in an unknown tongue?

Now all books and all conversation require in the reader or hearer the constant exercise of reason; or their true import is only to be obtained by continual comparison and inference. Human language, you well know, admits various interpretations; and every word and every sentence must be modified and explained according to the subject which is discussed, according to the purposes, feelings, circumstances and principles of the writer, and according to the genius and idioms of the language which he uses. These are acknowledged principles in the interpretation of human writings; and a man whose words we should explain without reference to these principles would reproach us justly with a criminal want of candor, and an intention of obscuring or distorting his meaning.

Were the Bible written in a language and style of its own, did it consist of words which admit but a single sense and of sentences wholly detached from each other, there would be no place for the principles now laid down. We could not reason about it as about other writings. But such a book would be of little worth; and perhaps, of all books, the Scriptures correspond least to this description. The word of God bears the stamp of the same hand which we see in His works. It has infinite connections and dependencies. Every proposition is linked with others, and is to be compared with others, that its full and precise import may be understood. Nothing stands alone. The New Testament is built on the Old. The Christian dispensation is a continuation of the Jewish, the completion of a vast scheme of providence requiring great extent of view in the reader. Still more, the Bible treats of subjects on which we receive ideas from other sources besides itself—such subjects as the nature, passions, relations, and duties of man—and it expects us to restrain and modify its language by the known truths which observation and experience furnish on these topics.

We profess not to know a book which demands a more frequent exercise of reason than the Bible. In addition to the remarks now made on its infinite connections, we may observe that its style nowhere affects the precision of science or the accuracy of definition. Its language is singularly glowing, bold and figurative, demanding more frequent departures from the literal sense than that of our own age and country, and consequently demanding more continual exercise of judgment. We find, too, that the different portions of this book, instead of being confined to general truths, refer perpetually to the times when they were written, to states of society, to modes of thinking, to controversies in the church, to feelings and usages which have passed away, and without the knowledge of which we are constantly in danger of extending to all times and places what was of temporary and local application. We find, too, that some of these books are strongly marked by the genius and character of their respective writers, that the Holy Spirit did not so guide the apostles as to suspend the peculiarities of their minds, and that a knowledge of their feelings, and of the influences under which they were placed, is one of the preparations for understanding their writings. With these views of the Bible, we feel it our bounden duty to exercise our reason upon it perpetually, to compare, to infer, to look beyond the letter to the spirit, to seek in the nature of the subject and the aim of the writer his true meaning; and, in general, to make use of what is known for explaining what is difficult and for discovering new truths.

Need I descend to particulars to prove that the Scriptures demand the exercise of reason? Take, for example, the style in which they generally speak of God, and observe how habitually they apply to him human passions and organs. Recollect the declarations of Christ: that he came not to send peace but a sword; that unless we eat his flesh and drink his blood we have no life in us; that we must hate father and mother, and pluck out the right eye; and a vast number of passages equally bold and unlimited. Recollect the unqualified manner in which it is said of Christians that they possess all things, know all things, and can do all things. Recollect the verbal contradiction between Paul and James, and the apparent clashing of some parts of Paul's writings with the general doctrines and end of Christianity. I might extend the enumeration indefinitely; and who does not see that we must limit all these passages by the known attributes of God, of Jesus Christ, and of human nature, and by the circumstances under which they were written, so as to give the language a quite different import from what it would require had it been applied to different beings, or used in different connections.

Enough has been said to show in what sense we make use of reason in interpreting Scripture. From a variety of possible interpretations we select that which accords with the nature of the subject and the state of the writer, with the connection of the passage, with the general strain of Scripture, with the known character and will of God, and with the obvious and acknowledged laws of nature. In other words, we believe that God never contradicts in one part of Scripture what He teaches in another; and never contradicts in revelation what he teaches in his works and providence. And we therefore distrust every interpretation which, after deliberate attention, seems repugnant to any established truth. We reason about the Bible precisely as civilians do about the constitution under which we live; who, you know, are accustomed to limit one provision of that venerable instrument by others, and to fix the precise import of its parts by inquiring into its general spirit, into the intentions of its authors, and into the prevalent feelings, impressions, and circumstances of the time when it was framed. Without these principles of interpretation, we frankly acknowledge that we cannot defend the divine authority of the Scriptures. Deny us this latitude, and we must abandon this book to its enemies. . . .

We indeed grant that the use of reason in religion is accompanied with danger. But we ask any honest man to look back on the history of the church and say whether the renunciation of it be not still more dangerous. Besides, it is plain fact that men reason as erroneously on all subjects as on religion. Who does not know the wild and groundless theories which have been framed in physical and political science? But who ever supposed that we must cease to exercise reason on nature and society because men have erred for ages in explaining them? We grant that the passions continually, and sometimes fatally, disturb the rational faculty in its inquiries into revelation. The ambitious contrive to find doctrines in the Bible which favor their love of dominion. The timid and dejected discover there a gloomy system, and the mystical and fanatical, a visionary theology. The vicious can find examples or assertions on which to build the hope of a late repentance, or of acceptance on easy terms. The falsely refined contrive to light on doctrines which have not been soiled by vulgar handling. But the passions do not distract the reason in religious any more than in other inquiries which excite strong and general interest; and this faculty, of consequence, is not to be renounced in religion unless we are prepared to discard it universally. The true inference from the almost endless errors which have darkened theology is not that we are to neglect and disparage our powers, but to exert them more patiently, circumspectly, uprightly. The worst errors, after all, have sprung up in that church which proscribes reason, and demands from its members implicit faith. The most pernicious doctrines have been the growth of the darkest times, when the general credulity encouraged bad men and enthusiasts to broach their dreams and inventions and to stifle the faint remonstrances of reason by the menaces of everlasting perdition. Say what we may, God has given us a rational nature and will call us to account for it. We may let it sleep, but we do so at our peril. Revelation is addressed to us as rational beings. We may wish, in our sloth, that God had given us a system demanding no labor of comparing, limiting and inferring. But such a system would be at variance with the whole character of our present existence; and it is the part of wisdom to take revelation as it is given to us, and to interpret it by the help of the faculties which it everywhere supposes and on which it is founded.

To the views now given an objection is commonly urged from the character of God. We are told that, God being infinitely wiser than men, His discoveries will surpass human reason. In a revelation from such a teacher we ought to expect propositions which we cannot reconcile with one another, and which may seem to contradict established truths; and it becomes us not to question or explain them away, but to believe, and adore, and to submit our weak and carnal reason to the divine word. To this objection we have two short answers. We say, first, that it is impossible that a teacher of infinite wisdom should expose those whom he would teach to infinite error. But if once we admit that propositions which in their literal sense appear plainly repugnant to one another, or to any known truth, are still to be literally understood and received, what possible limit can we set to the belief of contradictions? What shelter have we from the wildest fanaticism, which can always quote passages that, in their literal and obvious sense, give support to its extravagances? How can the Protestant escape from transubstantiation, a doctrine most clearly taught us, if the submission of reason, now contended for, be a duty? How can we even hold fast the truth of revelation, for if one apparent contradiction may be true, so may another, and the proposition that Christianity is false, though involving inconsistency, may still be a verity?

We answer again that if God be infinitely wise, He cannot sport with the understanding of His creatures. A wise teacher discovers his wisdom in adapting himself to the capacities of his pupils, not in perplexing them with what is unintelligible, not in distressing them with apparent contradictions, not in filling them with a skeptical distrust of their own powers. An infinitely wise teacher, who knows the precise extent of our minds and the best method of enlightening them, will surpass all other instructions in bringing down truth to our apprehension, and in showing its loveliness and harmony. We ought, indeed, to expect occasional obscurity in such a book as the Bible, which was written for past and future ages as well as for the present. But God's wisdom is a pledge that whatever is necessary for *us,* and necessary for salvation, is revealed too plainly to be mistaken, and too consistently to be questioned, by a sound and upright mind. It is not the mark of wisdom to use an unintelligible phraseology, to communicate what is above our capacities, to confuse and unsettle the intellect by appearances of contradiction. We honor our heavenly teacher too much to ascribe to him such a revelation. A revelation is a gift of light. It cannot thicken our darkness and multiply our perplexities.

[THE NATURE OF GOD]

. . . We believe in the *moral perfection of God*. We consider no part of theology so important as that which treats of God's moral character; and we value our views of Christianity chiefly as they assert His amiable and venerable attributes.

It may be said that in regard to this subject all Christians agree, that all ascribe to the Supreme Being infinite justice, goodness, and holiness. We reply that it is very possible to speak of God magnificently, and to think of Him meanly;

to apply to His person high-sounding epithets, and to His government principles which make Him odious. The heathens called Jupiter the greatest and the best, but his history was black with cruelty and lust. We cannot judge of men's real ideas of God by their general language, for in all ages they have hoped to soothe the Deity by adulation. We must inquire into their particular views of His purposes, of the principles of His administration, and of His disposition toward His creatures.

We conceive that Christians have generally leaned toward a very injurious view of the Supreme Being. They have too often felt as if He were raised, by His greatness and sovereignty, above the principles of morality, above those eternal laws of equity and rectitude, to which all other beings are subjected. We believe that in no being is the sense of right so strong, so omnipotent, as in God. We believe that His almighty power is entirely submitted to His perceptions of rectitude; and this is the ground of our piety. It is not because He is our Creator merely, but because He created us for good and holy purposes; it is not because His will is irresistible, but because His will is the perfection of virtue, that we pay Him allegiance. We cannot bow before a being, however great and powerful, who governs tyrannically. We respect nothing but excellence, whether on earth or in heaven. We venerate not the loftiness of God's throne, but the equity and goodness in which it is established.

We believe that God is infinitely good, kind, benevolent, in the proper sense of these words; good in disposition, as well as in act; good, not to a few, but to all; good to every individual, as well as to the general system.

We believe, too, that God is just; but we never forget that His justice is the justice of a good being, dwelling in the same mind, and acting in harmony, with perfect benevolence. By this attribute we understand God's infinite regard to virtue or moral worth, expressed in a moral government, that is, in giving excellent and equitable laws, and in conferring such rewards, and inflicting such punishments, as are best fitted to secure their observance. God's justice has for its end the highest virtue of the creation, and it punishes for this end alone, and thus it coincides with benevolence; for virtue and happiness, though not the same, are inseparably conjoined.

God's justice, thus viewed, appears to us to be in perfect harmony with His mercy. According to the prevalent systems of theology, these attributes are so discordant and jarring that to reconcile them is the hardest task, and the most wonderful achievement, of infinite wisdom. To us they seem to be intimate friends, always at peace, breathing the same spirit, and seeking the same end. By God's mercy we understand not a blind instinctive compassion, which forgives without reflection and without regard to the interests of virtue. This, we acknowledge, would be incompatible with justice, and also with enlightened benevolence. God's mercy, as we understand it, desires strongly the happiness of the guilty, but only through their penitence. It has a regard to character as truly as His justice. It defers punishment, and suffers long, that the sinner may return to his duty, but leaves the impenitent and unyielding to the fearful retribution threatened in God's word.

To give our views of God in one word, we believe in His Parental character. We ascribe to Him, not only the name, but the dispositions and principles of a father. We believe that He has a father's concern for His creatures, a father's desire for their improvement, a father's equity in proportioning His commands to their powers, a father's joy in their progress, a father's readiness to receive the penitent, and a father's justice for the incorrigible. We look upon this world as a place of education, in which He is training men by prosperity and adversity, by aids and obstructions, by conflicts of reason and passion, by motives to duty and temptations to sin, by a various discipline suited to free and moral beings for union with Himself, and for a sublime and evergrowing virtue in heaven.

Now we object to the systems of religion which prevail among us that they are adverse, in a greater or less degree, to these purifying, comforting, and honorable views of God, that they take from us our Father in heaven and substitute for Him a being whom we cannot love if we would, and whom we ought not to love if we could. We object particularly on this ground to that system which arrogates to itself the name of Orthodoxy, and which is now industriously propagated through our country. This system indeed takes various shapes, but in all it casts dishonor on the Creator. According to its old and genuine form, it teaches that God brings us into life wholly depraved, so that under the innocent features of our childhood is hidden a nature averse to all good and propense to all evil, a nature which exposes us to God's displeasure and wrath even before we have acquired power to understand our duties or to reflect upon our actions. According to a more modern exposition, it teaches that we came from the hands of our Maker with such a constitution, and are placed under such influences and circumstances, as to render certain and infallible the total depravity of every human being from the first moment of his moral agency; and it also teaches that the offense of the child, who brings into life this ceaseless tendency to unmingled crime, exposes him to the sentence of everlasting damnation. Now, according to the plainest principles of morality, we maintain that a natural constitution of the mind, unfailingly disposing it to evil and evil alone, would absolve it from guilt; that to give existence under this condition would argue unspeakable cruelty; and that to punish the sin of this unhappily constituted child with endless ruin would be a wrong unparalleled by the most merciless despotism.

This system also teaches that God selects from this corrupt mass a number to be saved and plucks them, by a special influence, from the common ruin; that the rest of mankind, though left without that special grace which their conversion requires, are commanded to repent under penalty of aggravated woe; and that forgiveness is promised them on terms which their very constitution infallibly disposes them to reject, and in rejecting which they awfully enhance the punishments of hell. These proffers of forgiveness and exhortations of amendment, to beings born under a blighting curse, fill our minds with a horror which we want words to express.

That this religious system does not produce all the effects on character which might be anticipated, we most joyfully admit. It is often, very often, counteracted by nature, conscience, common sense, by the general strain of Scripture, by the mild example and precepts of Christ, and by the many positive declarations of God's universal kindness, and perfect equity. But still we think that we see its unhappy influence. It tends to discourage the timid, to give excuses to the bad, to feed the vanity of the fanatical, and to offer shelter to the bad feelings of the malignant. By shocking, as it does, the fundamental principles of morality, and by exhibiting a severe and partial Deity, it tends strongly to pervert the moral faculty, to form a gloomy, forbidding, and servile religion, and to lead men to substitute censoriousness, bitterness, and persecution for a tender and impartial charity.

We think, too, that this system, which begins with degrading human nature, may be expected to end in pride; for pride grows out of a consciousness of high distinctions, however obtained, and no distinction is so great as that which is made between the elected and abandoned of God. . . .

[CHRISTIAN VIRTUE]

. . . We believe that all virtue has its foundation in the moral nature of man, that is, in conscience, or his sense of duty, and in the power of forming his temper and life according to conscience. We believe that these moral faculties are the grounds of responsibility and the highest distinctions of human nature, and that no act is praiseworthy any farther than it springs from their exertion. We believe that no dispositions infused into us without our own moral activity are of the nature of virtue, and therefore we reject the doctrine of irresistible divine influence on the human mind, molding it into goodness as marble is hewn into a statue. Such goodness, if this word may be used, would not be the object of moral approbation any more than the instinctive affections of inferior animals or the constitutional amiableness of human beings.

By these remarks we do not mean to deny the importance of God's aid or Spirit, but by His Spirit we mean a moral, illuminating, and persuasive influence, not physical, not compulsory, not involving a necessity of virtue. We object strongly to the idea of many Christians respecting man's impotence and God's irresistible agency on the heart, believing that they subvert our responsibility and the laws of our moral nature, that they make men machines, that they cast on God the blame of all evil deeds, that they discourage good minds and inflate the fanatical with wild conceits of immediate and sensible inspiration.

Among the virtues, we give the first place to the love of God. We believe that this principle is the true end and happiness of our being, that we were made for union with our Creator, that His infinite perfection is the only sufficient object and true resting place for the insatiable desires and unlimited capacities of the human mind, and that without Him, our noblest sentiments, admiration, veneration, hope, and love, would wither and decay. We believe, too, that the

love of God is not only essential to happiness but to the
strength and perfection of all the virtues; that conscience,
without the sanction of God's authority and retributive justice, would be a weak director; that benevolence, unless nourished by communion with His goodness, and encouraged
by His smile, could not thrive amidst the selfishness and
thanklessness of the world; and that self-government, without
a sense of the divine inspection, would hardly extend beyond an outward and partial purity. God, as He is essentially
goodness, holiness, justice, and virtue, so He is the life, motive, and sustainer of virtue in the human soul.

But whilst we earnestly inculcate the love of God, we believe that great care is necessary to distinguish it from
counterfeits. We think that much which is called piety is
worthless. Many have fallen into the error that there can be
no excess in feelings which have God for their object; and,
distrusting as coldness that self-possession without which virtue and devotion lose all their dignity, they have abandoned
themselves to extravagances which have brought contempt on
piety. Most certainly, if the love of God be that which often
bears its name, the less we have of it the better. If religion
be the shipwreck of understanding, we cannot keep too far
from it. On this subject we always speak plainly. We cannot
sacrifice our reason to the reputation of zeal. We owe it to
truth and religion to maintain that fanaticism, partial insanity, sudden impressions, and ungovernable transports are
anything rather than piety.

We conceive that the true love of God is a moral sentiment
founded on a clear perception, and consisting in a high
esteem and veneration of his moral perfections. Thus, it perfectly coincides, and is in fact the same thing, with the
love of virtue, rectitude, and goodness. You will easily
judge, then, what we esteem the surest and only decisive signs
of piety. We lay no stress on strong excitements. We esteem
him, and him only, a pious man who practically conforms
to God's moral perfections and government; who shows his
delight in God's benevolence by loving and serving his neighbor; his delight in God's justice by being resolutely upright;
his sense of God's purity by regulating his thoughts, imagination, and desires; and whose conversation, business, and domestic life are swayed by a regard to God's presence and authority. In all things else men may deceive themselves. Dis-
ordered nerves may give them strange sights and sounds and
impressions. Texts of Scripture may come to them as from

Heaven. Their whole souls may be moved, and their confidence in God's favor be undoubting. But in all this there is no religion. The question is, do they love God's commands, in which His character is fully expressed, and give up to these their habits and passions? Without this, ecstasy is a mockery. One surrender of desire to God's will is worth a thousand transports. We do not judge of the bent of men's minds by their raptures, any more than we judge of the natural direction of a tree during a storm. We rather suspect loud profession, for we have observed that deep feeling is generally noiseless, and least seeks display.

We would not, by these remarks, be understood as wishing to exclude from religion warmth, and even transport. We honor and highly value true religious sensibility. We believe that Christianity is intended to act powerfully on our whole nature, on the heart as well as the understanding and the conscience. We conceive of heaven as a state where the love of God will be exalted into an unbounded fervor and joy; and we desire, in our pilgrimage here, to drink into the spirit of that better world. But we think that religious warmth is only to be valued when it springs naturally from an improved character, when it comes unforced, when it is the recompense of obedience, when it is the warmth of a mind which understands God by being like Him, and when, instead of disordering, it exalts the understanding, invigorates conscience, gives a pleasure to common duties, and is seen to exist in connection with cheerfulness, judiciousness, and a reasonable frame of mind. When we observe a fervor called religious in men whose general character expresses little refinement and elevation, and whose piety seems at war with reason, we pay it little respect. We honor religion too much to give its sacred name to a feverish, forced, fluctuating zeal, which has little power over the life. . . .

William Ellery Channing

ON THE EVIDENCES OF REVEALED RELIGION* (1821)

. . . The great objection to Christianity—the only one which has much influence at the present day—meets us at the very threshold. We cannot, if we would, evade it, for it is founded on a primary and essential attribute of this religion. The objection is oftener felt than expressed, and amounts to this—that miracles are incredible, and that the supernatural character of an alleged fact is proof enough of its falsehood. So strong is this propensity to doubt of departures from the order of nature that there are sincere Christians who incline to rest their religion wholly on its internal evidence and to overlook the outward extraordinary interposition of God by which it was at first established. But the difficulty cannot in this way be evaded; for Christianity is not only confirmed by miracles, but is in itself, in its very essence, a miraculous religion. It is not a system which the human mind might have gathered in the ordinary exercise of its powers from the ordinary course of nature. Its doctrines, especially those which relate to its founder, claim for it the distinction of being a supernatural provision for the recovery of the human race. So that the objection which I have stated still presses upon us, and, if it be well grounded, it is fatal to Christianity. . . .

Whence, then, has this skepticism sprung? It may be explained by two principal causes. (1) It is now an acknowledged fact among enlightened men that in past times and in our own a strong disposition has existed and still exists to admit miracles without examination. Human credulity is found to have devoured nothing more eagerly than reports of prodigies. Now, it is argued that we discover here a principle of human nature, namely, the love of the supernatural and marvelous, which accounts sufficiently for the belief of mir-

* Discourse delivered before the University in Cambridge, at the Dudleian Lecture, 14 March, 1821.

acles wherever we find it; and that it is consequently un-
necessary and unphilosophical to seek for other causes, and
especially to admit that most improbable one, the actual
existence of miracles. This sweeping conclusion is a specimen
of that rash habit of generalizing which rather distinguishes
our times, and shows that philosophical reasoning has made
fewer advances than we are apt to boast. It is true that there
is a principle of credulity as to prodigies in a considerable
part of society, a disposition to believe without due scrutiny.
But this principle, like every other in our nature, has its
limits; acts according to fixed laws; is not omnipotent—cannot make the eyes see and the ears hear and the understanding credit delusions under all imaginable circumstances, but
requires the concurrence of various circumstances and of
other principles of our nature in order to its operation. For
example, the belief of spectral appearances has been very
common, but under what circumstances and in what state of
mind has it occurred? Do men see ghosts in broad day and
amidst cheerful society? Or in solitary places, in graveyards,
in twilights or mists, where outward objects are so undefined
as easily to take a form from imagination, and in other circumstances favorable to terror and associated with the delusion in question? The principle of credulity is as regular in
its operation as any other principle of the mind, and is so
dependent on circumstances and so restrained and checked
by other parts of human nature that sometimes the most
obstinate incredulity is found in that very class of people
whose easy belief on other occasions moves our contempt. It
is well known, for example, that the efficacy of the vaccine
inoculation has been encountered with much more unyielding skepticism among the vulgar than among the improved;
and in general, it may be affirmed that the credulity of the
ignorant operates under the control of their strongest passions and impressions, and that no class of society yields a
slower assent to positions which manifestly subvert their old
modes of thinking and most settled prejudices. It is, then,
very unphilosophical to assume this principle as an explanation of all miracles whatever. I grant that the fact that accounts of supernatural agency so generally prove false is a
reason for looking upon them with peculiar distrust. Miracles
ought on this account to be sifted more than common facts.
But if we find that a belief in a series of supernatural works
has occurred under circumstances very different from those
under which false prodigies have been received, under cir-

cumstances most unfavorable to the operation of credulity, then this belief cannot be resolved into the common causes which have blinded men in regard to supernatural agency. We must look for other causes, and if none can be found but the actual existence of the miracles, then true philosophy binds us to believe them.

(2) I proceed now to the second cause of the skepticism in regard to supernatural agency which has grown up, especially among the more improved, in later times. These later times are distinguished, as you well know, by successful researches into nature; and the discoveries of science have continually added strength to that great principle that the phenomena of the universe are regulated by general and permanent laws, or that the Author of the universe exerts His power according to an established order. Nature, the more it is explored, is found to be uniform. We observe an unbroken succession of causes and effects. Many phenomena, once denominated irregular and ascribed to supernatural agency, are found to be connected with preceding circumstances as regularly as the most common events. The comet, we learn, observes the same attraction as the sun and planets. When a new phenomenon now occurs, no one thinks it miraculous, but believes that when better understood, it may be reduced to laws already known, or is an example of a law not yet investigated.

Now this increasing acquaintance with the uniformity of nature begets a distrust of alleged violations of it, and a rational distrust too; for while many causes of mistake in regard to alleged miracles may be assigned, there is but one adequate cause of real miracles, that is, the power of God; and the regularity of nature forms a strong presumption against the miraculous exertion of this power, except in extraordinary circumstances and for extraordinary purposes to which the established laws of the creation are not competent. But the observation of the uniformity of nature produces in multitudes not merely this rational distrust of alleged violations of it, but a secret feeling as if such violations were impossible. That attention to the powers of nature which is implied in scientific research tends to weaken the practical conviction of a higher power; and the laws of the creation, instead of being regarded as the modes of divine operation, come insensibly to be considered as fetters on His agency, as too sacred to be suspended even by their Author. This secret feeling, essentially atheistical and at war with all sound philosophy, is the chief foundation of that skepticism which prevails in regard to miraculous agency, and deserves our particular consideration.

To a man whose belief in God is strong and practical, a miracle will appear as possible as any other effect, as the most common event in life; and the argument against miracles, drawn from the uniformity of nature, will weigh with him only as far as this uniformity is a pledge and proof of the Creator's disposition to accomplish His purposes by a fixed order or mode of operation. Now it is freely granted that the Creator's regard or attachment to such an order may be inferred from the steadiness with which He observes it; and a strong presumption lies against any violation of it on slight occasions, or for purposes to which the established laws of nature are adequate. But this is the utmost which the order of nature authorizes us to infer respecting its Author. It forms no presumption against miracles universally, in all imaginable cases, but may even furnish a presumption in their favor.

We are never to forget that God's adherence to the order of the universe is not necessary and mechanical but intelligent and voluntary. He adheres to it not for its own sake, or because it has a sacredness which compels Him to respect it, but because it is most suited to accomplish His purposes. It is a means and not an end, and like all other means must give way when the end can best be promoted without it. It is the mark of a weak mind to make an idol of order and method, to cling to established forms of business when they clog instead of advancing it. If, then, the great purposes of the universe can best be accomplished by departing from its established laws, these laws will undoubtedly be suspended; and though broken in the letter, they will be observed in their spirit, for the ends for which they were first instituted will be advanced by their violation. Now the question arises, For what purposes were nature and its order appointed? And there is no presumption in saying, that the highest of these is the improvement of intelligent beings. Mind (by which we mean both moral and intellectual powers) is God's first end. The great purpose for which an order of nature is fixed is plainly the formation of Mind. In a creation without order, where events would follow without any regular succession, it is obvious that Mind must be kept in perpetual infancy; for in such a universe there could be no reasoning from effects to causes, no induction to establish general truths, no adaptation of means to ends—that is, no science relating to God or matter or mind, no action, no virtue. The great purpose of God, then, I repeat it, in establishing the order of nature, is to form and advance the mind; and if the case should occur in which the interests of the mind could best be advanced by departing from this order or by miraculous agency, then the great purpose of the creation, the great end of its laws and regularity, would demand such departure, and miracles, instead of warring against, would concur with nature.

Now we Christians maintain that such a case has existed. We affirm that when Jesus Christ came into the world, nature had failed to communicate instructions to men in which, as intelligent beings, they had the deepest concern, and on which the full development of their highest faculties essentially depended; and we affirm that there was no prospect of relief from nature; so that an exigence had occurred in which additional communications, supernatural lights, might rationally be expected from the Father of spirits. Let me state two particulars out of many in which men needed intellectual aids not given by nature. I refer to the doctrine of one God and Father on which all piety rests; and to the doctrine of immortality, which is the great spring of virtuous effort. . . .

That a fixed order of nature, though a proof of the one God to reflecting and enlarged understandings, has yet a tendency to hide him from men in general, will appear, if we consider, first, that as the human mind is constituted, what is regular and of constant occurrence excites it feebly; and benefits flowing to it through fixed, unchanging laws seem to come by a kind of necessity, and are apt to be traced up to natural causes alone. Accordingly, religious convictions and feelings, even in the present advanced condition of society, are excited not so much by the ordinary course of God's providence as by sudden, unexpected events, which rouse and startle the mind and speak of a power higher than nature. There is another way in which a fixed order of nature seems unfavorable to just impressions respecting its Author. It discovers to us in the Creator a regard to general good rather than an affection to individuals. The laws of nature, operating as they do with an inflexible steadiness, never varying to meet the cases and wants of individuals, and inflicting much private suffering in their stern administration for the general weal, give the idea of a distant, reserved sovereign much more than of a tender parent; and yet this last view of God is the only effectual security from superstition and idolatry. Nature then, we fear, would not have brought back the world to its Creator. And as to the doctrine of immortality, the order of the natural world had little tendency to teach this, at least with clearness and energy. The natural world contains no provisions or arrangements for reviving the dead. The sun and the rain, which cover the tomb with verdure, send no vital influences to the moldering body. The researches of science detect no secret processes for restoring the lost powers of life. If man is to live again, he is not to live through any known laws of nature, but by a power higher than nature; and how then can we be assured of this truth but by a manifestation of this power, that is, by miraculous agency confirming a future life?

I have labored in these remarks to show that the uniformity of nature is no presumption against miraculous agency when employed in confirmation of such a religion as Christianity. Nature, on the contrary, furnishes a presumption in its favor. Nature clearly shows to us a power above itself, so that it proves miracles to be possible. Nature reveals purposes and attributes in its Author with which Christianity remarkably agrees. Nature too has deficiencies, which show that it was not intended by its Author to be His whole method of instructing mankind; and in this way it gives great confirmation to Christianity, which meets its wants, supplies its chasms, explains its mysteries, and lightens its heart-oppressing cares and sorrows. . . .

After the remarks now made to remove the objection to revelation in general, I proceed to consider the evidences of the Christian religion in particular; and these are so numerous that should I attempt to compress them into the short space which now remains, I could give but a syllabus, a dry and uninteresting index. It will be more useful to state to you, with some distinctness, the general principle into which all Christian evidences may be resolved, and on which the whole religion rests, and then to illustrate it in a few striking particulars.

All the evidences of Christianity may be traced to this great principle: that every effect must have an adequate cause. We claim for our religion a divine original because no adequate cause for it can be found in the powers or passions of human nature, or in the circumstances under which it appeared; because it can only be accounted for by the interposition of that Being to whom its first preachers universally ascribed it, and with whose nature it perfectly agrees.

Christianity, by which we mean not merely the doctrine of the religion, but everything relating to it, its rise, its progress, the character of its Author, the conduct of its propagators—Christianity, in this broad sense, can only be accounted for in two ways. It either sprang from the principles of human nature, under the excitements, motives, impulses of the age in which it was first preached, or it had its origin in a higher and supernatural agency. To which of these causes the religion should be referred is not a question beyond our reach; for being partakers of human nature, and knowing more of it than of any other part of creation, we can judge with sufficient accuracy of the operation of its principles and of the effects to which they are competent. It is indeed true that human powers are not exactly defined, nor can we state precisely the bounds beyond which they cannot pass; but still the disproportion between human nature and an effect ascribed to it may be so vast and palpable as to satisfy us at once that the effect is inexplicable by human power. I know not precisely what advances may be made by the intellect of an unassisted savage; but that a savage in the woods could not compose the Principia of Newton is about as plain as that he could not create the world. I know not the point at which bodily strength must stop; but that a man cannot carry Atlas or Andes on his shoulders is a safe position. The question, therefore, whether the principles of human nature, under the circumstances in which it was placed at Christ's birth, will explain his religion, is one to which we are competent, and is the great question on which the whole controversy turns.

Now we maintain that a great variety of facts belonging to this religion—such as the character of its Founder; its peculiar principles; the style and character of its records; its progress; the conduct, circumstances, and sufferings of its first propagators; the reception of it from the first on the ground of miraculous attestations; the prophecies which it fulfilled and which it contains; its influence on society, and other circumstances connected with it—are utterly inexplicable by human powers and principles, but accord with and are fully explained by the power and perfections of God.

These various particulars I cannot attempt to unfold. One or two may be illustrated to show you the mode of applying the principles which I have laid down. I will take first the character of Jesus Christ. How is this to be explained by the principles of human nature? We are immediately struck with this peculiarity in the Author of Christianity, that whilst all other men are formed in a measure by the spirit of the age, we can discover in Jesus no impression of the period in which he lived. We know with considerable accuracy the state of society, the modes of thinking, the hopes and expectations of the country in which Jesus was born and grew up; and he is as free from them, and as exalted above them, as if he had lived in another world, or with every sense shut on the objects around him. His character has in it nothing local or temporary. It can be explained by nothing around him. His history shows him to us a solitary being, living for purposes which none but himself comprehended, and enjoying not so much as the sympathy of a single mind. His apostles, his chosen companions, brought to him the spirit of the age; and nothing shows its strength more strikingly than the slowness with which it yielded in these honest men to the instructions of Jesus. . . .

Next to the character of Christ, his religion might be shown to abound in circumstances which contradict and repel the idea of a human origin. For example, its representations of the paternal character of God; its inculcation of a universal charity; the stress which it lays on inward purity; its substitution of a spiritual worship for the forms and ceremonies which everywhere had usurped the name and extinguished the life of religion; its preference of humility and of the mild, unostentatious, passive virtues to the dazzling qualities which had monopolized men's admiration; its consistent and bright discoveries of immortality; its adaptation to the wants of man as a sinner; its adaptation to all the conditions, capacities, and sufferings of human nature; its pure, sublime, yet practicable morality; its high and generous motives; and its fitness to form a character which plainly prepares for a higher life than the present—these are peculiarities of Christianity which will strike us more and more in proportion as we understand distinctly the circumstances of the age and country in which this religion appeared, and for which no adequate human cause has been or can be assigned.

Passing over these topics, each of which might be enlarged into a discourse, I will make but one remark on this religion, which strikes my own mind very forcibly. Since its introduction, human nature has made great progress and society experienced great changes; and in this advanced condition of the world, Christianity, instead of losing its appli-

cation and importance, is found to be more and more congenial and adapted to man's nature and wants. Men have
outgrown the other institutions of that period when Christianity appeared—its philosophy, its modes of warfare, its
policy, its public and private economy; but Christianity has
never shrunk as intellect has opened, but has always kept in
advance of men's faculties and unfolded nobler views in proportion as they have ascended. . . . This fitness of our religion
to more advanced stages of society than that in which it
was introduced, to wants of human nature not then developed, seems to me very striking. The religion bears the
marks of having come from a being who perfectly understood the human mind, and had power to provide for its
progress. This feature of Christianity is of the nature of
prophecy. It was an anticipation of future and distant ages;
and when we consider among whom our religion sprang,
where but in God can we find an explanation of this peculiarity?

I have now offered a few hints on the character of Christ
and on the character of his religion; and before quitting these
topics I would observe that they form a strong presumption
in favor of the miraculous facts of the Christian history.
These miracles were not wrought by a man whose character
in other respects was ordinary. They were acts of a being
whose mind was as singular as his works, who spoke and
acted with more than human authority, whose moral qualities
and sublime purposes were in accordance with superhuman
powers. Christ's miracles are in unison with his whole character, and bear a proportion to it like that which we observe
in the most harmonious productions of nature; and in this
way they receive from it great confirmation. And the same
presumption in their favor arises from his religion. That a
religion carrying in itself such marks of divinity, and so inexplicable on human principles, should receive outward con-
firmations from omnipotence is not surprising. The extraordinary character of the religion accords with, and seems to
demand, extraordinary interpositions in its behalf. Its miracles are not solitary, naked, unexplained, disconnected
events, but are bound up with a system which is worthy of
God, and impressed with God; which occupies a large space,
and is operating with great and increasing energy in human
affairs. . . .

William Ellery Channing

LIKENESS TO GOD* (1828)

* Discourse at the Ordination of the Rev. F. A. Farley, Providence, R. I., 1828.

. . . I begin with observing what all indeed will understand, that the likeness of God of which I propose to speak belongs to man's higher or spiritual nature. It has its foundation in the original and essential capacities of the mind. In proportion as these are unfolded by right and vigorous exertion, it is extended and brightened. In proportion as these lie dormant, it is obscured. In proportion as they are perverted and overpowered by the appetites and passions, it is blotted out. In truth, moral evil, if unresisted and habitual, may so blight and lay waste these capacities that the image of God in man may seem to be wholly destroyed.

The importance of this assimilation to our Creator is a topic which needs no labored discussion. All men, of whatever name, or sect, or opinion, will meet me on this ground. All, I presume, will allow that no good in the compass of the universe, or within the gift of omnipotence, can be compared to a resemblance of God, or to a participation of His attributes. I fear no contradiction here. Likeness to God is the supreme gift. He can communicate nothing so precious, glorious, blessed as Himself. To hold intellectual and moral affinity with the Supreme Being, to partake His spirit, to be His children by derivations of kindred excellence, to bear a growing conformity to the perfection which we adore, this is a felicity which obscures and annihilates all other good.

It is only in proportion to this likeness that we can enjoy either God or the universe. That God can be known and enjoyed only through sympathy or kindred attributes is a doctrine which even Gentile philosophy discerned. That the pure in heart can alone see and commune with the pure Divinity was the sublime instruction of ancient sages as well as of in-

54

spired prophets. It is indeed the lesson of daily experience. To understand a great and good being, we must have the seeds of the same excellence. How quickly, by what an instinct, do accordant minds recognize one another! No attraction is so powerful as that which subsists between the truly wise and good; whilst the brightest excellence is lost on those who have nothing congenial in their own breasts. God becomes a real being to us in proportion as His own nature is unfolded within us. To a man who is growing in the likeness of God, faith begins even here to change into vision. He carries within himself a proof of a Deity which can only be understood by experience. He more than believes, he feels the divine presence, and gradually rises to an intercourse with his Maker to which it is not irreverent to apply the name of friendship and intimacy. The apostle John intended to express this truth when he tells us that he in whom a principle of divine charity or benevolence has become a habit and life "dwells in God and God in him."

It is plain, too, that likeness to God is the true and only preparation for the enjoyment of the universe. In proportion as we approach and resemble the mind of God, we are brought into harmony with the creation; for in that proportion we possess the principles from which the universe sprang; we carry within ourselves the perfections of which its beauty, magnificence, order, benevolent adaptations, and boundless purposes are the results and manifestations. God unfolds Himself in His works to a kindred mind. It is possible that the brevity of these hints may expose to the charge of mysticism what seems to me the calmest and clearest truth. I think, however, that every reflecting man will feel that likeness to God must be a principle of sympathy or accordance with His creation; for the creation is a birth and shining forth of the Divine Mind, a work through which His spirit breathes. In proportion as we receive this spirit, we possess within ourselves the explanation of what we see. We discern more and more of God in everything, from the frail flower to the everlasting stars. Even in evil, that dark cloud which hangs over the creation, we discern rays of light and hope, and gradually come to see in suffering and temptation, proofs and instruments of the sublimest purposes of wisdom and love.

I have offered these very imperfect views that I may show the great importance of the doctrine which I am solicitous to enforce. I would teach that likeness to God is a good so unutterably surpassing all other good that whoever admits it as attainable must acknowledge it to be the chief aim of life. I would show that the highest and happiest office of religion is to bring the mind into growing accordance with God, and that by the tendency of religious systems to this end their truth and worth are to be chiefly tried.

I am aware that it may be said that the Scriptures, in speaking of man as made in the image of God and in calling us to imitate Him, use bold and figurative language. It may be said that there is danger from too literal an interpretation; that God is an unapproachable being; that I am not warranted in ascribing to man a like nature to the Divine; that we and all things illustrate the Creator by contrast, not by resemblance; that religion manifests itself chiefly in convictions and acknowledgments of utter worthlessness; and that to talk of the greatness and divinity of the human soul is to inflate that pride through which Satan fell, and through which man involves himself in that fallen spirit's ruin.

I answer that, to me, Scripture and reason hold a different language. In Christianity particularly, I meet perpetual testimonies to the divinity of human nature. This whole religion expresses an infinite concern of God for the human soul, and teaches that he deems no methods too expensive for its recovery and exaltation. Christianity, with one voice, calls me to turn my regards and care to the spirit within me, as of more worth than the whole outward world. It calls us to "be perfect as our Father in heaven is perfect"; and everywhere, in the sublimity of its precepts, it implies and recognizes the sublime capacities of the being to whom they are addressed. It assures us that human virtue is "in the sight of God of great price," and speaks of the return of a human being to virtue as an event which increases the joy of heaven. In the New Testament, Jesus Christ, the Son of God, the brightness of His glory, the express and unsullied image of the Divinity, is seen mingling with men as a friend and brother, offering himself as their example, and promising to his true followers a share in all his splendors and joys. In the New Testament, God is said to communicate His own spirit and all His fullness to the human soul. In the New Testament man is exhorted to aspire after "honor, glory, and immortality"; and Heaven, a word expressing the nearest approach to God and a divine happiness, is everywhere proposed as the end of his being. In truth, the very essence of

Christian faith is that we trust in God's mercy, as revealed in Jesus Christ, for a state of celestial purity in which we shall grow forever in the likeness and knowledge and enjoyment of the Infinite Father. Lofty views of the nature of man are bound up and interwoven with the whole Christian system. Say not that these are at war with humility; for who was ever humbler than Jesus, and yet who ever possessed such a consciousness of greatness and divinity? Say not that man's business is to think of his sin and not of his dignity; for great sin implies a great capacity; it is the abuse of a noble nature; and no man can be deeply and rationally contrite but he who feels that in wrongdoing he has resisted a divine voice, and warred against a divine principle, in his own soul. I need not, I trust, pursue the argument from revelation. There is an argument from nature and reason which seems to me so convincing, and is at the same time so fitted to explain what I mean by man's possession of a like nature to God, that I shall pass at once to its exposition.

That man has a kindred nature with God, and may bear most important and ennobling relations to him, seems to me to be established by a striking proof. This proof you will understand by considering for a moment how we obtain our ideas of God. Whence come the conceptions which we include under that august name? Whence do we derive our knowledge of the attributes and perfections which constitute the Supreme Being? I answer, we derive them from our own souls. The divine attributes are first developed in ourselves and thence transferred to our Creator. The idea of God, sublime and awful as it is, is the idea of our own spiritual nature, purified and enlarged to infinity. In ourselves are the elements of the Divinity. God, then, does not sustain a figurative resemblance to man. It is the resemblance of a parent to a child, the likeness of a kindred nature.

We call God a Mind. He has revealed himself as a spirit. But what do we know of mind but through the unfolding of this principle in our own breasts? That unbounded spiritual energy which we call God is conceived by us only through consciousness, through the knowledge of ourselves. We ascribe thought or intelligence to the Deity as one of His most glorious attributes. And what means this language? These terms we have framed to express operations or faculties of our own souls. The Infinite Light would be forever hidden from us did not kindred rays dawn and brighten within us. God is another name for human intelligence, raised above all error and imperfection, and extended to all possible truth.

The same is true of God's goodness. How do we understand this but by the principle of love implanted in the human breast? Whence is it that this divine attribute is so faintly comprehended but from the feeble development of it in the multitude of men? Who can understand the strength, purity, fullness, and extent of divine philanthropy but he in whom selfishness has been swallowed up in love?

The same is true of all the moral perfections of the Deity. These are comprehended by us only through our own moral nature. It is conscience within us, which, by its approving and condemning voice, interprets to us God's love of virtue and hatred of sin; and without conscience these glorious conceptions would never have opened on the mind. It is the lawgiver in our own breasts which gives us the idea of divine authority and binds us to obey it. The soul, by its sense of right, or its perception of moral distinctions, is clothed with sovereignty over itself, and through this alone it understands and recognizes the Sovereign of the Universe. Men, as by a natural inspiration, have agreed to speak of conscience as the voice of God, as the Divinity within us. This principle, reverently obeyed, makes us more and more partakers of the moral perfection of the Supreme Being, of that very excellence which constitutes the rightfulness of His scepter and enthrones Him over the universe. Without this inward law we should be as incapable of receiving a law from Heaven as the brute. Without this, the thunders of Sinai might startle the outward ear, but would have no meaning, no authority, to the mind. I have expressed here a great truth. Nothing teaches so encouragingly our relation and resemblance to God; for the glory of the Supreme Being is eminently moral. We blind ourselves to His chief splendor if we think only or mainly of His power and overlook those attributes of rectitude and goodness to which He subjects his omnipotence, and which are the foundations and very substance of His universal and immutable law. And are these attributes revealed to us through the principles and convictions of our own souls? Do we understand through sympathy God's perception of the right, the good, the holy, the just? Then with what propriety is it said that in His own image He made man!

I am aware that it may be objected to these views that we receive our idea of God from the universe, from His works, and not so exclusively from our own souls. The universe, I know, is full of God. The heavens and earth declare His glory. In other words, the effects and signs of power, wisdom, and goodness are apparent through the whole creation. But apparent to what? Not to the outward eye, not to the acutest organs of sense, but to a kindred mind, which interprets the universe by itself. It is only through that energy of thought by which we adapt various and complicated means to distant ends, and give harmony and a common bearing to multiplied exertions, that we understand the creative intelligence which has established the order, dependencies, and harmony of nature. We see God around us because He dwells within us. It is by a kindred wisdom that we discern His wisdom in His works. The brute, with an eye as piercing as ours, looks on the universe; and the page, which to us is radiant with characters of greatness and goodness, is to him a blank. In truth, the beauty and glory of God's works are revealed to the mind by a light beaming from itself. We discern the impress of God's attributes in the universe by accordance of nature, and enjoy them through sympathy. I hardly need observe that these remarks in relation to the universe apply with equal, if not greater force, to revelation.

I shall now be met by another objection which to many may seem strong. It will be said that these various attributes of which I have spoken exist in God in infinite perfection, and that this destroys all affinity between the human and the divine mind. To this I have two replies. In the first place, an attribute, by becoming perfect, does not part with its essence. Love, wisdom, power, and purity do not change their nature by enlargement. If they did, we should lose the Supreme Being through his very infinity. Our ideas of him would fade away into mere sounds. For example, if wisdom in God, because unbounded, have no affinity with that attribute in man, why apply to him that term? It must signify nothing. Let me ask what we mean when we say that we discern the marks of intelligence in the universe? We mean that we meet there the proofs of a mind like our own. We certainly discern proofs of no other; so that to deny this doctrine would be to deny the evidences of a God, and utterly to subvert the foundations of religious belief. What man can examine the structure of a plant or an animal, and see the adaptation of its parts to each other and to common ends, and not feel that it is the work of an intel-

ligence akin to his own, and that he traces these marks of
design by the same spiritual energy in which they had their
origin?

But I would offer another answer to this objection that
God's infinity places Him beyond the resemblance and approach of man. I affirm, and I trust that I do not speak too
strongly, that there are traces of infinity in the human mind,
and that in this very respect it bears a likeness to God.
The very conception of infinity is the mark of a nature
to which no limit can be prescribed. This thought indeed
comes to us not so much from abroad as from our own
souls. We ascribe this attribute to God because we possess
capacities and wants which only an unbounded being can
fill, and because we are conscious of a tendency in spiritual
faculties to unlimited expansion. We believe in the divine
infinity through something congenial with it in our own
breasts. I hope I speak clearly, and if not, I would ask
those to whom I am obscure to pause before they condemn.
To me it seems that the soul, in all its higher actions, in
original thought, in the creations of genius, in the soarings
of imagination, in its love of beauty and grandeur, in its
aspirations after a pure and unknown joy, and especially in
disinterestedness, in the spirit of self-sacrifice, and in enlightened devotion, has a character of infinity. There is often
a depth in human love which may be strictly called un-
fathomable. There is sometimes a lofty strength in moral
principle which all the power of the outward universe cannot overcome. There seems a might within which can more
than balance all might without. There is, too, a piety which
swells into a transport too vast for utterance, and into an
immeasurable joy. I am speaking indeed of what is uncommon, but still of realities. We see, however, the tendency
of the soul to the infinite in more familiar and ordinary
forms. Take for example the delight which we find in the
vast scenes of nature, in prospects which spread around us
without limits, in the immensity of the heavens and the
ocean, and especially in the rush and roar of mighty winds,
waves, and torrents, when, amidst our deep awe, a power
within seems to respond to the omnipotence around us. The
same principle is seen in the delight ministered to us by
works of fiction or of imaginative art, in which our own
nature is set before us in more than human beauty and
power. In truth, the soul is always bursting its limits. It
thirsts continually for wider knowledge. It rushes forward

to untried happiness. It has deep wants which nothing limited can appease. Its true element and end is an unbounded good. Thus God's infinity has its image in the soul, and through the soul much more than through the universe, we arrive at this conception of the Deity.

In these remarks I have spoken strongly. But I have no fear of expressing too strongly the connection between the divine and the human mind. My only fear is that I shall dishonor the great subject. The danger to which we are most exposed is that of severing the Creator from His creatures. The propensity of human sovereigns to cut off communication between themselves and their subjects, and to disclaim a common nature with their inferiors, has led the multitude of men, who think of God chiefly under the character of a king, to conceive of Him as a being who places His glory in multiplying distinctions between Himself and all other beings. The truth is that the union between the Creator and the creature surpasses all other bonds in strength and intimacy. He penetrates all things and delights to irradiate all with His glory. Nature, in its lowest and inanimate forms, is pervaded by His power; and when quickened by the mysterious property of life, how wonderfully does it show forth the perfections of its Author! How much of God may be seen in the structure of a single leaf, which, though so frail as to tremble in every wind, yet holds connections and living communications with the earth, the air, the clouds, and the distant sun; and, through these sympathies with the universe, is itself a revelation of an omnipotent mind. God delights to diffuse Himself everywhere. Through His energy, unconscious matter clothes itself with proportions, powers, and beauties which reflect His wisdom and love. How much more must He delight to frame conscious and happy recipients of His perfections in whom His wisdom and love may substantially dwell, with whom He may form spiritual ties, and to whom He may be an everlasting spring of moral energy and happiness. How far the Supreme Being may communicate His attributes to His intelligent offspring I stop not to inquire. But that His almighty goodness will impart to them powers and glories, of which the material universe is but a faint emblem, I cannot doubt. That the soul, if true to itself and its Maker, will be filled with God, and will manifest Him more than that sun, I cannot doubt. Who can doubt it that believes and understands the doctrine of human immortality?

The views which I have given in this discourse respecting man's participation of the divine nature seem to me to receive strong confirmation from the title or relation most frequently applied to God in the New Testament; and I have reserved this as the last corroboration of this doctrine because to my own mind it is singularly affecting. In the New Testament God is made known to us as a Father, and a brighter feature of that book cannot be named. Our worship is to be directed to Him as our Father. Our whole religion is to take its character from this view of the Divinity. In this He is to rise always to our minds. And what is it to be a Father? It is to communicate one's own nature, to give life to kindred beings; and the highest function of a Father is to educate the mind of the child, and to impart to it what is noblest and happiest in his own mind. God is our Father not merely because He created us, or because He gives us enjoyment, for He created the flower and the insect, yet we call Him not their Father. This bond is a spiritual one. This name belongs to God because He frames spirits like Himself and delights to give them what is most glorious and blessed in His own nature. Accordingly, Christianity is said with special propriety to reveal God as the Father because it reveals Him as sending His Son to cleanse the mind from every stain and to replenish it forever with the spirit and moral attributes of its Author. Separate from God this idea of His creating and training up beings after His own likeness, and you rob Him of the paternal character. This relation vanishes, and with it vanish the glory of the gospel and the dearest hopes of the human soul.

The great use which I would make of the principles laid down in this discourse is to derive from them just and clear views of the nature of religion. What then is religion? I answer, it is not the adoration of a God with whom we have no common properties, of a distinct, foreign, separate being, but of an all-communicating Parent. It recognizes and adores God as a being whom we know through our own souls, who has made man in His own image, who is the perfection of our own spiritual nature, who has sympathies with us as kindred beings, who is near us, not in place only like this all-surrounding atmosphere, but by spiritual influence and love, who looks on us with parental interest, and whose great design it is to communicate to us forever, and in freer and fuller streams, His own power, goodness, and joy. The conviction of this near and ennobling relation of God to the soul, and of His great purposes toward it, belongs to the very essence of true religion; and true religion manifests itself chiefly and most conspicuously in desires, hopes, and efforts corresponding to this truth. It desires and seeks supremely the assimilation of the mind to God, or the perpetual unfolding and enlargement of those powers and virtues by which it is constituted His glorious image. The mind, in proportion as it is enlightened and penetrated by true religion, thirsts and labors for a godlike elevation. What else indeed can it seek, if this good be placed within its reach? If I am capable of receiving and reflecting the intellectual and moral glory of my Creator, what else in comparison shall I desire? Shall I deem a property in the outward universe as the highest good when I may become partaker of the very mind from which it springs, of the prompting love, the disposing wisdom, the quickening power, through which its order, beauty, and beneficent influences subsist? True religion is known by these high aspirations, hopes, and efforts. And this is the religion which most truly honors God. To honor Him is not to tremble before Him as an unapproachable sovereign, nor to utter barren praise which leaves us as it found us. It is to become what we praise. It is to approach God as an inexhaustible fountain of light, power, and purity. It is to feel the quickening and transforming energy of His perfections. It is to thirst for the growth and invigoration of the divine principle within us. It is to seek the very spirit of God. It is to trust in, to bless, to thank Him for that rich grace, mercy, love which was revealed and proffered by Jesus Christ and which proposes as its great end the perfection of the human soul.

I regard this view of religion as infinitely important. It does more than all things to make our connection with our Creator ennobling and happy; and in proportion as we want it, there is danger that the thought of God may itself become the instrument of our degradation. That religion has been so dispensed as to depress the human mind, I need not tell you; and it is a truth which ought to be known that the greatness of the Deity, when separated in our thoughts from His parental character, especially tends to crush human energy and hope. To a frail, dependent creature an omnipotent Creator easily becomes a terror, and His worship easily degenerates into servility, flattery, self-contempt,

and selfish calculation. Religion only ennobles us in as
far as it reveals to us the tender and intimate connection
of God with His creatures, and teaches us to see in the very
greatness which might give alarm the source of great and
glorious communications to the human soul. You cannot,
my hearers, think too highly of the majesty of God. But
let not this majesty sever Him from you. Remember that His
greatness is the infinity of attributes which yourselves possess. Adore His infinite wisdom; but remember that this wisdom rejoices to diffuse itself, and let an exhilarating hope
spring up at the thought of the immeasurable intelligence
which such a Father must communicate to His children. In
like manner adore His power. Let the boundless creation
fill you with awe and admiration of the energy which sustains it. But remember that God has a nobler work than
the outward creation, even the spirit within yourselves; and
that it is His purpose to replenish this with His own energy
and to crown it with growing power and triumphs over the
material universe. Above all, adore His unutterable goodness.
But remember that this attribute is particularly proposed to
you as your model; that God calls you, both by nature and
revelation, to a fellowship in His philanthropy; that He has
placed you in social relations for the very end of rendering you ministers and representatives of His benevolence;
that He even summons you to espouse and to advance the
sublimest purpose of His goodness, the redemption of the
human race, by exerting the knowledge and power of Christian truth. It is through such views that religion raises up
the soul and binds man by ennobling bonds to his Maker.

To complete my views of this topic, I beg to add an
important caution. I have said that the great work of religion
is to conform ourselves to God, or to unfold the divine
likeness within us. Let none infer from this language that I
place religion in unnatural effort, in straining after excitements which do not belong to the present state, or in anything separate from the clear and simple duties of life. I
exhort you to no extravagance. I reverence human nature
too much to do it violence. I see too much divinity in its
ordinary operations to urge on it a forced and vehement
virtue. To grow in the likeness of God we need not cease to
be men. The likeness does not consist in extraordinary or
miraculous gifts, in supernatural additions to the soul, or
in anything foreign to our original constitution, but in our
essential faculties, unfolded by vigorous and conscientious

exertion in the ordinary circumstances assigned by God. To resemble our Creator we need not fly from society and entrance ourselves in lonely contemplation and prayer. Such processes might give a feverish strength to one class of emotions, but would result in disproportion, distortion, and sickliness of mind. Our proper work is to approach God by the free and natural unfolding of our highest power—of understanding, conscience, love and the moral will.

Shall I be told that by such language I ascribe to nature the effects which can only be wrought in the soul by the Holy Spirit? I anticipate this objection, and wish to meet it by a simple exposition of my views. I would on no account disparage the gracious aids and influences which God imparts to the human soul. The promise of the Holy Spirit is among the most precious in the sacred volume. Worlds could not tempt me to part with the doctrine of God's intimate connection with the mind, and of His free and full communications to it. But these views are in no respect at variance with what I have taught of the method by which we are to grow in the likeness of God. Scripture and experience concur in teaching that by the Holy Spirit we are to understand a divine assistance adapted to our moral freedom and accordant with the fundamental truth that virtue is the mind's own work. By the Holy Spirit I understand an aid which must be gained and made effectual by our own activity; an aid which no more interferes with our faculties than the assistance which we receive from our fellow beings; an aid which silently mingles and conspires with all other helps and means of goodness; an aid by which we unfold our natural powers in a natural order, and by which we are strengthened to understand and apply the resources derived from our munificent Creator. This aid we cannot prize too much, or pray for too earnestly. But wherein, let me ask, does it war with the doctrine that God is to be approached by the exercise and unfolding of our highest powers and affections in the ordinary circumstances of human life?

I repeat it, to resemble our Maker we need not quarrel with our nature or our lot. Our present state, made up as it is of aids and trials, is worthy of God, and may be used throughout to assimilate us to Him. For example, our domestic ties, the relations of neighborhood and country, the daily interchanges of thoughts and feelings, the daily occasions of kindness, the daily claims of want and suffering—

these and the other circumstances of our social state form
the best sphere and school for that benevolence which is
God's brightest attribute; and we should make a sad exchange
by substituting for these natural aids any self-invented artificial means of sanctity. Christianity, our great guide to
God, never leads us away from the path of nature, and
never wars with the unsophisticated dictates of conscience.
We approach our Creator by every right exertion of the
powers He gives us. Whenever we invigorate the understanding by honestly and resolutely seeking truth, and by with-
standing whatever might warp the judgment; whenever we
invigorate the conscience by following it in opposition to the
passions; whenever we receive a blessing gratefully, bear a
trial patiently, or encounter peril or scorn with moral courage; whenever we perform a disinterested deed; whenever we
lift up the heart in true adoration to God; whenever we war
against a habit or desire which is strengthening itself against
our higher principles; whenever we think, speak, or act with
moral energy and resolute devotion to duty, be the occasion
ever so humble, obscure, familiar—then the divinity is growing within us, and we are ascending toward our Author. True
religion thus blends itself with common life. We are thus to
draw nigh to God without forsaking men. We are thus, without parting with our human nature, to clothe ourselves with
the divine. . . .

Sampson Reed

ON GENIUS* (1821)

The world was always busy; the human heart has always had love of some kind; there has always been fire on the earth. There is something in the inmost principles of an individual, when he begins to exist, which urges him onward; there is something in the center of the character of a nation to which the people aspire; there is something which gives activity to the mind in all ages, countries, and worlds. This principle of activity is love: it may be the love of good or of evil; it may manifest itself in saving life or in killing; but it is love.

The difference in the strength and direction of the affections creates the distinctions in society. Every man has a form of mind peculiar to himself. The mind of the infant contains within itself the first rudiments of all that will be hereafter, and needs nothing but expansion, as the leaves and branches and fruit of a tree are said to exist in the seed from which it springs. He is bent in a particular direction, and as some objects are of more value than others, distinctions must exist. What it is that makes a man great depends upon the state of society: with the savage, it is physical strength; with the civilized, the arts and sciences; in heaven, the perception that love and wisdom are from the Divine.

There prevails an idea in the world that its great men are more like God than others. This sentiment carries in its bosom sufficient evil to bar the gates of heaven. So far as a person possesses it, either with respect to himself or others, he has no connection with his Maker, no love for his neighbor, no truth in his understanding. This was at the root of heathen idolatry: it was this that made men worship

* An oration delivered at the awarding of his M.A. degree. First published in *Aesthetic Papers* (1849), ed. by E. P. Peabody.

67

saints and images. It contains within itself the seeds of atheism, and will ultimately make every man insane by whom it is cherished. The life which circulates in the body is found to commence in the head, but unless it be traced through the soul up to God, it is merely corporeal, like that of the brutes.

Man has often ascribed to his own power the effects of the secret operations of divine truth. When the world is immersed in darkness, this is a judgment of the Most High, but the light is the effect of the innate strength of the human intellect.

When the powers of man begin to decay, and approach an apparent dissolution, who cannot see the Divinity? But what foreign aid wants the man who is full of his own strength? God sends the lightning that blasts the tree, but what credulity would ascribe to Him the sap that feeds its branches? The sight of idiotism leads to a train of religious reflections, but the face that is marked with lines of intelligence is admired for its own inherent beauty. The hand of the Almighty is visible to all in the stroke of death, but few see his face in the smiles of the newborn babe.

The intellectual eye of man is formed to see the light, not to make it; and it is time that, when the causes that cloud the spiritual world are removed, man should rejoice in the truth itself and that *he* has found it. More than once, when nothing was required but for a person to stand on this world with his eyes open, has the truth been seized upon as a thing of his own making. When the power of divine truth begins to dispel the darkness, the objects that are first disclosed to our view—whether men of strong understanding or of exquisite taste or of deep learning—are called geniuses. Luther, Shakespeare, Milton, Newton stand with the bright side toward us.

There is something which is called genius that carries in itself the seeds of its own destruction. There is an ambition which hurries a man after truth and takes away the power of attaining it. There is a desire which is null, a lust which is impotence. There is no understanding so powerful that ambition may not in time bereave it of its last truth, even that two and two are four. Know then that genius is divine not when the man thinks that he is God, but when he acknowledges that his powers are from God. Here is the link of the finite with the infinite, of the divine with the human: this is the humility which exalts.

The arts have been taken from nature by human invention; and as the mind returns to its God, they are in a measure swallowed up in the source from which they came. We see as they vanish the standard to which we should refer them. They are not arbitrary, having no foundation except in taste: they are only modified by taste, which varies according to the state of the human mind. Had we a history of music, from the war-song of the savage to the song of angels, it would be a history of the affections that have held dominion over the human heart. Had we a history of architecture, from the first building erected by man to the house not made with hands, we might trace the variations of the beautiful and the grand, alloyed by human contrivance, to where they are lost in beauty and grandeur. Had we a history of poetry, from the first rude effusions to where words make one with things and language is lost in nature, we should see the state of man in the language of licentious passion, in the songs of chivalry, in the descriptions of heroic valor, in the mysterious wildness of Ossian, till the beauties of nature fall on the heart as softly as the clouds on the summer's water. The mind, as it wanders from heaven, molds the art into its own form and covers its nakedness. Feelings of all kinds will discover themselves in music, in painting, in poetry, but it is only when the heart is purified from every selfish and worldly passion that they are created in real beauty, for in their origin they are divine.

Science is more fixed. It consists of the laws according to which natural things exist, and these must be either true or false. It is the natural world in the abstract, not in the concrete. But the laws according to which things exist are from the things themselves, not the opposite. Matter has solidity: solidity makes no part of matter. If, then, the natural world is from God, the abstract properties, as dissected and combined, are from Him also. If, then, science be from Him who gave the ten commandments, must not a life according to the latter facilitate the acquirement of the former? Can *he* love the works of God who does not love His commandments? It is only necessary that the heart be purified to have science, like poetry, its spontaneous growth. Self-love has given rise to many false theories because a selfish man is disposed to make things differently from what God has made them. Because God is love, nature exists; because God is love, the Bible is poetry. If, then, the love of God creates the scenery of nature, must not he whose mind is most open

to this love be most sensible of natural beauties? But in
nature both the sciences and the arts exist embodied.

Science may be learned from ambition, but it must be by
the sweat of the brow. The filthy and polluted mind *may*
carve beauties from nature, with which it has no allegiance:
the rose is blasted in the gathering. The olive and the vine
had rather live with God than crown the head of him whose
love for them is a lust for glory. The man is cursed who
would rob nature of her graces, that he may use them to
allure the innocent virgin to destruction.

Men say there is an inspiration in genius. The genius of the
ancients was the good or evil spirit that attended the man.
The moderns speak of the magic touch of the pencil and of
the inspiration of poetry. But this inspiration has been
esteemed so unlike religion that the existence of the one almost supposes the absence of the other. The spirit of God
is thought to be a very different thing when poetry is
written from what it is when the heart is sanctified. What
has the inspiration of genius in common with that of the
cloister? The one courts the zephyrs; the other flies them.
The one is cheerful; the other sad. The one dies; the other
writes the epitaph. Would the Muses take the veil? Would
they exchange Parnassus for a nunnery? Yet there has been
learning, and even poetry, under ground. The yew loves the
graveyard; but other trees have grown there.

It needs no uncommon eye to see that the finger of death
has rested on the church. Religion and death have in the
human mind been connected with the same train of associations. The churchyard is the graveyard. The bell which calls
men to worship is to toll at their funerals, and the garments
of the priests are of the color of the hearse and the coffin.
Whether we view her in the strange melancholy that sits on
her face, in her mad reasonings about truth, or in the occasional convulsions that agitate her limbs, there are symptoms, not of life, but of disease and death. It is not strange,
then, that genius, such as could exist on the earth, should
take its flight to the mountains. It may be said that great
men are good men. But what I mean is that, in the human
mind, greatness is one thing and goodness another; that
philosophy is divorced from religion; that truth is separated
from its source; that that which is called goodness is sad,
and that which is called genius is proud.

Since things are so, let men take care that the life which
is received be genuine. Let the glow on the cheek spring

from the warmth of the heart and the brightness of the eyes beam from the light of heaven. Let ambition and the love of the world be plucked up by their roots. How can he love his neighbor who desires to be above him? He may love him for a slave, but that is all. Let not the shrouds of death be removed till the living principle has entered. It was not till Lazarus was raised from the dead and had received the breath of life that the Lord said, "Loose him, and let him go."

When the heart is purified from all selfish and worldly affections, then may genius find its seat in the church. As the human mind is cleansed of its lusts, truth will permit and invoke its approach, as the coyness of the virgin subsides into the tender love of the wife. The arts will spring in full-grown beauty from Him who is the source of beauty. The harps which have hung on the willows will sound as sweetly as the first breath of heaven that moved the leaves in the garden of Eden. Cannot a man paint better when he knows that the picture ought not to be worshiped?

Here is no sickly aspiring after fame, no filthy lust after philosophy, whose very origin is an eternal barrier to the truth. But sentiments will flow from the heart warm as its blood, and speak eloquently, for eloquence is the language of love. There is a unison of spirit and nature. The genius of the mind will descend and unite with the genius of the rivers, the lakes, and the woods. Thoughts fall to the earth with power, and make a language out of nature.

Adam and Eve knew no language but their garden. They had nothing to communicate by words, for they had not the power of concealment. The sun of the spiritual world shone bright on their hearts, and their senses were open with delight to natural objects. In the eye were the beauties of paradise; in the ear was the music of birds; in the nose was the fragrance of the freshness of nature; in the taste was the fruit of the garden; in the touch, the seal of their eternal union. What had they to *say?*

The people of the golden age have left us no monuments of genius, no splendid columns, no paintings, no poetry. They possessed nothing which evil passions might not obliterate; and when their "heavens were rolled together as a scroll," the curtain dropped between the world and their existence.

Science will be full of life, as nature is full of God. She will wring from her locks the dew which was gathered in the wilderness. By science, I mean natural science. The science of the human mind must change with its subject. Locke's mind will not always be the standard of metaphysics. Had we a description of it in its present state, it would make a very different book from "Locke on the Human Understanding."

The time is not far distant. The cock has crowed. I hear the distant lowing of the cattle which are grazing on the mountains. "Watchman, what of the night? Watchman, what of the night? The watchman saith, The morning cometh."

Sampson Reed

OBSERVATIONS ON THE GROWTH OF THE MIND (1826)

Nothing is a more common subject of remark than the changed condition of the world. There is a more extensive intercourse of thought and a more powerful action of mind upon mind than formerly. The good and the wise of all nations are brought nearer together and begin to exert a power which, though yet feeble as infancy, is felt throughout the globe. Public opinion, that helm which directs the progress of events by which the world is guided to its ultimate destination, has received a new direction. The mind has attained an upward and onward look and is shaking off the errors and prejudices of the past. The gothic structure of the feudal ages, the ornament of the desert, has been exposed to the light of heaven, and continues to be gazed at for its ugliness as it ceases to be admired for its antiquity. The world is deriving vigor not from that which is gone by, but from that which is coming, not from the unhealthy moisture of the evening, but from the nameless influences of the morning. The loud call on the past to instruct us, as it falls on the rock of ages, comes back in echo from the future. Both mankind and the laws and principles by which they are governed seem about to be redeemed from slavery. The moral and intellectual character of man has undergone and is undergoing a change; and as this is effected it must change the aspect of all things, as when the position-point is altered from which a landscape is viewed. We appear to be approaching an age which will be the silent pause of merely physical force before the powers of the mind—the timid, subdued, awed condition of the brute gazing on the erect and godlike form of man. . . .

As all the changes which are taking place in the world originate in the mind, it might be naturally expected that nothing would change more than the mind itself, and what-

73

ever is connected with a description of it. . . . The powers of the mind are most intimately connected with the subjects by which they are occupied. We cannot think of the will without feeling, of the understanding without thought, or of the imagination without something like poetry. The mind is visible when it is active; and as the subjects on which it is engaged are changed, the powers themselves present a different aspect. New classifications arise and new names are given. . . . Thus it is that there is nothing fixed in the philosophy of the mind; it is said to be a science which is not demonstrative, and though now thought to be brought to a state of great perfection, another century under the providence of God and nothing will be found in the structure which has cost so much labor but the voice "he is not here, but is risen."

Is then everything that relates to the immortal part of man fleeting and evanescent, while the laws of physical nature remain unaltered? Do things become changeable as we approach the immutable and the eternal? Far otherwise. The laws of the mind are in themselves as fixed and perfect as the laws of matter; but they are laws from which we have wandered. There is a philosophy of the mind, founded not on the aspect it presents in any part or in any period of the world, but on its immutable relations to its first cause; a philosophy equally applicable to man before or after he has passed the valley of the shadow of death; not dependent on time or place, but immortal as its subject. The light of this philosophy has begun to beam faintly on the world, and mankind will yet see their own moral and intellectual nature by the light of revelation, as it shines through the moral and intellectual character it shall have itself created. It may be remarked also that the changes in the sciences and the arts are entirely the effect of revelation. To revelation it is to be ascribed that the genius which has taught the laws of the heavenly bodies and analyzed the material world did not spend itself in drawing the bow or in throwing the lance, in the chase or in war, and that the vast powers of Handel did not burst forth in the wild notes of the war-song. It is the tendency of revelation to give a right direction to every power of every mind; and when this is effected, inventions and discoveries will follow of course, all things assume a different aspect, and the world itself again becomes a paradise.

It is the object of the following pages not to be influenced by views of a temporal or local nature, but to look at the mind as far as possible in its essential revealed character, and beginning with its powers of acquiring and retaining truth, to trace summarily that development which is required in order to render it truly useful and happy. It is believed that they will not be found at variance with the state of the public mind on the subject of education, whether of the child or the man.

. . . There is a power of growth in the spiritual man, and if in his progress we be able to mark as in the grain of the oak the number of the years, this is only a circumstance, and all that is gained would be as real if no such lines existed. The mind ought not to be limited by the short period of its own duration in the body with a beginning and end comprising a few years; it should be poised on its own immortality, and what is learned should be learned with a view to that real adaptation of knowledge to the mind which results from the harmony of creation, and whenever or wherever we exist it will be useful to us. The memory has in reality nothing to do with time, any more than the eye has with space. As the latter learns by experience to measure the distance of objects, so the consciousness of the present existence of states of mind is referred to particular periods of the past. But when the soul has entered on its *eternal* state, there is reason to believe that the past and the future will be swallowed up in the present; that memory and anticipation will be lost in consciousness; that everything of the past will be comprehended in the present, without any reference to time, and everything of the future will exist in the divine effort of progression.

What is time? There is perhaps no question that would suggest such a variety of answers. It is represented to us from our infancy as producing such important changes, both in destroying some and in healing the wounds it has inflicted on others, that people generally imagine, if not an actual person, it is at least a real existence. We begin with time in the primer, and end with reasoning about the foreknowledge of God. What is time? The difficulty of answering the question (and there are few questions more difficult) arises principally from our having ascribed so many important effects to that which has no real existence. It is true that all things in the natural world are subject to change. But however these changes may be connected in our minds with time, it requires but a moment's reflection to see that time has no agency in them. They are the effects of chemical, or more properly perhaps, of natural decompositions and reorganizations. Time, or rather our idea of it, so far from having produced anything, is itself the effect of changes. There are certain operations in nature which, depending on fixed laws, are in themselves perfectly regular; if all things were equally so, the question "How long?" might never be asked. We should never speak of a late season, or of premature old age; but everything passing on in an invariable order, all the idea of time that would remain with respect to any object would be a sort of instinctive sense of its condition, its progress or decay. But most of the phenomena in the natural world are exceedingly irregular, for though the same combination of causes would invariably produce the same effect, the same combination very rarely occurs. Hence in almost every change, and we are conversant with nothing but changes, we are assisted in ascertaining its nature and extent by referring it to something in itself perfectly regular. We find this regularity in the apparent motions of the sun and moon. It is difficult to tell how much our idea of time is the effect of artificial means of keeping it, and what would be our feelings on the subject if left to the simple operations of nature—but they would probably be little else than a reference of all natural phenomena to that on which they principally depend, the relative situation of the sun and earth; and the idea of an actual succession of moments would be in a measure resolved into that of cause and effect.

Eternity is to the mind what time is to nature. We attain a perception of it by regarding all the operations in the world within us as they exist in relation to their first cause, for in doing this, they are seen to partake somewhat of the nature of that Being on whom they depend. We make no approaches to a conception of it by heaping day upon day or year upon year. This is merely an accumulation of time; and we might as well attempt to convey an idea of mental greatness by that of actual space as to communicate a conception of eternity by years or thousands of years. Mind and matter are not more distinct from each other than their properties; and by an attempt to embrace all time we are actually farther from an approach to eternity than when we confine ourselves to a single instant—because we merely collect the largest possible amount of natural changes, whereas that which is eternal approaches that which is immutable. . . . It is impossible to conceive of either time or space without matter. The reason is, they are the effect of matter; and as it is by creating matter that they are produced, so it is by thinking of it that they are conceived of. It need not be said how exceedingly improper it is to apply the usual ideas of time and space to the Divine Being, making him subject to that which he creates. . . . Time, then, is nothing real so far as it exists in our own minds.

Nor do we find a nearer approach to reality by any analysis of nature. Everything, as was said, is subject to change, and one change prepares the way for another by which there is growth and decay. There are also motions of bodies both in nature and art which in their operation observe fixed laws; and here we end. The more we enter into an analysis of things, the farther are we from finding anything that answers to the distinctness and reality which are usually attached to a conception of time; and there is reason to believe that when this distinctness and reality are most deeply rooted (whatever may be the theory), they are uniformly attended with a practical belief of the actual motion of the sun, and are indeed the effect of it. Let us then continue to talk of time as we talk of the rising and setting of the sun; but let us think rather of those changes in their origin and effect, from which a sense of time is produced. This will carry us one degree nearer the actual condition of things; it will admit us one step further into the temple of creation —no longer a temple created six thousand years ago, and deserted by him who formed it, but a temple with the hand of the builder resting upon it, perpetually renewing, perpetually creating—and as we bow ourselves to worship the "I am," "Him who liveth forever and ever, who created heaven and the things that are therein, and the earth and the things that are therein, and the sea and the things that are therein," we may hear in accents of divine love the voice that proclaims "that there shall be time no longer." . . .

Keeping in view what has been said on the subject of time, then, the mind is presented to us as not merely active in the acquirement of truth, but active in its possession. . . . There prevails a most erroneous sentiment that the mind is originally vacant, and requires only to be filled up; and there is reason to believe that this opinion is most intimately connected with false conceptions of time. The mind is originally a most delicate germ whose husk is the body, planted in this world that the light and heat of heaven may fall upon it with a gentle radiance and call forth its energies. The process of learning is not by synthesis or analysis. It is the most perfect illustration of both. As subjects are presented to the operation of the mind, they are decomposed and reorganized in a manner peculiar to itself, and not easily explained. . . .

Till the time of Newton, the motion of the heavenly bodies was in the strictest sense a miracle. It was an event which stood alone, and was probably regarded with peculiar reference to the Divine Being. The feeling of worship with which they had previously been regarded had subsided into a feeling of wonder, till at length they were received into the family of our most familiar associations. There is one step further. It is to regard gravitation wherever it may be found as an effect of the constant agency of the Divine Being, and from a consciousness of his presence and cooperation in every step we take, literally "to walk humbly with our God." It is agreeable to the laws of moral and intellectual progression that all phenomena, whether of matter or mind, should become gradually classified, till at length all things wherever they are found, all events, whether of history or experience, of mind or matter—shall at once conspire to form one stupendous miracle, and cease to be such. They will form a miracle in that they are seen to depend constantly and equally on the power of the Lord; and they will cease to be a miracle in that the power which pervades them is so constant, so uniform and so mild in its operation that it produces nothing of fear, nothing of surprise. From whatever point we contemplate the scene, we feel that we are still in our Father's house; go where we will, the paternal roof, the broad canopy of heaven is extended over us.

It is agreeable to our nature that the mind should be particularly determined to one object. The eye appears to be the point at which the united rays of the sun within and the sun without converge to an expression of unity; and accordingly the understanding can be conscious of but one idea or image at a time. Still there is another and a different kind of consciousness which pervades the mind, which is coextensive with everything it actually possesses. There is but one object in nature on which the *eye* looks directly, but the whole body is pervaded with nerves which convey perpetual information of the existence and condition of every part. So it is with the possessions of the mind; and when an object ceases to be the subject of this kind of consciousness, it ceases to be remembered. The memory, therefore, as was said, is not a dormant but an active power. It is rather the possession than the retention of truth. It is a consciousness of the will, a consciousness of character, a consciousness which is produced by the mind's preserving in effort whatever it actually possesses. It is the power which the mind has of preserving truth without actually making it the subject of thought, bearing a relation to thought analogous to what this bears to the actual perception of the senses or to language. Thus we remember a distant object without actually thinking of it, in the same way that we think of it without actually seeing it. . . .

It follows from these views of the subject that the true way to store the memory is to develop the affections. The mind must grow, not from external accretion, but from an internal principle. Much may be done by others in aid of its development; but in all that is done it should not be forgotten that even from its earliest infancy it posseses a character and a principle of freedom which *should be* respected and *cannot* be destroyed. Its peculiar propensities may be discerned and proper nutriment and culture supplied—but the infant plant, not less than the aged tree, must be permitted, with its own organs of absorption, to separate that which is peculiarly adapted to itself; otherwise it will be cast off as a foreign substance, or produce nothing but rottenness and deformity. . . .

What then is that development which the nature of the human mind requires? What is that education which has heaven for its subject, and such a heaven as will be the effect of the orderly growth of the spiritual man?

As all minds possess that in common which makes them human, they require to a certain extent the same general development by which will be brought to view the same powers however distinct and varied they may be found in different individuals; and as every mind possesses something peculiar to which it owes its character and its effect, it requires a particular development by which may be produced a full, sincere, and humble expression of its natural features, and the most vigorous and efficient exertion of its natural powers. These make one, so far as regards the individual.

Those sciences which exist embodied in the natural world appear to have been designed to occupy the first place in the development of all minds, or in that which might be called the general development of the mind. These comprise the laws of the animal, vegetable, and mineral kingdoms. The human mind, being as it were planted in nature by its heavenly Father, was designed to enter into matter and detect knowledge for its own purposes of growth and nutrition. This gives us a true idea of memory, or rather of what memory should be. We no longer think of a truth as being laid up in a mind for which it has no affinity, and by which it is perhaps never to be used; but the latent affections as they expand under proper culture absolutely require the truth to receive them, and its first use is the very nutriment it affords. It is not more difficult for the tree to return to the seed from which it sprang than for the man who has learned thus, to cease to remember. The natural sciences are the basis of all useful knowledge, alike important to man in whatever time, place, or condition he is found. . . . Natural philosophy seems almost essential to an enlightened independence of thought and action. A man may lean upon others, and be so well supported by an equal pressure in all directions as to be apparently dependent on no one, but his independence is apt to degenerate into obstinacy, or betray itself in weakness, unless his mind is fixed on this unchanging basis. A knowledge of the world may give currency to his sentiments and plausibility to his manners, but it is more frequently a knowledge of *the world* that gives light to the path and stability to the purposes. By the one he may learn what coin is current, by the other what possesses intrinsic value. The natural world was precisely and perfectly adapted to invigorate and strengthen the intellectual and moral man. Its first and highest use was not to support the vegetables which adorn, or the animals which cover, its surface, nor yet to give sustenance to the human body—it has a higher and holier object, in the attainment of which these are only means. It was intended to draw forth and mature the latent energies of the soul, to impart to them its own verdure and freshness, to initiate them into its own mysteries, and by its silent and humble dependence on its Creator, to leave on them, when it is withdrawn by death, the full impression of His likeness.

It was the design of Providence that the infant mind should possess the germ of every science. If it were not so, they could hardly be learned. The care of God provides for the flower of the field a place wherein it may grow, regale with its fragrance, and delight with its beauty. Is His providence less active over those to whom this flower offers its incense? No. The soil which produces the vine in its most healthy luxuriance is not better adapted to the end than the world we inhabit to draw forth latent energies of the soul and fill them with life and vigor. As well might the eye see with-

out light, or the ear hear without sound, as the human mind
be healthy and athletic without descending into the natural
world and breathing the mountain air. Is there aught in
eloquence which warms the heart? She draws her fire from
natural imagery. Is there aught in poetry to enliven the imagination? There is the secret of all her power. Is there aught in
science to add strength and dignity to the human mind? The
natural world is only the body of which she is the soul. In
books science is presented to the eye of the pupil as it were
in a dried and preserved state; the time may come when the
instructor will take him by the hand and lead him by the
running streams and teach him all the principles of science
as she comes from her Maker, as he would smell the
fragrance of the rose without gathering it.

This love of nature, this adaptation of man to the place
assigned him by his heavenly Father, this fullness of the mind
as it descends into the works of God, is something which
has been felt by everyone, though to an imperfect degree, and
therefore needs no explanation. It is the part of science that
this be no longer a blind affection, but that the mind be
opened to a just perception of what it is which it loves. The
affection which the lover first feels for his future wife may be
attended only by a general sense of her external beauty, but
his mind gradually opens to a perception of the peculiar features of the soul, of which the external appearance is only
an image. So it is with nature. Do we love to gaze on the
sun, the moon, the stars, and the planets? This affection contains in its bosom the whole science of astronomy, as the
seed contains the future tree. It is the office of the instructor
to give it an existence and a name by making known the
laws which govern the motions of the heavenly bodies, the
relation of these bodies to each other, and their uses. Have
we felt delight in beholding the animal creation, in watching their pastimes and their labors? It is the office of the instructor to give birth to this affection by teaching the different
classes of animals with their peculiar characteristics, which
inhabit the earth, air, and sea. Have we known the inexpressible pleasure of beholding the beauties of the vegetable
world? This affection can only expand in the science of
botany. Thus it is that the love of nature in the mass may
become the love of all the sciences; and the mind will grow
and bring forth fruit from its own inherent power of development. . . .

It is in this way the continual endeavor of Providence that

the natural sciences should be the spontaneous production of the human mind. To these should certainly be added poetry and music, for when we study the works of God as we should, we cannot disregard that inherent beauty and harmony in which these arts originate. These occasion in the mind its first glow of delight, like the taste of food as it is offered to the mouth; and the pleasure they afford is a pledge of the strength and manhood afterwards imparted by the sciences.

By poetry is meant all those illustrations of truth by natural imagery which spring from the fact that this world is the mirror of him who made it. Strictly speaking, nothing has less to do with fiction than poetry. The day will come, and it may not be far distant, when this art will have another test of merit than mere versification, or the invention of strange stories; when the laws by which poetry is tested will be as fixed and immutable as the laws of science; when a change will be introduced into taste corresponding to that which Bacon introduced into philosophy, by which both will be confined within the limits of things as they actually exist. It would seem that genius would be cramped, that the powers of invention would be destroyed, by confining the human mind, as it were, at home, within the bounds which nature has assigned. But what wider scope need it have? It reaches the throne of God; it rests on his footstool. All things spiritual and natural are before it. There is as much that is true as false; and truth presented in natural imagery is only dressed in the garments which God has given it.

The imagination was permitted for ages to involve the world in darkness by putting theory in the place of fact, till at length the greatest man revealed the simplest truth, that our researches must be governed by actual observation. God is the source of all truth. Creation (and what truth does not result from creation?) is the effect of the Divine Love and Wisdom. Simply to will and to think with the Divine Being result in creating, in actually producing those realities which form the groundwork of the thoughts and affections of man. But for the philosopher to desire a thing, and to think that it existed, produced nothing but his own theory. Hence it was necessary that he should bring his mind into coincidence with things as they exist, or in other words with the truth.

Fiction in poetry must fall with theory in science, for they depend equally on the works of creation. The word fiction, however, is not intended to be used in its most literal sense, but to embrace whatever is not in exact agreement with the creative spirit of God. It belongs to the true poet to feel this spirit and to be governed by it; to be raised above the senses; to live and breathe in the inward efforts of things; to feel the power of creation, even before he sees the effect; to witness the innocence and smiles of nature's infancy, not by extending the imagination back to chaos, but by raising the soul to nature's origin. The true poetic spirit, so far from misleading any, is the strongest bulwark against deception. It is the soul of science. Without it, the latter is a cheerless, heartless study, distrusting even the presence and power of Him to whom it owes its existence. Of all the poetry which exists, that only possesses the seal of immortality which presents the image of God which is stamped on nature. Could the poetry which now prevails be viewed from the future, when all partialities and antipathies shall have passed away and things are left to rest on their own foundations, when good works shall have dwindled into insignificance from the mass of useless matter that may have fallen from them, and bad ones shall have ceased to allure with false beauty; we might catch a glimpse of the rudiments of this divine art amid the weight of extraneous matter by which it is now protected and which it is destined to throw off. The imagination will be refined into a chaste and sober view of unveiled nature. It will be confined within the bounds of reality. It will no longer lead the way to insanity and madness by transcending the works of creation and, as it were, wandering where God has no power to protect it; but finding a resting place in every created object, it will enter into it and explore its hidden treasures, the relation in which it stands to mind, and reveal the love it bears to its Creator. . . . When there shall be a religion which shall see God in everything, and at all times; and the natural sciences not less than nature itself shall be regarded in connection with Him, the fire of poetry will begin to be kindled in its immortal part and will burn without consuming. The inspiration so often feigned will become real, and the mind of the poet will feel the spark which passes from God to nature. The veil will be withdrawn and beauty and innocence displayed to the eye, for which the lasciviousness of the imagination and the wantonness of desire may seek in vain.

There is a language not of words but of things. When this language shall have been made apparent, that which is human will have answered its end, and being as it were resolved into its original elements, will lose itself in nature. The use of language is the expression of our feelings and desires, the manifestation of the mind. But everything which is, whether animal or vegetable, is full of the expression of that use for which it is designed, as of its own existence. If we did but understand its language, what could our words add to its meaning? It is because we are unwilling to hear that we find it necessary to say so much; and we drown the voice of nature with the discordant jargon of ten thousand dialects. Let a man's language be confined to the expression of that which actually belongs to his own mind, and let him respect the smallest blade which grows and permit it to speak for itself. Then may there be poetry which may not be written, perhaps, but which may be felt as a part of our being. Everything which surrounds us is full of the utterance of one word, completely expressive of its nature. This word is its name; for God, even now could we but see it, is creating all things and giving a name to every work of his love in its perfect adaptation to that for which it is designed. But man has abused his power and has become insensible to the real character of the brute creation, still more so to that of inanimate nature, because in his selfishness he is disposed to reduce them to slavery. Therefore he is deaf. We find the animal world either in a state of savage wildness or enslaved submission. It is possible that as the character of man is changed, they may attain a midway condition equally removed from both. As the mind of man acknowledges its dependence on the Divine Mind, brutes may add to their instinct submission to human reason, preserving an unbroken chain from our Father in heaven to the most inanimate parts of creation. Such may be supposed to have been the condition of the animal on which the King of Zion rode into Jerusalem, at once free and subject to the will of the rider. Everything will seem to be conscious of its use, and man will become conscious of the use of everything.

It may be peculiar, and is said with deference to the opinions of others, but to my ear, rhymes add nothing to poetry, but rather detract from its beauty. They possess too strongly the marks of art, and produce a sameness which tires, and sometimes disgusts. We seek for them in vain in nature, and may therefore reasonably presume that they spring out of the peculiar state of the public taste, without possessing any real foundation in the mind itself; that they are rather the fashion of the dress than any essential part. In the natural world we find nothing which answers to them or

feels like them—but a happy assemblage of living objects
springing up not in straight lines and at a fixed distance, but
in God's own order, which by its apparent want of design
conveys the impression of perfect innocence and humility. It
is not for that which is human to be completely divested of the
marks of art, but every approach toward this end must be
an approach toward perfection. The poet should be free and
unshackled as the eagle whose wings, as he soars in the air,
seem merely to serve the office of a helm, while he moves
on simply by the agency of the will.

By music is meant not merely that which exists in the
rational world, whether in the song of angels or men; not
merely the singing of birds and the lowing of cattle, by
which the animal world express their affections and their
wants—but that harmony which pervades also all orders of
creation; the music of the harp of universal nature, which
is touched by the rays of the sun, and whose song is the morning, the evening, and the seasons. Music is the voice of God,
and poetry his language, both in His word and works. The one
is to the ear what the other is to the eye. Every child of nature must feel their influence. There was a time when the
human mind was in more perfect harmony with the Divine
Mind than the lower orders of creation and the tale of
the harp of Orpheus, to which the brutes, the vegetables, and
the rocks listened, is not altogether unfounded in reality—but
when the selfish and worldly passions usurped the place of
love to our God and our neighbor, the mind of man began to
be mute in its praise. The original order was reversed. The
very stones cry out, and we do well to listen to them.

There is a most intimate and almost inseparable connection
between poetry and music. This is indicated by the fact that
they are always united. Nothing is sung which has not some
pretensions to poetry; and nothing has any pretensions to
poetry in which there is not something of music. A good ear
is essential to rhythm, and rhythm is essential to verse. It is
the perfection of poetry that it addresses two senses at once,
the ear and the eye; that it prepares the affections for the
object before it is presented; that it sends light through the
understanding by forming a communication between the heart
of man and the works of God. The character of music must
have always harmonized with that of poetry. It is essential
to the former that it should be in agreement with our feelings,
for it is from this circumstance that it derives its power.
That music which is in unison with the Divine Mind alone

deserves the name. So various is it found in the different conditions of man that it is hardly recognized as the same thing.
There is music in the war-song of the savage and in the
sound for battle. Alas! how unlike that music which proclaimed peace on earth and good will toward men. Poetry and
music, like virtuous females in disguise, have followed our
race into the darkest scenes to which the fall has brought
them. We find them in the haunts of dissipation and vice, in
the song of revelry and lewdness. We meet them again kindling the fire of devotion at the altar of God, and find them
more and more perfect as we approach their divine origin. . . .

Enough has been said to illustrate generally the influence of
the natural world in the development of the mind. The
actual condition of society operates to produce the same effect,
with hardly less power. In this are comprised the religious and
civil institutions of one's own country; that peculiar character
in which they originate; and a knowledge of the past, as by
disclosing the origin and progress of things, it throws light on
the prospect actually before us. As the philosophy connected
with the natural world is that in which the mind may take
root, by which it may possess an independence worthy a being
whose eternal destiny is in his own hands—so the moral and
civil institutions, the actual condition of society, is the atmosphere which surrounds and protects it, in which it sends
forth its branches and bears fruit. The spiritual part of man
is as really a substance as the material, and is as capable of
acting upon spirit as matter is upon matter. It is not from
words of instruction and advice that the mind of the infant
derives its first impetus; it gathers strength from the warmth
of those affections which overshadow it, and is nourished by
a mother's love even before it has attained the power of
thought. It is the natural tendency of things that an individual
should be brought into a situation in which the external condition of the place and the circle of society in which he is
are particularly adapted to bring forth to view his hereditary
character. The actual condition of the human mind is, as it
were, the solid substance in which the laws of moral and
intellectual philosophy and political economy (whatever may
be their quality) exist embodied, as the natural sciences do
in the material world. A knowledge of those laws, such as
they exist, is the natural consequence of the development of
the affections by which a child is connected with those that
surround him. The connection of mind is not less powerful or
universal than that of matter. All minds, whatever may be

their condition, are not unconnected with God, and consequently not unconnected with each other. All nations, under whatever system of government, and in whatever state of civilization, are under the Divine Providence, surely but almost imperceptibly advancing to a moral and political order such as the world has not yet seen. They are guided by the same hand, and with a view to the same destiny. Much remains to be done, and more to be suffered, but the end is certain. The humblest individual may, nay *must* aid in the accomplishment of this consummation. It is not for time or space to set limits to the effects of the life of a single man. Let then the child be so initiated into a knowledge of the condition of mankind that the love at first indulged in the circle of his father's family shall gradually subside into a chaste and sober love of his country—and of his country not as opposed to other countries, but as aiding them in the same great object. Let the young mind be warmed and cherished by whatever is chaste and generous in the mind of the public, and be borne on to a knowledge of our institutions by the rich current of the disposition to preserve them. . . .

There is . . . another power which is necessary to the orderly development of the mind: the power of the Word of God. This indeed has been implied in all the preceding remarks. No possessions and no efforts of the mind are unconnected with it, whatever may be the appearance. Revelation so mingles with everything which meets us that it is not easy for us to measure the degree to which our condition is affected by it. Its effects appear miraculous at first, but after they have become established, the mind as in the ordinary operations of nature is apt to become unconscious of the power by which they are produced. All growth or development is effected from within, outward. It is so with animals; it is so with vegetables; it is so with the body; it is so with the mind. . . . It is not a mere metaphor, it is a plain and simple fact that the Spirit of God is as necessary to the development of the mind as the power of the natural sun to the growth of vegetables and in the same way. But let us remember that as in nature the heat and light may be converted into the most noxious poison, so the Spirit of God, in itself perfectly pure and holy, may be converted into passions the most opposite to its nature. It is left to us to open our hearts to its influence by obeying its commandments. . . .

The Bible can never be fully understood either by making it subservient to natural reason or by blindly adopting what

reason would reject, but by that illumination of the understanding and enlargement of the reason which will result from
a gradual conformity to its precepts. Reason now is something very different from what it was a few centuries past.
We are in the habit of thinking that the mode of reasoning
has changed, but this appears to be merely an indication of a
change which has taken place in the character of the mind itself. Syllogistic reasoning is passing away. It has left no permanent demonstration but that of its own worthlessness. It
amounts to nothing but the discernment and expression of
the particulars which go to comprise something more general;
and as the human mind permits things to assume a proper
arrangement from their own inherent power of attraction, it is
no longer necessary to bind them together with syllogisms.
Few minds can now endure the tediousness of being led
blindfold to a conclusion, and of being satisfied with the result merely from the recollection of having been satisfied on
the way to it. The mind requires to view the parts of a subject, not only separately but together; and the understanding
in the exercise of those powers of arrangement, by which a
subject is presented in its just relations to other things, takes
the name of reason. We appear to be approaching that condition which requires the union of reason and eloquence, and
will be satisfied with neither without the other. We neither
wish to see an anatomical plate of bare muscles nor the
gaudy daubings of finery, but a happy mixture of strength and
beauty. We desire language neither extravagant nor cold, but
blood-warm. Reason is beginning to learn the necessity of
simply tracing the relations which exist between created
things, and of not even touching what it examines lest it
disturb the arrangement in the cabinet of creation—and as in
the progress of moral improvement the imagination (which is
called the creative power of man) shall coincide with the
actively creative will of God, reason will be clothed with
eloquence as nature is with verdure. . . .

The insufficiency of reason to judge the Bible is obvious
on the very face of revelation from its miracles. The laws of
Divine Operation are perfectly uniform and harmonious;
and a miracle is a particular instance of Divine Power which
for a want of a more interior and extended knowledge of the
ways of God, appearing to stand alone and to have been the
result of an unusual ‘exertion of the Divine Will, creates
in the minds of men what its name implies, a sensation of
wonder. That there are miracles in the Bible proves that

there are laws of the Divine Operation and of the Divine Government which are not embraced within the utmost limits of that classification and arrangement which is the result of natural reason. . . . They are insulated examples of laws as boundless as the universe, and by the manner in which we are affected by them prove how much we have to learn, and how utterly incompetent we are to judge the ways of God from that reason which is founded on our own limited and fallacious observation. . . .

It is well known that at a certain period of life, the character of a man begins to be more distinctly marked. He appears to become separated from that which surrounds him —to stand in a measure aloof from his associates—to raise his head above the shadow of any earthly object into the light of heaven, and to walk with a more determined step on the earth beneath. This is the manifestation of a character which has always existed, and which has, as it were, been accumulating by little and little, till at length it has attained its full stature. . . .

Every individual . . . possesses peculiar powers which should be brought to bear on society in the duties best fitted to receive them. The highest degree of cultivation of which the mind of anyone is capable consists in the most perfect development of that peculiar organization which as really exists in infancy as in maturer years. The seed which is planted is said to possess in miniature the trunk, branches, leaves, and fruit of the future tree. So it is with the mind; and the most that can possibly be done is to afford facilities by which its development may be effected with the same order. In the process of the formation of our minds, there exists the spirit of prophecy; and no advancement can create surprise because we have always been conscious of that from which it is produced. We must not seek to make one hair white or black. It is in vain for us to attempt to add one cubit to our stature. All adventitious or assumed importance should be cast off as a filthy garment. We should seek an employment for the mind in which all its energies may be warmed into existence, which (if I may be allowed the expression) may bring every muscle into action. There is something which everyone can do better than anyone else, and it is the tendency and must be the end of human events to assign to each his true calling. Kings will be hurled from their thrones and peasants exalted to the highest stations by this irresistible tendency of mind to its true level. These effects may not be fully disclosed in the short period of this life, but even the most incredulous must be ultimately convinced that the truth is no respecter of persons, by learning the simple fact that a man cannot be other than what he is. Not that endless progression in moral goodness and in wisdom are not within the reach of anyone, but that the state will never arrive when he may not look back to the first rudiments—the original stamina of his own mind—and be almost able to say, I possessed all at the time of my birth. The more a person lives in singleness of heart, in simplicity and sincerity, the more will this be apparent.

It becomes us then to seek and to cherish this *peculium* of our own minds as the patrimony which is left us by our Father in heaven—as that by which the branch is united to the vine—as the forming power within us, which gives to our persons that by which they are distinguished from others —and by a life entirely governed by the commandments of God, to leave on the duties we are called to perform the full impress of our real characters. Let a man's ambition to be great disappear in a willingness to be what he is; then may he fill a high place without pride or a low one without dejection. As our desires become more and more concentrated to those objects which correspond to the peculiar organization of our minds, we shall have a foretaste of that which is coming, in those internal tendencies of which we are conscious. As we perform with alacrity whatever duty presents itself before us, we shall perceive in our own hearts a kind of preparation for every external event or occurrence of our lives, even the most trivial, springing from the all-pervading tendency of the Providence of God to present the opportunity of being useful wherever there is the disposition.

Living in a country whose peculiar characteristic is said to be a love of equal liberty, let it be written on our hearts that the end of all education is a life of active usefulness. We want no education which shall raise a man out of the reach of the understanding or the sympathies of any of his species. We are disgusted with that kind of dignity which the possessor is himself obliged to guard, but venerate that which, having its origin in the actual character of the man, can receive no increase from the countenance of power and suffer no diminution from the approach of weakness—that dignity in which the individual appears to live rather in the consciousness of the light which shines from above than in that of his own shadow beneath. There is a spiritual at-

mosphere about such a one which is at once its own
protection and the protection of him with whom it is
connected—which, while it is free as air alike to the most
powerful and the most humble, conveys a tacit warning that
too near an approach is not permitted. We acknowledge the
invisible chain which binds together all classes of society,
and would apply to it the electric spark of knowledge
with the hand of tenderness and caution. We acknowledge
the healthy union of mental and bodily exercise, and would
rather see all men industrious and enlightened than to see
one half of mankind slaves to the other, and these slaves to
their passions. We acknowledge that the natural world is one
vast mine of wisdom, and for this reason it is the scene of
the labors of man; and that in seeing this wisdom, there is
philosophy, and in loving it, there is religion. Most sensibly
do we feel that as the true end of instruction is to prepare
a man for some particular sphere of usefulness, that when
he has found this sphere his education has then truly commenced, and the finger of God is pointing to the very page of
the book of his oracles from which he may draw the profoundest wisdom. It was the design of Providence that
there should be enough of science connected with the calling
of each, for the highest and holiest purposes of heaven. It is
the natural world from which the philosopher draws his
knowledge; it is the natural world in which the slave toils
for his bread. Alas! when will they be one? When we are
willing to practice what we learn, and religion makes our
duty our delight. The mass of mankind must always labor;
hence it is supposed that they must be always ignorant.
Thus has the pride of man converted that discipline into an
occasion of darkness and misery which was intended only to
give reality to knowledge and to make happiness eternal.
Truth is the way in which we should act; and then only is a
man truly wise, when the body performs what the mind perceives. In this way, flesh and blood are made to partake
of the wisdom of the spiritual man; and the palms of our
hands will become the book of our life, on which is inscribed all the love and all the wisdom we possess. It is the
light which directs a man to his duty; it is by doing his duty
that he is enlightened—thus does he become identified with
his own acts of usefulness, and his own vocation is the silken
chord which directs to his heart the knowledge and the blessings of all mankind.

Bronson Alcott

JOURNALS (1826-1838)

December 6, 1826

It is not from books entirely that instruction is to be
drawn. They should only be subservient to our main purpose.
They should lie by us for occasional instruction only. When
doubts and uncertainties arise, they may sometimes explain
the difficulty and point to the truth. Frequently, however,
they lead us astray. They are imperfect. Adherence to them
has been the cause, and still continues to be, of perpetuating
error among men, and that to an alarming extent. Ideas,
when vended in a book, carry with them a kind of dignity and certainty which awe many into implicit belief. They
often impose the most irrational and absurd conclusions on
the fearful understanding. It dare not doubt. Fear keeps it
ignorant. Authority lifts her head and commands instant belief. Reason, thus hushed into slumber, sleeps in secure repose. To dare to think, to think for oneself, is denominated
pride and arrogance. And millions of human minds are in
this state of slavery and tyranny.

How shall they escape?

Rebel! Think for themselves! Let others grumble; dare to
be singular. Let others direct; follow Reason. Let others
dwell in the land of enchantments; be men. Let others prat-
tle; practice. Let others profess; do good. Let others define
goodness; act. Let others sleep; whatever thy hand findeth to
do, that do with all thy might, and let a gainsaying
calumniating world speculate on your proceedings.

September 21, 1828

The province of the instructor should be simple, awakening, invigorating, directing, rather than the forcing of the
child's faculties upon prescribed and exclusive courses of

thought. He should look to the child to see what is to be done, rather than to his book or his system. The child is the book. The operations of his mind are the true system. Let him study these carefully and his success is sure. Let him follow out the impulses, the thoughts, the volitions, of the child's mind and heart, in their own principles and rational order of expression, and his training will be what God designed it to be—an aid to prepare the child to aid himself.

April 24, 1834

To us [Americans] the past *is* of value. Not, however, in the way of example; for the parallel is wanting, the analogy is dim. Circumstances are widely different. Man is operating on vastly different external relations. We are spread over a wider space; we have freer air; Nature spreads itself around us on a wider scale; our situation is wholly new. Nor are *men* the same. Physical differences have molded us in accordance with their spirit. Our physical and intellectual make are national; and, despite the foreign associations of our ancestral education, Nature has assumed her rightful influence and has shaped us in her molds. Living on the accumulated treasures of the past in a new theater of action, we have monopolized the best of time and space, and stand on a vantage ground to which no people have ever ascended before.

June 18, 1834

May we not believe that thought gives life and meaning to external nature, that what we see, hear, feel, taste, and experience around us acquires these properties by the self-investing power of our spirits? Is not the living Spirit of all things in our spirits, and do they not, through the vivid action, the picturing, life-starting agency of this same Spirit, rise up, tinted and shaped, before us, even as in starting from the bed of rest the external world becomes visible to us with the opening of our eyes—not so much to let in the light as to let out our spirits upon the scene which they color and animate with beauty and life?

The reality is in the mind. Sense but gives us an outward type of it, an outward shaping to reduce it to the cognizance of the understanding, and in space and time to substantiate the indwelling forms of our spirits. We throw ourselves outward upon nature that we may the better look upon ourselves, and this process is rendered more conscious to us in the act of waking than in any other.

June 20, 1834

There is a world of true and lasting felicity into which my spirit sometimes strays, and catches glimpses of its soul-enkindling scenery. But there it stays not long. It is beckoned back again by some one of the thousand toils of the present and visible, to resume the little tasks of yesterday and complete what the present calls for. Would that it could remain longer where it so loves to dwell! Would that its toils might be *in* and *for* the relations of this sphere! Light might then be its pervading element, a clear and untroubled vision its constant privilege!

January, 1835

In the varied universe wherein man holdeth his individual being, is there aught more worthy of interest or study than himself, a member of this same wondrous fabric? We investigate the qualities or apprehend the laws of this universe to little purpose if the relations which they hold to our being are not made the primary objects of observation and thought. The true and the devout inquirer takes an humble stand in the grounds of his own being, and from this he goes forth to the survey of Nature and of Providence, being guided and illuminated by a faith that perceiveth in all things and in all beings the same sustaining, upholding Life that quickeneth and filleth his own conscious being. To him the universe is significant because of the self-conscious Life that actuateth his own individual spirit.

Hence it is that the spirit which is ever striving to find in the manifestations of Nature illustrations of its own being, its functions and laws, doth ever receive the ready and satisfactory answer. Nature willingly vouchsafes to such a one a reply. Docility, meekness, confiding trust, are rewarded. By seeking communion and fellowship with Nature, by proving constant to her requirements, such a one endoweth himself with her powers; and taketh all her meanings into himself, setting a value and a name upon her operations and subordinating these to his own spiritual activity. In the mighty Self within him he beholds energies whose ceaseless play shall overcome the kingdoms of Time and Space and establish an eternal dominion, making the universe the instrument of its power.

January 2, 1835

After a day of great interest in the duties of the school, I passed the evening with Dr. Channing. The conversation turned chiefly on the uses of history.

Dr. C., from the deficiency of his own knowledge on this subject and a still lingering tinge of that scholastic discipline by which his mind was formed, sets a much higher value on mere historical knowledge than belongs of right to it in a scale of human acquirement. He says that he is daily reminded of his own deficiencies and is compelled to recur to authorities, when, as I feel, he should have the facts in his own mind. History, he thinks, is one of the most effectual revelations of human nature—the facts of the past are the manifestations of the capacities of the human race. He thinks we cannot conceive of the dignity and destiny of man without the lights of history.

Now, while I would not take from his view of the importance of this knowledge, yet I think much knowledge of our nature can be derived from the study of individual life. History is rather the exhibition of the power of the individual than of the people. Enter into the subtle mechanism of the life of a great man, penetrate the secret by which he vivified and shaped the conceptions that thrill through the life of a people and spread themselves out in their institutions, and you have studied the true elements of history, you have viewed things in their universality, in their origin. All without, all that shapes itself in this external life, is contained in this individual life, and is but its product in time and space. Here is the mighty energy that awakened and saved, deadened or wrecked, a people. Biography is the only true historical record of human nature, for this is the history of spiritual causes, of which physical changes—all the vicissitudes of external life—are but the consequences. Events in the external world are so complex, so infracted as it were by the interventions of Providence, so far removed from the simple powers on which they depend, that they become perplexing and of dubious meaning unless seen in the light of a spiritual sense, and then they are of small value because they are seen in their insignificance.

In biography we are presented with life in its spirituality;

we behold humanity, and we see it not in the soiled glory of its original prerogatives but in its native dignity. For an individual becomes known and remembered because he retains his innate excellence, and, amid a world of contaminated spirits, shines forth as by contrast in all his brightness to their wondering, admiring eyes. The record of wickedness ceases to be interesting when we have penetrated its motives, and we feel that our common nature—so far from being represented in its true light—is deformed and dimmed; it is libeled, and we are indignant at the injustice. It is the sentiment of excellence that lifts our nature into the light of true perception, so that we can behold all its lineaments and penetrate our own individual being.

When God would reveal Himself to a people He entrusts the sacred truth not to that people in their aggregate capacity but to a gifted spirit among them, who transfuses it from himself into them.

January 21, 1835

I am more interested in the domestic and parental relations than I have been at any former period. Life is fuller of serene joy and steady purpose. I am happier, have more of the faith that reposes on Providence and the love that binds me to human nature, more of the assurance of progression, than I have been wont to enjoy. There is more unity in my life. Theory and practice are more harmoniously blended. The internal and external life constitute a whole to which thought, sentiment, and action form the parts.

My children are objects of great delight. They are both in health. Nature has given them good constitutions of body, fine endowments of mind, and the influences to which they have been subjected and the discipline pursued with them in their moral and spiritual culture has brought out their characters in interesting forms. They are indeed the charm of my domestic life. They keep alive and vivid the sentiment of humanity, and are living manifestations of the theories of my intellect; for they are the models of our common nature from whence these theories are in no small degree framed and delineated. So long as they move before me in the majestic dignity of human nature, unspoiled by dalliance with things, shall I have a strong bond to unite me to them, and in this union to find the tie that binds man to his race as well as to his Author. They are elements in the study of self—elements in the study of our nature—elements in the investigation of the Divinity that dwells within this nature. I know not how much the more spiritual I am from the parental relation, how much I have been indebted to them for the light that hath dawned upon my own mind from the radiance of their simple spirits. Certain it is that the more I associate with them in the simple ways that they love, the more do I see to revere, the profounder are my conceptions of our nature, the more glorious and solemn become the purposes and ends of its common destiny and the better do I appreciate the sentiment of Jesus, "of such is the Kingdom of Heaven."

Verily, had I not been called to associate with children . . . I should never have found the tranquil repose, the steady faith, the vivid hope that now shed a glory and a dignity around the humble path of my life. Childhood hath saved me. Once did I wander a little way from the Kingdom of Heaven, but childhood's sweet and holy voice hath recalled me, and now I am one with them in this same Kingdom, a child redeemed.

June 24, 1835

. . . Nothing can show itself in the exterior that has not a prior being and shaping within. We do not apprehend the spiritual kingdom by mere observation of external facts. We must enter within and find of what spiritual laws these phenomena are the exponents and signs. Infancy and childhood, yea, the life of every individual spirit, is the outraying of the inner life that first arrayeth its absolute will in the kingdom within. Except an adult be converted from the outward and his vision be turned inward to the life of the Spirit as it reveals itself in the consciousness of the little child yet in Spirit, he cannot apprehend the true life of humanity.

July 31, 1835

How, indeed, is it possible for the arts to assume their place among a people all whose ideas serve to check and keep under the sense of the beautiful as an element of our nature, whose manifestation "profiteth nothing"? Between beauty and utility there is a close affinity, and both serve their purpose in the great ends of human culture; but we have denied this affiance, and cut ourselves off from the goods that the contemplation of beauty hath in store for us. We acknowledge one God, even the God of Utility, and ask, as the grand test of all our efforts, "of what use is it?"— confining the term "use" to the outward interests of life instead of lifting it to its true place in the soul. As well might we inquire of what use is the soul, for in truth we find no use for it in the practical theories of the time. The soul is in our way. . . .

Divest the outward scene of beauty, cease to represent this in the arts, call it not forth in the social and actual relations of human life, and of what use is this life? How doth the charm and the glory of life fade away! How doth man degrade himself to a drudge—a thing among things!

September 21, 1835

Every visible, conscious thing is a revelation of the invisible, spiritual Creator. Matter is a revelation of Mind, the flesh of the Spirit, the world of God. All growth, production, progress, are but stages of the spiritual Being. They denote the Spirit struggling to represent, reveal, shadow forth itself to the sense and reason of man. They are tests of his faith in the infinite, invisible, spiritual life that flows through and quickens all things and beings.

The various kingdoms of matter, with all their array of forms and stages of growth, maturity, decay, are but so many modifications of the spiritual kingdom, whose laws they obey and by whose unseen yet ever-sustaining energy they are kept in their individual condition and attain to their absolute consummation and place. They are emblems and significant types of the Divine Spirit in whom alone is absolute Being and Life, Growth, and Vitality. They reveal the Latent One.

December 21, 1835

I set out from the wide ground of Spirit. This is; all else is its manifestation. Body is Spirit at its circumference. It denotes its confines to the external sense; it individualizes, defines Spirit, breaks the unity into multiplicity and places under the vision of man parts of the great whole which, standing thus separate, can be taken in by the mind—too feeble to apprehend the whole at once and requiring all save an individual thing to be excluded at a single view. Infinitude is too wide for man to take in. He is therefore permitted to take in portions and spread his vision over the wide circumference by little and little; and in these portions doth the Infinite shadow forth itself, God in all and all in God.

March 11, 1836

I am now finding an interest in the phenomena of the external world. I have a desire to apprehend the laws of which these phenomena are the pledge and appearance. This embraces the science of physiology. I have a dim yet assured instinct that these laws, when viewed from their true point in the vision of Spirit, will appear much more than has generally been supposed. Yes, I fancy that the hour is coming when all that moved in the mind of Jesus and prompted those sublime ideas on the soul's origin and immortality—that exposed nature and mastered its synthesis, that knew men and prescribed the healing of the human body as well as the soul—that all this shall come out as an actual distinct idea in the mind. I imagine that it will be possible, yea, certain, that the miracles, so called, wrought out by this faith in the spiritual and apprehension of the material, shall be made as common facts, the necessary and natural results of spiritual laws. The study of organs and functions will, I apprehend, become but another view of the Spirit's activity in body. Physiology is none other than the study of Spirit incarnate. We must wed the science of physiology and psychology, and from these shall spring the Divine Idea which, originally one in the mind of God, He saw fit to separate and spread throughout his twofold creation.

September 11, 1836

I have just finished reading *Nature,* by R. W. Emerson. It is a beautiful work. Mr. E. attempts to show the meaning of Nature to the minds of men. It is the production of a spiritualist, subordinating the visible and outward to the inward and invisible. Nature becomes a transparent emblem of the soul. Psyche animates and fills the earth and external things.

The book is small, scarce running to 100 pages, 12mo., but it is a gem throughout. I deem it the harbinger of an order of works given to the elucidation and establishment of the Spiritual. Mr. E. adverts, indirectly, to my "Psyche," now in his hands, in the work.[1]

[1] This corroborates the assertion, often made and as often denied, that Alcott was the "Orphic Poet" mentioned in the fifth paragraph from the end of *Nature.* The existing manuscript of "Psyche" has

January, Week III, *1837*

The lecture of Mr. Emerson on Thursday evening of this week was on Religion. . . . The speaker always kindles a sublime sentiment when, in those deep and oracular undertones which he knows when and how to use, he speaks of the divine entities of all being. A solemn and supernatural awe creeps over one as the serene pathos of his manner and the unaffected earnestness of his bearing come upon the senses. Here, I think, lies Emerson's power. At long intervals of remark bordering almost on coarseness—now the tones that he weaves into his diction and the pictures of vulgar life that he draws with a Shakespearean boldness of delineation depicting farmers, tradesmen, beasts, vermin, the rabid mob, the courtesan, the under as well as the upper vulgar, and now sliding into all that is beautiful, refined, elegant, both in thought, speech, action, and vocation—he bursts upon the hearers in strains of thought and charm and diction that affect the soul by their bewildering loftiness and grandeur. The burlesque is, in a twinkling, transformed into the serious. The bold and sketchy outline becomes a deep and sublime idea. This is the poet's, not the logician's, power. His ideas are clothed in bold, sharp, natural images. He states, pictures, sketches, but does not reason. His appeal is through the imagination and the senses to the mind. He leaves things in the place in which Nature put them, never deranging that order for a special logical analysis. All his ideas come orbed and winged. Footed and creeping things stand in contrast to give them effect; nor do slime and puddles become insignificant or unworthy in his creation. They occupy their place, as in great nature, serving as types and contrasts to the clean and solid ground of ideas. Nature shines serenely through the calm depths of his soul, and leaves upon its unruffled surface the images of all her works. . . .

---

no passages exactly corresponding to those which Emerson attributes to this "poet," although the thought and style of the paragraphs so attributed are Alcottian throughout. Emerson first saw "Psyche" only some five weeks before his book appeared, but he had seen an earlier version of it, called "Breath of Childhood," in the preceding February. What is perhaps more important, we know from his Journal entry of June 5, 1836, that he had just been reading Alcott's highly important Journal for 1835, in which the ideas of *Nature* are either expressed or clearly implied. Probably, however, Alcott's contribution to Emerson's first book was made not so much by any manuscript as by means of conversation. [Shepard's note.]

Honorable-notion and sham-image killer is he! Up-turner of all timeworn and vulgar associations thickly strewn over the soil of our land, now all exposed to the light of day by his shining and driving share. Drive on thy team, young and hopeful artist, till not ever a stone or sod shall not have been presented in a new aspect and new relation to the radiant orb of day! Break up the old and effete ground, and sow lavishly the seeds of new and refreshing nature, that thus, in due time, a rich spiritual harvest may be gathered and garnered!

March, Week XII, 1837

I spent Tuesday evening of this week with Dr. Channing. We conversed mostly on the connection of the Divine and Human Nature. I attempted to show the identity of the human soul, in its diviner action, with God. At this he expressed great dislike, even horror. He felt that doctrines of this character undermined the very foundations of virtue, confounded the nature of good and evil, destroyed human responsibility, and demolished free will. Singular perceptions this man has. He seems unable to take the views of another; and, though professedly free and declaring the doctrines of freedom, he binds himself to an imperfect creed and denies to others the assumption of views contrary to his own. . . . He is a disciple of the understanding, despite his professed reverence for the reason and spirit. He is not disenthralled from the slavery of sense and the visible. He asks demonstrations, where self-affirmation declares the truth to a nature in harmony with itself. He came too early to be the clear and lucid seer of the spiritual domain. . . . He cautions me as if I were a rash and sense-driven youth, liable to dash my brains against the dogmas and formulas I encounter. He fears for me.

I told him this evening that a good purpose, sustained by purity of life, always supplied the wisdom and the skill to carry its purposes through every conflict with the powers that be. Virtue endows the intellect with wisdom, and wisdom is valorous. It heeds not dogmas or conventions. It drives over their ruins to its own divine end.

May, Week XX, 1837

I spent a few days with Mr. Emerson at his own house in Concord. . . . Little difference of opinion seemed to exist between us. The means and method of communication with

the age were the chief points of difference. Emerson, true to
his genius, favors written works. He holds men and things
at a distance, pleases himself with using them for his own
benefit and as means of gathering materials for his works.
He does not believe in the actual. His sympathies are all intellectual. He persuades me to leave the actual, devote myself to the speculative, and embody my thoughts in written
works. . . .

Emerson idealizes all things. This idealized picture is the
true and real one to him. All else is naught. Even persons
are thus idealized, and his interest in them and their influence over him exists no longer than this conformity appears in his imagination. Beauty, beauty—this it is that
charms him. But beauty has pure and delicate tastes, and
hence all that mars or displeases this sense, with however
much of truth or of interest it may be associated, is of no
interest to his mind. Emerson seeks the beauty of truth:
it is not so much a quest of truth in itself as the beauty
thereof; not so much the desire of being holy and true as
of setting forth in fit and graceful terms the beauty of truth
and holiness. With him, all men and things have a beauty;
but this is the result of his point of vision, and often falls
wide of the actual truth. To give pleasure more than to impart truth is his mission. What is beautiful in man, nature,
or art—this he apprehends, and with the poet's power sets
forth.

His genius is high and commanding. He will do honor
to his age. As a man, however, this visit has somewhat modified my former notions of him. He seems not to be fully
in earnest. He writes and speaks for effect. Fame stands
before him as a dazzling award, and he holds himself somewhat too proudly, nor seeks the humble and sincere regard of his race. His life has been one of opportunity,
and he has sought to realize in it more of the accomplished
scholar than ·the perfect man.—A great intellect, refined by
elegant study, rather than a divine life radiant with the
beauty of truth and holiness. He is an eye more than a heart,
an intellect more than a soul.

November, Week XLV, *1837*

Let a thorough scholar—a man whose nature has not been
stolen away by precedent of books, but who sees man ever
above and of more value than the speech he employs—let
such a man leave the conventional city, wherein nature,

having profaned herself, is ashamed to acknowledge her mis-
deeds but sinks these out of hearing in speech, and visit a
rural retreat of simple people. Let him mark their speech,
observe their manners. Shall he not find himself again in
the presence of his proper nature, of which the city had
well-nigh bereft him?

These people put themselves into their speech. They do not
hide their souls. Words are things with them. Their souls
slide over their tongues. They are not hutched within and
hidden from sight. And in this simple, free state of being
their language is more true to nature. They speak it in
greater purity than the artificial citizen or closeted book-
worm. It is nearer to the soul, and the vocabulary of speech
is wider at the same time that it is more faithful to the soul.
I never hear a countryman speak without being reminded
of the dignity of our common nature and the richness of
our common tongue. He reminds me of Shakespeare. He has
retained his epithets. Language appears in its simpler, worthier forms. He deals with its staples. Its great words slip
from his tongue. The needs of the soul shine in his speech.
His vocabulary is not shorn of woods, winds, waters, sky,
toil, humanity. It hath a soul in it. Its images are of God's
shaping. It deals in the product of nature, and shames art—
save when she, like him, is faithful to the uses and ends
of nature. I would rather study simple countryman amidst
the scenes of nature, as dictionary of my native tongue,
then commune with citizen amidst his conventions, or read
with professor in college or hall, the tomes of a library.
There is life and meaning in it. It is devoid of pretense. It is
mother-tongue.

December, Week L, 1838

I received a letter on Monday of this week from Jones
Very of Salem, formerly Tutor in Greek at Harvard College
—which institution he left, a few weeks since, being deemed
insane by the faculty. A few weeks ago he visited me. . . .
He is a remarkable man. His influence at Cambridge on the
best young men was very fine. His talents are of a high
order. Some disquisitions of his on the genius and works of
Shakespeare I am soon to read. They are said to be composi-
tions of a pure and noble genius.

Is he insane? If so, there yet linger glimpses of wisdom in
his memory. He is insane with God—diswitted in the contemplation of the holiness of Divinity. He distrusts intel-

lect. He would have living in the concrete without the interposition of the meddling, analytic head. Curiosity he deems impious. He would have no one stop to account to himself for what he has done, deeming this hiatus of doing a suicidal act of the profane mind. Intellect, as intellect, he deems the author of all error. Living, not thinking, he regards as the worship meet for the soul. This is mysticism in its highest form. . . .

James Marsh

PRELIMINARY ESSAY TO COLERIDGE'S AIDS TO REFLECTION (1829)

. . . The only way in which it is possible for any one to learn the science of words, which is one of the objects to be sought in the present work, and the true import of those words especially which most concern us as rational and accountable beings, is by reflecting upon, and bringing forth into distinct consciousness, those mental acts which the words are intended to designate. We must discover and distinctly apprehend different meanings, before we can appropriate to each a several word or understand the words so appropriated by others. Now it is not too much to say that most men, and even a large proportion of educated men, do not reflect sufficiently upon their own inward being, upon the constituent laws of their own understanding, upon the mysterious powers and agencies of reason and conscience and will, to apprehend with much distinctness the objects to be named, or of course to refer the names with correctness to their several objects. Hence the necessity of associating the study of words with the study of morals and religion; and that is the most effectual method of instruction which enables the teacher most successfully to fix the attention upon a definite meaning, that is, in these studies, upon a particular act, or process, or law of the mind—to call it into distinct consciousness and assign to it its proper name, so that the name shall thenceforth have for the learner a distinct, definite, and intelligible sense. To impress upon the reader the importance of this, and to exemplify it in the particular subjects taken up in the work, is a leading aim of the author throughout; and it is obviously the only possible way by which we can arrive at any satisfactory and conclusive results on subjects of philosophy, morals, and religion. The first principles, the ultimate grounds of these, so far as they are possible objects of knowledge for us, must be sought and found in the laws of our being or they are not found at all. The knowledge of these terminates in the knowledge of ourselves, of our rational and personal being, of our proper and distinctive humanity, and of that Divine Being, in whose image we are created. . . .

In regard, then, to the distinguishing character and tendency of the work itself, it has already been stated to be didactic, and designed to aid reflection on the principles and grounds of truth in our own being; but, in another point of view, and with reference to my present object, it might rather be denominated A PHILOSOPHICAL STATEMENT AND VINDICATION OF THE DISTINCTIVELY SPIRITUAL AND PECULIAR DOCTRINES OF THE CHRISTIAN SYSTEM. . . .

In vindicating the peculiar doctrines of the Christian system . . . and a faith in the reality of agencies and modes of being essentially spiritual or supernatural, [the author] aims to show their consistency with reason and with the true principles of philosophy, and that indeed, so far from being irrational, *Christian faith is the perfection of human reason.* By reflection upon the subjective grounds of knowledge and faith in the human mind itself, and by an analysis of its faculties, he develops the distinguishing characteristics and necessary relations of the natural and the spiritual in our modes of being and knowing, and the all-important fact that although the former does not *comprehend* the latter, yet neither does it preclude its existence. He proves, that "the scheme of Christianity, though not discoverable by reason, is yet in accordance with it—that link follows link by necessary consequence—that religion passes out of the ken of reason only where the eye of reason has reached its own horizon—and that faith is then but its continuation." Instead of adopting, like the popular metaphysicians of the day, a system of philosophy at war with religion, and which tends inevitably to undermine our belief in the reality of anything spiritual in the only proper sense of that word, and then coldly and ambiguously referring us for the support of our faith to the *authority* of revelation, he boldly asserts the reality of something distinctively spiritual in man, and the futility of all those modes of philosophizing in which this is not recognized, or which are incompatible with it. He considers it the highest and most rational purpose of any system of philosophy, at least of one professing to be Christian, to investigate those higher and peculiar attributes which distinguish us from the brutes that perish—which are the image of God in us, and constitute our proper humanity. It is in his view the proper business and the duty of the Christian philosopher to remove all appearance of *contradiction* between the several manifestations of the one DIVINE WORD, to reconcile reason with revelation, and thus to justify the ways of God to man. . . . The key to his system will be found in the distinctions, which he makes and illustrates between *nature* and *free-will,* and between the *understanding* and *reason.* . . .

. . . I do not hesitate to express my conviction that the natural tendency of some of the leading principles of our prevailing system of metaphysics, and those which must unavoidably have more or less influence on our theoretical views of religion, are of an injurious and dangerous tendency, and that so long as we retain them, however we may profess to exclude their influence from our theological enquiries, and from the interpretation of Scripture, we can maintain no consistent system of Scriptural theology, nor clearly and distinctly apprehend the spiritual import of Scripture language. . . .

Let it be understood, then, without farther preface, that by the prevailing system of metaphysics, I mean the system of which in modern times Locke is the reputed author, and the leading principles of which, with various modifications, more or less important, but not altering its essential character, have been almost universally received in this country. . . . So long as we hold the doctrines of Locke and the Scotch metaphysicians respecting power, cause and effect, motives, and the freedom of the will, we not only can make and defend no essential distinction between that which is *natural* and that which is *spiritual,* but we cannot even find rational grounds for the feeling of *moral obligation* and the distinction between *regret* and *remorse.*

According to the system of these authors, as nearly and distinctly as my limits will permit me to state it, the same *law of cause and effect* is the *law of the universe.* It extends to the *moral* and *spiritual*—if in courtesy these terms may still be used—no less than to the properly *natural* powers and agencies of our being. The acts of the *free will* are predetermined by a cause *out of the will,* according to the same law of cause and effect which controls the changes in the physical world. We have no notion of *power* but uniformity of antecedent and consequent. The notion of a power in the will to act *freely* is therefore nothing more than an inherent capacity of *being acted upon* agreeably to its *nature* and according to a *fixed law* by the motives which are present in the *understanding.* . . .

I am aware that variations may be found in the mode of stating these doctrines, but I think every candid reader who is acquainted with the metaphysics and theology of this country will admit the above to be a fair representation of the form in which they are generally received. I am aware, too, that much has been said and written to make out consistently with these *general* principles, a distinction between *natural* and *moral* causes, natural and moral ability and inability, etc. But I beg all lovers of sound and rational philosophy to look carefully at the *general* principles and see whether there be, in fact, ground left for any such distinctions of this kind as are worth contending for. My first step in arguing with a defender of these principles, and of the distinctions in question as connected with them, would be to ask for his definition of *nature* and *natural*. And when he had arrived at a distinctive *general* notion of the import of these, it would appear, if I mistake not, that he had first subjected our whole being to the law of nature, and then contended for the existence of something which is *not* nature. For in their relation to the law of moral rectitude, and to the feeling of moral responsibility, what difference is there, and what difference can there be, between what are called *natural* and those which are called *moral* powers and affections, if they are all under the control of the *same universal law* of cause and effect? If it still be a mere nature, and the determinations of our will be controlled by causes out of the will, according to our nature, then I maintain that a moral nature has no more to do with the feeling of responsibility than any other nature.

Perhaps the difficulty may be made more obvious in this way. It will be admitted that brutes are possessed of various *natures,* some innocent or useful, others noxious, but all alike irresponsible in a moral point of view. But why? Simply because they act in accordance with their *natures.* They possess, each according to its proper nature, certain appetites and susceptibilities which are stimulated and acted upon by their appropriate objects in the world of the senses, and the relation—the law of action and reaction—subsisting between these specific susceptibilities and their corresponding outward objects *constitutes* their nature. They have a power of selecting and choosing in the world of sense the objects appropriate to the wants of their nature; but that nature is the *sole law* of their being. Their power of choice is *but a part of it*, instrumental in accomplishing its ends, but not capable of rising *above* it, of controlling its impulses, and of determining itself with reference to a purely *ideal law* distinct from their nature. They act in accordance with the law of cause and effect which constitutes their several natures, and cannot do otherwise. They are, *therefore*, not *responsible*—not capable of *guilt* or of *remorse*.

. . . So long as we refuse to admit the existence in the will of a power capable of rising *above this law,* and controlling its operation by an act of absolute *self*-determination, so long we shall be involved in perplexities both in morals and religion. At all events, the only method of avoiding them will be to adopt the creed of the necessitarians entire, to give man over to an irresponsible nature as a better sort of animal, and resolve the will of the Supreme Reason into a blind and irrational fate. . . .

It may perhaps be thought that the language used above is too strong and too positive. But I venture to ask every candid man, at least every one who has not committed himself by writing and publishing on the subject, whether, in considering the great questions connected with moral accountability and the doctrine of rewards and punishments, he has not felt himself pressed with such difficulties as those above stated; and whether he has ever been able fully to satisfy his reason, and there was not a lurking contradiction in the idea of a being created and placed under the law of its nature, and possessing at the same time a feeling of moral obligation to fulfil a law above its nature. . . . The *philosophical grounds* on which we are accustomed to defend our faith are unsafe, and . . . their *natural tendency* is to error. If the spirit of the gospel still exert its influence; if a truly spiritual religion be maintained, it is in *opposition* to our philosophy, and not at all by its aid. . . .

It must have been observed by the reader of the foregoing pages that I have used several words, especially *understanding* and *reason,* in a sense somewhat diverse from their present acceptation; and the occasion of this I suppose would be partly understood from my having already directed the attention of the reader to the distinction exhibited between these words in the work, and from the remarks made on the ambiguity of the word reason in its common use. I now proceed to remark that the ambiguity spoken of and the consequent perplexity in regard to the use and authority of reason have arisen from the habit of using, since the time of Locke, the terms understanding and reason indiscriminately, and thus confounding a distinction clearly marked in the philosophy and in the language of the older writers. . . . The powers of understanding and reason have not merely been blended and confounded in the view of our philosophy, the higher and far more characteristic, as an essential constituent of our proper humanity, has been as it were obscured and hidden from our observation in the inferior power which belongs to us in common with the brutes that perish. According to the old, the more spiritual, and genuine philosophy, the distinguishing attribute of our humanity—that "image of God" in which man alone was created of all the dwellers upon earth, and in virtue of which he was placed at the head of this lower world—was said to be found in the *reason* and *free will.* But understanding these in their strict and proper sense and according to the true *ideas* of them as contemplated by the older metaphysicians, we have literally, if the system of Locke and the popular philosophy of the day be true, neither the one nor the other of these—neither reason nor free will. What they esteemed the image of God in the soul and considered as distinguishing us specifically, and so vastly too, above each and all of the irrational animals, is found, according to this system, to have in fact no real existence. The reality neither of the free will, nor of any of those laws or ideas which spring from, or rather constitute, reason, can be authenticated by the sort of proof which is demanded, and we must therefore relinquish our prerogative and take our place with becoming humility among our more unpretending companions. . . .

We do indeed find in ourselves . . . certain powers of intelligence, which we have abundant reason to believe the brutes possess in common with us in a greater or less degree. The functions of the understanding as treated of in the popular systems of metaphysics, its faculties of attention, of abstraction, of generalization, the power of forethought and contrivance, of adapting means to ends, and the law of association may be, so far as we can judge, severally represented more or less adequately in the instinctive intelligence of the higher orders of brutes. But . . . do these, or any and all the faculties which we discover in irrational animals, satisfactorily account to a reflecting mind for all the phenomena which are presented to our observation in our own consciousness? Would any supposable addition to the *degree* merely of those powers which we ascribe to brutes render them *rational* beings and remove the sacred distinction, which law and reason have sanctioned, between things and persons? Will any such addition account for our having—what the brute is not supposed to have—the pure *ideas* of the geometrician, the power of ideal construction, the intuition of geometrical or other necessary and universal truths? Would it give rise, in irrational animals, to a *law of moral rectitude* and *to conscience*—to the feelings of moral *responsibility* and *remorse?* Would it awaken them to a reflective self-consciousness, and lead them to form and contemplate the *ideas* of the *soul,* of *free will,* of *immortality,* and of God. It seems to me that we have only to reflect for a serious hour upon what we mean by these, and then to compare them with our notion of what belongs to a brute, its inherent powers and their correlative objects, to feel that they are utterly incompatible—that in the possession of these we enjoy a prerogative which we cannot disclaim without a violation of reason and a voluntary abasement of ourselves—and that we must therefore be possessed of some *peculiar* powers—of some source of ideas *distinct* from the understanding, differing *in kind* from any and all of those which belong to us in common with inferior and irrational animals.

But what these powers are, or what is the precise nature of the distinction between the understanding and reason, it is not my province, nor have I undertaken, to show. My object is merely to illustrate its necessity, and the palpable obscurity, vagueness, and deficiency in this respect of the mode of philosophizing which is held in so high honor among us. The distinction itself will be found illustrated with some of its important bearings in the work and in the notes and Appendix attached to it, and cannot be too carefully studied—in connection with that between nature and the will—by the student who would acquire distinct and intelligible notions of what constitutes the truly spiritual in our being, or find rational grounds for the possibility of a truly spiritual religion. Indeed, could I succeed in fixing the attention of the reader upon this distinction in such a way as to secure his candid and reflecting perusal of the work, I should consider any personal effort or sacrifice abundantly recompensed. Nor am I alone in this view of its importance. A literary friend, whose opinion on this subject would be valued by all who know the soundness of his scholarship, says in a letter just now received, "If you can once get the attention of thinking men fixed on his distinction between the reason and the understanding, you will have done enough to reward the labor of a life. As prominent a place as it holds in the writings of Coleridge, he seems to me far enough from making too much of it." No person of serious and philosophical mind, I am confident, can reflect upon the subject enough to understand it in its various aspects without arriving at the same views of the importance of the distinction, whatever may be his conviction with regard to its truth. . . .

Samuel Taylor Coleridge

ON THE DIFFERENCE IN KIND OF REASON AND THE UNDERSTANDING* (1825)

. . . Reason is the power of universal and necessary convictions, the source and substance of truths above sense, and having their evidence in themselves. Its presence is always marked by the necessity of the position affirmed: this necessity being conditional, when a truth of reason is applied to facts of experience, or to the rules and maxims of the understanding; but absolute, when the subject matter is itself the growth or offspring of the reason. Hence arises a distinction in the reason itself, derived from the different mode of applying it and from the objects to which it is directed, accordingly as we consider one and the same gift, now as the ground of formal principles, and now as the origin of ideas. Contemplated distinctively in reference to formal (or abstract) truth, it is the speculative reason; but in reference to actual (or moral) truth, as the fountain of ideas, and the light of the conscience, we name it the practical reason. Whenever by self-subjection to this universal light, the will of the individual, the particular will, has become a will of reason, the man is regenerate, the reason is then the spirit of the regenerated man, whereby the person is capable of a quickening intercommunion with the Divine Spirit. And herein consists the mystery of Redemption, that this has been rendered possible for us. "And so it is written: the first man Adam was made a living soul, the last Adam a quickening Spirit." (1 Cor. xv. 45.) We need only compare the passages

*From *Aids to Reflection*.

in the writings of the Apostles Paul and John, concerning the spirit and spiritual gifts, with those in the Proverbs and in the Wisdom of Solomon respecting reason, to be convinced that the terms are synonymous. In this at once most comprehensive and most appropriate acceptation of the word, reason is preeminently spiritual, and a spirit, even *our* spirit, through an effluence of the same grace by which we are privileged to say Our Father!

On the other hand, the judgments of the understanding are binding only in relation to the objects of our senses, which we reflect under the forms of the understanding. It is, as Leighton rightly defines it, "the faculty judging according to sense." Hence we add the epithet "human," without tautology, and speak of the human understanding, in disjunction from that of beings higher or lower than man. But there is, in this sense, no human reason. There neither is nor can be but one reason, one and the same: even the light that lighteth every man's individual understanding (*Discursus*), and thus maketh it a reasonable understanding, discourse of reason—one only, yet manifold; it goeth through all understanding, and remaining in itself regenerateth all other powers. The same writer calls it likewise "an influence from the Glory of the Almighty," this being one of the names of the Messiah, as the *Logos*, or co-eternal Filial Word. And most noticeable for its coincidence is a fragment of Heraclitus, as I have indeed already noticed elsewhere: "To discourse rationally it behoves us to derive strength from that which is common to all men, for all human understandings are nourished by the one Divine Word." . . .

In no former part of this volume has the author felt the same anxiety to obtain a patient attention. For he does not hesitate to avow, that on his success in establishing the validity and importance of the distinction between reason and understanding, he rests his hopes of carrying the reader along with him through all that is to follow. . . .

UNDERSTANDING.	REASON.
1. Understanding is discursive.	1. Reason is fixed.
2. The understanding in all its judgments refers to some other faculty as its ultimate authority.	2. The reason in all its decisions appeals to itself, as the ground and *substance* of their truth. (Hebrews vi. 13.)

3. Understanding is the faculty of reflection.	3. Reason of contemplation. Reason indeed is much nearer to sense than to understanding, for reason (says our great Hooker) is a direct aspect of truth, an inward beholding, having a similar relation to the intelligible or spiritual, as sense has to the material or phenomenal.

. . . The understanding then (considered exclusively as an organ of human intelligence) is the faculty by which we reflect and generalize. Take, for instance, any objects consisting of many parts, a house, or a group of houses, and if it be contemplated as a whole, that is, as many constituting a one, it forms what in the technical language of psychology is called a total impression. Among the various component parts of this, we direct our attention especially to such as we recollect to have noticed in other total impressions. Then, by a voluntary act, we withhold our attention from all the rest to reflect exclusively on these; and these we henceforward use as common characters, by virtue of which the several objects are referred to one and the same sort. Thus, the whole process may be reduced to three acts, all depending on and supposing a previous impression on the senses: first, the appropriation of our attention; second (and in order to the continuance of the first), abstraction, or the voluntary withholding of the attention; and third, generalization. And these are the proper functions of the understanding, and the power of so doing is what we mean when we say we possess understanding, or are created with the faculty of understanding. . . .

Now, when a person speaking to us of any particular object or appearance refers it by means of some common character to a known class (which he does in giving it a name), we say that we understand him, that is, we understand his words. . . . Thus, in all instances it is words, names, or, if images, yet images used as words or names that are the only and exclusive subjects of understanding. In no instance do we understand a thing in itself, but only the name to which it is referred. Sometimes indeed, when several classes are recalled conjointly, we identify the words with the ob-

ject—though by courtesy of idiom rather than in strict
propriety of language. Thus we may say that we understand a rainbow, when, recalling successively the several
names for the several sorts of colors, we know that they are
to be applied to one and the same phenomenon, at once
distinctly and simultaneously; but even in common speech
we should not say this of a single color. No one would
say he understands red or blue. He *sees* the color, and had
seen it before in a vast number and variety of objects;
and he understands the word red as referring his fancy or
memory to this his collective experience.

If this be so, and so it most assuredly is—if the proper
functions of the understanding be that of generalizing the
notices received from the senses in order to the construction
of *names,* of referring particular notices (that is, impressions
or sensations) to their proper names, and, *vice versa,* names
to their correspondent class or kind of notices—then it follows of necessity that the understanding is truly and accurate-
ly defined in the words of Leighton and Kant, a "faculty
judging according to sense."

Now whether in defining the speculative reason (that is,
the reason considered abstractedly as an intellective power)
we call it "the source of necessary and universal principles,
according to which the notices of the senses are either
affirmed or denied," or describe it as "the power by which
we are enabled to draw from particular and contingent appearances universal and necessary conclusions," [1] it is
equally evident that the two definitions differ in their es-

[1] Take a familiar illustration. My sight and touch convey to me a
certain impression, to which my understanding applies its preconceptions
. . . of quantity and relation, and thus refers it to the class and
name of three-cornered bodies—we will suppose it the iron of a
turf-spade. It compares the sides and finds that any two measured
as one are greater than the third; and according to a law of the
imagination, there arises a presumption that in all other bodies of
the same figure (that is, three-cornered and equilateral) the same
proportion exists. After this, the senses have been directed successively
to a number of three-cornered bodies of *unequal* sides—and in these
too the same proportion has been found without exception, till at
length it becomes a fact of *experience* that in *all* triangles hitherto
seen the two sides together are greater than the third, and there will
exist no ground or analogy for anticipating an exception to a rule
generalized from so vast a number of particular instances. So far and
no farther could the understanding carry us, and as far as this "the
faculty judging according to sense" conducts many of the *inferior*

sential characters, and consequently the subjects differ in kind.

The dependence of the understanding on the representations of the senses, and its consequent posteriority thereto, as contrasted with the independence and antecedency of reason, are strikingly exemplified in the Ptolemaic system (that truly wonderful product and highest boast of the faculty judging according to the senses!) compared with the Newtonian, as the offspring of a yet higher power, arranging, correcting, and annulling the representations of the senses according to its own inherent laws and constitutive ideas.

---

animals, if not in the same, yet in instances analogous and fully equivalent.

The reason supersedes the whole process, and on the first conception presented by the understanding in consequence of the first sight of a triangular figure, of whatever sort it might chance to be, it affirms with an assurance incapable of future increase, with a perfect *certainty*, that in all possible triangles any two of the inclosing lines *will* and *must* be greater than the third. In short, understanding in its highest form of experience remains commensurate with the experimental notices of the sense from which it is generalized. Reason, on the other hand, either predetermines experience, or avails itself of a past experience to supersede its necessity in all future time, and affirms truths which no sense could perceive, nor experiment verify, nor experience confirm.

Yea, this is the test and character of a truth so unaffirmed, that in its own proper form it is *inconceivable*. For *to conceive* is a function of the understanding which can be exercised only on subjects subordinate thereto. And yet to the forms of the understanding all truth must be reduced, that is, to be fixed as an object of reflection and to be rendered expressible. And here we have a second test and sign of a truth so affirmed, that it can come forth out of the molds of the understanding only in the disguise of two contradictory conceptions, each of which is partially true, and the conjunction of both conceptions becomes the representative or expression (the exponent) of a truth beyond conception and inexpressible. Examples: Before Abraham *was*, I *am*. God is a circle, the center of which is everywhere and circumference nowhere. The soul is all in every part.

If this appear extravagant, it is an extravagance which no man can indeed learn from another, but which, (were this possible,) I might have learned from Plato, Kepler, and Bacon; from Luther, Hooker, Pascal, Leibnitz, and Fénelon. But in this last paragraph I have, I see, unwittingly overstepped my purpose, according to which we were to take reason as a simply intellectual power. Yet even as such, and with all the disadvantage of a technical and arbitrary abstraction, it has been made evident (1) that there is an *intuition* or *im*mediate beholding, accompanied by a conviction of the necessity and universality of the truth so beholden, not derived from the senses, which intuition, when it is *construed* by *pure* sense, gives birth to the science of mathematics, and when applied to objects supersensuous or spiritual is the organ of theology and philosophy; and (2) that there is likewise a reflective and discursive faculty, or *mediate* apprehension which, taken by itself and uninfluenced by the former, depends on the senses for the materials on which it is exercised and is contained within the sphere of the senses, constitutes sensible experience, and gives rise to maxims or rules which may become more and more *general,* but can never be raised into universal verities, or beget a consciousness of absolute certainty, though they may be sufficient to extinguish all doubt. . . .

Frederic Henry Hedge

COLERIDGE'S LITERARY CHARACTER—GERMAN METAPHYSICS* (1833)

. . . The characteristics of genius have been variously defined. To us it always seemed that, as there are two degrees of this mental quality, so there are also two characteristics, the one common to both degrees, the other peculiar to, and indeed constituting the highest. The first characteristic is originality. By this we mean not merely a disposition to think and act differently from the rest of mankind, but the power of imparting novelty and a sense of freshness to common thoughts and familiar objects. In poetry this faculty constitutes what is called the poetical feeling; it is that which distinguishes genuine poetry, whether metrical or unmetrical, from mere eloquence. In this quality Mr. Coleridge is by no means deficient. The following quotation may serve to illustrate our meaning; it is from the story of an orphan girl, contained in "The Friend":

> Maria followed Harlin, for that was the name of her guardian angel, to her home hard by. The moment she entered the door she sank down and lay at her full length, as if only to be motionless in a place of rest had been the fulness of delight. *As when a withered leaf that has long been whirled about by the gusts of autumn is blown into a cave or the hollow of a tree, it stops suddenly, and all at once looks the very image of quiet.* Such might this poor orphan girl appear to the eyes of a meditative imagination.

In the words which are here marked with italics we have a plain but accurate description of an incident familiar to all of us. Nothing can be simpler—perhaps some will think nothing could be less indicative of genius than the mention

* From *The Christian Examiner*, XIV (March, 1833).

of such a circumstance. And yet it is this faculty of seizing upon a natural incident, of presenting it exactly as it is, without embellishment or emotion, yet at the same time making it impressive by gently emphasizing its most distinctive feature, and by diffusing over the whole a kind of ideality—it is this faculty which gives life to poetry; it is this which gives to the poetry of the ancients in particular its strange and peculiar charm. Who has not seen a leaf whirled about by the wind and then lodged in the hollow of a tree? but who except a poet would have recalled the circumstance? who but a poet would have found in it an analogy to any thing in the moral world? This is to look upon nature with a poet's eye, and to interpret nature with a poet's sense. This is to clothe with new beauty, and as it were to sanctify a common sight, so that it can never more seem common nor pass unnoticed again. An incident thus selected from the daily spectacle of nature and associated with a particular state of mortal being becomes thenceforward and for ever a poetical image; by the poet's magic synthesis a natural object has become inseparably linked with a human feeling, so that the one must thenceforth always suggest the other. We feel assured that after reading this passage we shall never again behold the thing there described without a new sensation. . . .

The second characteristic of genius, that which distinguishes its highest degree, relates to form. It may be termed completeness, or the power of producing a well-proportioned whole. By a well-proportioned whole we mean a work of art in which one central idea pervades, connects, and determines all the parts; where the greatest diversity of matter is nicely balanced by unity of purpose; where the same leading thought shines visibly through every variety of attitude and scene; a work which, originating in a happy conception and grounded upon a rational plan, has all its parts proportioned to that plan, pursues a consistent course, has beginning, middle, and end, molds itself, as it were, by the self-determining power of its subject into a compact and pleasing form, and produces, when finished, a simple and undivided impression. Thus a good literary composition may be known by the same test by which we judge of an architectural work, unity of design and totality of effect. Some of Shakespeare's plays, *Othello,* for example, or *Romeo and Juliet,* will illustrate our meaning. Indeed, the greatest literary productions of ancient and modern times, whether dramatic, epic, or didactic, whether they be histories, orations, or systems of philosophy, all are marked with this characteristic. And not only literary productions, but all that is great in every department of intellectual exertion, a good painting, a masterpiece of sculpture, or in active life a masterpiece of policy, or in mechanics a useful invention, a well-contrived machine, any and every creation of the human mind, so far as it conforms to this standard—unity and completeness—is a work of genius. Genius, then, in its most perfect state, is known by its "perfect work." A writer in whom this quality is wanting betrays the defect in the loose and disjointed character of his composition. The difference between such a writer and one who possesses the quality we have described is like the contrast we may suppose between the *coup d'œil* of an eagle who surveys whole landscapes from his perch amid the clouds, and the vision of an insect to whose microscopic eye the minutest object divides itself into numberless fragments. The difference in the productions of these men resembles that which distinguishes the growth of an organic from that of a mineral product—the one develops itself into determinate forms by the evolution of a single germinal principle, the other irregularly swells its bulk by heterogeneous accretions. Mr. Coleridge is one of those in whom this quality of completeness, the power of producing a whole, is entirely wanting. We have never met with a writer whose works are so patched and ill made up. There does not occur to us at this moment a single production of his which has the least pretensions to shape.

As to the charge of obscurity, so often and obstinately urged against Mr. Coleridge's prose writings, we cannot admit it in anything like the extent in which it has been applied. So far as there is *any* ground for this complaint, it is owing to the author's excessive anxiety to make himself intelligible, an anxiety which leads him to present a subject in so many points of view that we are sometimes in danger of losing the main topic amid the variety of collateral and illustrative matter which he gathers round it. We are inclined, however, to suspect that the greater part of this alleged obscurity exists in the mind of the reader, and not in the author. In an age when all classes read, and when a consequent demand for popular works has rendered everything superficial that could be made superficial, and excluded almost everything that could not, when the best books in the language are the least read, when such works as Butler's

Analogy and others of the same stamp are confined within the narrow circle of professional reading—while at the same time complaints are heard that we have no good books to put into the hands of infidels—when in religion and philosophy superficial treatises and books of amusement have almost supplanted scientific inquiry; when, even in the department of taste, novels and tales supersede Shakespeare and Milton; in such an age we are not surprised to hear the charge of obscurity preferred against books whose only fault is that they deserve, and therefore require, a little more study than we are compelled to bestow upon a novel or a tract. It is to be feared that the men of this generation have been spoiled by the indulgence shown to their natural indolence, and made tender by the excessive pains which have been taken to render everything easy and smooth. Our intellects are dwarfed and stunted by the constant stimulus of amusement which is mixed up with all our literary food. There is no taste for hardy application, no capacity for vigorous and manly efforts of the understanding. Whatever taxes the mind, instead of exciting it, is deemed a burden. A hard word scares us; a proposition which does not explain itself at first glance troubles us; whatever is *supersensual* and cannot be made plain by images addressed to the senses is denounced as obscure or beckoned away as mystical and extravagant. Whatever lies beyond the limits of ordinary and outward experience is regarded as the ancient geographers regarded the greater portion of the globe, as a land of shadows and chimæras. In a treatise on mechanics or astronomy many things would be unintelligible to one who is ignorant of mathematics; but would it be fair in such a one to charge the author with a difficulty which arises from his own ignorance? Some writers are clear because they are shallow. If it be complained that Mr. Coleridge is not one of these, we shall not deny a charge which is applicable also, and in a much greater degree, to much wiser men. He is certainly not a shallow writer, but, as we think, a very profound one, and his style is for the most part as clear as the nature of his thoughts will admit. To those only is he obscure who have no depths within themselves corresponding to his depths, and such will do well to consider, as Bishop Butler has said in reference to his own work, "that the question is not whether a more intelligible book might have been written, but whether the subjects which he handles will admit of greater perspicuity in the treatment of them."

In a review of Mr. Coleridge's literary life, we must not omit to notice that marked fondness for metaphysics, and particularly for German metaphysics, which has exercised so decisive an influence over all his writings. . . .

[GERMAN METAPHYSICS]

While we are on this ground, we beg leave to offer a few explanatory remarks respecting German metaphysics which seem to us to be called for by the present state of feeling among literary men in relation to this subject. We believe it impossible to understand fully the design of Kant and his followers without being endowed to a certain extent with the same powers of abstraction and synthetic generalization which they possess in so eminent a degree. In order to become fully master of their meaning, one must be able to find it in himself. Not all are born to be philosophers or are capable of becoming philosophers, any more than all are capable of becoming poets or musicians. The works of the transcendental philosophers may be translated word for word, but still it will be impossible to get a clear idea of their philosophy unless we raise ourselves at once to a transcendental point of view. Unless we take our station with the philosopher and proceed from his ground as our starting-point, the whole system will appear to us an inextricable puzzle. As in astronomy the motions of the heavenly bodies seem confused to the geocentric observer and are intelligible only when referred to their heliocentric place, so there is only one point from which we can clearly understand and decide upon the speculations of Kant and his followers: that point is the interior consciousness, distinguished from the common consciousness by its being an active and not a passive state. In the language of the school, it is a free intuition and can only be attained by a vigorous effort of the will. It is from an ignorance of this primary condition that the writings of these men have been denounced as vague and mystical. Viewing them from the distance we do, their discussions seem to us like objects half enveloped in mist; the little we can distinguish seems most portentously magnified and distorted by the unnatural refraction through which we behold it, and the point where they touch the earth is altogether lost. The effect of such writing upon the uninitiated is like being in the company of one who has inhaled an exhilarating gas. We witness the inspiration and are astounded at the effects, but we can form no conception of the feeling until we ourselves have experienced it. To those who are without the veil, then, any *exposé* of transcendental views must needs be unsatisfactory. Now if any one chooses to deny the point which these writers assume, if any one chooses to call in question the metaphysical existence of this interior consciousness and to pronounce the whole system a mere fabrication or a gross self-delusion—to such a one the disciples of this school have nothing further to say; for him their system was not conceived. Let him content himself, if he can, with "that compendious philosophy which talking of mind, but thinking of brick and mortar or other images equally abstracted from body, contrives a theory of spirit by nicknaming matter, and in a few hours can qualify the dullest of its disciples to explain the *omne scibile* by reducing all things to impressions, ideas, and sensations." The disciples of Kant wrote for minds of quite another stamp; they wrote for minds that seek with faith and hope a solution of questions which that philosophy meddles not with, questions which relate to spirit and form, substance and life, free will and fate, God and eternity. Let those who feel no interest in these questions, or who believe not in the possibility of our approaching any nearer to a solution of them, abstain forever from a department of inquiry for which they have neither talent nor call. There are certain periods in the history of society when, passing from a state of spontaneous production to a state of reflection, mankind are particularly disposed to inquire concerning themselves and their destination, the nature of their being, the evidence of their knowledge, and the grounds of their faith. Such a tendency is one of the characteristics of the present age, and the German philosophy is the strongest expression of that tendency; it is a striving after information on subjects which have been usually considered as beyond the reach of human intelligence, an attempt to penetrate into the most hidden mysteries of our being. In every philosophy there are three things to be considered: the object, the method, and the result. In the transcendental system, the *object* is to discover in every form of finite existence an infinite and unconditioned as the ground of its existence, or rather as the ground of our knowledge of its existence, to refer all phenomena to certain *noumena,* or laws of cognition. It is not a *ratio essendi,* but a *ratio cognoscendi;* it seeks not to explain the existence of God and creation, objectively considered, but to explain our knowledge of their existence. It is not a skeptical philosophy; it seeks not to overthrow, but to build up; it wars not with the common opinions and general experience of mankind, but aims to place these on a scientific basis and to verify them by scientific demonstrations.

The method is synthetical, proceeding from a given point, the lowest that can be found in our consciousness, and deducing from that point "the whole world of intelligences, with the whole system of their representations." The correctness or philosophical propriety of the construction which is to be based upon this given point, this absolute thesis, must be assumed for a while, until proved by the successful completion of the system which it is designed to establish. The test by which we are to know that the system is complete, and the method correct, is the same as that by which we judge of the correct construction of the material arch—continuity and self-dependence. The last step in the process, the keystone of the fabric, is the deduction of time, space, and variety, or, in other words, (as time, space, and variety include the elements of all empiric knowledge) the establishing of a coincidence between the facts of ordinary experience and those which we have discovered within ourselves, and scientifically derived from our first fundamental position. When this step is accomplished, the system is complete, the hypothetical framework may then fall, and the structure will support itself.

. . . [Kant] did not himself create a system, but he furnished the hints and materials from which all the systems of his followers have been framed. In his preface to the second edition of the *Critique of Pure Reason,* he makes us acquainted with the train of reasoning which led to the course he has adopted in his metaphysical inquiries. "He had been struck with the fact that, while other departments of knowledge, availing themselves of scientific method, were constantly and regularly advancing, intellectual philosophy alone, although the most ancient of all sciences and the one which would remain though all the rest should be swallowed up in the vortex of an all-engulfing barbarism—intellectual philosophy alone appears to be still groping in the dark, sometimes advancing and sometimes receding, but making on the whole little actual progress. How are we to account for this fact? Is a science of metaphysics impossible? Why then has nature implanted within us this ardent longing after certain and progressive knowledge on subjects of all others the most interesting to the human soul; or how can we place any confidence in our reason when it fails us in the investigation of such topics as these? But perhaps the fault lies with us. May not our want of success be owing to a wrong method? The science of geometry was probably for some time in the same condition that metaphysical inquiry is now; but ever since the demonstration of the equilateral triangle commonly ascribed to Thales, it has advanced in regular and rapid progression. Physical science has done the same since Bacon. It is evident that both these branches of knowledge are indebted for the success with which they have been cultivated to the fortunate discovery of a right method. May not the want of such a method constitute the sole obstacle to the progress of metaphysical science? Hitherto philosophers have assumed that our cognitions are determined by the objects they represent. On this assumption it is evident that every attempt to establish anything *a priori* concerning them (the objects) must be vain. Let us therefore try whether, in metaphysical problems, we may not succeed better by assuming that the objects without us are determined by our cognitions. Copernicus, when he found that he could not explain the motions of the heavenly bodies on the supposition that the starry host revolves around the observer, changed his theory and made the observer revolve and the stars stand still. Reversing this process, let us, since the supposition that our intuitions depend on the nature of the world without will not answer, assume that the world without depends on the nature of our intuitions. Thus perhaps we shall be enabled to realize that great desideratum—*a priori* knowledge."

We have here the key to the whole critical philosophy, the very essence of which consists in proposing an absolute self as unconditionally existing, incapable of being determined by anything higher than itself but determining all things through itself. . . .

If now it be asked, as probably it will be asked, whether any definite and substantial good has resulted from the labors of Kant and his followers, we answer, much. More than metaphysics ever before accomplished these men have done for the advancement of the human intellect. It is true the immediate, and if we may so speak, the calculable results of their speculations are not so numerous nor so evident as might have been expected—these are chiefly comprised under the head of method. Yet even here we have enough to make us rejoice that such men have been, and that they have lived and spoken in our day. We need mention only the sharp and rightly dividing lines that have been drawn within and around the kingdom of human knowledge; the strongly marked distinctions of subject and object, reason and understanding, phenomena and noumena; the categories established by Kant; the moral liberty proclaimed by him as it had never been proclaimed by any before; the authority and evidence of law and duty set forth by Fichte; the universal harmony illustrated by Schelling. But in mentioning these things, which are the direct results of the critical philosophy, we have by no means exhausted all that that philosophy has done for liberty and truth. The preeminence of Germany among the nations of our day in respect of intellectual culture is universally acknowledged; and we do fully believe that whatever excellence that nation has attained in science, in history, or poetry is mainly owing to the influence of her philosophy, to the faculty which that philosophy has imparted of seizing on the spirit of every question, and determining at once the point of view from which each subject should be regarded—in one word, to the transcendental method. In theology this influence has been most conspicuous. We are indebted to it for that dauntless spirit of inquiry which has investigated, and for that amazing erudition which has illustrated, every corner of biblical lore. Twice it has saved the religion of Germany, once from the extreme of fanatic extravagance, and again from the verge of speculative infidelity. But, though most conspicuous in theology, this influence has been visible in every department of intellectual exertion to which the Germans have applied themselves for the last thirty years. It has characterized each science and each art, and all bear witness to its quickening power. A philosophy which has given such an impulse to mental culture and scientific research, which has done so much to establish and to extend the spiritual in man, and the ideal in nature, needs no apology; it commends itself by its fruits, it lives in its fruits, and must ever live, though the name of its founder be forgotten, and not one of its doctrines survive. . . .

2

THE NEW SCHOOL

Bronson Alcott

THE DOCTRINE AND DISCIPLINE OF HUMAN CULTURE (1836)

Idea of Man

Man is the noblest of the Creator's works. He is the most richly gifted of all his creatures. His sphere of action is the broadest; his influence the widest; and to him is given nature and life for his heritage and his possession. He holds dominion over the outward. He is the rightful sovereign of the earth, fitted to subdue all things to himself, and to know of no superior, save God. And yet he enters upon the scene of his labors a feeble and wailing babe, at first unconscious of the place assigned him, and needs years of tutelage and discipline to fit him for the high and austere duties that await him.

Idea of Education

The art which fits such a being to fulfil his high destiny is the first and noblest of arts. Human culture is the art of revealing to a man the true idea of his being, his endowments, his possessions and of fitting him to use these for the growth, renewal, and perfection of his spirit. It is the art of completing a man. It includes all those influences and disciplines by which his faculties are unfolded and perfected. It is that agency which takes the helpless and pleading infant from the hands of its Creator, and, apprehending its entire nature, tempts it forth—now by austere, and now by kindly influences and disciplines—and thus molds it at last into the image of a perfect man, armed at all points to use the body, nature, and life for its growth and renewal, and

131

to hold dominion over the fluctuating things of the outward. It seeks to realize in the soul the image of the Creator. Its end is a perfect man. Its aim, through every stage of influence and discipline, is self-renewal. The body, nature, and life are its instruments and materials. Jesus is its worthiest ideal. Christianity its purest organ. The Gospels its fullest textbook. Genius its inspiration. Holiness its law. Temperance its discipline. Immortality its reward.

History and Type of This Idea

This divine art, including all others or subordinating them to its idea, was never apprehended in all its breadth and depth of significance till the era of Jesus of Nazareth. He it was that first revealed it. Over his divine intellect first flitted the idea of man's endowments and destiny. He set no limits to the growth of our nature. "Be ye perfect even as my Father in Heaven is perfect," was the high aim which he placed before his disciples; and in this he was true to our nature, for the sentiment lives in every faculty and function of our being. It is the ever-sounding trump of duty, urging us to the perpetual work of self-renewal. It is the deep instinct of the spirit. And his life gives us the promise of its realization. In his attributes and endowments he is a type of our common nature. His achievements are a glimpse of the apotheosis of humanity. They are a glorious unfolding of the Godlike in man. They disclose the idea of spirit. And if he was not, in himself, the complete fulfillment of Spirit, he apprehended its law, and set forth its conditions. He bequeathed to us the phenomena of its manifestation, for in the Gospels we have the history of spirit accomplishing its mission on the earth. We behold the Incarnate One, dealing with flesh and blood—tempted, and suffering—yet baffling and overcoming the ministries of evil and of pain.

Idea and Type Misapprehended

Still this idea, so clearly announced, and so fully demonstrated in the being and life of Jesus, has made but little advance in the minds of men. Men have not subdued it to themselves. It has not become the ground and law of human consciousness. They have not married their nature to it by a living faith. Nearly two millenniums have elapsed since its announcement, and yet, so slow of apprehension have been the successors of this divine genius that even at this day the deep and universal significance of his idea has not been fully taken in. It has been restricted to himself alone. He stands in the minds of this generation as a phenomenon which God, in the inscrutable designs of His Providence, saw fit to present to the gaze and wonder of mankind, yet as a being of unsettled rank in the universe whom men may venture to imitate but dare not approach. In him, the human nature is feebly apprehended, while the Divine is lifted out of sight and lost in the ineffable light of the Godhead. Men do not deem him as the harmonious unfolding of spirit into the image of a perfect man—as a worthy symbol of the Divinity, wherein human nature is revealed in its fullness. Yet, as if by an inward and irresistible instinct, all men have been drawn to him; and, while diverse in their opinions, explaining his idea in different types, they have given him the full and unreserved homage of their hearts. They have gathered around the altars inscribed with his perfections, and, through his name, delighted to address the God and Father of spirits. Disowning him in their minds, unable to grasp his idea, they have deified him in their hearts. They have worshiped the holiness which they could not define.

Era of Its Revival

It is the mission of this age, to revive his idea, give it currency, and reinstate it in the faith of men. By its quickening agency, it is to fructify our common nature and reproduce its like. It is to unfold our being into the same divine likeness. It is to reproduce perfect men. The faded image of humanity is to be restored and man reappear in his original brightness. It is to mold anew our institutions, our manners, our men. It is to restore Nature to its rightful use, purify life, hallow the functions of the human body, and regenerate philosophy, literature, art, society. The divine idea of a man is to be formed in the common consciousness of this age, and genius mold all its products in accordance with it.

Means of Its Revival

The means for reinstating this idea in the common mind, in order to conduce to these results, are many. Yet all are simple. And the most direct and effectual are by apprehending the genius of this divine man from the study of those records wherein his career is delineated with so much fidelity, simplicity, and truth. Therein have we a manifestation of spirit while undergoing the temptations of this corporeal life, yet faithful to the laws of its renovation and its end. The divine idea of humanity gleams forth through every circumstance of his terrestrial career. The fearful agencies of the spirit assert their power. In him nature and life are subordinated to the spiritual force. The Son of God appears on earth enrobed in flesh and looks forth serenely upon man. We feel the significance of the Incarnation, the grandeur of our nature. We associate Jesus with our holiest aspirations, our deepest affections; and thus does he become a fit mediator between the last age and the new era of which he was the herald and the pledge. He is to us the prophet of two millenniums. He is the brightest symbol of a man that history affords, and points us to yet fuller manifestations of the Godhead.

Ideal of a Teacher

And the Gospels are not only a fit textbook for the study of spirit, in its corporeal relations, but they are a specimen also of the true method of imparting instruction. They give us the practice of Jesus himself. They unfold the means of addressing human nature. Jesus was a teacher; he sought to renovate humanity. His method commends itself to us. It is a beautiful exhibition of his genius, bearing the stamp of naturalness, force, and directness. It is popular. Instead of seeking formal and austere means, he rested his influence chiefly on the living word rising spontaneously in the soul and clothing itself at once in the simplest yet most commanding forms. He was a finished extemporaneous speaker. His manner and style are models. In these, his ideas became like the beautiful, yet majestic nature, whose images he wove so skillfully into his diction. He was an artist of the highest order. More perfect specimens of address do not elsewhere exist. View him in his conversation with his disciples. Hear him in his simple colloquies with the people. Listen to him when seated at the well-side discoursing with the Samaritan woman on the idea of worship, and at night with Nicodemus on spiritual renewal. From facts and objects the most familiar, he slid easily and simply into the highest and holiest themes, and, in this unimposing guise, disclosed the great doctrines, and stated the divine ideas, that it was his mission to bequeath to his race. Conversation was the form of utterance that he sought. Of formal discourse but one specimen is given, in his Sermon on the Mount; yet in this the inspiration bursts all forms, and he rises to the highest efforts of genius at its close.

Organ of Instruction

This preference of Jesus for conversation as the fittest organ of utterance is a striking proof of his comprehensive idea of education. He knew what was in man, and the means of perfecting his being. He saw the superiority of this exercise over others for quickening the spirit. For in this all the instincts and faculties of our being are touched. They find full and fair scope. It tempts forth all the powers. Man faces his fellow man. He holds a living intercourse. He feels the quickening life and light. The social affections are addressed, and these bring all the faculties in train. Speech comes unbidden. Nature lends her images. Imagination sends abroad her winged words. We see thought as it springs from the soul, and in the very process of growth and utterance. Reason plays under the mellow light of fancy. The genius of the soul is waked, and eloquence sits on her tuneful lip. Wisdom finds an organ worthy her serene yet imposing products. Ideas stand in beauty and majesty before the soul.

Organ of Genius

And genius has ever sought this organ of utterance. It has given us full testimony in its favor. Socrates—a name

that Christians can see coupled with that of their divine sage
—descanted thus on the profound themes in which he delighted. The marketplace, the workshop, the public streets were
his favorite haunts of instruction. And the divine Plato has
added his testimony also in those enduring works wherein he
sought to embalm for posterity both the wisdom of his master and the genius that was his own. Rich textbooks these
for the study of philosophic genius. They rank next in finish
and beauty to the specimens of Jesus as recorded by his own
beloved John.

Genius Alone Renews

It is by such organs that human nature is to be unfolded
into the idea of its fullness. Yet to do this, teachers must be
men in possession of their idea. They must be men of their
kind, men inspired with great and living ideas, as was
Jesus. Such alone are worthy. They alone can pierce the customs and conventions that hide the soul from itself. They
alone can release it from the slavery of the corporeal life and
give it back to itself. And such are ever sent at the call of
humanity. Some God, instinct with the idea that is to regenerate his era, is ever vouchsafed. As a flaming herald he appears in his time and sends abroad the idea which it is the
mission of the age to organize in institutions, and quicken
into manners. Such mold the genius of the time. They revive
in humanity the lost idea of its destiny, and reveal its fearful
endowments. They vindicate the divinity of man's nature, and
foreshadow on the coming time the conquests that await it.
An age preexists in them, and history is but the manifestation and issue of their wisdom and will. They are the prophets
of the future.

Genius Misapprehended

At this day, men need some revelation of genius to arouse
them to a sense of their nature, for the divine idea of a
man seems to have died out of our consciousness. En-
cumbered by the gluts of the appetites, sunk in the corporeal senses, men know not the divine life that stirs within

them yet hidden and enchained. They revere not their own nature. And when the phenomenon of genius appears, they marvel at its advent. They cannot own it. Laden with the gifts of the Divinity it touches their orb. At intervals of a century it appears. Some nature, struggling with vicissitude, tempts forth the idea of spirit from within, and unlooses the Promethean God to roam free over the earth. He possesses his idea and brings it as a blessed gift to his race. With awe-struck visage the tribes of semi-unfolded beings survey it from below, deeming it a partial or preternatural gift of the Divinity, into whose life and being they are forbidden, by a decree of the Eternal, from entering; whose law they must obey, yet cannot apprehend. They dream not that this phenomenon is but the complement of their common nature, and that in this admiration and obedience which they proffer is both the promise and the pledge of the same powers in themselves; that this is but their fellow creature in the flesh. And thus the mystery remains sealed, till at last it is revealed—that this is but the unfolding of human nature in its fullness working free of every encumbrance by possessing itself.

Idea of Genius

For genius is but the free and harmonious play of all the faculties of a human being. It is a man possessing his idea and working with it. It is the whole man—the central will—working worthily, subordinating all else to itself, and reaching its end by the simplest and readiest means. It is human nature rising superior to things and events and transfiguring these into the image of its own spiritual ideal. It is the spirit working in its own way, through its own organs and instruments, and on its own materials. It is the inspiration of all the faculties of a man by a life conformed to his idea. It is not indebted to others for its manifestation. It draws its life from within. It is self-subsistent. It feeds on holiness, lives in the open vision of truth, enrobes itself in the light of beauty, and bathes its powers in the fount of temperance. It aspires after the perfect. It loves freedom. It dwells in unity. All men have it, yet it does not appear in all men. It is obscured by ignorance, quenched by evil; discipline does not reach it, nor opportunity cherish it. Yet there it is—an original, indestructible element of every spirit; and sooner or later, in this corporeal, or in the spiritual era—at some period of the soul's development—it shall be tempted forth, and assert its claims in the life of the spirit. It is the province of education to wake it and discipline it into the perfection which is its end and for which it ever thirsts. Yet genius alone can wake it. Genius alone inspire it. It comes not at the incantation of mere talent. It respects itself. It is strange to all save its kind. It shrinks from vulgar gaze and lives in its own world. None but the eye of genius can discern it, and it obeys the call of none else. . . .

Faith of Genius

To work worthily, man must aspire worthily. His theory of human attainment must be lofty. It must ever be lifting him above the low plain of custom and convention in which the senses confine him, into the high mount of vision and of renovating ideas. To a divine nature, the sun ever rises over the mountains of hope and brings promises on its wings; nor does he linger around the dark and depressing valley of distrust and fear. The magnificent bow of promise ever gilds his purpose, and he pursues his way steadily, and in faith to the end. For faith is the soul of all improvement. It is the will of an idea. It is an idea seeking to embody and reproduce itself. It is the all-proceeding Word going forth, as in the beginning of things, to incarnate itself and become flesh and blood to the senses. Without this faith an idea works no good. It is this which animates and quickens it into life. And this must come from living men.

Genius Alone Inspires

And such faith is the possession of all who apprehend ideas. Such faith had Jesus, and this it was that empowered him to do the mighty works of which we read. It was this which inspired his genius. And genius alone can inspire others. To nurse the young spirit as it puts forth its pinions in the fair and hopeful morning of life, it must be placed under the kindly and sympathizing agency of genius—Heaven-inspired and hallowed—or there is no certainty that its aspirations will not die away in the routine of formal tuition or spend themselves in the animal propensities that coexist with it. Teachers must be men of genius. They must be men inspired. The divine idea of a man must have been unfolded from their being and be a living presence. Philosophers and sages and seers—the only real men—must come as of old, to the holy vocation of unfolding human nature. Socrates and Plato and the diviner Jesus must be raised up to us, to breathe their wisdom and will into the genius of our era, to recast our institutions, remold our manners, and regenerate our men. Philosophy and religion, descending from the regions of cloudy speculation, must thus become denizens of our common earth, known among us as friends, and uttering their saving truths through the mouths of our little ones. Thus shall our being be unfolded. Thus the idea of a man be reinstated in our consciousness. Thus Jesus be honored among us. And thus shall man grow up as the tree of the primeval woods, luxuriant, vigorous—armed at all points to brave the winds and the storms of the finite and the mutable —bearing his fruit in due season.

Idea of Inspiration

To fulfill its end, instruction must be an inspiration. The true teacher, like Jesus, must inspire in order to unfold. He must know that instruction is something more than mere impression on the understanding. He must feel it to be a kindling influence; that in himself alone is the quickening, informing energy; that the life and growth of his charge preexist in him. He is to hallow and refine as he tempts forth the soul. He is to inform the understanding by chastening the appetites, allaying the passions, softening the affections, vivifying the imagination, illuminating the reason, giving pliancy and force to the will; for a true understanding is the issue of these powers working freely and in harmony with the genius of the soul, conformed to the law of duty. He is to put all the springs of being in motion. And to do this, he must be the personation and exemplar of what he would unfold in his charge. Wisdom, truth, holiness must have preexistence in him, or they will not appear in his pupils. These influence alone in the concrete. They must be made flesh and blood in him, to reappear to the senses, and reproduce their like. And thus shall his genius subordinate all to its own force. Thus shall all be constrained to yield to its influence, and this, too, without violating any law, spiritual, intellectual, corporeal—but in obedience to the highest agency, coworking with God. Under the melting force of his genius, thus employed, mind shall become fluid, and he shall mold it into types of heavenly beauty. His agency is that of mind leaping to meet mind, not of force acting on opposing force. The soul is touched by the live coal of his lips. A kindling influence goes forth to inspire, making the mind think, the heart feel, the pulse throb with his own. He arouses every faculty. He awakens the Godlike. He images the fair and full features of a man. And thus doth he drive at will the drowsy brute, that the Eternal hath yoked to the chariot of life to urge man across the finite!

Hallowed Genius

To work worthily in the ministry of instruction requires not only the highest gifts, but that these should be refined by holiness. This is the condition of spiritual and intellectual clearness. This alone unfolds genius and puts nature and life to their fit uses. "If any man will know of the doctrine, let him do the will of my Father," said Jesus; and he who does not yield this obedience shall never shine forth in the true and full glory of his nature.

Quenching of Genius

Yet this truth seems to have been lost sight of in our measures of human culture. We encumber the body by the gluts of the appetites, dim the senses by self-indulgence, abuse nature and life in all manner of ways, and yet dream of unfolding genius amidst all these diverse agencies and influences. We train children amidst all these evils. We surround them by temptations which stagger their feeble virtue, and they fall too easily into the snare which we have spread. Concupiscence defiles their functions, blunts the edge of their faculties, obstructs the passages of the soul to the outward, and blocks it up. The human body, the soul's implement for acting on nature in the ministry of life, is thus depraved, and the soul falls an easy prey to the tempter. Self-indulgence too soon rings the knell of the spiritual life as the omen of its interment in the flesh. It wastes the corporeal functions, mars the divine image in the human form, estranges the affections, paralyzes the will, clouds the intellect, dims the fire of genius, seals conscience, and corrupts the whole being. Lusts entrench themselves in the soul; unclean spirits and demons nestle therein. Self-subjection, self-sacrifice, self-renewal are not made its habitual exercises, and it becomes the vassal of the body. The idea of spirit dies out of the consciousness, and man is shorn of his glories. Nature grows over him. He mistakes images for ideas and thus becomes an idolater. He deserts the sanctuary of the indwelling spirit and worships at the throne of the outward. . . .

Self-apprehension

Man's mission is to subdue nature, to hold dominion over his own body, and use both these and the ministries of life for the growth, renewal, and perfection of his being. As did Jesus, he must overcome the world by passing through its temptations and vanquishing the tempter.

But before he shall attain this mastery he must apprehend himself. In his nature is wrapped up the problem of all power reduced to a simple unity. The knowledge of his own being includes, in its endless circuit, the alphabet of all else. It is a universe wherein all else is imaged. God—nature—are the extremes of which he is the middle term, and through his being flow these mighty forces, if, perchance, he shall stay them as they pass over his consciousness, apprehend their significance—their use—and then conforming his being to the one, he shall again conform the other to himself.

Childhood a Type of the Godhead

Yet, dimmed as is the divine image in man, it reflects not the full and fair image of the Godhead. We seek it alone in Jesus in its fullness, yet sigh to behold it with our corporeal senses. And this privilege God ever vouchsafes to the pure and undefiled in heart, for he ever sends it upon the earth in the form of the child. Herein have we a type of the Divinity. Herein is our nature yet despoiled of none of its glory. In flesh and blood he reveals his presence to our senses and pleads with us to worship and revere.

Misapprehension of Childhood

Yet few there are who apprehend the significance of the divine type. Childhood is yet a problem that we have scarce studied. It has been and still is a mystery to us. Its pure and simple nature, its faith and its hope, are all unknown to us. It stands friendless and alone, pleading in vain for sympathy and aid. And, though wronged and slighted, it still retains its trustingness; still does it cling to the adult for renovation and light. But thus shall it not be always. It shall be apprehended. It shall not be a mystery and made to offend. "Light is springing up and the dayspring from on high is again visiting us." And, as in times sacred to our associations, the star led the Wise Men to the Infant Jesus to present their reverent gifts, and was at once both the herald and the pledge of the advent of the Son of God on the earth, even so is the hour approaching, and it lingers not on its errand, when the wise and the gifted shall again surround the cradles of the newborn babe, and there proffer, as did the Magi, their gifts of reverence and of love to the holiness that hath visited the earth and shines forth with a celestial glory around their heads; and these, pondering well, as did Mary, the divine significance, shall steal from it the art—so long lost in our consciousness—of unfolding its powers into the fullness of the God.

Renovation of Nature

And thus man, repossessing his idea, shall conform nature to himself. Instructions shall bear the fruits of his regenerate being. They shall flourish in vigor and beauty. They shall circulate his genius through nature and life and repeat the story of his renewal.

Human Renewal

Say not that this era is distant. Verily, it is near. Even at this moment the heralds of the time are announcing its approach. Omens of good hover over us. A deeper and holier faith is quickening the genius of our time. Humanity awaits the hour of its renewal. The renovating fiat has gone forth to revive our institutions and remold our men. Faith is lifting her voice, and, like Jesus near the tomb of Lazarus, is uttering the living words, "I am the Resurrection and the Life, and he that believeth, though dead in doubts and sins, shall be reassured of his immortality, and shall flourish in unfading youth! I will mold nature and man according to my will. I will transfigure all things into the image of my ideal." And by such faith and such vision shall education work its mission on the earth. Apprehending the divine significance of Jesus—yet filled with the assurance of coming messiahs to meet the growing nature of man—shall inspired genius go forth to renovate his era; casting out the unclean spirits and the demons that yet afflict the soul. And then shall humanity, leaving her infirmities, her wrongs, her sufferings, and her sins in the corrupting grave, reappear in the consciousness of physical purity, inspired genius, and spotless holiness. Men shall be one with God, as was the Man of Nazareth.

Orestes A. Brownson

COUSIN'S PHILOSOPHY* (1836)

Whoever would see the American people as remarkable for their philosophy as they are for their industry, enterprise, and political freedom must be gratified that these works have already attracted considerable attention among us and are beginning to exert no little influence on our philosophical speculations. It is a proof that our philosophical speculations are taking a wholesome direction, and especially that the great problems of mental and moral science are assuming in our eyes a new importance and calling to their solution a greater and an increasing amount of mind. We are, in fact, turning our attention to matters of deeper interest than those which relate merely to the physical well-being of humanity. We are beginning to perceive that Providence, in the peculiar circumstances in which it has placed us, in the free institutions it has given us, has made it our duty to bring out the ideal man, and to prove, by a practical demonstration, what the human race may be, when and where it has free scope for the full and harmonious development of all its faculties. In proportion as we perceive and comprehend this duty, we cannot fail to inquire for a sound philosophy, one which will enumerate and characterize all the faculties of the human soul and determine the proper order and most efficient means of their development.

These works will, we think, afford us important aid in rescuing the Church and religious matters in general from their present lamentable condition. Religion subsists among us, and always will, for it has its seat in the human heart; but to a great extent it has lost its hold upon the understanding. Men are no longer satisfied with the arguments by

* From *The Christian Examiner*, XXI (Sept. 1836). Published as a review of Cousin's *Introduction to the History of Philosophy, Elements of Psychology*, and *Fragmens Philosophiques*.

which it has heretofore been defended; the old forms in which it has been clothed fail to meet the new wants which time and events have developed, and there is everywhere in a greater or less degree, a tendency to doubt, unbelief, indifference, infidelity. We have outgrown tradition, and authority no longer seems to us a valid argument. We demand conviction. We do not, as in the Middle Ages, go to religion to prove our philosophy, but to our philosophy to prove our religion. This may or may not be an evil, but it is unavoidable. We must accept and conform to it. Henceforth religion must, if sustained at all, except as a vague, intangible sentiment, be sustained by philosophy. To doubt this is to prove ourselves ignorant of the age in which we live.

But the philosophy which has hitherto prevailed and whose results now control our reasonings, cannot sustain religion. Everybody knows that our religion and our philosophy are at war. We are religious only at the expense of our logic. This accounts for the fact that, on the one hand, we disclaim logic, unchurch philosophy, and pronounce it a dangerous thing to reason, while, on the other, we reject religion, declaim against the clergy, and represent it exceedingly foolish to believe. This opposition cannot be concealed. It is found not only in the same community, but to a great extent in the same individual. The result cannot be doubtful. Philosophy will gain the victory. The friends of religion may seek to prevent it, labor to divert men's minds from inquiry by engaging them in vast associations for practical benevolence, or to frighten them from philosophizing by powerful appeals to hopes and fears, but the desire to philosophize, to account to ourselves for what we believe, cannot be suppressed. Instead, then, of quarreling with this state of things, instead of denouncing the religious as do professed free inquirers, or the philosophizers, as is the case with too many of the friends of religion, we should reexamine our philosophy and inquire if there be not a philosophy true to human nature and able to explain and verify, instead of destroying, the religious belief of mankind? We evidently need such a philosophy; such a philosophy we believe there is, and we know of no works so well fitted to assist us in finding it as those of M. Cousin. . . .

What has been known, and what is now considered by many, in an especial sense, as French philosophy, is sensualism, so called from its professing to trace back all the facts of consciousness to sensation. France was ready for this philosophy when Voltaire introduced it to her acquaintance from England, where he had borrowed it from Locke and his disciples. Condillac simplified it, gave it systematic unity, constructed its logic, and fitted it for empire, which it obtained and held for nearly a century, without contradiction and without example in the whole history of philosophy. . . . But its reign is now ended and its glory departed. The works before us, together with their popularity in France, and that of their author, are sufficient proof of it. Providence doubtless assigned it an important mission; but that mission ended with the destruction of the old Catholic Church and the feudal monarchy, and though it continued to reign some time after, it was as a tradition rather than as a living system. . . .

M. Cousin calls the system of philosophy which he and his friends profess and advocate, Eclecticism, because it recognizes the leading principles of all the great schools into which the philosophical world has been divided and attempts to mold them into one grand whole which shall include them all and yet be itself unlike any of them. It went into power with the king of the barricades, and will undoubtedly preside over the new system of schools and instruction which the government is preparing for France. We already see it in the most popular French journals and in many of the most fashionable literary productions; and we can hardly persuade ourselves but that (in these and other ways) its influence on the destinies of France is at present, and must be for the future, very great. But without going into any speculations on the influence and prospects of this philosophy, we proceed to give our readers as clear and as satisfactory a statement of what it is as we can within the limits to which we are necessarily restricted. In doing this we shall draw liberally from the Preface to the second edition of the Philosophical Fragments . . . in which the author has given us a summary of his system together with answers to some objections which are raised against it and some account of its formation and growth in his own mind. We shall arrange what we have to offer under the heads of (1) Method; (2) Application of Method to Psychology; (3) Passage from Psychology to Ontology; (4) Passage from God to Nature; and (5) General Views on the History of Philosophy.

I. The adoption of a method decides the destinies of a philosophy, for any given system of philosophy is only the development and application of a given method. The method of all sound philosophy is that of observation and induction.

Our first step is to study human nature, by observation to ascertain what is in the consciousness; our next and last step is to draw from observation by induction, by reasoning, all the consequences contained in the facts it has collected. Philosophy is the science of facts, and also the science of reasoning. It begins with observation, but it ends only with the limits of the reason itself. It observes and it reasons. In physical science we begin with observation of facts, but we do not end with it; we rise from observation, by reasoning, to general laws and to the system of the world. We should pursue the same method in mental and moral science. If we receive as true whatever legitimately follows from the facts of the external world which we have observed, we should do the same with whatever legitimately follows from the facts of the internal world which we have scrupulously observed and profoundly analyzed. . . . There is, in fact, no difference between philosophy and physical science except in the nature of the phenomena to be observed. The proper phenomena of physical science are those of external nature, of that vast world of which man makes so small a part; the proper phenomena of philosophy are those of internal nature, of that world which each man carries within himself, and which is observed by that inward light called consciousness in like manner as the other is observed by the senses. . . .

Psychology, an exact classification of the mental phenomena, is the first part, the foundation, but not the whole of philosophy. This is a point of great importance. The principal peculiarity of M. Cousin's system results from the fact that he makes psychology the foundation, but not the superstructure, the beginning, but not the end, of philosophy. By making psychology the basis of philosophy, he connects his philosophical enterprise with modern philosophy itself, which from Descartes, Bacon, and Locke tolerates only the experimental method. In this he does not dissent from the philosophy which reigned in France during the last century. That philosophy was indeed sensualism, but it was also experimental; as experimental M. Cousin accepts and, though he modifies, continues it. . . .

II. There is, undoubtedly, a class or order of phenomena in the consciousness which may be traced back to sensation. That this class exists, and is of large extent, is incontestable. The manner in which the phenomena it includes are generated, although somewhat complicated, is easily comprehended; and they have the advantage of reposing on a primitive fact which, by connecting them with the physical sciences, seems to vouch for their reality. This fact is that of the impression produced on the organs of sensation and reproduced by the brain in the consciousness. The illusion of believing that this order includes all the phenomena of which we can be conscious was therefore very natural. If there be only a single order of phenomena in the consciousness, there can be only a single faculty to which we can refer those phenomena, and which in its transformations must produce all the others. This faculty is that of sensation, or, if we may adopt the etymological instead of the common meaning of the word, the sensibility; but if the sensibility be the root of all our intellectual faculties, it must be the root of all our moral faculties. This reduces man to a mere creature of sensation. He can then know nothing which is not cognizable by some one or all of his five senses. Our senses can take cognizance of only material objects; if other objects exist we cannot know them; they are for us as though they were not. When we recognize only material existences, thought itself becomes materialized; painting, sculpture, poetry, all the fine arts, take a tinge of materiality, cease to reveal the infinite, and merely represent some small portions of the finite. All our notions of God, of the soul, of the beautiful, the right, inasmuch as they are not copies of outward material objects which are observed alike by the senses, are illusions, mere fantasies, no more to be trusted than the dreams which disturb our nightly slumbers; religion withers into a mere form, hardens into a petrifaction, or entirely disappears—or at least can be retained only as an inconsequence or as an instrument; morality freezes into selfishness; pleasure and pain become the synonyms of right and wrong; and that alone which gives pleasure—not to the soul but to the senses —can be dignified with the name of *good;* the soul, having no longer any employment, takes its departure, and the man sinks in the animal, recognizing and laboring only for animal wants. This is the unavoidable result of recognizing in the consciousness the phenomena of the sensibility alone, and of reducing the whole nature of man to the faculty of receiving a sensation. . . .

M. Cousin recognizes in the consciousness three classes of phenomena, which result from the great elementary faculties which comprehend and explain all the rest. These faculties are sensibility, activity, and reason. They are never found isolated one from another. Yet they are essentially distinct, and a scrupulous analysis distinguishes them in the complex phenomena of intellectual life without dividing them. To sensibility belong all the internal phenomena which are derived from sensation through our senses, from the external world; to the activity belong those which we are conscious that we ourselves produce; and under the head of reason must be arranged all our ideas of the absolute, the supersensible, and all the internal facts which are purely intellectual, which we know we do not produce, and which cannot be derived through sensation from external nature. The activity is developed only by sensation. Activity and sensibility can generate no idea without the reason; and without sensibility and activity the reason would have no office. . . . The reason, though appearing in us, is not our *self*. It is independent of us, and in no sense subject to our personality. If it depended on our personality, or if it constituted our personality, we could control its conceptions, prescribe its laws, and compel it to speak according to our pleasure. Its conceptions would be ours, as much and in the same sense as our intentions; its revelations would be our revelations, that is, revelations of ourselves, and its truths would be our truths. Who is prepared to admit such a conclusion? We may say "my actions, my crimes, my virtues," for we consider ourselves very justly as their cause; we may even say "my error," for our errors are in some degree attributable to ourselves; but who dare say *"my* truth"? Who does not feel, who does not know, that the truth is not his—is nobody's—but independent of everybody? If, then, we are conscious that the conceptions of the reason are not ours, that the truths it reveals are not our truths, are not truths which are in any sense dependent on us, we must admit that the reason is independent of us, and, though appearing in us, is not ours, is not our *self*.

Nobody doubts the independence of the reason in the consciousness itself. Who doubts the reality of the mental phenomena of which we are directly conscious? Who doubts the apperceptions of consciousness, apperceptions on which is founded the knowledge of our own existence? No skeptic doubts these, for no skeptic doubts that he doubts. But not to doubt that we doubt is to know that we doubt, is to know something, is, in fine, *to know*. Now, what is it that *knows?* What is that inward light we call consciousness which has these apperceptions in which we confide, which knows in any degree—which knows at all? Is it not the reason? If the

reason may be trusted in one case, why not in another?
If the knowledge which the reason gives us of what is passing
within us be undeniable, why shall not all other knowledge,
which the same reason gives, be considered equally certain?
The reason is the same in all its degrees, and we have no
right arbitrarily to restrict or extend its limits.

III. The reason, once established in its true nature and
independence, becomes a legitimate authority for whatever it
reveals. A true analysis of it shows that, instead of being
imprisoned in the consciousness and compelled to turn forever within the sphere of the subjective, it extends far beyond,
and attains to beings as well as to phenomena. It reveals to us
God and the world on precisely the same authority as our
own existence, or the slightest modification of it. Ontology
thus becomes as legitimate as psychology, since it is psychology which, by disclosing to us the true nature of the
reason, conducts of itself to ontology.

. . . The psychological truth of God and the world, we
think, has been demonstrated over and over again, in a manner that must be satisfactory to the most skeptical, who are
not ignorant of the demonstrations which have been given;
but no philosopher with whom we are acquainted, unless
it be M. Cousin, has demonstrated their ontological truth.
M. Cousin professes to have demonstrated that we not only
have the belief, and cannot help having it, but that it is well
founded, that there is something out of us to respond to it.
This he supposes he has done by establishing the independence of the reason; by proving that the reason is objective in
relation to our personality, he thinks he has obtained a legitimate witness of the objective; and since this witness unquestionably deposes to the existence of God and of the world,
he thinks he has proved their validity. . . .

Can there be any fact of consciousness without some attention? . . .

Now is not every act of the attention more or less voluntary? Is not every voluntary act marked with this character,
that we consider ourselves its cause? And is it not this cause,
whose effects may vary while it remains itself unvaried, this
power, which its acts alone reveal to us, and which its acts
do not exhaust—is it not this cause, power, force that we
call *I, me,* our individuality, our personality, that personality
of which we never doubt, which we never confound with any
other, because we never refer to any other the voluntary acts
which give us an intimate sentiment and an unalterable con-

viction of it? The *I*, the personality, is then given us in every fact of consciousness. There can be no fact of consciousness without a conception of our own existence.

We find *ourselves* then, in the fact of consciousness, and we find ourselves a cause, a creative force. This is the radical idea which we have of ourselves. We know ourselves under no other character than that of a cause, and we exist for ourselves no farther than we are a cause. The bounds of our causality are the bounds of our existence. Can this cause, which we are, do whatever it will? Meets it no resistance, no obstacles? It does, at every step, and of every kind. To the sentiment of our strength is ever added that of our weakness. Thousands of impressions from without continually assail us. If we do not attend to them, they come not to the consciousness; but as soon as we attend to them, sensation begins. Now, here is the intervention of a new element. We refer to ourselves the act of attending to the impressions made upon our organs of sense, but we do not, and we cannot, refer to ourselves, as their cause, the impressions to which we attend. We receive sensations, we do not cause them. But if we cannot refer them to ourselves as their cause, we cannot help referring them to some cause, and necessarily to a cause which is out of us, exterior. The existence of this exterior cause is as certain to us as our own existence; for the phenomenon—sensation—which suggests it, is as certain to us as the phenomenon—act of attention—which suggests to us our existence. Both, too, are given together, in the same phenomenon. There is, then, in every fact of consciousness, not only a conception of our own existence, of our personality, but also a conception of something which is not ourselves, something independent of our personality and exterior to it—external nature.

If anyone should doubt this, he is required to conceive of himself without also conceiving of that which is not himself, or of that which is not himself without conceiving of himself. I cannot have a clear conception of myself without distinguishing myself from all other existences. To assert that I exist is to assert that I am, and that I am myself and not another. In the complex phenomena of consciousness, we have seen there necessarily intervene activity and sensibility. There are the impressions from a cause which we are not, and attention, which is our act applied to those impressions, giving us a consciousness of them. These two causes, one of which we are, the other of which we are not (external nature) are

then unquestionable in every fact of consciousness, and both
equally certain. But with what characters do we find these
two causes? Certainly they appear as relative, imperfect,
bounded, finite. The cause which we are meets resistance,
obstacles, bounds, in that variety of causes to which we refer the phenomena of which we are conscious, which we
do not produce and which are purely affective and involuntary; and these causes themselves are limited and bounded by
that voluntary cause which we are. We resist them as they
resist us and, to a certain extent, limit their action as they
limit ours. It is only in the meeting, the clashing of the two
causes, it is only in their conflict that either is revealed to
us. There is no question that we always conceive of them,
and cannot help conceiving of them, as relative and as
finite causes. Now, what is it to conceive of these two causes
as relative and finite? It is to distinguish them in our minds
as such; it is to assert that they are not absolute, infinite
causes but relative and finite causes. If, then, whenever these
two causes are in the consciousness, they are there as relative,
as finite, they must be there as contrasted with the infinite,
the absolute. But they cannot be contrasted with, or distinguished from, the infinite and the absolute without a conception of the infinite and the absolute; and without being so
contrasted or distinguished they cannot be conceived as relative and finite. In every fact of consciousness, then, there is a
conception of ourselves, or of personality, and of something
which is not ourselves, external nature, both as relative, finite
causes; and of the infinite, the absolute, to which they are
by the reason necessarily referred, and with which they must
be contrasted in order to be conceived. . . .

If this analysis of a fact of consciousness be accurate, we
are authorized to say that no fact of consciousness is possible
without the conception of our own existence, the existence of
the world, and that of God. The ideas of ourselves as a free
personality, of nature, and of God as the substance, the cause,
of both us and nature, constitute a single fact of the consciousness, are its inseparable elements, and without them
consciousness is impossible. Ourselves, nature, and God are,
then, necessarily asserted in every word, in every affirmation,
in every thought. The skeptic who professes to doubt their
existence, in that he can assert that he doubts, asserts that
they exist. Atheism is, then, impossible; some men may want
the term, the word, but all men believe in God. . . .

The whole matter, then, turns on the credit due the reason.

Grant reason tells the truth, we know the absolute, the un-conditioned—God. Deny the reason, or declare the reason unworthy to be believed, and we neither know God, the world, ourselves, nor anything else. We are reduced to a worse strait than to "doubt that doubt itself be doubting," a strait in which we cannot possibly remain even in thought so long as it takes to name it. Thus much, we think, M. Cousin has done, and, we believe, it is all that he considers himself as having done, though he calls it a demonstration, which we contend it is not. The demonstration would require him to prove the credibility of the reason, a thing which he cannot do because he has only the reason with which to establish the truth of the reason. But this is no cause of regret. We want no higher authority than the reason. The reason in all its essential elements is in every man. It is the light, "the true light that lighteneth every man that cometh into the world." As it reveals spontaneously in every man's consciousness the vast world of reality, the absolute God, the cause and sub-stance of all that *appears*, it follows that every man has the witness of the spiritual world, of the absolute, the infinite, God, in himself.

IV. The reason can reveal nothing which it has not in it-self. If it reveal the absolute, it must itself be absolute. If absolute, it must be the Being of beings, God himself. The elements of the reason are then the elements of God. And analysis of the reason gives, as its elements, the ideas of the infinite, the finite, and their relation as cause and effect. Then these ideas are the elements of all thought, of thought in it-self, of God. God, then, is thought, reason, intelligence in it-self. An intelligence which does not manifest itself is a dead intelligence, a dead thought; but a dead thought, a dead in-telligence, is inconceivable. To live, to exist, intelligence must manifest itself. God, being thought, intelligence in itself, must necessarily manifest himself. To manifest himself is to create, and his manifestation is creation. . . .

But God can manifest only what is in Himself. He is thought, intelligence itself. Consequently there is in creation nothing but thought, intelligence. In nature, as in humanity, the supreme reason is manifested, and there, where we had fancied all was dead and without thought, we are now enabled to see all living and essentially intellectual. There is no dead matter, there are no fatal causes; nature is thought, and God is its personality. This enables us to see God in nature in a new and striking sense, and gives a sublime meaning to the

words of Paul: "The invisible things of Him from the creation of the world, even His eternal power and Godhead, are
clearly seen, being understood by the things which are made."
Well may we study nature, for as a whole and in the minutest
of its parts it is a manifestation of the infinite, the absolute,
the everlasting, the perfect, the universal reason—God. It
should be loved, should be reverenced, not merely as a piece
of mechanism, but as a glorious shining out of the infinite
and the perfect. How much more, however, should we study,
love, reverence and stand in awe of humanity, the still brighter manifestation, more perfect type, image of the supreme
intelligence, the true God—our Father! . . .

This is not pantheism. Pantheism considers the universe as
God; but this presents God as the cause and the universe as
the effect. God is as inseparable from the universe as the
cause is inseparable from the effect; but no one who can discern any distinction between an appearance and that which
appears, between the phenomenon and being, the manifestation and that which is manifested, can ever confound Him
with the universe. The cause is always in the effect. I am in
my intention but I am not my intention. All there is in the
intention is of me, but it does not exhaust me. I create an
intention, and I remain with all my creative energy. So of
God. The universe is His intention. It is what He wills, and
He is in it, the substance of His volition; it is what He
speaks, and He is in it as a man is in his words, but He is
distinct from it by all the distinction there is between the
energy that wills and that which is willed, between him who
speaks and the words he utters.

The reason, taken absolutely, we have said is identical
with God. The consequences of this are numerous and grand.
The reason is God; it appears in us, therefore God appears
in us. The light of reason, the light by which we see and
know all that we do see and know, is truly the light of God.
The voice of the spontaneous reason is the voice of God;
those who speak by its authority speak by the authority of
God, and what they utter is a real revelation. This explains
inspiration, accounts for the origin of prophecies, pontificates,
and religious rites, and justifies the human race for having
believed that some men had been the confidants and interpreters of God. He in whom the spontaneous reason was more
active than in his fellow beings had a closer communion with
God, could better interpret him than they, and was rightly
termed the inspired, for he was inspired—not indeed in a

sense different from the rest of mankind, but in a different, a special, degree. . . .

V. Man's intellectual life begins with the spontaneous reason. We believe, we confide before we reflect . . . Philosophy begins the day that man begins to reflect; it is the creation of reflection, and, since reflection is our act, it is our creation. It is to humanity what nature and humanity are to God. As there can be nothing in nature and humanity which is not in God, so there can be nothing in philosophy which is not in humanity. He who comprehends humanity comprehends not only true philosophy but all systems of philosophy which have heretofore obtained, or which can obtain hereafter. He who comprehends all the systems of philosophy which have been comprehends humanity as far as it is now developed. The study of human nature, then, throws light on the history of philosophy, and the study of the history of philosophy in return throws light on human nature. Since all the systems of philosophy which have been embrace the entire development of humanity in the past, it follows that he who should comprehend those systems would comprehend thus far the whole history of our race. History in general, as throwing light on humanity, the history of philosophy in particular, as enlightening all other branches of history, and as the practical, the experimental test of a philosophy, should be ranked among the very highest objects of human study. . . .

A philosophy which accepts the entire history of humanity, and which finds itself precisely the same number of elements as in that history, excluding nothing, owning and enlightening all, may be pronounced the true philosophy, that which exactly represents the development of humanity. No philosophy does this except that which finds in each system, creed, event, an element of the true, which it extracts and brings together into one vast, harmonious whole. This philosophy is Eclecticism. Every sound philosopher, then, must be an Eclectic. . . .

We must be Eclectics, excluding no element of humanity, but accepting and melting all into one vast system which will be a true representative of humanity so far as it has yet developed. We must take broad and liberal views, expect truth and find it in all schools, in all creeds, in all ages, and in all countries. The great mission of our age is to unite the infinite and the finite. Union, harmony, whence proceed peace and love, are the points to be aimed at. We of the nineteenth century appear in the world as mediators. In philosophy, theology, government, art, industry, we are to conciliate hostile feelings and harmonize conflicting principles and interests. We must bind together the past and the future, reconcile progress and immobility, by preserving what is good and studying to advance, that is by meliorating instead of destroying; enable philosophy and theology to walk together in peace and love by yielding to theology the authority of the spontaneous reason—inspiration—and vindicating for philosophy the absolute freedom of reflection. . . .

George Ripley

MARTINEAU'S RATIONALE*
(1836)

We believe . . . in opposition to Mr. Martineau, that the mental state of the Apostles involved, among other elements, that of divine inspiration. They professed to have received not the gift of infallibility, but an extraordinary illumination from on high. This claim, we think, is substantiated by all that we know of their character and history.

We will briefly indicate the process by which we arrive at this conclusion. The first step in the proof of supernatural inspiration is the admission of natural inspiration. The foundation for this is laid in the primitive elements of our being. The power of the soul by which it gains the intuitive perception of spiritual truth is the original inspiration that forms the common endowment of human nature. This, we maintain, is established by the testimony of the absolute and intuitive reason in man. Our own consciousness assures us that a revelation of great spiritual truths is made to the soul. There are certain primitive and fundamental ideas which compose the substance of reason that exist, with more or less distinctness, in every intelligent mind. These ideas are the intuitive perceptions on which all moral and religious truth is founded, just as the whole science of mathematics is built up on a few simple definitions and axioms which neither require nor are susceptible of demonstration. These ideas, by the necessity of our nature, we refer to an origin out of ourselves. They are not created by us but they command us. They are not the products of our own will but should be its sovereigns. They are not limited to our own personality but bear the signatures of universal and everlasting authority. Now psychology and the history of man alike compel us to trace back their origin to God. We are conscious that they

* From *The Christian Examiner*, XXI (Nov. 1836). A review of James Martineau's *The Rationale of Religious Enquiry*.

do not proceed from any act of volition, the personal causality which acts within us, nor from the influence of nature, the material causality which acts without us; and we are, therefore, compelled, by the authority of our reason, to refer them to the Absolute Causality—the Infinite Author of truth and good. Hence they are not human but divine. They do not grow out of any deductions of our understandings, but are the fruits of a spontaneous and original inspiration, without which the understanding would have no materials to work upon.

The revelations of this natural inspiration are the absolute ideas of reason, which lay claim to necessary and universal validity. The primary truths which are independent of experience and demonstration, the perception of the just, the holy, the perfect, the infinite, upon which all religious faith is founded, proceed from this source.

Now when these ideas are developed in any mind so as to create a predominant conviction of the reality of spiritual truth, we say of that mind, by way of emphasis and distinction, that it is inspired. And just in the proportion in which the supremacy of these ideas transcends the ordinary, the natural effects of culture and reflection, we pronounce them supernatural. We say of the mind in which the essential ideas of religious truth exist in signal perfection, independent of human agency, that it is supernaturally inspired. This we believe can be asserted of our Saviour without any limitation. His soul was a sea of light. All that was human in the Son of the Virgin, all that belonged to his personality as a Jewish teacher, all that marks the secondary, derived, and fallible in the nature of man, as distinguished from the primitive, the original, the infallible, the divine, was swallowed up and, as it were, annihilated in the fullness of the Spirit which dwelt in him, in those kingly ideas of truth and good which sustain the authority of the Eternal Throne, and authenticated the man of Nazareth as the Son of God, the visible tabernacle of the Word which was made flesh and dwelt among us. . . .

With regard to the criterion of such an inspiration, it can be no other than its agreement with the primitive and universal dictates of the absolute reason in man. In this way and in no other can it be distinguished from the fancies of enthusiasm or the reveries of superstition. Everything which claims to be of an immediate divine origin in history must be brought to the test of that which is admitted to be of immediate divine origin in the facts of consciousness. The natural inspiration which is possessed by all must sit in judgment on the supernatural inspiration which is imparted to an elect few. As a common degree of poetical genius is qualified to decide upon the merits of the great masters of song, so the divine sense of truth which is the property of the race must pass sentence on the claim of its prophets and teachers to supernatural endowments. The light of the soul is of a kindred nature with the light of the spiritual sun which irradiates the universe of thought; and it enables man to recognize between the reflections of the primal luminary and the meteors, which, of impure and earthly origin, often flash over the gloom of night. We submit to the observer of his own nature whether this be not a more convincing proof of the reality of inspiration than any testimony of an external character . . . We are led by similar considerations with those which we have here suggested to take a different view of the position and relative value of miracles in a system of divine revelation from that advanced by our author. It is rather a singular combination of opinions to deny the inspiration of the sacred writers and to defend the miracles which they record as the essential foundation of the Christian faith. He attaches so great importance to these outward signs as to make a belief in them the exclusive ground of a title to the name of Christian. In our opinion, this criterion depends upon an erroneous view of the connection between Christianity and the miracles which accompanied its introduction into the world.

We think no one will hesitate to admit that miracles do not compose the essence of Christian revelation, but were intended to facilitate its reception and establish its authority; that the revelation is not for the sake of the miracles, but the miracles for the sake of the revelation. Our Saviour explicitly declared that he came into the world to bear witness to the truth, not to exercise a marvelous power over the agencies of physical nature; and he more than intimates that they who cherished the love of truth in pure hearts would hear his voice and acknowledge his sovereignty without reference to wonders and prodigies addressed to the outward eye. Hence we infer that whoever believes the truth which it was the mission of Christ to announce is entitled to the name of a disciple, whatever be the foundation on which he has been led to rest his faith. Christianity, as we understand it, is a revelation of spiritual life and truth, an exhibition of the grand moral laws of the universe, a development of the relation between the finite and the infinite, between humanity and Providence. The soul of man and the primal spirit; and whoever accepts this revelation as it was announced by Jesus Christ may claim to be a Christian for reasons which human decisions can do little to invalidate. . . .

It may be said that a profound and hearty faith in Christianity cannot be produced except by the evidence of miracles. But this assertion involves a fallacy in the logical procedure. It takes for granted the very point which we deny. We present an example of apparent Christian faith, where the reality of the miracles is not admitted; but the genuineness of the faith is denied because the evidence of the miracles is not perceived. But this is to oppose an arbitrary definition to the testimony of consciousness and experience. It is bringing facts to the test of our theory rather than framing our theory in accordance with facts. The question can be settled in no other way than by an appeal to universal Christian experience, so far as we are in a condition to avail ourselves of its testimony.

We ask then if there be the least shadow of proof that all the primitive believers were converted to Christianity on the evidence of miracles? We find that among the throngs who crowded around our Saviour when a miracle was to be exhibited, few became convinced of his claims and attached to his cause. They gazed as a crowd gazes on any other spectacle, but the hidden springs of faith within the soul were not touched. As far as we can judge at this distance of time, it was the truth which Jesus Christ announced rather than the wonderful works which he wrought that called forth the faith of his disciples and gave it vigor and steadfastness. At all events, we are not authorized to maintain the contrary. We must know the secret workings of the heart when the words of Christ fell upon the ear; we must be admitted to the retirement in which deep and solemn thoughts crowded together when the voice of the Son of God searched its dark places; we must see the movement of consciousness when it was first awakened to religious life by the touch of light from above, before we can pronounce with certainty that there was no faith in the Saviour except that which was founded on the contemplation of his dominion over external nature. . . .

With regard to our Saviour himself, we think it will appear, that his miracles of majesty and love were the free expressions of his character, rather than the formal supports of his mission. He exercised the divine power with which God had endowed him, not in the way of demonstration, but of philanthropy. He did not say, "Look at these miracles and believe what I declared"; on the contrary, he left his works to produce their own blessed effects on the body, while he put forth his truth to operate, in a similar manner, upon the soul. In some instances, it may be thought that he appealed to his miracles as an evidence that he was the messenger of God, and, therefore, entitled to be heard; but even this was not in confirmation of the truth of his doctrine, but of the authority with which he announced it. In the final appeal, he rested the claim of his truth on its intrinsic divinity and power.

Indeed, we do not see how our Lord could have adopted a different method, under the circumstances in which he was placed. The apparent performance of miracles was not peculiar to him. It was not sufficient to authenticate his mission as divine without reference to other sources of conviction. The very records which describe the miracles of Christ inform us that similar works were performed by others who did not acknowledge his authority but acted in their own name. It was an age in which portents and prodigies were not uncommon. How, then, was a true miracle to be distinguished from a false one? The Pharisees accused our Saviour of casting out devils through the Prince of the devils; how could this accusation be set aside but by establishing the divinity of his mission on independent evidence. If it had previously been made clear that God was with him, there would be no difficulty in admitting that his miracles were wrought by the finger of God. The evidence of the miracles alone will not sustain the test of a searching examination; for in themselves considered, they afford us no criterion to decide between the miracles of Christ and the miracles of a pretender. We must view them from a higher point of vision before they are made to stand out in contrast with all others, in their own peculiar beauty and grandeur.

In like manner, we know of no unerring test by which to distinguish a miracle of religion from a new manifestation of natural powers, without a previous faith in the divinity of the performer. The phenomena of electricity and magnetism exhibit wonders surpassing the ordinary agencies of nature.

Upon their first discovery they presented all the characteristics by which we designate miracles, except their application to religious purposes. If a miracle is said to have been wrought by one whom we already know to be in possession of supernatural gifts, there is a strong presumption that it may be true; but if the evidence of supernatural endowments is made to depend on the miracle, we ask how we are to know that what appears to be a miracle is, in fact, supernatural, and not a new development of nature.

If, then, a firm faith in Christianity may be cherished independently of miracles; if the purpose of miracles be to operate within the sphere of action rather than of thought; and if there be great difficulties in the proof of miracles without a previous conviction of the divine authority of him who is said to exhibit them, we hold it to be an unsound method to make a belief in them the essential foundation of Christian faith, or the ultimate test of Christian character.

It will be perceived that in the foregoing remarks we have not been inclined to controvert the truth of the Christian miracles. They are subjects of historical inquiry, and are to be settled by historical considerations, including that of the character and position of their author. We wish only to maintain what we deem a better mode of examining the evidences of Christianity than that which is usually pursued in the study of theology. The adoption of this mode, we are persuaded, would remove some of the strongest objections of infidels, and convert the timid and wavering faith of multitudes into strong and masculine conviction. Let the study of theology commence with the study of human consciousness. Let us ascertain what is meant by the expression, often used, but little pondered—the Image of God is the soul of man. Let us determine whether our nature has any revelation of the Deity within itself, and, if so, analyze and describe it. If we there discover, as we firmly believe we shall, a criterion of truth by which we can pass judgment on the spiritual and infinite, we shall then be prepared to examine the claims of a divine revelation in history. If our inward eye is unsealed, we shall discern the glory of God in the Person of his Son. Our faith will embrace him with a vital sympathy and certainty as the bearer of the highest inspiration of Heaven. We shall experience in our own souls the miracles of redemption and grace which he daily works therein, and with his conscious perception of his divine power, it will be easy to believe that he who has quelled our earthly passions and raised us from the death of sin to a life in God had authority to still the elements and restore Lazarus from the grave.

Orestes A. Brownson

NEW VIEWS OF CHRISTIANITY, SOCIETY, AND THE CHURCH
(1836)

Religion is natural to man and he ceases to be man the moment he ceases to be religious.

This position is sustained by what we are conscious of in ourselves and by the universal history of mankind.

Man has a capacity for religion, faculties which are useless without it, and wants which God alone can satisfy. Accordingly, wherever he is, in whatever age or country, he has—with a few individual exceptions easily accounted for—some sort of religious notions and some form of religious worship.

But it is only religion, as distinguished from religious institutions, that is natural to man. The religious sentiment is universal, permanent, and indestructible; religious institutions depend on transient causes, and vary in different countries and epochs.

As distinguished from religious institutions, religion is the conception, or sentiment, of the holy, that which makes us think of something as reverend, and prompts us to revere it. It is that indefinable something within us which gives a meaning to the words venerable and awful, which makes us linger around the sacred and the time-hallowed, the graves of heroes or of nations—which leads us to launch away upon the boundless expanse, or plunge into the mysterious depths of being, and which, from the very ground of our nature, like the Seraphim of the prophet, is forever crying out, "Holy, holy, holy, is the Lord of hosts; the whole earth is full of His glory."

Religious institutions are the forms with which man clothes his religious sentiment, the answer he gives to the question, What is the holy? Were he a stationary being, or could he take in the whole of truth at a single glance, the answer once given would be always satisfactory, the institution once adopted would be universal, unchangeable, and eternal. But neither is the fact. Man's starting-point is the low valley, but he is continually—with slow and toilsome effort it may be—ascending the sides of the mountain to more favorable positions, from which his eye may sweep a broader horizon of truth. He begins in ignorance, but he is ever growing in knowledge. . . .

All things change their forms. Literature, art, science, governments change under the very eye of the spectator. Religious institutions are subject to the same universal law. Like the individuals of our race, they pass away and leave us to deck their tombs, or in our despair, to exclaim that we will lie down in the grave with them. But as the race itself does not die, as new generations crowd upon the departing to supply their places, so does the reproductive energy of religion survive all mutations of forms, and so do new institutions arise to gladden us with their youth and freshness, to carry us further onward in our progress, and upward nearer to that which "is the same yesterday, today, and forever."

. . . Christianity, as it existed in the mind of Jesus, was the type of the most perfect religious institution to which the human race will, probably, ever attain. It was the point where the sentiment and the institution, the idea and the symbol, the conception and its realization appear to meet and become one. But the contemporaries of Jesus were not equal to this profound thought. They could not comprehend the God-Man, the deep meaning of his assertion, "I and my Father are one." He spake as never man spake, uttered truths for all nations and for all times; but what he uttered was necessarily measured by the capacity of those who heard him—not by his own. The less never comprehends the greater. Their minds must have been equal to his in order to have been able to take in the full import of his words. They might—as they did—apprehend a great and glorious meaning in what he said; they might kindle at the truths he revealed to their understandings, and even glory in dying at the stake to defend them; but they would invariably and inevitably narrow them down to their own inferior intellects, and interpret them by their own previous modes of thinking and believing. . . .

To comprehend Jesus, to seize the holy as it was in him, and consequently the true idea of Christianity, we must, from the heights to which we have risen by aid of the church, look back and down upon the age in which he came, ascertain what was the work which there was for him to perform, and from that obtain a key to what he proposed to accomplish.

Two systems then disputed the empire of the world; spiritualism[1] represented by the Eastern world, the old world of Asia, and materialism represented by Greece and Rome. Spiritualism regards purity or holiness as predicable of spirit alone, and matter as essentially impure, possessing and capable of receiving nothing of the holy—the prison house of the soul, its only hindrance to a union with God or absorption into His essence, the cause of all uncleanliness, sin, and evil, consequently to be contemned, degraded, and as far as possible annihilated. Materialism takes the other extreme, does not recognize the claims of spirit, disregards the soul, counts the body everything, earth all, heaven nothing, and condenses itself into the advice, "Eat and drink for tomorrow we die."

This opposition between spiritualism and materialism presupposes a necessary and original antithesis between spirit and matter. When spirit and matter are given as antagonist principles, we are obliged to admit antagonism between all the terms into which they are respectively convertible. From spirit is deduced by natural generation, God, the priesthood, faith, heaven, eternity; from matter, man, the state, reason, the earth, and time; consequently, to place spirit and matter in opposition is to make an antithesis between God and man, the priesthood and the state, faith and reason, heaven and earth, and time and eternity.

This antithesis generates perpetual and universal war. It is necessary then to remove it and harmonize or unite the spirit and matter, the representative of both—God-Man—two terms. Now, if we conceive Jesus as standing between the point where both meet and lose their antithesis, laying a hand on each and saying, "Be one, as I and my Father are one," thus sanctifying both and marrying them in a mystic and holy union, we shall have his secret thought and the true idea of Christianity.

The Scriptures uniformly present Jesus to us as a mediator, the middle term between two extremes, and they call

---

[1] I use these terms, spiritualism and materialism, to designate two social, rather than two philosophical systems. They designate two orders, which, from time out of mind, have been called *spiritual* and *temporal* or *carnal, holy* and *profane, heavenly* and *worldly*, etc. [Brownson's note.]

his work a mediation, a reconciliation—an atonement. The church has ever considered Jesus as making an atonement. It has held on to the term at all times as with the grasp of death. The first charge it has labored to fix upon heretics has been that of rejecting the atonement, and the one all dissenters from the predominant doctrines of the day have been most solicitous to repel is that of "denying the Lord who bought us." The whole Christian world, from the days of the Apostles up to the moment in which I write, have identified Christianity with the atonement, and felt that in admitting the atonement that admitted Christ, and that in denying it they were rejecting him.

Jesus himself always spoke of his doctine, the grand idea which lay at the bottom of all his teaching, under the term "Love." "A new commandment give I unto you, that ye love one another." . . . The nature of love is to destroy all antagonism. It brings together; it begetteth union, and from union cometh peace. Where there is but one term there is no union. There is no harmony with but one note. It is mockery to talk to us of peace where one of the two belliger-ant parties is annihilated. That were the peace of the grave. Jesus must then save both parties. The church has, therefore, with a truth it has never comprehended, called him God-Man. But if the two terms and their products be originally and essentially antagonistic; if there be between them an in-nate hostility, their union, their reconciliation cannot be effected. Therefore in proposing the union, in attempting the atonement, Christianity declares as its great doctrine that there is no essential, no original antithesis between God and man; that neither spirit nor matter is unholy in its nature; that all things, spirit, matter, God, man, soul, body, heaven, earth, time, eternity, with all their duties and interests, are in themselves holy. All things proceed from the same holy fountain, and no fountain sendeth forth both sweet waters and bitter. It therefore writes "Holiness to the Lord" upon every thing, and sums up its sublime teaching in that grand synthesis, "Thou shalt love the Lord thy God with all thy heart and mind and soul and strength, and thy neighbor as thyself."

The aim of the church was to embody the holy as it existed in the mind of Jesus, and had it succeeded, it would have realized the atonement, that is, the reconciliation of spirit and matter and all their products.

But the time was not yet. The Paraclete was in expectation. The church could only give currency to the fact that it was the mission of Jesus to make an atonement. It from the first misapprehended the conditions on which it was to be effected. Instead of understanding Jesus to assert the holiness of both spirit and matter, it understood him to admit that matter was rightfully cursed, and to predicate holiness of spirit alone. In the sense of the church, then, he did not come to atone spirit and matter, but to redeem spirit from the consequences of its connection with matter. His name therefore was not the Atoner, the Reconciler, but the Redeemer, and his work not properly an atonement but a redemption. This was the original sin of the church.

By this misapprehension the church rejected the mediator. The Christ ceases to be the middle term uniting spirit and matter, the *hilasterion*, the mercy-seat, or point where God and man meet and lose their antithesis, the Advocate with the Father for humanity, and becomes the Avenger of spirit, the manifestation of God's righteous indignation against man. He dies to save mankind, it is true, but he dies to pay a penalty. God demands man's everlasting destruction; Jesus admits that God's demand is just, and dies to discharge it. Hence the symbol of the cross signifying to the church an original and necessary antithesis between God and man which can be removed only by the sacrifice of justice to mercy. In this the church took its stand with spiritualism, and from a mediator became a partisan.

By taking its stand with spiritualism the church condemned itself to all the evils of being exclusive. It obliged itself to reject an important element of truth, and it became subject to all the miseries and vexations of being intolerant. It became responsible for all the consequences which necessarily result from spiritualism. The first of these consequences was the denial that Jesus came in the flesh. If matter be essentially unholy, then Jesus, if he had a material body, must have been unholy; if unholy, sinful. Hence all the difficulties of the Gnostics—difficulties hardly adjusted by means of a Virgin Mother and the Immaculate Conception, for this mode of accommodation really denied the God-Man, the symbol of the great truth the church was to embody. It left the God indeed, but it destroyed the man, inasmuch as it separated the humanity of Jesus by its very origin from common humanity.

Man's inherent depravity, his corruption by nature, followed as a matter of course. Man by his very nature partakes of matter, is material, then unholy, then sinful, corrupt, depraved. He is originally material, therefore originally a sinner. Hence original sin. Sometimes original sin is indeed traced as a primitive disobedience, to the fall; but then the doctrine of the fall itself is only one of the innumerable forms which is assumed by the doctrine of the essential impurity of matter.

From this original, inherent depravity of human nature necessarily results that antithesis between God and man which renders their union impossible and which imperiously demands the sacrifice of one or the other. "Die he or justice must." Man is sacrificed on the cross in the person of Jesus. Hence the vicarious atonement, the conversion of the atonement into an expiation. But if man was sacrificed, if he died as he deserved in Jesus, his death was eternal. Symbolically then he cannot rise. The body of Jesus after his resurrection is not material in the opinion of the church. He does not rise God-Man, but God. Hence the absolute Deity of Christ, which under various disguises has always been the sense of the church.

From man's original and inherent depravity it results that he has no power to work out his own salvation. Hence the doctrine of human inability. By nature man is enslaved to matter; he is born in sin and shapen in iniquity. He is sold to sin, to the world, to the devil. He must be ransomed. Matter cannot ransom him; then spirit must, and "God the mighty Maker" dies to redeem his creature—to deliver the soul from the influence of matter. . . .

God has indeed died to ransom sinners from the grave of the body, to redeem them from the flesh, to break the chains of the bound and to set the captive free; but the effects of the ransom must be secured; agents must be appointed to proclaim the glad tidings of salvation, to bid the prisoner hope and the captive rejoice that the hour of release will come. Hence the church. Hence too the authority of the church to preach salvation—to save sinners. And the church is composed of all who have this authority and of none others, therefore the dogma, "Out of the church there is no salvation.". . .

Everything must have its time. The church abused, degraded, vilified matter, but could not annihilate it. It existed in spite of the church. It increased in power, and at length rose against spiritualism and demanded the restoration of its rights. This rebellion of materialism, of the material order against the spiritual, is Protestantism.

Matter always exerted a great influence over the practice of the church. In the first three centuries it was very powerful. It condemned the Gnostics and Manicheans as heretics, and was on the point of rising to empire under the form of Arianism. But the oriental influence predominated, and the Arians became acknowledged heretics. . . .

The accession of Leo X. to the papal throne is a remarkable event in the history of the church. It marks the predominance of material interests in the very bosom of the church itself. . . . Now all this was in direct opposition to the theory of the church. Materialism was in the papal chair, but it was there as a usurper, as an illegitimate. It reigned in fact, but not in right. The church was divided against itself. In theory it was spiritualist, but in practice it was materialist. It could not long survive this inconsistency, and it needed not the attacks of Luther to hasten the day of its complete destruction . . . .

The dominant character of Protestantism is then the insurrection of materialism, and what we call the Reformation is really a revolution in favor of the material order. Spiritualism had exhausted its energies; it had done all it could for humanity; the time had come for the material element of our nature, which spiritualism had neglected and grossly abused, to rise from its depressed condition and contribute its share to the general progress of mankind. It rose, and in rising it brought up the whole series of terms the church had disregarded. It brought up the state, civil liberty, human reason, philosophy, industry, all temporal interests.

In Protestantism, Greece and Rome revived and again carried their victorious arms into the East. The Reformation connects us with classical antiquity, with the beautiful and graceful forms of Grecian art and literature, and with Roman eloquence and jurisprudence, as the church had connected us with Judea, Egypt, and India.

By means of the classics, the scholars of the fifteenth century were introduced to a world altogether unlike and much superior to that in which they lived—to an order of ideas wholly diverse from those avowed or tolerated by the church. They were enchanted. They had found the ideal of their dreams. They became disgusted with the present; they repelled the civilization effected by the church, looked with contempt on its fathers, saints, martyrs, schoolmen, troubadours, knights, and minstrels, and sighed and yearned and labored to reproduce Athens or Rome.

And what was that Athens and that Rome which seemed to them to realize the very ideal of the perfect? . . . In Athens and Rome all this is reversed. Human interests, the interests of mankind in time and space, predominate. Man is the most conspicuous figure in the group. He is everywhere and his imprint is upon everything. Industry flourishes; commerce is encouraged; the state is constituted, and tends to democracy; citizens assemble to discuss their common interests; the orator harangues them; the aspirant courts them; the warrior and the statesman render them an account of their doings and await their award. The *people*—not the gods —will, decree, make, unmake, or modify the laws. Divinity does not become incarnate as in the Asiatic world, but men are deified. History is not theogony, but a record of human events and transactions. Poetry sings heroes, the great and renowned of earth, or chants at the festal board and the couch of voluptuousness. Art models its creations after human forms for human pleasure or human convenience. They are human faces we see, human voices we hear, human dwellings in which we lodge and dream of human growth and human melioration. . . .

Under the reign of spiritualism all questions are decided by authority. The church prohibited reasoning. It commanded, and men were to obey or be counted rebels against God. Materialism, by raising up man and the state, makes the reason of man, or the reason of the state, paramount to the commands of the church. Under Protestantism, the state in most cases, the individual reason in a few, imposes the creed upon the church. The king and parliament in England determine the faith which the clergy must profess and maintain; the Protestant princes in Germany have the supreme control of the symbols of the church, the right to enact what creed they please. . . .

But the tendency, however arrested by the state, has been steadily toward the most unlimited freedom of thought and conscience. Our fathers rebelled against the authority of the state in religious matters as well as against the authority of the pope. In political and industrial speculations, the English and Americans give the fullest freedom to the individual reason; Germany has done it to the greatest extent in historical, literary and philosophical, and, to a very great extent, in theological matters, and France does it in everything. All modern philosophy is built on the absolute freedom and independence of the individual reason, that is, the reason of humanity, in opposition to the reason of the church or the state. Descartes refused to believe in his own existence but upon the authority of his reason; Bacon allows no authority but observation and induction; Berkeley finds no ground for admitting an external world, and therefore denies it; and Hume, finding no certain evidence of anything outward or inward, doubted—philosophically—of all things. . . .

The same tendency to exalt the terms depressed by the church is to be observed in the religious aspect of Protestantism. Properly speaking, Protestantism has no religious character. As Protestants, people are not religious, but co-existing with their Protestantism, they may indeed retain something of religion. Men often act from mixed motives. They bear in their bosoms sometimes two antagonist principles, now obeying the one, and now the other, without being aware that both are not one and the same principle. With Protestants, religion has existed; but as a reminiscence, a tradition. Sometimes, indeed, the remembrance has been very lively, and seemed very much like reality. . . .

If the religion of the Protestant world be a reminiscence, it must be the religion of the church. It is, in fact, only Catholicism continued. The same principle lies at the bottom of all Protestant churches, in so far as they are churches, which was at the bottom of the church of the Middle Ages. But materialism modified their rites and dogmas. In the practice of all there is an effort to make them appear reasonable. Hence commentaries, expositions, and defenses without number. Even where the authority of reason is denied, there is an instinctive sense of its authority and a desire to enlist it. In mere forms, pomp and splendor have gradually disappeared, and dry utility and even baldness have been consulted. In doctrines, those which exalt man and give him some share in the work of salvation have gained in credit and influence. Pelagianism, under some thin disguises or undisguised, has become almost universal. The doctrine of man's inherent total depravity, in the few cases in which it is asserted, is asserted more as a matter of duty than of conviction. Nobody who can help it preaches the old-fashioned doctrine of God's sovereignty expressed in the dogma of unconditional election and reprobation. The vicarious Atonement has hardly a friend left. The deity of Jesus is questioned, his simple humanity is asserted and is gaining credence. Orthodox is a term which implies as much reproach as commendation; people are beginning to laugh at the claims of councils and synods and to be quite merry at the idea of excommunication.

In literature and art there is the same tendency. Poetry in the last century hardly existed, and was, so far as it did exist, mainly ethical or descriptive. It had no revelations of the Infinite. Prose writers under Protestantism have been historians, critics, essayists, or controversalists; they have aimed almost exclusively at the elevation or adornment of the material order, and in scarcely an instance has a widely popular writer exalted God at the expense of man, the church at the expense of the state, faith at the expense of reason, or eternity at the expense of time. Art is finite, and gives us busts and portraits or copies of Greek and Roman models. The physical sciences take precedence of the metaphysical, and faith in railroads and steamboats is much stronger than in ideas. . . .

Industry has received in Protestant countries its grandest developments. Since the time of Luther, it has been performing one continued series of miracles. Every corner of the globe is explored; the most distant and perilous seas are navigated; the most miserly soil is laid under contribution; manufactures, villages and cities spring up and increase as by enchantment; canals and railroads are crossing the country in every direction; the means of production, the comforts, conveniences, and luxuries of life are multiplied to an extent hardly safe to relate.

Such, in its most general aspect, in its dominant tendency, is Protestantism. It is a new and much improved edition of the classics. . . . The real character of Protestantism, the result to which it must come, wherever it can have its full development, may be best seen in France at the close of the last century. The church was converted into the Pantheon and made a resting place for the bodies of the great and renowned of earth; God was converted into a symbol of the human reason and man into the man-machine; spiritualism fell, and the revolution marked the complete triumph of materialism.

What I have said of the Protestant world cannot be applied to the present century without some important qualifications. Properly speaking, Protestantism finished its work and expired in the French revolution at the close of the last century. Since then there has been a reaction in favor of spiritualism. . . .

In consequence of this reaction, men again despaired of

the earth, and when they despair of the earth, they always take refuge in heaven; when man fails them, they always fly to God. They had trusted materialism too far—they would now not trust it at all. They had hoped too much—they would now hope nothing. The future which had been to them so bright and promising was now overspread with black clouds; the ocean on which they were anxious to embark was lashed into rage by the storm and presented only images of dismasted or sinking ships and drowning crews. They turned back and sighed for the serene past, the quiet and order of old times, for the mystic land of India, where the soul may dissolve in ecstasy and dream of no change. . . .

Indeed everywhere is seen a decided tendency to spiritualism. The age has become weary of uncertainty. It sighs for repose. Controversy is nearly ended, and a sentiment is extensively prevailing that it is a matter of very little consequence what a man believes or what formulas of worship he adopts if he only have a right spirit. Men who a few years ago were staunch rationalists now talk of spiritual communion; and many, who could with difficulty be made to admit the inspiration of the Bible, are now ready to admit the inspiration of the sacred books of all nations, and instead of stumbling at the idea of God's speaking to a few individuals, they see no reason why he should not speak to everybody. Some are becoming so spiritual that they see no necessity of matter; others so refine matter that it can offer no resistance to the will, making it indeed move as the spirit listeth; others still believe that all wisdom was in the keeping of the priests of ancient India, Egypt, and Persia, and fancy the world has been deteriorating for four thousand years instead of advancing. Men go out from our midst to Europe, and come back half Catholics, sighing to introduce the architecture, the superstition, the rites, and the sacred symbols of the Middle Ages.

A universal cry is raised against the frigid utilitarianism of the last century. Money-getting, desire for worldly wealth and renown are spoken of with contempt, and men are evidently leaving the outward for the inward, and craving something more fervent, living, and soul-kindling. All this proves that we have changed from what we were, that, though materialism yet predominates and appears to have lost none of its influence, it is becoming a tradition, and that there is a new force collecting to expel it. Protestantism passes into the condition of a reminiscence. Protestant America cannot be aroused against the Catholics. A mob may burn a convent from momentary excitement, but the most protestant of the Protestants among us will petition the legislature to indemnify the owners. Indeed, Protestantism died in the French revolution and we are beginning to become disgusted with its dead body. The East has reappeared and spiritualism revives; will it again become supreme? Impossible.

We cannot go back either to exclusive spiritualism or to exclusive materialism. Both these systems have received so full a development, have acquired so much strength, that neither can be subdued. Both have their foundation in our nature, and both will exist and exert their influence. Shall they exist as antagonist principles? Shall the spirit forever lust against the flesh and the flesh against the spirit? Is the bosom of humanity to be eternally torn by these two contending factions? No. It cannot be. The war must end. Peace must be made.

This discloses our mission. We are to reconcile spirit and matter, that is, we must realize the atonement. Nothing else remains for us to do. Stand still we cannot. To go back is equally impossible. We must go forward, but we can take not a step forward but on the condition of uniting these two hitherto hostile principles. Progress is our law and our first step is union. . . .

The "second coming" of Christ will be when the idea which he represents, that is, the idea of atonement, shall be fully realized. That idea will be realized by a combination, a union, of the two terms which have received thus far from the church only a separate development. This union the church has always had a presentiment of; it has looked forward to it, prayed for it, and we are still praying for it, for we still say, "Let thy kingdom come." Nobody believes that the Gospel has completed its work. The church universal and eternal is not yet erected. The corner stone is laid, the materials are prepared. Let then the workmen come forth with joy and bid the Temple rise. Let them embody the true idea of the God-Man, and Christ will then have come a second time; he will have come in power and great glory, and he will reign, and the whole earth will be glad.

This age must realize the atonement, the union of spirit and matter, the destruction of all antagonism and the production of universal peace.

God has appointed us to build the new church, the one

which shall bring the whole family of man within its sacred enclosure, which shall be able to abide the ravages of time, and against which "the gates of hell shall not prevail." . . .

The great doctrine, which is to realize the atonement and which the symbol of the God-Man now teaches us, is that all things are essentially holy, that everything is cleansed, and that we must call nothing common or unclean.

"And God saw everything that he had made, and behold it was very good." And what else could it have been? God is wise, powerful and good; and how can a wise, powerful and good being create evil? God is the great fountain from which flows everything that is; how then can there be anything but good in existence?

Neither spiritualism nor materialism was aware of this truth. Spiritualism saw good only in pure spirit. God was pure spirit and therefore good; but all which could be distinguished from Him was evil, and only evil, and that continually. Our good consisted in resemblance to God, that is, in being as like pure spirit as possible. Our duty was to get rid of matter. All the interests of the material order were sinful. St. Augustine declared the flesh, that is the body, to be sin; perfection then could be obtained only by neglecting and, as far as possible, annihilating it. Materialism, on the other hand, had no recognition of spirit. It considered all time and thought and labor bestowed on that which transcends this world as worse than thrown away. It had no conception of inward communion with God. It counted fears of punishment or hopes of reward in a world to come mere idle fancies, fit only to amuse or control the vulgar. It laughed at spiritual joys and griefs, and treated as serious affairs only the pleasures and pains of sense.

But the new doctrine of the atonement reconciles these two warring systems. This doctrine teaches us that spirit is real and holy, that matter is real and holy, that God is holy and that man is holy, that spiritual joys and griefs and the pleasures and pains of sense, are alike real joys and griefs, real pleasures and pains, and in their places are alike sacred. Spirit and matter, then, are saved. One is not required to be sacrificed to the other; both may and should coexist as separate elements of the same grand and harmonious whole.

The influence of this doctrine cannot fail to be very great. It will correct our estimate of man, of the world, of religion, and of God, and remodel all our institutions. It must in fact create a new civilization as much in advance of ours as ours is in advance of that which obtained in the Roman empire in the time of Jesus.

Hitherto we have considered man as the antithesis of all good. We have loaded him with reproachful epithets and made it a sin in him even to be born. We have uniformly deemed it necessary to degrade him in order to exalt his Creator. But this will end. The slave will become a son. Man is hereafter to stand erect before God as a child before its father. Human nature, at which we have pointed our wit and vented our spleen, will be clothed with a high and commanding worth. It will be seen to be a lofty and deathless nature. It will be felt to be divine, and the infinite will be found traced in living characters on all its faculties.

We shall not treat one another then as we do now. Man will be sacred in the eyes of man. To wrong him will be more than crime, it will be sin. To labor to degrade him will seem like laboring to degrade the Divinity. Man will reverence man.

Slavery will cease. Man will shudder at the bare idea of enslaving so noble a being as man. It will seem to him hardly less daring than to presume to task the motions of the Deity and to compel him to come and go at our bidding. When man learns the true value of man, the chains of the captive must be unloosed and the fetters of the slave fall off.

Wars will fail. The sword will be beaten into the plowshare and the spear into the pruning hook. Man will not dare to mar and mangle the shrine of the divinity. The God looking out from human eyes will disarm the soldier and make him kneel to him he had risen up to slay. The warhorse will cease to bathe his fetlocks in human gore. He will snuff the breeze in the wild freedom of his native plains, or quietly submit to be harnessed to the plow. The hero's occupation will be gone, and heroism will be found only in saving and blessing human life.

Education will destroy the empire of ignorance. The human mind, allied as it is to the divine, is too valuable to lie waste or to be left to breed only briars and thorns. Those children, ragged and incrusted with filth, which throng our streets, and for whom we must one day build prisons, forge bolts and bars, or erect gibbets, are not only our children, our brother's children, but they are children of God; they have in themselves the elements of the Divinity and powers which when put forth will raise them above what the tallest archangel now is. And when this is seen and felt, will those children be left to fester in ignorance or to grow up in vice and crime? The whole energy of man's being cries out against such folly, such gross injustice.

Civil freedom will become universal. It will be everywhere felt that one man has no right over another which that other has not over him. All will be seen to be brothers and equals in the sight of their common Father. All will love one another too much to desire to play the tyrant. Human nature will be reverenced too much not to be allowed to have free scope for the full and harmonious development of all its faculties. Governments will become sacred; and while on the one hand they are respected and obeyed, on the other it will be felt to be a religious right and a religious duty to labor to make them as perfect as they can be.

Religion will not stop with the command to obey the laws, but it will bid us make just laws, such laws as befit a being divinely endowed like man. The church will be on the side of progress, and spiritualism and materialism will combine to make man's earthly condition as near like the lost Eden of the eastern poets as is compatible with the growth and perfection of his nature.

Industry will be holy. The cultivation of the earth will be the worship of God. Workingmen will be priests, and as priests they will be reverenced, and as priests they will reverence themselves and feel that they must maintain themselves undefiled. He that ministers at the altar must be pure, will be said of the mechanic, the agriculturist, the common laborer, as well as of him who is technically called a priest.

The earth itself and the animals which inhabit it will be counted sacred. We shall study in them the manifestation of God's goodness, wisdom, and power, and be careful that we make of them none but a holy use.

Man's body will be deemed holy. It will be called the temple of the living God. As a temple it must not be desecrated. Men will beware of defiling it by sin, by any excessive or improper indulgence, as they would of defiling the temple or the altar consecrated to the service of God. Man will reverence himself too much, he will see too much of the holy in his nature ever to pervert it from the right line of truth and duty.

"In that day shall there be on the bells of the horses, *Holiness unto the Lord;* and the pots in the Lord's house shall be as the bowls before the altar. Yea, every pot in Jerusalem and in Judah shall be Holiness unto the Lord of

Hosts." The words of the prophet will be fulfilled. All things proceed from God and are therefore holy. Every duty, every act necessary to be done, every implement of industry, or thing contributing to human use or convenience, will be treated as holy. We shall recall even the reverence of the Indian for his bow and arrow, and by enlightening it with a divine philosophy, preserve it.

"Pure religion, and undefiled before God and the Father is this, To visit the fatherless and the widows in their affliction, and to keep one's self unspotted from the world." Religious worship will not be the mere service of the sanctuary. The universe will be God's temple, and its service will be the doing of good to mankind, relieving suffering and promoting joy, virtue, and well-being. By this, religion and morality will be united, and the service of God and the service of man become the same. Our faith in God will show itself by our good works to man. Our love to the Father, whom we have not seen, will be evinced by our love for our brother whom we have seen.

Church and state will become one. The state will be holy, and the church will be holy. Both will aim at the same thing, and the existence of one as separate from the other will not be needed. The church will not be then an outward visible power coexisting with the state, sometimes controlling it and at other times controlled by it; but it will be within, a true spiritual—not spiritualistic—church, regulating the heart, conscience, and the life.

And when this all takes place the glory of the Lord will be manifested unto the ends of the earth, and all flesh will see it and rejoice together. The time is yet distant before this will be fully realized. We are now realizing it in our theory. We assert the holiness of all things. This assertion becomes an idea, and ideas, if they are true, are omnipotent. As soon as humanity fully possesses this idea, it will lose no time in reducing it to practice. Men will conform their practice to it. They will become personally holy. Holiness will be written on all their thoughts, emotions, and actions, on their whole lives. And then will Christ really be formed within, the hope of glory. He will be truly incarnated in universal humanity, and God and man will be one.

George Ripley

DISCOURSES ON THE
PHILOSOPHY OF RELIGION
(1836)

"FOR HE ENDURED, AS SEEING HIM WHO IS INVISIBLE."—HE-
BREWS xi, 27.

These words are applied by the writer of the Epistle to
the Hebrews, to the ancient lawgiver of their nation, as
descriptive of the principle of faith which formed a prominent element in his character. They may be regarded as
describing with no less justice and force the peculiar character of every truly religious man. For there is nothing which
more strongly marks the believer in religious truth than his
firm conviction of the reality of a vast range of subjects
which do not come under the cognizance of any of the
senses. His thoughts are not confined to the contemplation
of facts which are presented to the notice of the outward
eye. His mind is not limited to the gross and material objects
with which he is now surrounded, but passing over the
boundaries of space and time, is conversant with truths which
bear the stamp of infinity and eternity. He is conscious of
an inward nature which is the source of more important and
comprehensive ideas than any which the external senses suggest, and he follows the decision of these ideas as the inspir-
ing voice of God with none the less confidence because they
lead him into the region of the infinite and invisible. The principle of faith in the truth and reality of these ideas exerts
such a strong influence over his mind that he acts as if
their objects were now present with him; he proceeds upon
their certainty with as much assurance as if they had been exhibited to his bodily eye; he endures as seeing him who is
invisible. This, indeed, is so obvious and essential a trait
in the character of the truly religious man, that it has led

those who are blind to the destiny of our nature to charge
him with being a visionary, and devoted to objects that lie
beyond the cognizance of the human mind. A religious man
is one, it is said, who is taken up with objects that no one
has ever seen, and which, it is further argued, are unworthy
the attention of a rational being. We wish for facts, it is
repeated by persons of this way of thinking; we can have
no knowledge beyond the evidence of our senses; we can
believe nothing except what we have actually seen. The religious man, they contend, is in a great error because he is
not content with that, but wishes to obtain truth from the
testimony of his inward nature as well as from his outward
senses.

Now we admit that remarks like these are correct so far
as they indicate the direction which religion gives to our
minds toward the "things which are unseen and eternal";
but they are incorrect, as we think, in supposing that this direction does not lead to as clear and certain truth as that
which is opposed to it. The religious man is, indeed, conversant with invisible objects. His thoughts expatiate in regions
which eye hath not seen, but which God has revealed to him
by his spirit. He reposes as firm faith in those ideas which
are made known to him by his reason, as in those facts
which are presented to his notice by the senses. He has no
belief that human nature is so shackled and hemmed in,
even in its present imperfect state, as to be confined to the
objects made known by the eye of sense, which is given us
merely for the purposes of our temporal existence, and incapable of ascending to those higher spheres of thought
and reality to which the eternal elements of our being belong.

But, allowing this, it by no means follows that the religious man is a visionary in any just sense of that word, because, in the first place, he need not neglect the objects with
which he is at all times surrounded, and which are appropriate to the province of sense, and in the second place, the invisible objects with which he is conversant have no less
truth and reality than those which are seen. . . .

In pursuing this subject, I would first remark that the
things which are unseen possess the only independent reality. This assertion, I know, is contrary to our usual modes
of conception. The objects of sense make so early and so
strong an impression upon our minds that we soon learn to
regard them as more real than any others. Our first connection is with the material universe. . . . But, in truth, the things

which are seen were not made of things which do appear. The material universe is the expression of an Invisible Wisdom and Power. It has its origin in the will of the Infinite, Who has made it what it is, endowed it with all its properties, impressed it with all its tendencies, assigned it all its laws, and by whose energy it is ever constantly sustained. The creation in itself, without reference to the Almighty Spirit from which it sprung, is formless and without order— a mass of chaotic objects of whose uses we are ignorant, and whose destiny we cannot imagine. It is only when its visible glory leads our minds to its unseen Author, and we regard it as a manifestation of Divine Wisdom, that we can truly comprehend its character and designs. . . .

The things that are seen, moreover, are dependent, in a great measure, upon our own souls. We have another instance, here, of the relation between the visible and the invisible, and the subjection of the former to the latter. It is often said, I am aware, that the soul is dependent for its character and growth, on the external forms of matter with which it is connected, and that it is greatly influenced by them is a fact which no observer of human nature can deny; but it is no less true that the outward universe is to a great degree dependent upon our souls for its character and influence, and that by changes in our inward condition a corresponding change is produced in the objects with which we are surrounded. It is from the cast and disposition of our souls that external nature derives its hues and conformation. Place two men of different character in the same outward scenes, how different is the effect which takes place. To one, perhaps, whose heart is tuned to the praises of his Maker, everything suggests the presence of Divine Wisdom and Love. The voice of God is heard in the rushings of the wind and the whisperings of the breeze, in the roar of the thunder and the fall of the rain; His hand is visible in the glories of the midnight sky and the splendor of the opening morn, in the fierce majesty and might of winter, and in the greenness and beauty of the returning spring; every object is an image of the goodness of God; every sound, a call for His adoration; every spot a hallowed temple for His praise. But to the heart of the other, no such feelings are suggested. He looks coldly on amid the fair scene of things in which he is placed. No emotions of admiration or of gratitude penetrate his soul. No sound comes to him from the depths of nature, answering to an accordant sound within the depths of his own heart. He views all that is before him with a spirit of calculation or a spirit of indifference. Yet he sees precisely the same objects with his companion. . . .

When it is said that man may become a partaker of the divine nature, let us be careful to understand what is meant by the assertion. We shall otherwise fall into the region of extravagance and mysticism. To be a partaker of the divine nature is to possess, in some degree, the qualities which we attribute to the Supreme Divinity. Now it is plain that man possesses many qualities of an opposite character. With regard to this fact there can be no doubt, and there is no controversy. These qualities force themselves upon the attention of everyone. They are exhibited in the daily experience of life, and we cannot escape noticing them. But we must not look merely at one side of man's nature. We must not direct our attention so fixedly to certain qualities which it displays, as to lose sight of others, which are less prominent, of a contrary character. If man can become a partaker of the divine nature, there must be a basis for such participation in his own nature. If he can acquire any of the qualities which we attribute to the Supreme Divinity, there must be an original capacity for their cultivation. There must be a foundation to work upon, or the building cannot be erected. Let us see if there is anything in the nature of man which may enable him to become a partaker of the divine nature—any capacities which may be the germ of qualities in his character similar to those which we reverence in the character of God.

When we examine the nature which we possess, we perceive at once that it has a power of a remarkable character which seems to bear some resemblance to one of the divine attributes—the power of perceiving truth. Man has a faculty which enables him not merely to count, to weigh, and to measure, to estimate probabilities and to draw inferences from visible facts, but to ascertain and determine certain principles of original truth. He sees not merely that one thing is and another is not, that one object of sense is present and another is absent, but that one proposition, relating to abstract and invisible subjects of thought, is true, and another is false. An assertion may be made concerning an object which he has never seen and never can see—which cannot be submitted to the cognizance of the senses—and yet he has the power which enables him to say with absolute certainty whether it is true or false. It is this power by which all science is created. It was the possession of this power in a remarkable degree which enabled the solitary thinkers, in the retirement of their closets, whose labors have shed the greatest light on science, to make those discoveries by which the arts of life have been promoted, and aid given in the pursuit of the great interests of society. This power is reason. It gives us the immediate perception of truth. It is the ultimate standard in judging on all subjects of human inquiry. Whatever appears to be true to our reason, we believe to be true; whatever appears false to that, we believe to be false. Existing in different degrees in different men, it is found in some degree in all. There are certain points on which the judgment of all men is alike—certain propositions which everyone would pronounce true, certain others which all would declare false. We are compelled to this by the nature of our reason. It is not subject to the control of our will. We cannot say that we choose to have two and two appear equal to five, and therefore they are so in the sight of reason; but this faculty exercises its own judgment, announces its own decisions, enforces its own authority, from which there is no appeal. Does not this show that reason though within us is not created by us; though belonging to human nature, originates in a higher nature; though shining in the mind of man, is an emanation from the mind of God? Is not the faculty of reason similar to the wisdom of God? As He has the power of perceiving the pure and absolute truth on all subjects has He not endowed man with the similar power of perceiving truth on a limited number of subjects? In this respect, then, I believe that the nature of man has powers by which he may become a partaker of the divine nature—may exhibit qualities of a similar character to those which we reverence in God.

Again, man has the faculty of recognizing moral distinctions. Of two courses of conduct that are presented to his choice, he is able to say that one is right and that the other is wrong. He perceives not merely what would be for his advantage, his interest, what will gratify his passions, or promote the happiness of society, but he sees that certain actions, though they might gratify his selfish inclinations, are forbidden by the law of duty, and he feels an inward obligation to obey that law. Man does not obtain this knowledge through the medium of any of his senses. It is not the result of that part of his nature which calculates and compares. It is not subject to his own will. . . . Is not conscience in the human soul a quality similar to that attribute of God which makes him the righteous judge of all the earth? Is not conscience the voice of God, the word of Him who is of purer eyes than to behold iniquity, and Who separates between the evil and the good? As God discerns with His all-seeing eye the real character of every action, so has He imparted to the human soul a portion of his spirit which gives it a similar power, and arms the decisions of conscience with a divine authority. Here, then, is an element by the cultivation of which man may become a partaker of the divine nature. Let him reverence his conscience, and it will acquire a power similar to that justice which we adore in God. Let him listen to the faintest whispers of that voice which speaks in his moral nature, and he will preserve, in its original brightness, the image of his Maker which has been impressed upon his soul.

The purpose of Christianity . . . is to elevate the human soul to a resemblance to God, to make it a partaker of the divine nature. But this is accomplished, as we have seen, by calling forth the native powers of the soul itself, not by forcing upon it any constraint or violence from without. The growth of the soul may be compared to the growth of a plant. In both cases, no new properties are imparted by the operation of external causes, but only the inward tendencies are called into action and clothed with strength. The fragrance of the plant is elicited by the effect of the air, it opens its colors to the descending light, and assumes a form of beauty and grace according to the secret law of its organization, under the influence of surrounding circumstances. In like manner, the original properties of the soul are revealed under the influence of external causes, and in the light and strength of the Divine Spirit, which streams forth from the Primal Fountain on all created things, its divine elements are quickened into life and activity, and it becomes a partaker of the divine nature. Now this influence which the soul needs to give it a divine life and strength is imparted in a peculiar manner in the Gospel of Christ. Let it be brought under the power of Christianity, all that it has of the Divine, the Godlike, will be called forth; its original capacity for religion will become religion in reality, and it will exhibit a true resemblance to God.

. . . We perceive . . . from this subject, the true manner in which the evidences of Christianity are to be understood. It is the correspondence between the divine spirit of Christianity and the divine spirit in man that gives it the power of commanding a just and rational belief. If we are insensible to the divine spirit of Christianity—if its real character, as breathing the same spirit which we love and adore in God, has not been revealed to our minds, we can have no clear and distinct perception of its truth. On the other hand, if the divine spirit in our own hearts has been quenched—if the elements in our nature which ally us to God have never been called into life and action, we can have no hearty faith in Christianity. As face answereth to face in a mirror, so the divine in the Gospel answers to the divine in the heart of man. Let Christianity be clearly understood—let the heart of man be pure and alive—and they rush forward to meet each other—each as bearing the image of God and emanating from His Holy Spirit. . . .

When it is said that Christianity coincides with the higher nature of man, it is of the utmost importance to the success of the argument that we obtain a correct and clear idea of what Christianity really is. . . . We are to understand by Christianity the doctrine which our Saviour taught. In him, it pleased the Father that all fullness should dwell; in his person, the fullness of the divine character; in his instructions, the fullness of divine truth. Whatever he taught in his precepts or in his life, in his briefest hints, or his copious expositions, we regard as the essence of Christianity. The views of religion which he cherished himself are the views of religion which every Christian should cherish; the spirit which he breathed should be breathed by his followers; the faith which he taught himself, and about which there is no difficulty, should be the faith for which we contend as the substance of revelation, "the glorious Gospel of the Blessed God." . . . As the image of God is displayed in the divine elements of our nature, a similar image is presented in the revelations of the Gospel. Shall we not recognize the likeness? Are not the spirit which breathes in the human soul and the spirit which breathes in the religion of Christ brother-spirits that have come down from their native heaven to conduct the creatures of earth to their home with God? Yes, they are of a kindred origin, they know and love each other, and as soon as the spirit of man becomes conscious of its affinity with God, and beholds the same image in Jesus Christ, it utters what it cannot but feel—By this we know that thou camest forth from God. We are thus made free from the heavy burden of doubt, and enabled to embrace a faith that will satisfy the soul—a faith, that is not merely a form of lifeless words, but the strong conviction of our hearts—a faith that is so incorporated with the deepest elements of our nature that no earthly power can destroy it —a faith that will sustain us in the temptations of life, and reveal to us an unchanging home in the hour of death.

Elizabeth Palmer Peabody

RECORD OF A SCHOOL* (1836)

To contemplate spirit in the Infinite Being has ever been acknowledged to be the ground of true religion. To contemplate spirit in external nature is universally allowed to be the true science. To contemplate spirit in ourselves and in our fellowmen is obviously the means of understanding social duty, and quickening within ourselves a wise humanity. In general terms, contemplation of spirit is the first principle of human culture, the foundation of self-education.

This principle Mr. Alcott begins with applying to the education of the youngest children, considering early education as a leading of the young mind to self-education.

. . . But perhaps it will be admitted that Mr. Alcott is somewhat peculiar in the faith which he puts in this principle, or in his fearless and persevering application of it, and especially in his not setting the child to look for spirit *first* in the vast and varied field of external nature, as seems to be the sole aim of common education. For in common education, as is well known, the attention is primarily and principally directed to the part of language which consists of the names of outward things, as well as to books which scientifically class and explain them, or which narrate events in a matter-of-fact manner.

One would think that there has been proof enough that this common plan is a bad one, in the universally acknowledged difficulty of making children study those things to which they are first put without artificial stimulus; also in the absolute determination with which so many fine minds turn aside from word-knowledge and dry science to play and fun, and to whatever interests the imagination or heart; and, finally, in the very small amount of acquisition which, after

* *Record of a School* was first published in 1835. This "explanatory" chapter appeared in a new edition the following year.

all the pains taken, is generally laid up from school days. Besides, is it not *a priori* absurd? Is not external nature altogether too vast a field for the eye of childhood to command? And is it not impossible for the mind to discover the spirit in unity, unless the field is, as it were, commanded? The result of the attempt has generally been that no spiritual culture has taken place at school. In most cases, the attention has been bewildered, discouraged, or dissipated by a variety of objects; and in the best cases the mind has become one-sided and narrow by being confined to some particular department. Naturalists are apt to be full of oddities.

Instead, therefore, of making it his aim to make children investigate external nature after spirit, Mr. Alcott leads them, in the first place, to the contemplation of spirit as it unveils itself within themselves. He thinks there is no intrinsic difficulty in doing this, inasmuch as a child can as easily perceive and name pleasure, pain, love, anger, hate, and any other exercises of soul to which himself is subjected, as he can see the objects before his eyes; and thus a living knowledge of that part of language which expresses intellectual and moral ideas, and involves the study of his own consciousness of feelings and moral law, may be gained, external nature being chiefly made use of as imagery, to express the inward life which he experiences. Connected with this self-contemplation, and constantly checking any narrowing effect of egotism or self-complacency which it may be supposed to engender, is the contemplation of God that can so easily be associated with it. For as the word *finite* gives meaning to the word *infinite*, so the finite virtue always calls up in the mind an idea which is henceforth named and becomes an attribute of the Eternal Spirit. Thus a child, having felt what a just action is, either in himself or another, henceforth has an idea of justice which is pure and perfect in the same ratio as he is unsophisticated, and is more and more comprehensive of particular applications as his reason unfolds. How severe and pure it often is in a child, thousands have felt. . . .

But some say that the philosophy of the spirit is a disputed philosophy; that the questions—what are its earliest manifestations upon earth, and what are the means and laws of its growth—are unsettled; and therefore it is not a subject for dogmatic teaching.

Mr. Alcott replies to this objection that his teaching is

not dogmatic; that nothing more is assumed by him than that spirit exists, bearing a relation to the body in which it is manifested analogous to the relation which God bears to the external creation. And it is only those persons who are spiritual so far as to admit this whom he expects to place children under his care.

At this point his dogmatic teaching ends, and here he takes up the Socratic mode. He begins with asking questions upon the meanings of the words which the children use in speaking, and which they find in their spelling lessons, requiring illustrations of them in sentences composed or remembered. This involves the study of spirit. He one day began with the youngest of thirty scholars to ask illustrations of the word *brute,* and there were but three literal answers. A brute was a man who killed another; a drunken man; a man who beats his wife; a man without any love; but it was always a man. In one instance it was a boy beating a dog. Which is the brute, said Mr. Alcott, the boy or the dog? The boy, said the little girl, with the gravest face. This case indicates a general tendency of childhood, and is an opening therefore for speaking of the outward as the sign of the inward, and for making all the reading and spelling lessons exercises for defining and illustrating words. The lessons on language given in the Record, have generally been admitted to be most valuable. Most persons seem to be struck with the advantages necessarily to be derived from the habit of inquiring into the history of words from their material origin and throughout the spiritual applications of them which the imagination makes. . . .

Some objections have been made, however, to the questioning upon consciousness, of which specimens are given in the lessions on self-analysis. It is said that their general tendency must be to produce egotism. This might be if, in self-analysis, a perfect standard were not always kept before the mind by constant reference to Jesus Christ as the "truth of our nature"; and by means of that generalizing tendency, which I have noticed before, which always makes children go from finite virtue to the idea of the perfect. We have found the general influence of the lessons on self-analysis to be humbling to the self-conceited and vain, though they have also encouraged and raised up the depressed and timid in one or two instances. The objection seems to me to have arisen from taking the word *self* in a too limited signification. The spirit within is what is meant by *self,* when considered as an object of philosophical investigation. I think that the lessons would more appropriately have been styled analysis of human nature than self-analysis; for, excepting the first one, they were of a very general character, and constantly became more so in their progress. . . .

Having spoken thus elaborately of the school with respect to its principles and methods of moral culture, I will proceed to speak of it with respect to its intellectual effects; and here, I for one have never had any doubts in any particular. I think it can be proved *a priori* and *a posteriori* that the intellectual influences are in all respects salutary. . . .

The first object of investigation is . . . in the highest degree fruitful for the intellect. Spirit as it appears within themselves, whether in the form of feeling, law, or thought, is universally interesting. No subject interests children so much as self-analysis. To give name to inward movements of heart and mind, whether in themselves or others, is an employment of their faculties which will enchain the attention of the most volatile. There is no one class of objects in external Nature which interests all children, for children are very differently gifted with respect to their sympathies with Nature. But all are conscious of something within themselves which moves, thinks, and feels; and as a mere subject of curiosity, and of investigation for the sake of knowledge, it may take place of all others. In order to investigate it, a great many things must be done which are in themselves very agreeable. Mr. Alcott reads and tells stories calculated to excite various moral emotions. On these stories he asks questions, in order to bring out from each, in words, the feelings which have been called forth. These feelings receive their name and history and place in the moral scale. Then books and passages from books are read, calculated to exercise various intellectual faculties, such as perception, imagination, judgment, reason, conscience, and these various exercises of mind are discriminated and named. There can be no intellectual action more excellent than this, whether we consider the real exercise given to the mind, or its intrinsic interest to the children, and consequently the naturalness of the exercise. And its good influence with respect to preparing for the study of science is literally incalculable. There is not a single thing that cannot be studied with comparative ease by a child who can be taught what faculties he must use, and how they are to be brought to bear on the subject, and what influence on those faculties the subject will have after it is mastered.

But Mr. Alcott would not sequestrate children from Nature, even while this preparatory study of spirit is going on. He would be very thankful to throw all the precious influences of a country life, its rural employments, its healthful recreations, its beautiful scenery, around his scholars' minds. He thinks that the forms of Nature, as furniture for the imagination and an address to the sentiments of wonder and beauty, and also as a delight to the eye and as models for the pencil, cannot be too early presented, or too lovingly dwelt upon. In lieu of these circumstances, which of course cannot be procured in Boston, he reads to them of all in Nature which is calculated to delight the imagination and heart. He surrounds them also with statuary and pictures in his schoolroom; and he has drawing taught to all his scholars by a gentleman who probably possesses the spirit of art more completely than any instructor who has ever taught in this country.

Nor is the study of books excluded from the school. This is so common a mistake with respect to Mr. Alcott's plan, that perhaps I could not do better than to enter into some details respecting the precise manner in which the studying from books in its various departments is conducted. In the first place, with respect to

The English Language

As the analysis of English words into letters, and the unfolding of the meanings contained in them, constitute the foundation of an English education, spelling and defining words are the most prominent intellectual exercises of the school. The children learn the spelling lesson by writing the given number of words on their slates, or in manuscript books with pencils; those who do not yet write the script, hand print, or endeavor to print them. The spelling book they use is Pike's, which was selected because it contains the primitive words of the language, together with such derivatives as are roots in relation to other words. But a spelling book containing the roots of the language and nothing more is yet a desideratum with us, which Mr. Alcott hopes to supply when he gets leisure to study the Anglo-Saxon language, whence the life of our tongue undoubtedly springs.

After writing the words, the children spell them to themselves, and when they think they can arrange the letters rightly, they look out their meanings in their Johnson's dictionaries, a copy of which is placed at each desk. They are also directed to imagine sentences in which the words can be used, or to remember any sentences which contain them, that they may have heard or read. Those who are too young to manage a bulky dictionary, Mr. Alcott orally teaches, as may be seen in the Record. Grammatical exercises, which consist of the analysis of sentences and the classification of words according to their meanings, also constitute a regular exercise. Children soon become expert in abstracting and classifying words in this way, although quite unacquainted with the technicalities of grammatical science.

Composition

From the foregoing remarks it will be evident that book learning is not entirely neglected by Mr. Alcott. Yet it is true that he lays himself out rather to prepare his scholars to receive it after they have left him, than to give it to them himself at the early age when they are under his care. His main object is to produce activity of mind and taste for intellectual pursuits. And for the purpose of activity he uses one means which is very much neglected in common schools, and that is, he leads them to express their thoughts on paper as soon as they can write the script hand so as to be read.

Several of his pupils commenced their journals as soon as they came, but it was some time before these became any record of the inward life. The children were entirely unused to composition, and at first only set down the most dry and uninteresting circumstances.

Mr. Alcott, however, contented himself with expressing the hope that by and by we should have more thoughts mingled with the record of facts; and he made no criticisms on the language, or even on the spelling, knowing that courage is easily checked, in these first efforts, by criticism, and wishing to produce a sense of freedom as a condition of free expression. He did not expect interesting views from them, until their minds were more thoroughly trained to self-inspection and inward thought. He has little reliance on any method of producing the impulse to composition, except the indirect one of leading children to think vividly and consecutively, which leads of itself to expression. And still less has he any reliance upon the power of a composition which was not the result of an inward impulse. A mere mechanical exercise leads to a tame and feeble style, which it is a misfortune to acquire, and which generates no desire to write more; but it is spontaneous to endeavor to express energetically what one feels vividly and conceives clearly; and any degree of success in this inspires ardor for new attempts. . . . The objections made against the intellectual influences of Mr. Alcott's school by those who do not know much about it are chiefly of the negative character which the foregoing pages have attempted to answer. There is one, however, of a positive character, on which I wish to make some observations, and then I shall close this protracted essay.

It is said that Mr. Alcott cultivates the imagination of his scholars inordinately by leading them to the works of the poets and to the prose creations of such writers as Krummacher, Bunyan, Carova, etc. It is thought that by exercising the minds of the children in following authors of this class, requiring them to picture out all the imagery of their language, and leading them to consider, also, the inward life which this imagery is intended to symbolize, the energy of the imagination is increased. But I apprehend that all this is but guiding the imagination, freeing it from the dominion of the senses and passions, and placing it under its true lawgiver— the idea of beauty; and that it does not increase its natural energy, which is always a gift of Nature. The decision does not lie with us whether there shall be imagination or not, or what degree of it there shall be. It exists equally energetic, whether cultivated or not. It presides over the sports of childhood just in the same ratio as that of the spirit to the body of the child. In acts in every walk of the most prosaic business. The victims of uncultivated imagination are all around us—in the wild speculators of commercial life, in the insane pursuers of outward goods to the destruction of all inward peace, in the fanatics of all sects of religion, and all parties of politics, and all associations for general objects. Nothing is to be gained by neglecting to use this faculty, or by omitting to give name to its movements, or by checking the soul's natural tendency to gratify it. Could we succeed in doing this, yet events would wake it up from its slumber, and might do so at any time; and it will be all the more liable to deem itself some god or demon from the hidden world because it does not understand itself. To cultivate the imagination is rather to disarm its energy than to increase it; but in lieu of mere energy, cultivation gives beauty, safety, and elevating influences to all its movements.

But Mr. Alcott has no intention of cultivating one faculty more than another. His plan is to follow the natural order of the mind. He begins with analyzing the speech the children use. In doing this, they are led immediately to consider the action of the imagination, since it is this faculty which has formed language. We find that language clothes thoughts and emotions with the forms of nature, its staple being the imagery of outward nature, as truly as the staple of sculptures and paintings is the material of outward nature, and all are Psyche's drapery. Mr. Alcott asks a child questions in order to turn his attention upon what passes within his own mind; and what the child says, when making this inward survey, will determine what faculties are most active in his nature for the time being. Or, if his words must be taken with caution—and it is true that they sometimes must, since some children learn words by rote so easily—his inward state can be determined by taking a wide range of reading and constantly observing what character of books interests him most strongly. He will like those books best which exercise the faculties and feelings that are already in agreeable activity; and these should be cherished and nurtured in a full confidence that they will wake up in due time the other faculties of the soul. Mr. Alcott, by pursuing this course faithfully, has found that the imagination is the first faculty which comes forth, leading all the others in its train. He has therefore not failed to meet it and give it food. If he were to give it other than the healthy food supplied by Nature, Providence, and that true Genius which embodies Nature and Providence in its creations; or if he were to allow it to degenerate into fancy, or fantasy, or stray from the principle of beauty, which is the law of the imagination, I should be the last to defend it. But, wisely fed and governed, the imagination need not be feared. It is the concentration of profound feeling, reason, and the perception of outward nature

into one act of the mind, and prepares the soul for vigorous
effort in all the various departments of its activity.

[LESSONS]

Thirty words were spelled; and then they were taken up
one by one, and not merely defined, but illustrations of all
their meanings, literal and imaginative, were given, either by
original or remembered sentences which contained the word
in question. This course led often to disquisitions on the subject to which the word was typically applied.

During this lesson on words, which Mr. Alcott considers
one of the most important exercises in the school, he requires
profound attention from every scholar. A whisper, a movement, a wandering look arrests him in what he says, and he
immediately calls the scholar by name. When he asks a question, everyone who can answer it must raise a hand and he
selects one—sometimes he asks every member of the class—
to give what is in his mind upon the word. The most general
and strict attention is the result. . . .

Look was defined. "How does the soul look out?" said Mr.
Alcott. "Through the eyes." "How does the soul look in?"
A very little boy said, "By the thoughts turning round." A
large boy said, "The soul looks in with the eyes as well as
out." Mr. Alcott said, "Is not the soul itself an eye? And
what is reflection?" "Reflection," said a girl twelve years
old, "seems to imply a looking glass." Mr. Alcott replied, "It
is not the best name for the act of mind I was speaking of;
there is a better word for this—thought." One of the little
boys asked what was the name of the soul's look upon things.
Mr. Alcott said it was commonly named Perception, and
added, "Perhaps all the shapes we see without pre-exist in
the mind, and are perfect, whether the shape without is so
or not." He illustrated this by asking them if the man who
made the Temple did not have a picture in his mind of
the Temple before it was made, etc. . . .

Afterward Mr. Alcott remarked that when they obtained
one thought, they possessed more than a person who had
earned many thousand dollars. The oldest boy said he thought
five thousand dollars was better than a thought. Another boy
said that he should rather have five thousand dollars than all
the thoughts he had had this last hour. Mr. Alcott said, "Here
is a boy that prefers five thousand dollars to his mind." The
boy replied that he did not do that, but only to the thoughts

of this last hour. Mr. Alcott said that the thoughts even of this hour were mind. The boy replied that the thoughts of the last hour were not all his mind. Mr. Alcott said that was very true, and possibly he had thought no thoughts in the last hour; but he was going on the supposition that he had had thoughts, when he said that the last hour was worth more to him than five thousand dollars. One boy said he should prefer five thousand dollars to the thoughts of this last hour, even if he had had any. Mr. Alcott said it was very often the case that the desire for the latter interfered with that of the former; Jesus had said it was easier for a camel to go through the eye of a needle than for a rich man to be a Christian, which, in those times, involved giving up his riches, and putting them in a common stock. One boy said he wanted money for his relations. There was a good deal of conversation on this subject, and as it closed, Mr. Alcott asked them if they were sorry to hear such kind of conversation. If any of them did not like it, he wished they would hold up their hands. No one held up his hands.

One boy in school (who is a lately entered scholar) asked if [a] story was true. Mr. Alcott said, "There are two sorts of truth—the truth of what is in the mind, and the truth of what is out of the mind. But there are some boys who do not understand that there are realities *in* the mind; and, when I shape out the realities of the mind by means of outward things that represent them, these boys think it is not true. They cannot believe any truth but the outward truth. Now the inward truth is the first truth; there would never have been a single outward thing, not a thing in the world, no world at all, if God had not had thoughts *in* his mind first. The world existed as a thought in God's mind before a single particle of it existed in such a way as to be seen or heard or felt." He then addressed one boy eight years old: "Tell me, when you do anything outside of you, anything which others see you do, does it not exist first within your mind? Do you not feel it first really existing within your mind?" "Yes." "Well, can any of you tell me of a single thing that you see with your eyes that did not first exist really within some spirit?" One boy said, "Did that bust of Shakespeare exist really in a mind before it existed out of a mind?" He was soon convinced that the form of it did exist in the mind of the molder.

In the subsequent spelling lesson, when the word *tale* came up, it elicited a good deal of conversation. It was seen that a tale, a fable, etc., might be the medium of conveying truth. Mr. Alcott went on to show that the things that we see tell us a tale all the time. And he asked what the world was a tale of? After a moment's reflection, several of the children said, of God. Then he asked what the things that happen in the outward world were tales of. It was answered that there was not a thing that happened that had not existed in some mind, either in God's mind or in some man's mind. He then said, "The world is a tale, and life is a tale."

At the hour of dismissal, the whole school was brought together. One or two boys had been punished on their hands during the school hours, and one of the larger boys remarked that a certain gentleman (naming him) had said that he was sorry Mr. Alcott had found it necessary to use the ferule. Mr. Alcott said, "Such of you as have been punished with the ferule may rise." Several did so. He then said, "Such of you as have been made better, have been assisted in self-control and in your memory, by being so punished, may sit down." All sat down but one. Mr. Alcott then remarked that he was sorry thoughts were not realized as they might be, to govern their actions. But as sometimes they were not, and many boys deemed thoughts to be unreal, it was necessary for outward things, which they did believe real, to take the side of conscience, and help to make them seem real and visible; and he believed not one boy had been punished without acknowledging beforehand that he felt it would do him good, and that it was Mr. Alcott's duty to give him that help.

Birth was the first word. Mr. Alcott remarked that we had once before talked of birth, and their ideas had been brought out. "Now I am going to speak of it again, and we shall read Wordsworth's ode." He then asked the youngest child present how old he was, and found he was four. The oldest was twelve. He said, "That little boy, in four years, has not had time to make that comparison of thoughts and feelings which makes up conscious life." He asked those who understood him to hold up their hands. Several held up their hands. "Those who do not understand these words may hold up their hands." A great many of the younger ones held up their hands.

"I am not surprised that you did not understand; but perhaps you will understand some things I am going to say. Do you feel," said he to the oldest, "that any change has taken place in you in twelve years? Do things seem the same

to you as they did six years ago?" She recognized a change.
A boy of ten said that he did also. "Wordsworth had lived,
when he wrote this ode, many years, and consequently had
felt changes, and he expresses this in the lines I am about
to read." He then began and read the first stanza:

> There was a time when meadow, grove, and stream,
>   The earth and every common sight,
>   To me did seem
>   Apparelled in celestial light,
>   The glory and the freshness of a dream.
>   It is not now as it has been of yore;
>   Turn wheresoe'er I may,
>   By night or day,
> The things which I have seen I now can see no more.

He here stopped, and asked why Wordsworth could not see
the things which he had seen before; had they changed, or
had he changed? He had changed, said a boy of ten. "Have
you had any degree of this change?" "Yes, and more in
this last year than in all my life before."

He then said, "But let us all look back six months; how
many of you look at things, and feel about them, differently from what you did six months ago? How many of you
feel that this schoolroom is a different place from what it
was the first week you were here?" Almost everyone immediately, with great animation, held up his hand. He then asked
those who knew why this was to hold up their hands. Many
did. And when called on to answer, they severally said, "Because we know more, because we think more, because we
understand you, because you know us, because you have
looked inside of us." Mr. Alcott said, "The place is very different to me, and why?" They gave similar answers, but he
said they had not hit it. At last one said, "Because we be-
have better." "Yes," said he, "you have it now; knowledge is
chaff of itself, but you have taken the knowledge and used
it to govern yourselves, and to make yourselves better. If I
thought I gave you knowledge only, and could not lead you
to use it to make yourselves better, I would never enter this
schoolroom again."

He went on and read the next stanza of the ode:

> The rainbow comes and goes,
> And lovely is the rose,
> The moon doth with delight
> Look round her when the heavens are bare.

> Waters on a starry night
> Are beautiful and fair.
> The sunshine is a glorious birth;
> But yet I know, where'er I go,
> That there hath passed away a glory from the earth;

stopping to ask them about the effects of the rainbow, the rose, the waters on a starry night, on themselves; remarking, "There are some minds which live in the world, and yet are insensible, which do not see any beauty in the rainbow, the moon, the waters on a starry night." As he went on through the next stanza, so descriptive of the animation and beauty of spring, he paused on every line, and asked questions. "Why are 'the cataracts said to blow their trumpets'?" A little girl said, "Because the waters dash against the rocks." "The echoes thronging through the woods" led out to recollections of the sound in the woods in spring, to echoes which they had severally heard. As the animating pictures of "children pulling flowers on May-day," the "child springing up on the mother's arm," etc., came up, every countenance expressed the most vivid delight, and one girl exclaimed, "What a succession of beautiful pictures!" "All full of life," said Mr. Alcott; and he went on:

> But there's a tree of many one,
> A single field which I have looked upon;
> Both of them speak of something that is gone:
> The pansy at my feet
> Doth the same tale repeat:
> Whither is fled the visionary gleam?
> Where is it now, the glory and the dream?

When he had read these lines, he said, "Was that a thought of life?" "No, a thought of death," said several. "Yes," said Mr. Alcott, "Wordsworth had lived long enough to feel changes; he had known death, as well as life." He then went on:

> Our birth is but a sleep and a forgetting,

and stopped and asked how that was. After a pause, one of the most intelligent boys, eight years old, said he could not imagine. The two oldest girls said they understood it, but could not explain it in words. "Do you understand it?" said Mr. Alcott to a little boy of five who was holding up his hand. "Yes." "Well, what does it mean?" "Why, you know," said he very deliberately, "that, for all that our life seems so long to us, it is a very short time to God, and so when we die it seems all a sleep to God." He repeated this at Mr. Alcott's request, and I said to him, "So Mr. Wordsworth was thinking of God, and how God felt on seeing that a child was born into the world?" He paused, looked a little confused, and repeated the word *forgetting*. I said, "Wait, and tell me your thought." "Why, you know," said he, "God knows us, but we don't." He looked at me with a look of doubt, whether I should understand him. "And our knowledge of ourselves, in comparison with what God knows about us," said I, "seems like forgetfulness itself?" "Yes," said he, "that is it" (with a cleared up countenance). All the rest listened with interest and an expression of great pleasure, and then one girl said, "The soul comes from heaven; it goes to sleep in that world, and wakes up in this." Mr. Alcott then read on to the line

Heaven lies about us in our infancy,

when he shut up the book, and asked every child separately what he understood by birth. They all answered; and many repeated the definitions which they gave the other day. When they had answered all round, Mr. Alcott observed that there was one striking difference in their answers; some expressed the idea that the soul shaped and made the body; others that the body was made, and the soul put into it. "Which is right?" said one boy. "That is more than I can tell, but I incline to the first opinion. You are all nearly right, however; you have the important ideas; birth is not the beginning of the spirit; life is the remembrance, or a waking up of spirit. All the life of knowledge is the waking up of what is already within,

The rising of life's star, that had elsewhere its setting.

"What is life's star?" "The soul," said they. "But birth is sometimes the prelude to the death of the soul," said Mr. Alcott. "How?" said one boy. "Because the soul becomes the slave of the body, is governed, darkened, shut up, and buried in it; and it is necessary that it should be born again, born out of the body; do you understand that?" "Yes." "Some of you have needed to be born again into your new life," said Mr. Alcott. Then he asked, "Do you know what *pulp* means?" Several said, "Yes." Mr. Alcott continued, "It is the part of the fruit round the seed; and its use is to cherish the seed, and give it life, and make it fit to become the beginning of a new tree or plant. Well, do you understand my figure when I say that the body is a pulp, and that its use is to cherish and protect the spiritual seed?" Many of them said, "Yes." "Well, suppose that we take the seed of a plant and put it in the ground, what happens to it?" They were silent, and he added, "It bursts, and some parts shoot down into the earth, and some parts shoot up toward the light. Now can you understand this, that *the soul* is a seed placed in the midst of the world, represented by the ground; and that the shoots which go down into the earth, to fasten the plant in the earth awhile, are the bodily feelings and appetites; and that the shoots which go upward toward the light are the affections and better feelings that seek Heaven?" They said, "Yes." "Well, suppose that more of the seed shoots downward than is necessary, and that no shoots go upward, would there be any flower and fruit? No. It would all be *root;* all would be under the earth. Well, can you understand that if the soul loves the body only, and only uses its animal appetites, and does not seek the light and Heaven, it will have no beauty nor fruit, but will be an earthly, dark thing, a root?" Yes, they understood that. "Well," said he, "now you know why I wish to check your animal appetites, your love of the body, when that interferes with the mind's growth. It is right to love your body in a degree—the body has its uses; but it is one thing to take care of your body and another to indulge it. The plant must have root enough to make it stand steady in the earth, but that is enough."

Andrews Norton

A DISCOURSE ON THE LATEST FORM OF INFIDELITY (1839)

. . . The latest form of infidelity is distinguished by assuming the Christian name, while it strikes directly at the root of faith in Christianity, and indirectly of all religion, by denying the miracles attesting the divine mission of Christ. The first writer, so far as I know, who maintained the impossibility of a miracle was Spinoza, whose argument, disengaged from the use of language foreign from his opinions, is simply this, that the laws of nature are the laws by which God is bound, Nature and God being the same, and therefore laws from which Nature or God can never depart. The argument is founded on atheism. The denial of the possibility of miracles must involve the denial of the existence of God; since, if there be a God, in the proper sense of the word, there can be no room for doubt that He may act in a manner different from that in which He displays His power in the ordinary operations of nature. It deserves notice, however, that in Spinoza's discussion of this subject we find that affectation of religious language, and of religious reverence and concern, which is so striking a characteristic of many of the irreligious speculations of our day, and of which he, perhaps, furnished the prototype; for he has been regarded as a profound teacher, a patriarch of truth, by some of the most noted among the infidel philosophers and theologians of Germany. . . .

There is one, however, among the writings against the miracles of Christianity, of a different kind, the famous essay of Hume. None has drawn more attention, or has more served as a groundwork for infidelity. Yet, considering the sagacity of the author, and the celebrity of his work, it is remarkable that, in his main argument, the whole point to be proved is broadly assumed in the premises. "It is a miracle," he says, "that a dead man should come to life;

because that has never been observed, in any age or country. There must, therefore, be a uniform experience against every miraculous event; otherwise the event would not merit that appellation." The conclusion, if conclusion it may be called, is easily made. If a miracle has never been observed in any age or country, if uniform experience shows that no miracle ever occurred, then it follows that all accounts of past miracles are undeserving of credit. But if there be an attempt to stretch this easy conclusion, and to represent it as involving the intrinsic incredibility of a miracle, the argument immediately gives way. "Experience," says Hume, "is our only guide in reasoning concerning matters of fact." Experience is the foundation of such reasoning, but we may draw inferences from our experience. We may conclude from it the existence of a power capable of works which we have never known it to perform; and no one, it may be presumed, who believes that there is a God, will say that he is convinced by his experience that God can manifest His power only in conformity to the laws which He has imposed upon nature. . . .

To deny that a miracle is capable of proof, or to deny that it may be proved by evidence of the same nature as establishes the truth of other events, is, in effect, as I have said, to deny the existence of God. A miracle can be incapable of proof only because it is physically or morally impossible, since what is possible may be proved. To deny that the truth of a miracle may be established involves the denial of creation, for there can be no greater miracle than creation. It equally implies that no species of being that propagates its kind ever had a commencement; for if there was a first plant that grew without seed, or a first man without parents, or if of any series of events there was a first without such antecedents as the laws of nature require, then there was a miracle. So far is a miracle from being incapable of proof that you can escape from the necessity of believing innumerable miracles only by believing that man and all other animals and all plants have existed from eternity upon this earth without commencement of propagation, there never having been a first of any species. No one at the present day will maintain with Lucretius that they were generated from inanimate matter by the fermentation of heat and moisture. Nothing can seem more simple or conclusive than the view we have taken, but we may render it more familiar by an appeal to fact. The science of geology has shown us that man is but a late inhabitant of the earth.

The first individuals of our race, then, were not produced as all others have been. They were formed by a miracle, or, in other words, by an act of God's power exerted in a different manner from that in which it operates according to the established laws of nature. Creation, the most conspicuous, is at the same time the most undeniable of miracles.

By anyone who admits that God exists, in the proper sense of the words, His power to effect a miracle cannot be doubted; and it would be the excess of human presumption and folly to affirm that it would be inconsistent with His wisdom and goodness ever to exert His power except in those modes of action which He has prescribed to Himself in what we call the laws of nature.

On the contrary, a religious philosopher may regard the uniformity of the manifestations of God's power in the course of nature as solely intended by Him to afford a stable ground for calculation and action to His rational creatures, which could not exist if the antecedents that we call causes were not, in all ordinary cases, the signs of consequent effects. This uniformity is necessary to enable created beings to be rational agents. . . .

But, if the uniformity of the laws of nature, so far as they fall within our cognizance, is ordained by God for the good of His creatures, then, should a case occur in which a great blessing is to be bestowed upon them, the dispensing of which requires that He should act in other modes, no presumption would exist against His so acting. So far as we are able to discern, there would be no reason to doubt that He would so act. A miracle is improbable when we can perceive no sufficient cause in reference to His creatures why the Deity should vary His modes of operation; it ceases to be so when such a cause is assigned. But Christianity claims to reveal facts, a knowledge of which is essential to the moral and spiritual regeneration of men; and to offer, in attestation of the truth of those facts, the only satisfactory proof, the authority of God, evidenced by miraculous displays of His power. The supposed interposition of God corresponds to the weighty purpose which it is represented as effecting. If Christianity profess to teach truths of infinite movement; if we perceive that such is the character of its teachings, if, indeed, they are true; and if we are satisfied, from the exercise of our own reason and the history of the world, that they relate to facts concerning our relations and destiny of which we could otherwise obtain no assurance, then this character of our religion removes all presumption against its claims to a miraculous origin. . . .

If it were not for the abuse of language that has prevailed, it would be idle to say that, in denying the miracles of Christianity, the truth of Christianity is denied. It has been vaguely alleged that the internal evidences of our religion are sufficient, and that miraculous proof is not wanted; but this can be said by no one who understands what Christianity is, and what its internal evidences are. On this ground, however, the miracles of Christ were not indeed expressly denied, but were represented by some of the founders of the modern school of German infidelity as only prodigies adapted to rouse the attention of a rude people like the Jews, but not required for the conviction of men of more enlightened minds. By others, the accounts of them in the Gospels have been admitted as in the main true, but explained as only exaggerated and discolored relations of natural events. But now, without taking the trouble to go through this tedious and hopeless process of misinterpretation, there are many who avow their disbelief of all that is miraculous in Christianity, and still affect to call themselves Christians. But Christianity was a revelation from God, and, in being so, it was itself a miracle. Christ was commissioned by God to speak to us in His name, and this is a miracle. No proof of His divine commission could be afforded but through miraculous displays of God's power. Nothing is left that can be called Christianity, if its miraculous character be denied. Its essence is gone; its evidence is annihilated. Its truths, involving the highest interests of man, the facts which it makes known, and which are implied in its very existence as a divine revelation, rest no longer on the authority of God. . . .

The proposition that the history of Jesus is miraculous throughout is to be understood in all its comprehensiveness. It is not merely that his history is full of accounts of his miracles; it is that everything in his history, what relates to himself and what relates to others, is conformed to this fact, and to the conception of him as speaking with authority from God. This is what constitutes the internal evidence of Christianity, a term, as I have said, often used of late with a very indistinct notion of any meaning attached to it. . . . .

The words of Christ, equally with his miracles, imply his mission from God. They are accordant only with the conception of him as speaking with authority from God. They would be altogether unsuitable to a merely human teacher of religious truth. So considered, if not the language of an impostor, they become the language of the most daring and crazy fanaticism. I speak of the general character of his discourses, a character of the most striking peculiarity. In ascribing them to one not miraculously commissioned by God, they must be utterly changed and degraded. What is most solemn and sublime must either be rejected as never having been spoken by him, or its meaning must be thoroughly perverted; it must be diluted into folly, that it may not be blasphemy. . . .

The rejection of Christianity, in any proper sense of the word, the denial that God revealed Himself by Christ, the denial of the truth of the Gospel history, or, as it is called in the language of the sect, the rejection of *historical* Christianity, is, of course, accompanied by the rejection of all that mass of evidence which, in the view of a Christian, establishes the truth of his religion. This evidence, it is said, consists only of probabilities. We want certainty. The dwellers in the region of shadows complain that the solid earth is not stable enough for them to rest on. They have firm footing on the clouds.

To the demand for certainty, let it come from whom it may, I answer that I know of no absolute certainty beyond the limit of momentary consciousness, a certainty that vanishes the instant it exists, and is lost in the region of metaphysical doubt. Beyond this limit, absolute certainty, so far as human reason may judge, cannot be the privilege of any finite being. When we talk of certainty, a wise man will remember what he is, and the narrow bounds of his wisdom and of his powers. A few years ago he was not. A few years ago he was an infant in his mother's arms, and could but express his wants and move himself and smile and cry. He has been introduced into a boundless universe, boundless to human thought in extent and past duration. An eternity had preceded his existence. Whence came the minute particle of life that he now enjoys? Why is he here? Is he only with other beings like himself that are continually rising up and sinking in the shoreless ocean of existence; or is there a Creator, Father, and Disposer of all? Is he to continue a conscious being after this life and undergo new changes; or is death, which he sees everywhere around him, to be the real, as it is the apparent end of what would then seem to be a purposeless and incomprehensible existence? He feels happiness and misery, and would understand how he may avoid the one and secure the other. He is restlessly urged on in pursuit of one object after another, many of them hurtful, most of them such as the changes of life, or possession itself, or disease, or age will deprive of their power of gratifying; while, at the same time, if he be unenlightened by revelation, the darkness of the future is rapidly closing round him. What objects should he pursue? How, if that be possible, is happiness to be secured? A creature of a day, just endued with the capacity of thought, at first receiving all his opinions from those who have preceded him, entangled among numberless prejudices, confused by his passions, perceiving, if the eyes of his understanding are opened, that the sphere of his knowledge is hemmed in by an infinity of which he is ignorant, from which unknown region clouds are often passing over and darkening what seemed clearest to his view—such a being cannot pretend to attain by his unassisted powers any assurance concerning the unseen and the eternal, the great objects of religion. If men had been capable of comprehending their weakness and ignorance, and of reflecting deeply on their condition here, a universal cry would have risen from their hearts, imploring their God, if there were one, to reveal Himself and to make known to them their destiny. Their wants have been answered by God before they were uttered. Such is the belief of a Christian; and there is no question more worthy of consideration than whether this belief be well founded. It can be determined only by the exercise of that reason which God has given us for our guidance in all that concerns us. There can be no intuition, no direct perception, of the truth of Christianity, no metaphysical certainty. But it would be folly, indeed, to reject the testimony of God concerning all our higher relations and interests, because we can have no assurance that He has spoken through Christ, except such as the condition of our nature admits of. . . .

Of the form of infidelity which we have been considering, there can be but one opinion among honest men. Great moral offenses in individuals are, indeed, commonly connected with the peculiar character of their age, and with a prevailing want of moral sentiment in regard to such offenses in the community in which they are committed. This may be pleaded in excuse for the individual; but the essential nature of the offenses remains. It is a truth which few among us will question that for anyone to pretend to be a Christian teacher who disbelieves the divine origin and authority of Christianity, and would undermine the belief of others, is treachery toward God and man. If I were to address such a one, I would implore him by all his remaining self-respect, by his sense of common honesty, by his regard to the well-being of his fellow-men, by his fear of God, if he believe that there is a God, and by the awful realities of the future world, to stop short in his course, and, if he cannot become a Christian, to cease to be a pretended Christian teacher, and to assume his proper character. . . .

George Ripley

THE LATEST FORM OF INFIDELITY EXAMINED (1839)

I . . . hasten to the discussion of the chief topic which I conceive worthy of attention in the statements of your discourse. I refer to your adoption and defense of the exclusive principle in an address before an assembly of liberal clergymen. By the exclusive principle, I mean the assumption of the right for an individual, or for any body of individuals, to make their own private opinions the measure of what is fundamental in the Christian faith. As liberal Christians, we have long contended against this principle as contrary to the very essence of Protestantism; we have claimed the inherent right of private judgment as essential to Christian freedom; we have resisted to the uttermost every attempt to impose controverted points of opinion on the universal belief of the Church. We have welcomed every man as a brother who acknowledged Christ as his Master; we have not presumed to sit in judgment on any Christian's claim to discipleship; we have refused to entertain the question whether he were entitled to the Christian name; we have felt that it was not ours to give or to withhold, and that the decision in all cases must rest with himself. . . .

I have thus far confined my remarks to your adoption of the exclusive principle, without a direct consideration of the doctrine in support of which you have given that principle the sanction of your authority. It would be a glaring inconsistency with all our modes of thought, with all our practical usages as liberal Christians for an individual to make any speculative opinion the standard of Christian faith, however true and important the opinion might be in itself. But the inconsistency is aggravated when the doctrine which is maintained on exclusive grounds can easily be shown to be almost peculiar to the individual by whom it is announced, at variance with the general belief of Christians in every age, incapable of support from the teachings of Scripture and right reason, and involving consequences of an irreligious and alarming character. . . .

The doctrine to which I allude, and which I now mean to discuss, is that THE MIRACLES RECORDED IN THE NEW TESTAMENT ARE THE ONLY PROOF OF THE DIVINE ORIGIN OF CHRISTIANITY. . . .

"Christianity is a revelation by God of the truths of religion." This is a distinct, independent proposition. I may admit it without being obliged to admit any other which it does not logically include; but that this revelation "is attested by miraculous displays of God's power" is a quite different proposition; there is no necessary connection between them; and any argument which you attempt to build on the supposition of such a connection, falls to the ground. The question in the first case is whether I believe that Christianity is a revelation by God of the truths of religion; how that revelation is attested is another question; and because I do not accept your answer to the last, you have no right to conclude that I give a negative answer to the first. . . .

The distinction which is now insisted on cannot be set aside by the assertion that the divine mission of Christ is itself a miracle. For in that case, you change the question at issue, which relates not to the divine mission of Christ, but to the evidence by which it is supported. If you say that a belief in the divine mission of Christ is all the belief in miracles you contend for, you acknowledge that you have brought a groundless charge against your opponents, for the divine mission of Christ they have never denied. But if you say that the divine mission of Christ cannot be separated from the miracles usually alleged as proof, you confound two points which, as we have seen, are essentially distinct; this confusion can be justified only by the principle that "miracles are the sole proof of a divine revelation"; but in assuming this principle, you assume what is not yet settled, and what . . . has no evidence in its favor. . . .

There are several objections however, of a practical character that apply to the doctrine of your discourse, and the connection in which it is presented, which I cannot pass over without notice.

The doctrine that miracles are the only evidence of a divine revelation, if generally admitted, would impair the religious influence of the Christian ministry. It would separate the pastor of a church from the sympathies of his people, confine him in a sphere of thought remote from their usual interests, and give an abstract and scholastic character to his services in the pulpit. The great object of his endeavors would be to demonstrate the truth of the Christian history; the weapons of his warfare would be carnal, and not spiritual, drawn from grammars and lexicons and moldy traditions, not from the treasures of the human heart. The miracles being established to the satisfaction of an inquisitive generation, nothing would remain but to announce the truth on their authority, for as all other evidence is without value, and this alone sufficient, it would be a waste of time to direct the attention to the divine glory of Christ and his revelation; this is beyond the reach of human "perception"; none but enthusiasts can make use of it. The minister would rely for success on his skill in argument, rather than on his sympathy with man, on the knowledge he gains within the walls of the university, rather than on the experience which may be learned in the homes of his people. He would trust more to his logical demonstration of the evidences of Christianity, than to the faithful exhibition of Christian truth to the naked human heart. But, I believe, not a wise and experienced pastor can be found who will not say that, as a general rule, the discussion of the historical evidence is ill adapted to the pulpit, and that the effects of such preaching on society at large, or on the individual conscience, are too minute to be estimated. . . .

On the contrary, I have known great and beneficial effects to arise from the simple exhibition of the truth of the Gospel to the heart and conscience, by earnest men who trusted to the intuitive power of the soul for the perception of its divinity. The revelation of Christ is addressed to the better nature of man; "my sheep," said he, "hear my voice, and follow me, and I give unto them eternal life"; "the light shines in darkness, and the darkness comprehendeth it not," but the "children of light" look upward and are blessed; it meets with a cordial reception from those who are burdened with the consciousness of sin, who are seeking for higher things, who are "feeling after God, if haply they may find him"; and this fact is the foundation of the minister's success. If you confine him to the demonstration of the miracles; if you deny him intimate access to the soul, by the truth which he bears; if you virtually tell him that the internal evidence of Christianity is a delusion, that our personal experience of

its power is no proof of its divinity, and that the glorious
Gospel of the blessed God is to be believed only because
learned men vouchsafe to assure the humble Christian of its
truth, you deprive the minister of all inward force; you
make him little better than a logical machine; and much as
I value a sound logic in its proper place, I am sure it is not
the instrument which is mighty through God to the pulling
down of the strongholds of sin. It may detect error; but it
cannot give so much as a glimpse of the glory of Christ. It
may refute fallacies; but it cannot bind the heart to the love
of holiness. A higher power is necessary for this purpose, and
such a power God has granted to man in the divine gift of
Christianity, which corresponds to his inmost wants and bears
the pledge of its truth in its effects on the soul. . . .

The preceding views suggest another fatal objection to
the doctrine of your discourse. It removes Christianity from
its stronghold in the common mind, and puts it into the
keeping of scholars and antiquaries. I have already hinted at
this objection, but it deserves a more particular consideration.
It follows as the necessary consequence of your exclusive
hypothesis. For if the truth of Christianity rests entirely on
the foundation of historical evidence; if there be nothing in
its intrinsic character to commend it to the soul as the revelation of God; if the uneducated inquirer must make up his
mind, either from his own investigations or from the testimony
of others, in regard to the subtlest questions of literary criticism before he can cherish a vital faith in the doctrines of
Christ, of course, he resigns his opinions to the guidance of
the learned. He must give up his birthright as a man before
he can establish his faith as a Christian. For he cannot enter
into such investigations himself; he has neither the ability, the
leisure, nor the apparatus that is requisite; he must sue at
the feet of the scholar for the light which he needs for the
salvation of the soul. The "grace and truth" revealed by the
Saviour become "as the words of a book that is sealed; the
book is delivered to him that is not learned, saying, 'Read this,
I pray thee'; and he saith, 'I cannot, for I am not learned.'"
The dark hour of God's displeasure has come back; we hear
the prophetic denunciation repeated: "forasmuch as this people have removed their heart far from me, and their fear toward me is *taught by the precept of men;* therefore, behold,
I will proceed to do a marvelous work among this people,
even a marvelous work and a wonder; for the wisdom of

their wise men shall perish, and the understanding of their prudent men shall be hid." . . .

Christian truth has always been addressed to the "intuitive perceptions" of the common mind. The Gospel was first preached to the poor; and with the "poor in spirit," those who renounced the pride of learning, who "loved to lie low in God's power," and listen to his secret voice within the heart, it has always found its most faithful friends. A shallow and presumptuous philosophy—presumptuous, because shallow— usurps the place of the simplicity of Christ, and would fain smother the breathing life of heavenly truth. Creeds came into the Church with the dreams of speculation; they have been handed down through the dust of the schools; they have sought their principal defense in the subtle, shadowy, and artificial distinctions of the learned; and the most vigorous attacks they have received have come from the unarmed strength of plebeian sects. The sword of the Spirit is not wielded after the tactics of a university; and even a shepherd's sling has often proved more powerful than the spear of a giant. . . .

George Ripley

A THIRD LETTER TO
MR. ANDREWS NORTON (1840)

... I cannot close this letter without adding a few words
in regard to the character of the theology which is presented
in your "Discourse" and "Remarks." Its radical defect, in my
opinion, proceeds from the influence of the material philosophy on which it is founded. The error with which it starts,
that there is no faculty in human nature for perceiving spiritual truth, must needs give rise to the other errors which I
have formerly pointed out, and which will be rejected, one
would hope, as soon as their character and tendency are
understood.

You maintain that "there can be no intuition, no direct
perception of the truth of Christianity," and that "the feeling or direct perception of religious truth" is an "imaginary
faculty." Revolting as this statement appears when presented in its naked form, it is the legitimate and unavoidable consequence of the philosophical system which grounds
all possible certainty on the testimony of the senses and
allows no distinct and independent reality to the testimony
of the soul. I honor the mental consistency which accepts
and asserts this consequence far more than the effeminate
timidity which shrinks from it and would fain keep it out of
sight. Truth is usually promoted, by following out every path
to its ultimate limit. We thus learn to what it leads, or that
it leads to nothing; and in either case, we may be induced
to retrace our steps.

The principle that the soul has no faculty to perceive
spiritual truth is contradicted, I believe, by the universal
consciousness of man. God has never left himself without
witness in the human heart. The true light has shone, more
or less brightly, on every man that cometh into the world.
This Divine Spirit has never ceased to strive with the children of earth; it has helped their infirmities, given them

just and elevated conceptions, touched their eyes with celestial light, and enabled them to see the beauty and glory of divine things. God has ever manifested himself to his intelligent creatures; but have they had no faculty to behold this manifestation? Did the ray from above fall on sightless eyeballs? Not so. There has always been truth in the world; man has never been quite shut out from intercourse with his Maker; the early patriarchs communed with the unseen Father as they wandered over the verdant plains of the East; the meek spirits that yearned after divine knowledge, among oriental bards and Grecian sages, were not blind to the heavenly vision; "the ignorant savage has believed in God without the aid of metaphysics"; and when the full-orbed Sun of Righteousness and Truth arose upon the world, in the soul of Jesus of Nazareth, it was hailed by the unlettered fishermen of Galilee, and has been reverenced by the most faithful spirits in every succeeding age as the visible manifestation of the eternal glory. Must there not have been an eye for this? Does the body see, and is the spirit blind? No. Man has the faculty for "feeling and perceiving religious truth." So far from being imaginary, it is the highest reality of which the pure soul is conscious. Can I be more certain that I am capable of looking out and admiring the forms of external beauty, "the frail and weary weed in which God dresses the soul that He has called into time," than that I can also look within, and commune with the fairer forms of truth and holiness, which plead for my love, as visitants from Heaven?

In the exercise of this faculty, man is able to behold the presence of God in the phenomena of the universe. The glory of the invisible Spirit beams from the visible creation, and is recognized as such, by those "whose eye is single, and whose whole body is full of light." The same faculty reveals to them the sacredness of their moral nature, invests conscience with divine authority, shows them the baseness, as well as the guilt of sin, makes them meekly grateful in view of their affinity with the Supreme Power, and enables them to read the law of God which is written on the heart. This perception, moreover, gives them "the knowledge of the glory of God in the face of Jesus Christ." They see the Father in the person of the Son. They feel that God was with him who displayed such divine grace and truth. They perceive the express image of his perfections in the character of Jesus, and embrace him as the Saviour of their souls, and the light of the world.

The denial of this faculty in the higher nature of man, of course, leads to the endeavor to make truth dependent on external support. It will thus be valued, not for what it is in itself, but for the circumstances in which it appears. Its intrinsic authority will fail to be recognized; its affinity with the soul, if admitted at all, will be only as a barren formula; and all inward feeling of its reality, "the tasting that the Lord is gracious," "the judging for ourselves what is right," will be rejected as visionary or presumptuous. Religion is thus removed from the sphere of consciousness and subjected to historical conditions. The certainty of faith must proceed from reliance on others, not from a spiritual witness in ourselves. The humble Christian can put no trust in his Redeemer till he is assured of its safety from the lips of the learned. The researches of the critic are deemed of greater importance than the experience of the believer. The royal priesthood of faith is dishonored, and a hierarchy of scholars installed. The wise after the flesh must sit in judgment on the teachings of the spirit. The character of a revelation is no proof of its divinity; the signatures of an heavenly origin borne on its front are unworthy of account; nothing is valid but the evidence of miracles; the prophets and divine messengers of old who uttered the burden of the Lord without external attestation had no claims to inspiration; and even "the glorious Gospel of the blessed God," which, in every word of its promises, every tone of its rebuke, every expression of its truth, exhibits "the power of God, and the wisdom of God to salvation," must rely for its support on the fact that "it was authenticated by miracles as coming from God."

A faith thus founded on historical testimony, with no reliance on the inward feeling or perception of truth, can never attain to positive certainty. I do not see how any mind can derive from it the repose which our nature craves. Without a higher faith than this, I know that to many life would be a burden, duty but a name, and religion a dream. The serene assurance of the reality of immortal truth, which is imparted by the contrary doctrine, cannot rest on such a basis. Hence the confession that "there is no absolute certainty beyond the limit of momentary consciousness, a certainty that vanishes the instant it exists, and is lost in the region of metaphysical doubt."

The soul of the Christian, as I understand Christianity, seeks a higher boon than this. He demands a certainty of a different character from that which can be enjoyed in the unstable affairs of this life, in the transactions of earthly business, "in the establishment of a manufactory, or the building of a railroad." "The things which are seen," he knows, "are temporal," subject to manifold fluctuations, perpetually eluding the firmest grasp, incapable of giving assurance or repose to the immortal soul. "But the things which are not seen," he is equally certain, "are eternal"; when everything earthly has passed away, they will remain; and in the worship of undying truth, of spiritual beauty and goodness, he finds a source of sustaining convictions and a perpetual and "exceeding great reward."

The enlightened believer, it seems to me, cannot rest satisfied with a mere balance of probability decided by intellectual researches. This would leave his heart dry and impoverished. It is the nature of faith to cling to its objects with earnest grasp, to throw around them the warm light of the affections, and to incorporate them with the deepest and most sincere experiences of life. Its tone is that of confidence; in its best moments, of triumph; habitually, of serene and joyful trust. It discards negations; it will accept nothing but truth; it acknowledges the efficacy of the Divine Spirit to inform the soul, not as a theological phrase, but as a daily reality. Its language is, "I know in whom I have believed; I know that my Redeemer liveth"; and in perpetual communion with the spirit of holiness and love, it beholds the presence of God. . . .

James Freeman Clarke

JONES VERY (1839)

. . . We had the pleasure of meeting Mr. Very, a few
months since, in the city of Boston. We had heard of him
before, from various quarters, as a young man of much intelligence and of a remarkably pure character, whose mind
had become extremely interested within a few months upon
the subject of religion. He was said to have adopted some
peculiar views on this important theme, and to consider
himself inspired by God to communicate them. Such pretensions had excited the fears of his friends, and by many
he was supposed to be partially deranged. The more intelligent and larger sort of minds, however, who had conversed
with him dissented from this view, and although they might
admit a partial derangement of the lower intellectual organs,
or perhaps an extravagant pushing of some views to their
last results, were disposed to consider his main thoughts
deeply important and vital.

And here we may remark that the charge of insanity is
almost always brought against any man who endeavors to
introduce to the common mind any very original ideas. And
especially is this the case with moral and religious truths.
He who insists on taking us out of the sphere of thought
which is habitual to us, into a higher and purer one, is
regarded by us with alarm and dissatisfaction. We must
either yield ourselves to him and suffer our minds to be
taken out of their customary routine, which is always painful—or we must find some way to set aside his appeals to
our reason and conscience and disarm them of their force.
The easiest way is to call him insane. It is a short and ready
explanation of his whole conduct. It relieves us at once of all
further trouble about him. Nobody is obliged to attend to
the "insane ravings" of a maniac. The moment, therefore, this word is applied to a man, were he sage, prophet,
or apostle—were he Socrates or Solon, were he Jesus or

Paul—all men are authorized to look down upon him with pity. And it is so much more soothing to our vanity to look down than to look up that it is no wonder that the worldly-minded, the men of sluggish and shallow intellects, and those who have arranged and systematized their opinions, are pleased with this excuse for pitying the man whom they ought to reverence. With them too go all those teachers, priests and prophets who have attained an influence over the public mind and love the exercise of that better than the attainment of new truth. The fear of innovation, error, change allies itself to these other motives, and so by common consent the prophet is declared a maniac. "He has a devil, and is mad, why hear ye him?" was said of the Saviour of men. "Paul, thou art beside thyself, much learning has made thee mad." And so have many other earnest souls who spurn the worldly and mean thoughts and practices of those about them, who longed for an introduction to a brighter day into the darkness of time, reformers and enthusiastic philanthropists, Wesleys, Penns, Foxes, been called delirious by their own age, and been deified by the following one. "Your fathers stoned the prophets, and ye build their sepulchres."

It is also, however, to be remarked that the intense contemplation of any vast theme is apt to disturb the balance of the lower intellectual faculties. While the reason, which contemplates absolute truth, is active and strong, the understanding, which arranges and gives coherence to our thoughts, may be weakened and reduced to a state of torpor. When this reaches an extreme point, it becomes delirium or monomania.

But even in these cases it may be a question which is the worst delirium, that by which a man possessing some great truth has lost the use of his practical intellect, or that other widespread delirium, in which the mind is enslaved to the lowest cares and meanest aims, and all that is loftiest and greatest in the soul is stupefied and deadened in worldliness. When, for instance, we have seen a man in whose intellect all other thoughts have become merged in the great thought of his connection with God, we have had the feeling very strongly, which we once heard thus expressed, "Is this monomania, or is it monosania?"

With respect to Mr. Very, we have only to say that the intercourse we have ourselves had with him has given no evidence ever of such partial derangement. We have heard him converse about his peculiar views of religious truth, and saw only the workings of a mind absorbed in the loftiest contemplations, and which utterly disregarded all which did not come into that high sphere of thought. We leave it to our readers to decide whether there is any unsoundness in these sonnets. To us, they seem like wells of thought, clear and pellucid, and coming up from profound depths.

Mr. Very's views in regard to religion, as we gathered them from himself, were not different from those heretofore advocated by many pure and earnest religionists. He maintains, as did Fénelon, Mme. Guion and others, that all sin consists in self-will, all holiness in an unconditional surrender of our own will to the will of God. He believes that one whose object is not to do his will in anything, but constantly to obey God, is led by Him, and taught by Him in all things. He is a Son of God, as Christ was the Son, because he *always* did the things which pleased his Father. He professes to be himself guided continually by this inward light, and he does not conjecture, speculate, or believe, but he *knows* the truth which he delivers. In this confidence, however, there is nothing of arrogance, but much modesty of manner.

Jones Very

EPIC POETRY (1839)

The poets of the present day who would raise the epic song cry out, like Archimedes of old, "give us a place to stand on and we will move the world." This is, as we conceive, the true difficulty. Glancing for a moment at the progress of epic poetry, we shall see that the obscurity of fabulous times could be adapted to the earliest development only of the heroic character. There is an obvious incongruity in making time so far remote the theater on which to represent the heroism of a civilized age; and it adds still more to the difficulty that, although the darkness of fable still invests them, reason will no longer perceive the beings which the infant credulity of man once saw there.

To men in the early stages of society their physical existence must seem almost without end, and they live on through life with as little reference to another state of being as we ourselves do in childhood. To minds in this state there was a remoteness in an event which had taken place one or two centuries before, of which we cannot conceive, and which rendered the time that Homer had chosen for his subject, though not materially differing in character, sufficiently remote for his purpose. If to these advantages possessed by Homer we add those which belonged to him from the religion of his times and from tradition, whose voice is to the poet more friendly than the plain written records of history, we must confess that the spot on which he built up his scenes of heroic wonder was peculiarly favorable. . . .

The simplest conception of the origin and plan of the *Iliad* must, we think, prove the most correct. It originated, doubtless, in that desire, which every great poet must especially feel, of revealing to his age forms of nobler beauty and heroism than dwell in the minds of those around him. Wandering, as his active imagination must have led him to do, in the days of the past, Homer must have been led by the fitness of the materials presented to him in the siege of Troy, by their remoteness from his own time, and the interest with which they would be viewed by the mass of his countrymen, as descendants of the Grecian heroes, to the choice of a subject which seemed to present a worthy form in which to manifest the workings of his soul. His enthusiasm would doubtless prompt him to the execution of detached parts before he had completed his general plan, and the various incidents, which constitute so much of the charm and interest of his poem as they suggested themselves to his mind, would also direct him to the great point round which they all revolved. The influence upon the several parts, resulting from the contemplation of the chief character, would thus give all the unity to the subject which we find in fact to belong to the earliest forms of a nation's poetry. . . .

Homer's machinery, as all epic machinery must be, was founded on the popular belief in the visible appearance of the gods; and on account of this belief he was not less favored by the circumstances under which he introduced them than he was by those which enabled him to represent his heroes. It cast around his whole subject a sublimity which it could not otherwise have had, giving occasion to noble description, and tending to excite that admiration which is the leading aim of the epic.

We have made this analysis of the *Iliad* to show in what way all things combined in Homer's age to assist him in giving a perfect outward manifestation of the heroic character of his times. He wrote in that stage of society when man's physical existence assumed an importance in the mind like that of our immortality, and gave to all without a power and dignity not their own. . . .

This state of things gave to the *Iliad* and *Odyssey* that intense epic interest which we fail to find in later heroic poems. As the mind advances, a stronger sympathy with the inner man of the heart is more and more felt and becomes more and more the characteristic of literature. In the expanded mind and cultivated affections, a new interest is awakened, *dramatic* poetry succeeds the *epic,* thus satisfying the want produced by the farther development of our nature. For the interest of the epic consists in that character of greatness that in the infancy of the mind is given to physical action and the objects associated with it; but the interest of the drama consists in those mental struggles which precede physical action, and to which in the progress of man the greatness of the other becomes subordinate. For as the mind expands and the moral power is developed, the mightiest conflicts are born within—outward actions lose their grandeur, except to the eye, for the soul looks upon them but as results of former battles won and lost, upon whose decision, and upon whose alone, its destiny hung. This is the mystery of that calm, more awful than the roar of battle, which rests on the spirits of the mighty, and which the hands of the Grecian sculptor strove to fix on the brow of his god. . . .

It is in the greatness of the epic action that the poets succeeding Homer, if we except Milton, have failed; and the causes which have operated against them will always operate with increasing force against every attempt to represent the present or future development of the heroic character in action. It is in the childhood of the human mind alone that the interval between thought and action is the widest, and therefore it is then alone that the events occupying that interval can be best described. The great struggle of the epic poets since the time of Homer has been against the narrowing of their field of action, and making the instruments there employed less visible, less tangible. The wonder and interest of the world is now transferred to the mind, whose thought is action, and whose word is power. . . .

The effect of Christianity was to make the individual mind the great object of regard, the center of eternal interest, and transferring the scene of action from the outward world to the world within, to give to all modern literature the dramatic tendency—and as the mind of Homer led him to sing of the physical conflicts of his heroes with *visible* gods *without,* so the soul of the modern poet, feeling itself contending with motives of godlike power *within,* must express that conflict in the dramatic form, in the poetry of sentiment. Were the present a fit opportunity, Shakespeare might afford us still farther illustrations of this truth, and especially in the character of Hamlet, of whom a critic has truly said, "We love him not, we think of him not, because he was witty, because he was melancholy, because he was filial; but we love him because he existed and was himself. This is the sum total of the impression. I believe that of every other character, either in tragic or epic poetry, the story makes part of the conception; but of Hamlet the deep and permanent interest is the conception of himself. This seems to belong not to the character being more perfectly drawn, but to there being a more intense conception of individual human life, than perhaps in any other human composition." . . .

By removing the bounds of time, Christianity has, I think, rendered every finite subject unsuited for an epic poem. The Christian creed, in opening the vista of eternity before the poet's view and leaving him unrestrained by prescriptive forms, while it freed him from the bonds of history by giving him a place beyond its limits where he might transfer the heroic spirit of his age and surround his heroes with supernatural agents capable of raising for his action the highest admiration, subjected him to a far greater difficulty than any yet experienced by former poets, that of finding a subject, an action to fill those boundless realms of space, and call forth the energies of the spirits that people it. In considering the efforts which Christian poets have made to overcome this difficulty and bridge the space between time and eternity, we shall find the great reason for not expecting another attempt so successful as that made by Milton arising from circumstances which have rendered the difficulty far more formidable since his time. . . .

The . . . highest development of the heroic character yet shown in action was that exhibited by the sublime genius of Milton. The mind had taken a flight above the materiality of Dante, and resting between that and the pure spirituality of the present day, afforded him a foundation for his action. He could not adopt altogether the material or the immaterial system, and he therefore raised his structure on the then debatable ground. The greatest objective which our minds urge against his agents is the incongruity between their spiritual properties and the human modes of existence, he was obliged to ascribe to them. But this is an objection of our own times, of men requiring a more spiritual representation of the mind's action, which, if it cannot be given, must preclude the possibility of another great epic. In fact, Milton's poem but confirms more strongly the conclusion . . . that dramatic is supplying the place of epic interest. His long deliberation in the choice of a subject suited to his conceptions shows the difficulty then lying in the way of an epic; and his first intention of making *Paradise Lost* a tragedy shows whence this difficulty originated. The tendency of the mind to which we have before alluded, and which had grown yet stronger in Milton's time than before, compelled him to make choice of the Fall of Man as his subject, a subject exclusive in its nature, being the only one which to our minds possesses a great epic interest. The interest of his poem depends upon the strong feeling we have of our own free agency, and of the almost infinite power it is capable of exercising. An intense feeling of this kind seems to have pervaded Milton's whole life, and by this he was probably directed in the choice of his theme. . . .

This sense of free agency is what constitutes Adam the hero of *Paradise Lost,* and makes him capable of sustaining the immense weight of interest which in this poem is made to rest upon him. But that which renders Adam the hero of the poem makes Satan still more so, for Milton has opened to our gaze, within his breast of flame, passions of almost infinite growth, burning with intensest rage. There is seen a conflict of "those thoughts that wander through eternity," at the sight of which we lose all sense of the material terrors of that fiery hell around him, and compared with which the physical conflict of the archangels is a mockery. It is not so much that battles present less a subject for description than they did in the time of Homer, that they fail to awaken those feelings of admiration they did then, but because we have become sensible of a power within which bids the tide of war roll back upon its foundations. For the same reason it is that the manners of civilized nations are unsuited for heroic song. They are no longer the representatives of greatness; for the heroism of Christianity is not seen so much in the outward act, as in the struggle of the will to control the springs of action. It is this which gives to tragedy its superiority over the epic at the present day; it strikes off the chains of wonder by which man has been so long fettered to the objects of sense and, instead of calling upon him to admire the torrent-streams of war, it bids the bosom open whence they rushed, and points him downward to their source, the ocean might of the soul,

> Dark—heaving—boundless, endless, and sublime—
> The image of eternity—the throne
> Of the invisible.

Thus Milton's poem is the most favorable model we can have of a Christian epic. The subject of it afforded him the only field of great epic interest where the greatest power could be shown engaged in bringing about the greatest results. Adam is not so much the Achilles as the Troy of the poem. And there is no better proof that greatness has left the material throne, which she has so long held, for a spiritual one, than that Milton, in putting in motion that vast machinery which he did to effect his purpose, seems as if he made, like Ptolemy, the sun and all the innumerable hosts of heaven again to revolve about this little spot of earth. Though he has not made the Fall of Man a tragedy in form, as he first designed, he has yet made it tragic in *spirit*, and the epic form it has taken seems but the drapery of another interest. This proves that, however favored by his subject the epic poet of our day may be, he must by the laws of his own being possess an introspective mind, and give that which Bacon calls an inwardness of meaning to his characters, which in proportion as the mind advances, must diminish that greatness once shown in visible action. . . .

Jones Very

SHAKESPEARE (1839)

... With other writers, at our very first acquaintance with
their thoughts, we recognize our relationship with the swiftness
of intuition; but who of us, however familiar he may have
been with his writings, has yet caught a glance of Shakespeare's self, so that he could in any way identify himself
with him and feel himself a sharer in his joys and sorrows,
his motives and his life? With views narrowed down to our
own peculiar and selfish ends, we cannot well conceive, for
we feel little within us that answers to a being like him—whose
spirit seemed the antagonist of matter; whose life was as
various and all-embracing as nature's; and in whom the individual seemed lost and blended with the universal. In him
we have a gift not of a world of matter but one of mind—a
spirit to whom time and place seemed not to adhere; to
whom all seasons were congenial; the world a home; who
was related to us all in that which is most ourselves; and
whose life and character, the more we lay aside what in us
is provincial and selfish, the more deeply shall we understand. In speaking of him and what he did as an exception
to ordinary rules, we only confess our ignorance of the
great law of his existence. If he was natural, and by a common
nature kindred with us, as we all confess, that ignorance,
which only exists by our own sufferance, will clear up as
we lay aside all that is false and artificial in our characters,
and Shakespeare and his creations will stand before us in
the clear bright sunlight of our own consciousness.

My object is to show, by an analysis of the character of
Shakespeare, that a desire of action was the ruling impulse of
his mind; and consequently a sense of existence, its permanent state. That this condition was natural, not the result felt
from a submission of the will to it, but bearing the will
along with it; presenting the mind as phenomenal and un-

228

conscious, and almost as much a passive instrument as the material world.

I shall thus be led to find excuse for much that has seemed impure in his writings, and to change that admiration which has hitherto regarded him as a man, into one which would look upon him and love him as the unconscious work of God.

By doing this I shall show that there is a higher action than that we witness in him, where the will has not been borne down and drawn along by the mind's own original impulse, but, though capable of resistance, yields flexibly to all its natural movements, presenting that higher phenomenon which genius and revelation were meant to forward in all men—conscious nature. . . .

There is a desire of mental activity felt by such a mind as Shakespeare's corresponding with that impulse to physical action felt by all men. . . .The main action of all such minds must evidently be as independent of the will as is the life in a plant or a tree; and, as they are but different results of the same great vital energy in nature, we cannot but feel that the works of genius are as much a *growth* as are the productions of the material world. Such minds act as if all else but the sense of their existence was an accident, and, under the influence of this transforming power, all is plastic—marble becomes flexible and shapes itself into life; words partake as it were of motion, form and speech; and matter, like the atoms on the magnetic plate, feels instinct with order and design. The stream of life—which, in other men, obstructed and at last stationary as the objects that surround it, seems scarcely to deserve the name—in them rolls ever onward its rich and life-giving waters as if unconscious of the beautiful banks it has overflowed with fertility. With most men it requires a continual effort of the will to prevent the objects which were only intended to give exercise to their souls from detaining them, as it were, and holding them in a torpid inanimation. . . . As we resist this process, the resulting state must evidently be one with which we may interpret the mind of Shakespeare—a sense of eternal life, an activity communicated to all else, and not merely one communicated to us from without; we are no longer the servants of sin, but the free followers of Christ.

As, therefore, the activity of the mind, freed by an exertion of the will, must ever be connected with the sense of eternal life, so is there joined with the mind's involuntary freedom a sense of existence that constitutes its innocent happiness, and makes it the natural teacher to us of the wide principle which is its mission. In Claudio's reflections on death, the poet unconsciously lays bare the texture of his own mind. Claudio regrets not, as we should suppose he would, the loss of his sister, or the good things of this world, nor feels a doubt of another; but all his horrors are but the negations of these two great characteristics of Shakespeare's own mind—the barring up of his varied activity, and the losing in kneaded clod of the sensible warm motion of life.

> Ay, but to die, and go we know not where;
> To lie in cold obstruction, and to rot;
> This sensible warm motion to become
> A kneaded clod; and the delighted spirit
> To bathe in fiery floods, or to reside
> In thrilling regions of thick-ribbed ice;
> To be imprisoned in the viewless winds,
> And blown with restless violence round about
> The pendent world; or to be worse than worst
> Of those lawless and uncertain thoughts
> Imagine howling!—'tis too horrible!
> The weariest and most loathed worldly life,
> That age, ache, penury, and imprisonment
> Can lay on nature, is a paradise
> To what we fear of death.

And again, in Clarence's dream of death so strongly is the resistance of the soul to this imprisoning of it expressed, that we feel a sense of suffocation in reading it.

> Often did I strive
> To yield the ghost: but still the envious flood
> Kept in my soul, and would not let it forth
> To seek the empty, vast, and wand'ring air;
> But smother'd it within my panting bulk,
> Which almost burst to belch it in the sea.

The play of *Hamlet* is founded on these two characteristics, and they are apparent throughout, as we shall endeavor to show by a separate analysis of it. We are continually hearing the poet himself speaking out through the words of Hamlet. As we become more and more conscious of that state of mind

which our Saviour calls eternal life, we shall the better understand the natural superiority of such a mind as Shakespeare's to the narrowing influences which we have to resist,
but which his involuntary activity rendered powerless. That a
sense of life would be the accompaniment of this activity
would then be apparent; for how could that childlike love
of variety and joyous sympathy with all things exist, save
from that simple happiness which in him ever flowed from
the consciousness of being, but which, alas, by most of us
is known but in youth? Between the dignified and trivial,
between decay and bloom, how else could he have felt that
connecting link, of which we are insensible, enabling him
to present them all united as in the moving panorama that
encircles us. This life of his in all objects and scenes was
the simple result of the movements of a mind which found
only in all it saw around it something to correspond with
its own condition. Its own activity was its possession; circumstances and things seemed to be, because it was; these
were accidents, and not, as with other men, realities. His
power, while exerted on every thing, seems independent of
its objects. Like the ocean, his mind could fill with mur-
muring waves the strangely indented coast of human existence from the widest bay to the smallest creek; then ebbing,
retire within itself, as if form was but a mode of its limitless
and independent being. . . .

In this activity of mind, then, in this childlike superiority
to the objects by which it was attracted, we find Shakespeare.
This was his genius, for genius is nothing but this natural action of the mind rendering obedient to itself by a higher
principle those objects to whose power it might otherwise
have been subjected. This it was that enabled him like a boy
"to toss creation like a bauble from hand to hand, embody-
ing in turn each capricious shade of thought." Thus it was,
that, while others were making ends of things, he gave to
them their deeper significance of life and death, of time and
eternity. In this view, the acts of Shakespeare seem but natural movements. With the ever-surprised mind of a child, he
was always transformed into the object he saw. This condition of mind might perhaps be designated as an impersonal
one, so strongly is it always possessed by that which is
before it, as to seem for the time to have no other individuality. It is the unconscious possessor of all things, and, like the
mythological Greek, gives personality and voice even to the

objects of inanimate creation. This is that primeval state of innocence from which we have fallen. . . .

This view of Shakespeare will lead us to look upon his characters as the natural expression of his own, as its necessary growths or offshoots. We shall then see a reason for their being as they actually appear to be, facts, real events which you could no more alter or improve than you can the branch of a tree or the visible realities themselves. Such being the foundations on which his characters rest, we may see why it is that they stand in the front of mental achievements, and that we speak and think of them as those with whom we are acquainted, whom we have seen and addressed. . . .

Each of the characters that Shakespeare has left us . . . was his own; the impulse by which he moved was so universal that it rendered his being coincident with that of all. He actually lived what he represented. We cannot speak of him as breaking away from his own egotism and throwing himself into his characters; he had no egotism other than that which would arise from that childlike state of mind which robes itself in no particular shape, but in all shapes. . . . He delighted in all men of high as well as low estate—we had almost said, in the licentious as in the virtuous. But how different is that playful and childlike spirit with which he acted a vicious character from that which seems to have actuated a Byron. The one represents an abandoned man as he actually exists, with the joys of sense and the anguish of the spirit alternately agitating his troubled breast; and the contemplation of such a character, if it does not make us as good as it might have done had he drawn it with higher motives, will yet make us better as the sight of it does in actual life. But the latter was not innocent; he imparted something of himself to what he describes; he would not and could not, like Shakespeare, put before us a virtuous man with the same pleasure as he does a vicious one; he has not, like him, held a pure and untarnished mirror up to nature, but reflected her back upon us from his own discolored and passion-stained bosom. . . .

Shakespeare was gifted with the power of the poet; a power which, though he may have employed for the purposes intended, does not seem to have been accompanied by that sense of responsibility which would have lent them their full and perfect effect. His creations are natural, but they are unconsciously so. He could but give to them his own life, which was one of impulse and not of principle. Man's brightest dignity is conscious nature; and virtue when deprived of this is robbed of her nobility; and without it vice is but a pardonable weakness. Shakespeare is not to be esteemed so much a man, as a natural phenomenon. We cannot say of him that he conformed to God's will; but that the Divine Will in its ordinary operations moved his mind as it does the material world. *He* was natural from an unconscious obedience to the will of God; *we,* if it acts not so strongly upon us but has left us the greater freedom, must become natural by a conscious obedience to it. He that is least in the kingdom of heaven, is greater than he. . . .

Jones Very

HAMLET (1839)

The play of Hamlet, when viewed with reference to the character of Shakespeare, which we have given, will no longer stand in that unique relation to the rest of his performances it has hitherto held, but will be found to be more vitally connected than any of them with the great characteristics of the poet's mind. We have chosen this, therefore, because it illustrates our previous remarks, and because these, in their turn, afford the position from which it is to be viewed. . . . There is, to use his own words, "something more than natural" in this tragedy, "if philosophy could find it out." That which makes it so is the playing up, in a peculiar manner, of the great features of Shakespeare's own mind—that sense of existence which must have been, as we have said, the accompanying state of so much and so varied activity. Hence the darkness which has so long hung over it, a darkness which, for us, can only be dispelled when we too rest on the same simple basis. . . . Shakespeare was, as I have said, the childlike embodiment of this sense of existence. It found its natural expression in the many forms of his characters; in the circumstances of Hamlet, its peculiar one. As has been well observed, the others we love for something that may be called aventitious; but we love him not, we think not of him because he was witty, because he is melancholy, but because he existed and was himself; this is the sum total of the impression. The great fore-plane of adversity has been driven over him, and his soul is laid bare to the very foundation. It is here that the poet is enabled to build deep down on the clear groundwork of being. It is because the interest lies here, that Shakespeare's own individuality becomes more than usually prominent. We here get down into his deep mind, and the thoughts that interested him interest us. Here is where our Shakespeare suffered, and, at times, a golden vein of his own fortune penetrates to the surface of Hamlet's character, and enriches, with a new value, the story of his sorrows.

If Shakespeare's master passion then was, as we have seen it to be, the love of intellectual activity for its own sake, his continual satisfaction with the simple pleasure of existence must have made him more than commonly liable to the fear of death; or, at least, made that change the great point of interest in his hours of reflection. Often and often must he have thought that to be or not to be forever was a question which must be settled, as it is the foundation, and the only foundation, upon which we feel that there can rest one thought, one feeling, or one purpose worthy of a human soul. Other motives had no hold upon him—place, riches, favors, the prizes of accident, he could lose and still exclaim "Fortune and I are friends," but the thought of death touched him in his very center. However strong the sense of continued life such a mind as his may have had, it could never reach that assurance of eternal existence which Christ alone can give—which alone robs the grave of victory, and takes from death its sting. Here lie the materials out of which this remarkable tragedy was built up. From the wrestling of his own soul with the great enemy, comes that depth and mystery which startles us in Hamlet.

It is to this condition that Hamlet has been reduced. This is the low portal of grief to which we must stoop, before we can enter the heaven-pointing pile that the poet has raised to his memory. Stunned by the sudden storm of woes, he doubts, as he looks at the havoc spread around him whether he himself is left, and fears lest the very ground on which he lies prostrate may not prove treacherous. Stripped of all else, he is sensible on this point alone. Here is the life from which all else grows. Interested in the glare of prosperity around him only because he lives, he is ever turning his eyes from it to the desolation in which he himself stands. His glance ever descends from the lofty pinnacle of pride and false security to the rotten foundation—and tears follow smiles. He raises his eye to heaven, and "the brave o'erhanging firmament" seems to him but "a pestilential congregation of vapors"; it descends to earth, and "its goodly frame seems a sterile promontory." He fixes it on man, and his noble apostrophe: "what a piece of work is a man! How noble in reason! How infinite in faculties, in form and moving, how express and admirable! in action, how like an angel! in apprehension, how like a god!" is followed fast upon by the sad confession, "Yet man delights me not, nor woman neither." He does not, as we say, "get accustomed to his situation." He holds fast by the wisdom of affliction, and will not let her go. He would keep her, for she is his life. The storm has descended, and all has been swept away but the rock. To this he clings for safety. He will not return, like the dog to his vomit. He will not render unavailing the lessons of Providence by "getting accustomed" to feed on that which is not bread, on which to live is death. He fears nothing save the loss of existence. But this thought thunders at the very base of the cliff on which, shipwrecked of every other hope, he had been thrown. That which to everybody else seems common presses upon him with an all-absorbing interest; he struggles with the mystery of his own being, the root of all other mysteries, until it has become an overmastering element in his own mind, before which all others yield and seem as nothing.

This is the hinge on which his every endeavor turns. Such a thought as this might well prove more than an equal counterpoise to any incentive to what we call action. The obscurity that lies over these depths of Hamlet's character arises from this unique position in which the poet exhibits him, a position which opens to us the basis of Shakespeare's own being, and which, though dimly visible to all, is yet familiar to but few. There is action indeed, but projected on so gigantic a scale that, like the motion of some of the heavenly bodies from whom we are inconceivably removed, it seems a perpetual rest. With Dr. Johnson and other commentators, we are at first inclined to blame Hamlet's inactivity and call him weak and cowardly; but as we proceed, and his character and situation open upon us, such epithets seem least of all applicable to him. So far is he from being a coward, in the common meaning of that term, that he does not set this life at a pin's fee. He is contending in thought with the great realities beyond it—the dark clouds that hang over the valley of the shadow of death and float but dimly and indistinct before *our* vision have, like his father's ghost, become fixed and definite "in *his* mind's eye"; he has looked them into shape, and they stand before him wherever he turns with a presence that will not be put by. Thus it is that to most he seems a coward, and that enterprises which to others appear of great pith and moment,

With this regard, their currents turn awry
And lose the name of action.

This view will account for Hamlet's indecision. With him the next world, by the intense action of his thoughts, had become as real as the present, and, whenever this is the case, thought must always at first take precedence of action. We have said at first, for it ends in giving the strength of the spirit to the arm of flesh. Hamlet frequently accuses himself of cowardice and indecision, yet is fully conscious, at the same time, of faultlessness. We too go with him, and at first accuse him of it, and afterward rest in as full a conviction as he himself that he is not a coward. Could we view him from the position in which Shakespeare must have seen him, he would appear a hero of loftier stature and nobler action than any other that now wins our admiration from among his numberless creations. . . . We may, by and by, come to see that there may be more of true heroic action in a mental conflict that never results in a deed than in a thousand that do; that it is at the root of the tree of self within the heart that Christ has laid the axe; and that here fall the blows that sound loudest and farthest through the kingdom of Satan. We have to do with this world only, and the objects of sense which are our daily care, unmodified by the great ideas of death and eternity, stand before us in a light and greatness not their own. Hamlet, on the other hand, is dealing with both worlds at once; and, under the influence of those spiritual realities which should qualify our thoughts, he describes objects in a manner which from our position appears very strange and distorting. Under the transforming power of such ideas, what seems to us of permanent shape and coloring, to him is like a many-tinted cloud continually varying in hue and form.

> *Hamlet.* Do you see yonder cloud, that's almost in the shape of a camel?
> *Polonius.* By the mass, and 'tis like a camel indeed.
> *Hamlet.* Methinks, it is like a weasel.
> *Polonius.* It is backed like a weasel.
> *Hamlet.* Or, like a whale?
> *Polonius.* Very like a whale.

After all that has been said to explain the apparent inactivity of Hamlet, we must still feel that, although we have accounted for, and shown the naturalness of his delay, yet the character of the son, and he "the son of a dear father murdered," is still somewhat less earnest in Hamlet than we should have expected. This particular view of his circumstance which we have given is pressed too far home to be entirely natural. It seems as if Shakespeare, feeling a more than common sympathy with the situation he had assumed for the expression of his own feelings, put too much of himself, so to speak, in the composition. We feel that Hamlet is rather such a son as Shakespeare would have made than the Hamlet of the king's own household. The poet's intention in this play was not, we think, as Goethe says, "to exhibit the effects of a great action imposed as a duty on a mind too feeble for its accomplishment"; nor, as Coleridge expresses it, "to exhibit a character flying from the sense of reality and seeking a reprieve from the pressure of its duties in that ideal activity, the overbalance of which with the consequent indisposition to action is Hamlet's disease." These are but accidents, and had the design been such as these suppose in Shakespeare, this play would have never been written. No, it was not for ends like these, but for an end of which these should prove but accidents. Was he strongly sensible of a purpose—it must have been to open to our view that wild tumultuous sea of thoughts which was rolling in the breast of Hamlet, when the idea of death and the presence of things invisible stood sensible to sight and touch before him. This thought, breaking upon him, in so terrible and unexpected a form, tore from life, at one rude grasp, the gaudy and alluring attire with which it is arrayed to the eye of sense, and, blotting out "all trivial fond records, all saws of books," it fronted him in its own grim reality. Well might he feel, if this was all there was of living, to him it was valueless. Unlike Claudio and Macbeth, the goods of this world, were they all, appeared not to him of consequence enough to deserve a moment's regard—in the wide firmament of his vision, time and space had dwindled to what they really are, but golden points of an immensity. . . .

We need not go farther to show what will now be apparent, the tendency of Shakespeare to overact this particular part of Hamlet, and thus give it an obscurity from too close a connection with his own mind—a state so difficult to approach. It is plain that to him the thought of death, and the condition of being to which that change might subject him, would ever be his nearest thoughts, and that, wherever there exists the strong sense of life, these ideas must follow hard upon it. In the question of Hamlet, the thoughts as well as the words have their natural order, when "to be" is followed by "not to be." And we think that no one can read the words of Claudio, or the soliloquy of Hamlet, without thinking that, for Shakespeare, they must have had no common meaning. . . .

The thoughts of the soliloquy are not found to belong to a particular part of this play, but to be the spirit of the whole. "To be or not to be" is written over its every scene from the entrance of the ghost to the rude inscription over the gateway of the churchyard; and, whenever we shall have built up, in ourselves, the true conception of this the greatest of the poets, "To be or not to be," will be found to be chiseled in golden letters on the very keystone of that arch which tells us of his memory. . . .

Jones Very

POEMS (1839)

The Forms of Nature and the Unity of Their Origin

Seek not in outward things,
The origin and birth
Of animal, and plant, and seed,
In air, or sea, or earth;
In vain their history we trace
Through ages vast, through time and space.

From One Eternal Mind
Have come the forms we see;
Those countless forms, whose difference make
Nature's variety;
Each stamped with impress of its kind
And each to its own sphere confined.

No atom but obeys
The One Creative Will;
Whose Word, beneficent and good,
The universe doth fill;
Without which naught was made, or born,
Which was before Creation's morn.

Globule and secret cell
A history contain;
Which Science, with its marvelous powers,
Still seeks to read in vain;
To the All Perfect Mind alone
Their origin, and types are known.

In Nature's primal plan
Prophetic types are seen;
Which lead us onward up to Man,
Their end, and destiny;
A unity of mind and thought
Through every form and being wrought.

But, in her labyrinth lost,
Too oft we miss the clue;
Which, midst her ever varying forms,
Runs through the old and new;
And in phenomena we rest,
As of the truth itself possessed.

Rest not, O Soul, till thou
That clue, that thread shall find;
Without whose constant, guiding help,
We wander dark and blind;
In endless mazes led astray,
Missing the strait and narrow way.

For this still upward leads;
Steep is the Mount of Thought,
Which we, aspiring still, must climb,
Till to the summit brought;
Where, with clear vision, we discern
Nature's vast realm, her mysteries learn.

THE EAGLES

The eagles gather on the place of death
So thick the ground is spotted with their wings,
The air is tainted with the noisome breath
The wind from off the field of slaughter brings;
Alas! no mourners weep them for the slain,
But all unburied lies the naked soul;
The whitening bones of thousands strew the plain,
Yet none can now the pestilence control;
The eagles gathering on the carcass feed,
In every heart behold their half-formed prey;
The battened wills beneath their talons bleed,
Their iron beaks without remorse must slay;
Till by the sun no more the place is seen,
Where they who worshiped idol gods have been.

WINTER

There is a winter in the godless heart
More cold than that which creeps upon the year;
That will not with the opening spring depart,
But presses on though summer's heats are near.
Its blasts are words that chill the living soul,
Though heard in pleading phrase and learned sound;
Their chilling breath nor triple folds control,
They pierce within though flesh and blood surround.
How dead the heart whence drives the arrowy shower!
The full-blown rose hangs drooping at its breath,
The bursting buds of promise feel its power,
And fixed stand encased in icy death;
And e'en the soul which Christ's warm tears fill,
Its sleety accents falling thick can chill.

THE HAND AND FOOT

The hand and foot that stir not, they shall find
Sooner than all the rightful place to go:
Now in their motion free as roving wind,
Though first no snail so limited and slow;
I mark them full of labor all the day,
Each active motion made in perfect rest;
They cannot from their path mistaken stray,
Though 'tis not theirs, yet in it they are blessed;
The bird has not their hidden track found out,
The cunning fox though full of art he be;
It is the way unseen, the certain route,
Where ever bound, yet thou art ever free;
The path of Him, whose perfect law of love
Bids spheres and atoms in just order move.

THE RIVER

Oh! swell my bosom deeper with thy love,
That I some river's widening mouth may be;
And ever on, for many a mile above,
May flow the floods that enter from thy sea;
And may they not retreat as tides of earth,

Save but to show from Thee that they have
     flown;
Soon may my spirit find that better birth,
Where the retiring wave is never known;
But Thou dost flow through every channel wide,
With all a Father's love in every soul;
A stream that knows no ebb, a swelling tide
That rolls forever on and finds no goal,
Till in the hearts of all shall opened be
The ocean depths of thine eternity.

THE GARDEN

I saw the spot where our first parents dwelt;
And yet it wore to me no face of change,
For while amid its fields and groves, I felt
As if I had not sinned, nor thought it strange;
My eye seemed but a part of every sight,
My ear heard music in each sound that rose;
Each sense forever found a new delight,
Such as the spirit's vision only knows;
Each act some new and ever-varying joy
Did by my Father's love for me prepare,
To dress the spot my ever fresh employ,
And in the glorious whole with Him to share;
No more without the flaming gate to stray,
No more for sin's dark stain the debt of death to
     pay.

THE LOST

The fairest day that ever yet has shone,
Will be when thou the day within shalt see;
The fairest rose that ever yet has blown,
When thou the flower thou lookest on shalt be.
But thou art far away among Time's toys;
Thyself the day thou lookest for in them,
Thyself the flower that now thine eye enjoys,
But wilted now thou hang'st upon thy stem.
The bird thou hearest on the budding tree,
Thou hast made sing with thy forgotten voice;
But when it swells again to melody,
The song is thine in which thou wilt rejoice;

And thou new risen 'midst these wonders live,
That now to them dost all thy substance give.

THE DEAD

I see them—crowd on crowd they walk the
    earth,
Dry leafless trees no autumn wind laid bare;
And in their nakedness find cause for mirth,
And all unclad would winter's rudeness dare;
No sap doth through their clattering branches
    flow.
Whence springing leaves and blossoms bright
    appear;
Their hearts the living God have ceased to know
Who gives the spring-time to th' expectant year.
They mimic life, as if from Him to steal
His glow of health to paint the livid cheek;
They borrow words for thoughts they cannot
    feel,
That with a seeming heart their tongue may
    speak;
And in their show of life more dead they live
Than those that to the earth with many tears
    they give.

THY BROTHER'S BLOOD

I have no brother. They who meet me now
Offer a hand with their own wills defiled,
And, while they wear a smooth, unwrinkled brow,
Know not that Truth can never be beguiled.
Go wash the hand that still betrays thy guilt;
Before the Spirit's gaze what stain can hide?
Abel's red blood upon the earth is spilt,
And by thy tongue it cannot be denied.
I hear not with the ear—the heart doth tell
Its secret deeds to me untold before;
Go, all its hidden plunder quickly sell,
Then shalt thou cleanse thee from thy brother's
    gore,

Then will I take thy gift—that bloody stain
Shall not be seen upon thy hand again.

THE WILD ROSE OF PLYMOUTH

Upon the Plymouth shore the wild rose blooms,
As when the Pilgrims lived beside the bay,
And scents the morning air with sweet perfumes;
Though new this hour, more ancient far than
      they;
More ancient than the wild, yet friendly race,
That roved the land before the Pilgrims came,
And here for ages found a dwelling-place,
Of whom our histories tell us but a name!
Though new this hour, out from the past it springs,
Telling this summer morning of earth's prime;
And happy visions of the future brings,
That reach beyond, e'en to the verge of time;
Wreathing earth's children in one flowery chain
Of love and beauty, ever to remain.

Orestes A. Brownson

AMERICAN LITERATURE* (1840)

. . . Of American literature as it has been, and even as
it now is, not much is to be said flattering to our national
vanity. We have produced some works respectable for their
practical aims and utility; we have brought forth much which
passes for poetry, but there is no great poem of American
origin unless we call Barlow's Columbiad such—our only
national epic—and we could make up but a meager collection of national songs. Latterly, we have given birth to
some tolerable novels and made a good beginning in history. But, aside from the newspaper press, which we are
somewhat prone to underrate, we have produced nothing in
the literary way whereof to boast. We have no literature that
can begin to compare with the literature of England, the
literature of Germany, or that of France.

To what are we to ascribe this? Many are somewhat
prone to ascribe it to the fact that we are a young people,
and have not lived long enough to create a literature. They
may not be wholly wrong in this. In a political sense, and
in relation to the long future before us, we are undoubtedly
a young people. But there is a sense in which we are an
old people. We did not begin in this country as savages or
as barbarians. Our fathers were of a civilized race. They
brought with them to these western wilds the polity, arts,
and refinements of civilized life. They could boast one of
the richest literatures of the world. Chaucer, Shakespeare,
Spenser, Bacon, Milton were among our ancestors, and the
literatures of the old world have ever been open to us. The
Bible and the classics have been in our possession, and these
lie at the bottom of all modern literature. I have, therefore,
not much confidence in this plea of minority, on which our

* From *The Boston Quarterly Review*, III (Jan. 1840).

countrymen are so much disposed to rely. We must seek the cause of the meagerness of our literature elsewhere.

This cause is sometimes looked for in the democratic institutions which we have adopted. We have, it is said, no court the center of fashion and elegance to exalt the imagination and give laws to taste; no long line of titled nobility raised far above the people and presenting us models of excellence. We see, it is said, nothing great among us, no elevated rank to which we may aspire, and therefore can have no lofty ambition; and having no ambition to be great, we can produce nothing great. Our minds and deeds of a necessity sink down to the level of our conditions. This is the Tory version of the matter, repeated with sickening frequency in the *London Quarterly* and kindred prints in the old world and the new. But there is nothing in democratic institutions to hinder the expansion of mind, to check the play of fancy and imagination, or to impede free thought and free utterance. . . .

One of the real causes of the meagerness of our literature is to be looked for, I apprehend, in the fact that we were for a long time dependent as colonies on England. The condition of colonists which so long continued generated a feeling of dependence, a habit of looking to England for direction in nearly all cases, which we have not yet wholly surmounted. Colonists almost invariably regard the mother country as their moral and intellectual superior. It is their native land, their home, to which they look back as exiles, with deep yearning and tender recollection. In it are the objects with which they are most familiar, which are dear to the heart, and around which cluster all the hallowed associations of childhood and youth. They borrow its language, its laws, its customs, fashions, sentiment, and opinion. Through these the mother country exerts an almost absolute spiritual dominion over the colonies, which may be continued long after events shall have severed the political ties which bind them together. . . .

Here, if I mistake not, is a chief cause why we have made no greater advances in literature. With this feeling toward England, we must needs regard her literature as the model of excellence, and anxious to commend ourselves to her grace, we must needs conclude that, in order to do it, we must write as much like Englishmen as possible. Feeling ourselves inferior, we could have no confidence in our own taste or judgment, and therefore could not think and speak

freely. We could not be ourselves. We could not trust the
workings of our own minds. We were safe only when we
thought as the English thought, wrote as the English wrote,
or sang as the English sang. But how the English thought,
wrote, or sang, we could, at the distance we were placed,
and the little intercourse we had with good English society,
know but imperfectly. When, therefore, we attempted to
write, we were like those who write in a foreign language
which they have studied only late in life, and which they
have but imperfectly acquired. The energy of mind due to
the subject we proposed to treat was wasted in avoiding
Americanisms, and in trying to conceal the place of our
birth and education. We sank of necessity into servile im-
itators, into mere copyists, and in seeking to write as Englishmen, abdicated our power to write as Americans and
as men.

Whoever would attain to excellence in anything must repose a generous confidence in himself. He must feel that he
is equal to what he undertakes. He must proceed calmly
and with a conscious strength to his task. If he doubts himself, if he feels that he must make an effort, that he must
strain, he will do nothing but betray his weakness. We Americans in literary matters have had no self-confidence. There
is no repose in our literature. There is ever a straining
after effect, a labor to be eloquent, striking, or profound.
This proceeds in a great measure from the fact that we
have found our model of excellence, not in our own minds
and hearts, nor in human nature generally, but in the literature of that land from which our forefathers came. Instead
of studying man, we have studied English literature; instead of drawing our inspirations from the universal reason
which glows within and agitates the American heart not
less than the English heart, we have sought them in the productions of the English muse. We have written and sung,
or at least aimed to write and sing, for Englishmen, and to
gain the applause or escape the censure of the English
critic. Hence our minds have been crippled, and our literature has been tame and servile. . . .

Another cause of the meagerness of our literature, nearly
akin to the one just mentioned if not growing out of it, is
to be found in the fact that our literary men have been but
slow to accept our democratic institutions and conform to
the order of things which our fathers established. Educated
in schools modeled after the English, early accustomed by

the literature they study and the lessons of their professors to distrust the people, to look upon democratic institutions as unfavorable to the development of genius, and to regard the institutions of their own country as a doubtful experiment, they have failed to imbibe the national spirit, and have therefore been able to fetch but a feeble echo from the national heart. Till quite recently, the literary men of our country have not sympathized with the people, and have had in their hearts no deep and abiding love, as they have had in their minds no clear conceptions of the great doctrine of equal rights and social equality to which this nation stands pledged. They may have had a tender concern for the people; they may have been willing to labor to enlighten them; they may even have preferred a republican form of government, but they have not been true democrats in their hearts. There has been a great gulf between them and the American people.

Now nothing is more certain than that the men who create a national literature must be filled with the spirit of their nation, be the impersonations of its wishes, hopes, fears, sentiments. The American people are democratic—I use the word in its etymological and philosophical sense—and consequently the creators of American literature must be democrats. It is not I that says this; it is truth, it is philosophy, and therefore if you dislike it, blame not me. No man who studies attentively the American people can doubt that their souls, however defective their utterance or crude their notions, are wedded to democracy. No party not believed to be democratic can rise in the nation to even a respectable minority; and no measure believed to be antidemocratic can stand any chance of success. We may deny this, we may quarrel with it and declare it altogether wrong, but so it is, and it is only they who conform to it, not from policy, but from the heart, from the real love of democracy, and a full understanding of what it is, that can do much to advance American literature. The fact that the majority of our literary men have been distrustful of the democracy, or opposed to it, is one reason why our literature has not attained to a larger growth and become more honorable to the country.

Another cause why our literature has continued so meager, is to be found in the circumstances of our country which have made no great literary demands, and which have turned out mental energies almost altogether in another direction. Literature is not a nation's first want any more than reading and writing is the first want of the individual. We are not, properly speaking, as I have said, a young people, but ours is a young country. We received it at a comparatively recent period, fresh from the hands of nature. We have had the primitive forests to clear away, the virgin soil to cultivate, commerce and manufactures to call into existence and encourage, cities and villages to erect, roads, canals, and railways to construct; in a word, our whole material interests to provide for and the field of our future glory to prepare. Here was our first work, and in this work we have shown our creative powers, displayed our skill and energy, and done that whereof it is permitted us to boast. While engaged in this work, we could not turn our attention to the cultivation of a national literature. . . .

Literature springs up only in those epochs when there is some great work to be performed for the human race, when there are great moral, philosophical, or social problems up for solution, and when all minds and hearts are busy with them. . . . Whoever has eyes to see or ears to hear cannot fail to perceive that grave questions, problems of immense magnitude, are coming up among us and demanding a solution in tones which it is not in man to resist. The old world is still engaged in the old war between the plebeians and the patricians. The great struggle going on there need not indeed alarm us, for it cannot come here. That struggle has for its object on the part of the people not republicanism in the state, nor equal wealth among the members of society, but the abolition of rank founded on birth. It has never existed with us, and, as I have said, never can, for here birth confers no distinction. The struggle which is coming up here is not between the highborn and the lowborn, between the gentlemen and the simplemen, for, thank God, we have learned that all who are born at all are wellborn. It is to be a struggle between MAN and MONEY. This struggle has not yet fairly commenced in the old world, but it must come there and ultimately make the tour of the globe.

In the old world, the interests of labor are, to a great extent, lost in the interests of the rich commoner, and will be so long as the rich commoner finds an hereditary nobility above him. But here we have no hereditary nobility, no titled rank, no privileges of birth. We have established political equality, declared the lists open to all, and the prize to the swiftest runner. But we have not obtained in practice the equality we have established in theory. There are distinc-

tions amongst us, inequalities, not without a long train of
grievous evils which an increasing party will hold to be
compatible neither with the principles of our political institutions nor with the true interests of humanity. The question has already been asked, What are the boasted advantages of a democratic government if the people under it
are to be in point of fact cursed with all the evils of social
inequality? What avails it that I am declared equal to my
neighbor, when in fact, I am regarded by him, and by
myself, and by all others, as his social inferior, when he may
task my labor almost at will, and fix himself the wages he
shall pay me? when, in fact, he may live in ease and luxury
without labor, and I, an able-bodied man and well skilled
in all kinds of labor, can, by my simple labor, but barely
keep myself and family from starving? The question has been
asked, too, Can a rich man, a man who has accumulated
and possesses great wealth, be a good Christian? There are
those among us who begin to suspect that Jesus meant
something when he said, "It is easier for a camel to go
through the eye of a needle, than for a rich man to enter the
kingdom of heaven." There are those who ask themselves,
when they see the extremes of wealth and poverty which
meet us in our cities, bloated luxury and pining want side
by side, if this be a Christian order of things, if indeed this
order of things is to last forever? As a Christian, am I not
bound to love my fellow men, even the lowest and most polluted, well enough, if need be, to die for them as Jesus
died on the cross for me? Am I then permitted to avail myself of the labors of others, so as to accumulate an immense
estate; am I then permitted to live in luxury, to feast on the
rarities of every clime which commerce procures me, while
my brother languishes in poverty, while the poor mother at
my next door is watching, pale and emaciated, over her
starving boy, and the poor sempstress is prostituting herself
so as not to die of famine? You will see at once that these
are fearful and searching questions such as cannot be put in
a tone of solemn earnest without shaking society to its center.

Questions like these are coming up amongst us. We may
deny it, may seek to suppress them, or to hush the matter
up; but come they will, and come they must. It is not in my
power nor in yours to suppress these questions. We may regret as much as we will that they must come, but nothing
remains for us but to meet them. The whole matter of
wealth and labor, of the means by which wealth is accumu-

lated, of the relations between capitalists and laborers, of wages, which a French nobleman has pronounced "a prolonged slavery," must come up, be discussed and disposed of. To my view, questions relating to this matter are the most fearful questions which can be asked, and they seem to me to involve a revolution to which all preceding revolutions were but mere child's play. . . .

In the struggle of these two elements, true American literature will be born. This struggle, which has already commenced, presents the conditions of its birth and its growth. We have now to solve, not the question of political equality, but the problem of social equality. This problem, if I have not wholly misconceived its magnitude and bearing, will present work for whomsoever has a hand, a head, or a heart; and in the effort to finish this work, a literature will be born before which all the literature now extant may, perhaps, shrink into insignificance. . . .

What will be the destiny of American literature I know not, and pretend not to foretell. But this much you will permit me to say in conclusion, that God in his providence has given the American people a great problem to work out. He has given it us in charge to prove what man may be, when and where he has free and full scope to act out the almightiness that slumbers within him. Here, for the first time since history began, man has obtained an open field and fair play. Everywhere else, up to the present moment, he has been borne down by kings, priests, and nobles; the loftier aspirations of his nature have been suppressed, and the fire of his genius smothered by unhallowed tyranny. Long, long ages has he struggled under every disadvantage; and under every disadvantage, though oft defeated, he has never despaired, or bated a jot of heart or hope, but always rallied himself anew with fresh courage and strength to the combat. Here, at length, he has gained the vantage ground. No longer must he struggle for every existence; no longer must he make a wall of his dead body to protect his wife and little ones. His domestic hearth is sacred, his fields are safe from the invader, and his flocks and herds may graze unmolested. He can now choose his ground. He may now abandon the attitude of defense and assume that of attack. He has no longer to defend his right to free thought and free speech, to the possession and use of himself. Here, thank God, we have no apologies to offer for speaking out for man, for truth, for justice, for freedom, for equality. We carry the war into the enemy's country. We summon the oppressor to judgment; the adherents to arbitrary governments, to superannuated creeds, and hoary abuses, to stand forth and show cause, if they can, why sentence shall not be pronounced against them. We call upon those recreants to their race, who believe all made for one, or the many for the few, to stand forth and give us a reason for the faith they avow. Here democracy is the order of the day, the PEOPLE are the orthodox party, and to them the aristocrat must answer for his heresy.

Such is the position we now occupy, such the progress we have made in working out the problem committed to us. Shall we stop here? I do not believe we shall. I do not believe that we shall prove false to our trust, or slight our work. I seem to myself to see many proofs around me that we are beginning to comprehend more fully our mission and to prepare ourselves to engage in earnest for its execution. I see this in the wide and deep agitation of the public mind; I see it in the new parties and associations which every day is forming; I see it in the weighty problems, moral, religious, social, political, economical, which both the learned and the unlearned are discussing; I feel it in the new spirit which has been of late breathed into American publications, and I recognize it in the increasing depth and earnestness of American writers. No, I cannot be mistaken. America will not be false to her mission. She will be true to that cause which landed our fathers on Plymouth Rock, which sustained the free mind and warm heart of Roger Williams, in which Warren fell, for which Washington fought, to which Franklin and Jefferson gave their lives. Sacerdocy has had its day; monarchy has had its day; nobility has had its day; and MAN, if there be justice in Heaven, shall have his day. . . .

Orestes A. Brownson

THE LABORING CLASSES* (1840)

... No one can observe the signs of the times with much care, without perceiving that a crisis as to the relation of wealth and labor is approaching. It is useless to shut our eyes to the fact, and like the ostrich fancy ourselves secure because we have so concealed our heads that we see not the danger. We or our children will have to meet this crisis. The old war between the king and the barons is well nigh ended, and so is that between the barons and the merchants and manufacturers—landed capital and commercial capital. The businessman has become the peer of my lord. And now commences the new struggle between the operative and his employer, between wealth and labor. Every day does this struggle extend further and wax stronger and fiercer; what or when the end will be God only knows. . . .

What we would ask is, throughout the Christian world, the actual condition of the laboring classes viewed simply and exclusively in their capacity of laborers? They constitute at least a moiety of the human race. We exclude the nobility, we exclude also the middle class, and include only actual laborers, who are laborers and not proprietors, owners of none of the funds of production, neither houses, shops, nor lands, nor implements of labor, being therefore solely dependent on their hands. We have no means of ascertaining their precise proportion to the whole number of the race; but we think we may estimate them at one half. In any contest they will be as two to one, because the large class of proprietors who are not employers but laborers on their own lands or in their own shops will make common cause with them.

Now we will not so belie our acquaintance with political economy as to allege that these alone perform all that is

* From *The Boston Quarterly Review*, III (July-Oct. 1840).

necessary to the production of wealth. We are not ignorant of the fact that the merchant, who is literally the common carrier and exchange dealer, performs a useful service and is therefore entitled to a portion of the proceeds of labor. But make all necessary deductions on his account, and then ask what portion of the remainder is retained, either in kind or in its equivalent, in the hands of the original producer, the workingman? All over the world this fact stares us in the face, the workingman is poor and depressed, while a large portion of the nonworkingmen, in the sense we now use the term, are wealthy. It may be laid down as a general rule, with but few exceptions, that men are rewarded in an inverse ratio to the amount of actual service they perform. Under every government on earth the largest salaries are annexed to those offices which demand of their incumbents the least amount of actual labor either mental or manual. And this is in perfect harmony with the whole system of repartition of the fruits of industry which obtains in every department of society. Now here is the system which prevails, and here is its result. The whole class of simple laborers are poor, and in general unable to procure anything beyond the bare necessaries of life.

In regard to labor two systems obtain; one that of slave labor, the other that of free labor. Of the two, the first is, in our judgment, except so far as the feelings are concerned, decidedly the least oppressive. If the slave has never been a free man, we think, as a general rule, his sufferings are less than those of the free laborer at wages. As to actual freedom one has just about as much as the other. The laborer at wages has all the disadvantages of freedom and none of its blessings, while the slave, if denied the blessings, is freed from the disadvantages. We are no advocates of slavery, we are as heartily opposed to it as any modern abolitionist can be; but we say frankly that, if there must always be a laboring population distinct from proprietors and employers, we regard the slave system as decidedly preferable to the system at wages. It is no pleasant thing to go days without food, to lie idle for weeks, seeking work and finding none, to rise in the morning with a wife and children you love, and know not where to procure them a breakfast, and to see constantly before you no brighter prospect than the almshouse. Yet these are no unfrequent incidents in the lives of our laboring population. . . .

We pass through our manufacturing villages; most of

them appear neat and flourishing. The operatives are well dressed, and we are told, well paid. They are said to be healthy, contented, and happy. This is the fair side of the picture; the side exhibited to distinguished visitors. There is a dark side, moral as well as physical. Of the common operatives, few, if any, by their wages acquire a competence. A few of what Carlyle terms not inaptly the *body-servants* are well paid, and now and then an agent or an overseer rides in his coach. But the great mass wear out their health, spirits, and morals, without becoming one whit better off than when they commenced labor. The bills of mortality in these factory villages are not striking, we admit, for the poor girls when they can toil no longer go home to die. The average life, working life we mean, of the girls that come to Lowell, for instance, from Maine, New Hampshire, and Vermont, we have been assured, is only about three years. What becomes of them then? Few of them ever marry; fewer still ever return to their native places with reputations unimpaired. "She has worked in a factory," is almost enough to damn to infamy the most worthy and virtuous girl. We know no sadder sight on earth than one of our factory villages presents, when the bell at break of day, or at the hour of breakfast, or dinner, calls out its hundreds or thousands of operatives. We stand and look at these hardworking men and women hurrying in all directions, and ask ourselves, where go the proceeds of their labors? The man who employs them, and for whom they are toiling as so many slaves, is one of our city nabobs, reveling in luxury; or he is a member of our legislature, enacting laws to put money in his own pocket; or he is a member of Congress, contending for a high tariff to tax the poor for the benefit of the rich; or in these times he is shedding crocodile tears over the deplorable condition of the poor laborer, while he docks his wages twenty-five per cent; building miniature log cabins, shouting Harrison and "hard cider." And this man too would fain pass for a Christian and a republican. He shouts for liberty, stickles for equality, and is horrified at a Southern planter who keeps slaves.

One thing is certain: that of the amount actually produced by the operative, he retains a less proportion than it costs the master to feed, clothe, and lodge his slave. Wages is a cunning device of the devil, for the benefit of tender consciences who would retain all the advantages of the slave system, without the expense, trouble, and odium of being slave-holders. . . .

Now, what is the prospect of those who fall under the operation of this system? We ask, is there a reasonable chance that any considerable portion of the present generation of laborers shall ever become owners of a sufficient portion of the funds of production to be able to sustain themselves by laboring on their own capital, that is, as independent laborers? We need not ask this question, for everybody knows there is not. Well, is the condition of a laborer at wages the best that the great mass of the working people ought to be able to aspire to? Is it a condition—nay, can it be made a condition—with which a man should be satisfied; in which he should be contented to live and die?

In our own country this condition has existed under its most favorable aspects, and has been made as good as it can be. It has reached all the excellence of which it is susceptible. It is now not improving but growing worse. The actual condition of the workingman today, viewed in all its bearings, is not so good as it was fifty years ago. If we have not been altogether misinformed, fifty years ago health and industrious habits constituted no mean stock in trade, and with them almost any man might aspire to competence and independence. But it is so no longer. The wilderness has receded, and already the new lands are beyond the reach of the mere laborer, and the employer has him at his mercy. If the present relation subsist, we see nothing better for him in reserve than what he now possesses, but something altogether worse.

We are not ignorant of the fact that men born poor become wealthy, and that men born to wealth become poor; but this fact does not necessarily diminish the number of the poor, nor augment the numbers of the rich. The relative numbers of the two classes remain, or may remain, the same. But be this as it may; one fact is certain, no man born poor has ever, by his wages as a simple operative risen to the class of the wealthy. Rich he may have become, but it has not been by his own manual labor. He has in some way contrived to tax for his benefit the labor of others. He may have accumulated a few dollars which he has placed at usury, or invested in trade; or he may, as a master workman, obtain a premium on his journeymen; or he may have from a clerk passed to a partner, or from a workman to an overseer. The simple market wages for ordinary labor has never been adequate to raise him from poverty to wealth. This fact is decisive of the whole controversy, and proves that the system of wages must be supplanted by some other system, or else one half of the human race must forever be the virtual slaves of the other.

Now the great work for this age and the coming is to raise up the laborer, and to realize in our own social arrangements and in the actual condition of all men that equality between man and man which God has established between the rights of one and those of another. In other words, our business is to emancipate the proletaries, as the past has emancipated the slaves. This is our work. There must be no class of our fellow men doomed to toil through life as mere workmen at wages. If wages are tolerated it must be, in the case of the individual operative, only under such conditions that by the time he is of a proper age to settle in life, he shall have accumulated enough to be an independent laborer on his own capital—on his own farm or in his own shop. Here is our work. How is it to be done?

Reformers in general answer this question, or what they deem its equivalent, in a manner which we cannot but regard as very unsatisfactory. They would have all men wise, good, and happy; but in order to make them so, they tell us that we want not external changes, but internal; and therefore instead of declaiming against society and seeking to disturb existing social arrangements, we should confine ourselves to the individual reason and conscience, seek merely to lead the individual to repentance, and to reformation of life; make the individual a practical, a truly religious man, and all evils will either disappear or be sanctified to the spiritual growth of the soul.

This is doubtless a capital theory, and has the advantage that kings, hierarchies, nobilities—in a word, all who fatten on the toil and blood of their fellows will feel no difficulty in supporting it. Nicholas of Russia, the Grand Turk, His Holiness the Pope, will hold us their especial friends for advocating a theory which secures to them the odor of sanctity even while they are sustaining by their anathemas or their armed legions a system of things of which the great mass are and must be the victims. If you will only allow me to keep thousands toiling for my pleasure or my profit, I will even aid you in your pious efforts to convert their souls. I am not cruel; I do not wish either to cause, or to see suffering; I am therefore disposed to encourage your labors for the souls of the workingman, providing you will secure to me the products of his bodily toil. So far as the salvation of his soul will not interfere with my income, I hold it worthy of being sought; and if a few thousand dollars will aid you, Mr. Priest, in reconciling him to God, and making fair weather for him hereafter, they are at your service. I shall not want him to work for me in the world to come, and I can indemnify myself for what your salary costs me by paying him less wages. A capital theory this, which one may advocate without incurring the reproach of a disorganizer, a jacobin, a leveler, and without losing the friendship of the rankest aristocrat in the land.

This theory, however, is exposed to one slight objection, that of being condemned by something like six thousand years' experience. For six thousand years its beauty has been extolled, its praises sung, and its blessings sought under every advantage which learning, fashion, wealth, and power can secure; and yet under its practical operations, we are assured that mankind, though totally depraved at first, have been growing worse and worse ever since.

For our part, we yield to none in our reverence for science and religion; but we confess that we look not for the regeneration of the race from priests and pedagogues. They have had a fair trial. They cannot construct the temple of God. They cannot conceive its plan, and they know not how to build. They daub with untempered mortar, and the walls they erect tumble down if so much as a fox attempt to go up thereon. In a word they always league with the people's masters, and seek to reform without disturbing the social arrangements which render reform necessary. They would change the consequents without changing the antecedents, secure to men the rewards of holiness, while they continue their allegiance to the devil. We have no faith in priests and pedagogues. They merely cry peace, peace, and that too when there is no peace, and can be none.

We admit the importance of what Dr. Channing in his lectures on the subject we are treating recommends as "self-culture." Self-culture is a good thing, but it cannot abolish inequality, nor restore men to their rights. As a means of quickening moral and intellectual energy, exalting the sentiments, and preparing the laborer to contend manfully for his rights, we admit its importance, and insist as strenuously as anyone on making it as universal as possible; but as constituting in itself a remedy for the vices of the social state, we have no faith in it. As a means it is well, as the end it is nothing.

The truth is, the evil we have pointed out is not merely individual in its character. It is not, in the case of any single individual, of any one man's procuring, nor can the efforts of any one man, directed solely to his own moral and religious perfection, do aught to remove it. What is purely individual in its nature, efforts of individuals to perfect themselves may remove. But the evil we speak of is inherent in all our social arrangements, and cannot be cured without a radical change of those arrangements. Could we convert all men to Christianity in both theory and practice, as held by the most enlightened sect of Christians among us, the evils of the social state would remain untouched. Continue our present system of trade, and all its present evil consequences will follow, whether it be carried on by your best men or your worst. Put your best men, your wisest, most moral, and most religious men at the head of your paper money banks, and the evils of the present banking system will remain scarcely diminished. The only way to get rid of its evils is to change the system, not its managers. The evils of slavery do not result from the personal characters of slave masters. They are inseparable from the system, let who will be masters. Make all your rich men good Christians, and you have lessened not the evils of existing inequality in wealth. The mischievous effects of this inequality do not result from the personal characters of either rich or poor, but from itself, and they will continue just so long as there are rich men and poor men in the same community. You must abolish the system or accept its consequences. No man can serve both God and Mammon. If you will serve the devil, you must look to the devil for your wages; we know no other way. . . .

The evil we have pointed out, we have said, is not of individual creation, and it is not to be removed by individual effort, saving so far as individual effort induces the combined effort of the mass. But whence has this evil originated? How comes it that all over the world the working classes are depressed, are the low and vulgar, and virtually the slaves of the nonworking classes? This is an inquiry which has not yet received the attention it deserves. It is not enough to answer that it has originated entirely in the inferiority by nature of the working classes; that they have less skill and foresight, and are less able than the upper classes to provide for themselves, or less susceptible of the highest moral and intellectual cultivation. Nor is it sufficient for our purpose to be told that Providence has decreed that some shall be poor and wretched, ignorant and vulgar; and that others shall be rich and vicious, learned and polite, oppressive and miserable. We do not choose to charge this matter to the will of God. "The foolishness of man perverteth his way, and his heart fretteth against the Lord." God has made of one blood all the nations of men to dwell on all the face of the earth, and to dwell there as brothers, as members of one and the same family; and although he has made them with a diversity of powers, it would perhaps, after all, be a bold assertion to say that he has made them with an inequality of powers. There is nothing in the actual difference of the powers of individuals which accounts for the striking inequalities we everywhere discover in their condition. The child of the plebeian, if placed early in the proper circumstances, grows up not less beautiful, active, intelligent, and refined than the child of the patrician; and the child of the patrician may become as coarse, as brutish as the child of any slave. So far as observation on the original capacities of individuals goes, nothing is discovered to throw much light on social inequalities.

The cause of the inequality we speak of must be sought in history, and be regarded as having its root in Providence, or in human nature, only in that sense in which all historical facts have their origin in these. We may perhaps trace it in the first instance to conquest, but not to conquest as the ultimate cause. . . . For our part we are disposed to seek the cause of the inequality of conditions of which we speak in religion and to charge it to the priesthood. And we are confirmed in this by what appears to be the instinctive tendency of every, or almost every, social reformer. Men's instincts, in a matter of this kind, are worthier of reliance than their reasonings. Rarely do we find in any age or country a man feeling himself commissioned to labor for a social reform who does not feel that he must begin it by making war upon the priesthood. This was the case with the old Hebrew reformers, who are to us the prophets of God; with Jesus, the Apostles, and the early Fathers of the Church; with the French democrats of the last century; and is the case with the young Germans, and the Socialits [sic], as they call themselves in England, at the present moment. Indeed it is felt at once that no reform can be effected without resisting the priests and emancipating the people from their power.

Historical research, we apprehend, will be found to justify this instinct, and to authorize the eternal hostility of the reformer, the advocate of social progress, to the priesthood. How is it, we ask, that man comes out of the savage state? In the savage state, properly so called, there is no inequality of the kind of which we speak. The individual system obtains there. Each man is his own center, and is a whole in himself. There is no community, there are no members of society, for society is not. This individuality, which, if combined with the highest possible moral and intellectual cultivation, would be the perfection of man's earthly condition, must be broken down before the human race can enter into the path of civilization or commence its career of progress. But it cannot be broken down by material force. It resists by its own nature the combination of individuals necessary to subdue it. It can be successfully attacked only by a spiritual power, and subjugated only by the representatives of that power, that is to say, the priests. . . .

Mankind came out of the savage state by means of the priests. Priests are the first civilizers of the race. For the wild freedom of the savage, they substitute the iron despotism of the theocrat. This is the first step in civilization, in man's career of progress. It is not strange then that some should prefer the savage state to the civilized. Who would not rather roam the forest with a free step and unshackled limb, though exposed to hunger, cold, and nakedness, than crouch an abject slave beneath the whip of a master? As yet civilization has done little but break and subdue man's natural love of freedom; but tame his wild and eagle spirit. In what a world does man even now find himself when he first awakes and feels some of the workings of his manly nature? He is in a cold, damp, dark dungeon, and loaded all over with chains, with the iron entering into his very soul. He cannot make one single free movement. The priest holds his conscience, fashion controls his tastes, and society with her forces invades the very sanctuary of his heart, and takes command of his love, that which is purest and best in his nature, which alone gives reality to his existence, and from which proceeds the only ray which pierces the gloom of his prisonhouse. Even that he cannot enjoy in peace and quietness, nor scarcely at all. He is wounded on every side, in every part of his being, in every relation in life, in every idea of his mind, in every sentiment of his heart. O, it is a sad world, a sad world to the young soul just awakening to its diviner instincts! A sad world to him who is not gifted with the only blessing which seems compatible with life as it is—absolute insensibility. But no matter. A wise man never murmurs. He never kicks against the pricks. What is is, and there is an end of it; what can be may be, and we will do what we can to make life what it ought to be. Though man's first step in civilization is slavery, his last step shall be freedom. The free soul can never be wholly subdued; the etherial fire in man's nature may be smothered, but it cannot be extinguished. Down, down deep in the center of his heart it burns inextinguishable and forever, glowing intenser with the accumulating heat of centuries; and one day the whole mass of humanity shall become ignited, and be full of fire within and all over, as a live coal; and then—slavery, and whatever is foreign to the soul itself, shall be consumed.

But, having traced the inequality we complain of to its origin, we proceed to ask again what is the remedy? The remedy is first to be sought in the destruction of the priest. We are not mere destructives. We delight not in pulling down; but the bad must be removed before the good can be introduced. Conviction and repentance precede regeneration. Moreover we are Christians, and it is only by following out the Christian law, and the example of the early Christians, that we can hope to effect anything. Christianity is the sublimest protest against the priesthood ever uttered, and a protest uttered by both God and man; for he who uttered it was God-Man. In the person of Jesus both God and Man protest against the priesthood. What was the mission of Jesus but a solemn summons of every priesthood on earth to judgment, and of the human race to freedom? He discomfited the learned doctors, and with whips of small cords drove the priests, degenerated into mere money changers, from the temple of God. He instituted himself no priesthood, no form of religious worship. He recognized no priest but a holy life, and commanded the construction of no temple but that of the pure heart. He preached no formal religion, enjoined no creed, set apart no day for religious worship. He preached fraternal love, peace on earth, and good will to men. He came to the soul enslaved, "cabined, cribbed, confined," to the poor child of mortality, bound hand and foot, unable to move, and said in the tones of a God, "Be free; be enlarged; be there room for thee to grow, expand, and overflow with the love thou wast made to overflow with."

In the name of Jesus we admit there has been a priesthood instituted, and considering how the world went, a priesthood could not but be instituted; but the religion of Jesus repudiates it. It recognizes no mediator between God and man but him who dies on the cross to redeem man; no propitiation for sin but a pure love which rises in a living flame to all that is beautiful and good, and spreads out in light and warmth for all the chilled and benighted sons of mortality. In calling every man to be a priest, it virtually condemns every possible priesthood, and in recognizing the religion of the new covenant, the religion written on the heart, of a law put within the soul, it abolishes all formal worship. . . .

We object not to religious instruction; we object not to the gathering together of the people on one day in seven, to sing and pray, and listen to a discourse from a religious teacher; but we object to everything like an outward, visible church; to everything that in the remotest degree partakes of the priest. A priest is one who stands as a sort of mediator between God and man; but we have one mediator, Jesus Christ, who gave himself a ransom for all, and that is enough. It may be supposed that we, Protestants, have no priests; but for ourselves we know no fundamental difference between a Catholic priest and a Protestant clergyman, as we know no difference of any magnitude, in relation to the principles on which they are based, between a Protestant church and the Catholic church. Both are based on the principle of authority; both deny in fact, however it may be in manner, the authority of reason and war against freedom of mind; both substitute dead works for true righteousness, a vain show for the reality of piety, and are sustained as the means of reconciling us to God without requiring us to become godlike. Both therefore ought to go by the board. . . .

The next step in this work of elevating the working classes will be to resuscitate the Christianity of Christ. . . . According to the Christianity of Christ no man can enter the kingdom of God who does not labor with all zeal and diligence to establish the kingdom of God on the earth; who does not labor to bring down the high, and bring up the low; to break the fetters of the bound and set the captive free; to destroy all oppression, establish the reign of justice, which is the reign of equality, between man and man; to introduce new heavens and a new earth, wherein dwelleth righteousness, wherein all shall be as brothers, loving one another, and no one possessing what another lacketh. No man can be a Christian who does not labor to reform society, to mold it according to the will of God and the nature of man; so that free scope shall be given to every man to unfold himself in all beauty and power, and to grow up into the stature of a perfect man in Christ Jesus. No man can be a Christian who does not refrain from all practices by which the rich grow richer and the poor poorer, and who does not do all in his power to elevate the laboring classes, so that one man shall not be doomed to toil while another enjoys the fruits; so that each man shall be free and independent, sitting under "his own vine and figtree with none to molest or to make afraid." . . .

Having, by breaking down the power of the priesthood and the Christianity of the priests, obtained an open field and freedom for our operations, and by preaching the true Gospel of Jesus, directed all minds to the great social reform needed, and quickened in all souls the moral power to live for it or to die for it, our next resort must be to government, to legislative enactments. Government is instituted to be the agent of society, or more properly the organ through which society may perform its legitimate functions. It is not the master of society; its business is not to control society, but to be the organ through which society effects its will. Society has never to petition government; government is its servant, and subject to its commands.

Now the evils of which we have complained are of a social nature. That is, they have their root in the constitution of society as it is, and they have attained to their present growth by means of social influences, the action of government, of laws, and of systems and institutions upheld by society, and of which individuals are the slaves. This being the case, it is evident that they are to be removed only by the action of society, that is, by government, for the action of society is government.

But what shall government do? Its first doing must be an *un*doing. There has been thus far quite too much government, as well as government of the wrong kind. The first act of government we want is a still further limitation of itself. It must begin by circumscribing within narrower limits its powers. And then it must proceed to repeal all laws which bear against the laboring classes, and then to enact such laws as are necessary to enable them to maintain their equality. We have no faith in those systems of elevating the working classes which propose to elevate them without calling in the aid of the government. We must have government, and legislation expressly directed to this end.

But again what legislation do we want so far as this country is concerned? We want first the legislation which shall free the government, whether State or Federal, from the control of the banks. The banks represent the interest of the employer, and therefore of necessity interests adverse to those of the employed; that is, they represent the interests of the business community in opposition to the laboring community. So long as the government remains under the control of the banks, so long it must be in the hands of the natural enemies of the laboring classes, and may be made, nay, will be made, an instrument of depressing them yet lower. . . .

Following the destruction of the banks must come that of all monopolies, of all privilege. There are many of these. We cannot specify them all; we therefore select only one, the greatest of them all, the privilege which some have of being born rich while others are born poor. It will be seen at once that we allude to the hereditary descent of property, an anomaly in our American system which must be removed or the system itself will be destroyed. We cannot now go into a discussion of this subject, but we promise to resume it at our earliest opportunity. We only say now that as we have abolished hereditary monarchy and hereditary nobility, we must complete the work by abolishing hereditary property. A man shall have all he honestly acquires, so long as he himself belongs to the world in which he acquires it. But his power over his property must cease with his life, and his property must then become the property of the state, to be disposed of by some equitable law for the use of the generation which takes his place. Here is the principle without any of its details, and this is the grand legislative measure to which we look forward. We see no means of elevating the laboring classes which can be effectual without this. And is this a measure to be easily carried? Not at all. It will cost infinitely more than it cost to abolish either hereditary monarchy or hereditary nobility. It is a great measure, and a startling. The rich, the business community, will never voluntarily consent to it, and we think we know too much of human nature to believe that it will ever be effected peaceably. It will be effected only by the strong arm of physical force. It will come, if it ever come at all, only at the conclusion of war, the like of which the world as yet has never witnessed, and from which, however inevitable it may seem to the eye of philosophy, the heart of humanity recoils with horror. . . .

II

An objection which we have heard urged against our views is that we would abolish the priesthood, and dispense with all religious instruction, and all religious worship. To this objection we reply that the inference drawn from what we have said against priests is unwarranted. . . .

But what are our views of the priesthood? To what did we in reality object, when we objected to the priesthood? These questions we can answer only by giving at some length our views of Christianity, as an outward, visible institution.

The mission of Jesus was twofold. One purpose of his mission was to atone for sin and prepare the soul for heaven in the world to come. The other purpose was to found a holy kingdom on the earth, under the dominion of which all men should finally be brought. This last purpose is the only one which concerns us in our present inquiry.

This Holy kingdom which Christ came to found on the earth has been mistaken for the outward, visible Church; and the Church has therefore been held to be a spiritual body, a body corporate, independent in itself, and distinct from the body politic, civil society, or the State. This has given rise to a double organization of mankind: one for material interests called the State, and under the control of the civil government proper; the other for spiritual purposes, called the Church, and governed by laws and officers of its own, distinct from those of the State.

Now to this we strenuously object. We would establish the kingdom of God on the earth, but we would not have a *double* organization of mankind. We would have but a single organization, and this organization we would call not the Church, but the State. This organization should be based on the principles of the Gospel, and realize them as perfectly as finite man can realize them.

The kingdom of God is an inward, spiritual kingdom. In plain language, it is the dominion of truth, justice, and love. Now, we would build up this kingdom not by founding an outward visible Church, but by cultivating the principles of truth, justice, and love in the soul of the individual, and by bringing society and all its acts into perfect harmony with them. Our views, if carried out, would realize not a union, but the unity, the identity, of Church and State. They would indeed destroy the Church as a *separate* body, as a distinct organization, but they would do it by transferring to the State the moral ideas on which the Church was professedly founded and which it has failed to realize. They would realize that idea of a "Christian Commonwealth," after which our Puritan fathers so earnestly and perseveringly struggled. They are nothing but the views of the first settlers of this state, developed and systematized, and freed from the theological phraseology in which they were then expressed. We are true to their idea, to their spirit, and are laboring to realize that which they most desired. We therefore remind those who profess to reverence our Puritan ancestors that they would do well to study the history and opinions of those ancestors, and forbear to censure us till they are prepared to condemn them. . . .

The great evil of all modern society in relation to the material order is the separation of the capitalist from the laborer—the division of the community into two classes, one of which owns the funds, and the other of which performs the labor of production. . . .

. . . It is in our cities, large towns, and manufacturing villages that the condition of the laboring population is the most unfavorable. The distinction between the capitalist and the proletary in these is as strongly marked as it is in the old world. The distance between the wife and daughters of an Abbot Lawrence and the poor factory girl employed in his mills is as great as that between the wife and daughters of an English nobleman and the daughter of one of his tenants, and the intercourse less frequent. Intermarriage between the families of the wealthy factory owners and those of the operatives is as much an outrage on the public sense of propriety as it was in ancient Rome between the patricians and plebeians—almost as much as it would be at the South between the family of a planter and that of one of his slaves.

Still, taking our country throughout, the condition of the proletary population has been, and is, altogether superior here to what it is in any other part of the civilized world. We do not, however, attribute this fact to our democratic institutions, nor to the adoption of more enlightened systems of social, political, or domestic economy than are adopted elsewhere. It is owing to causes purely accidental and which are rapidly disappearing. The first of these accidental causes may be traced to the original equality of the first settlers of this country. But this equality no longer exists. Fortunes are said to be more unequal with us than they are in France. The second cause, and the main one, has consisted in the low price of land. The ease with which individuals have been able to procure them farms, and pass from the class of proletaries to that of proprietors, has had a constant tendency to diminish the number of proletaries and to raise the price of labor. But this cause becomes less and less powerful. Few, comparatively speaking, of the proletaries in any of the old states can ever become land-owners. Land there is already too high for that. The new lands are rapidly receding to the west, and can even now be reached only by the those who have some little capital in advance. Moreover, these new lands are not inexhaustible. Fifty years to come, if emigration go on at the rate it has for fifty years past, will leave very little for the new emigrant.

The causes removed which have hitherto favored the workingman and lessened the distance between him and the proprietor, what is to prevent the reproduction here, in our land of boasted equality, of the order of things which now exists in the old world? As yet, that order does not exist here in all its revolting details, but who can fail to see that there is a strong tendency to it? Our economical systems are virtually those of England; our passions, our views, and feelings are similar; and what is to prevent the reproduction of the same state of things in relation to our laboring population with that which gangrenes English society? We confess, we cannot see any causes at work among us likely to prevent it.

The remedies relied on by the political reformers are free trade and universal suffrage; by the moral reformers, universal education and religious culture. We agree with both, and sustain them as far as they go; but they are insufficient. These measures are all good and necessary, but inadequate, unless something more radical still be adopted along with them. Alone they are mere palliatives. They may serve to conceal the sore, perhaps assuage its pain, but they cannot cure it.

Universal suffrage is little better than a mockery where the voters are not socially equal. No matter what party you support, no matter what men you elect, property is always the

basis of your governmental action. No policy has ever yet
been pursued by our government, state or federal, under one
party or another, notwithstanding our system of universal
suffrage, which has had for its aim the elevation of man
independent of his relation as a possessor of property. In no
instance have the rights of the proletary prevailed over the
interests of the proprietor. To separate power from property
we hold to be impossible under our present system. Its interests will always predominate in the measures of government, though they may sometimes be defeated in elections. . . .
Still, universal suffrage is a right, and is worth something.
All we mean to say is that in itself it by no means constitutes a sovereign remedy for the evils under which the
laboring classes suffer. It by no means gives them that degree
of political power which theorists imagine. To be rendered
efficient, it must be coupled with something like equality of
fortunes. The proprietors may indeed sometimes be outvoted
in an election, but their interests will invariably triumph in
the legislative halls and at the tribunals of justice. At least,
this has been the experience of this country thus far. We will
hope that the future will furnish a different experience.

The system of free trade, so far as it has as yet been
advocated in this country, we approve as a means of social
amelioration; but we cannot reply on it as alone sufficient. Because, to amount to much the competitors must start even,
and with nearly equal chances of success, which cannot be
with our present constitution of property, nor, indeed, with
our present constitution of human nature. Moreover, if the
system of free trade be pushed to its last results, it becomes
the introduction of a system of universal competition, a system of universal strife, where each man is for himself and no
man for another. It would be a return to the pure individuality
of the savage state, the abolition of all government, and the
adoption, as the practical rule of conduct, of the maxim
"save who can." We have not yet advanced far enough in
moral or social science to adopt this rule. We would indeed
restrict as much as possible the sphere of government, and
enlarge that of the individual; but government, as the organ
and agent of society, is a positive good, and can never be
dispensed with. We have, moreover, no faith in bringing about
the social order we desire by the agency of selfishness and
strife. True democracy can never rest permanently on the
maxim "I am as good as you," but it must resort to this
other maxim, "You are as good as I." The spirit by which it

must ultimately be sustained is not the spirit that will not submit to tyranny, but the spirit that will not tyrannize.

In universal education and religious culture, we have faith indeed, but not as final measures. Their office is to generate the moral force needed, but the generation of that force is not the reform. Mind is undoubtedly superior to matter, and all reforms must come from within; but the mental and moral reform effected in the interior of man will prove insufficient unless it come out of the interior and remodel the exterior. What we contend is not that free trade, universal suffrage, universal education, and religious culture are not essential, indispensable means to the social regeneration we are in pursuit of; but that, if we stop with them and leave the material order of society untouched, they will prove inadequate. We make no war on the political reformer, nor on the moral reformer. Our plan includes all they propose, and more too. Ours includes that without which theirs would accomplish little.

With this view of the case, it becomes necessary to seek something more ultimate, more radical than our most approved reformers have as yet ventured upon. This something we have professed to find in the abolition of hereditary property, a measure foreshadowed in the first number of this Journal, and implied, at least in our own mind, by almost every article we have ever written on the subject of social reform. We have long been thoroughly convinced that, without resorting to some such measure, it would be useless to talk of social progress or to speak in behalf of the laborer.

The doctrine we have long labored to maintain is that the work of this country is to emancipate labor by raising up the laborer from a mere workman without capital to be a proprietor and a workman on his own farm, or in his own shop. . . .

Now we would ask how is it possible to gain the end here implied, without a change in the present consitution of property? . . . Hereditary property is either a privilege or it is not. If it is not, if it confer no social advantage on him who inherits it over him who does not, then there can be no harm in seeking to abolish it, for what we propose to abolish is declared to be valueless. . . .

But hereditary property, unless the amount inherited by each individual could be rendered equal, is unquestionably a privilege. It gives, and always must give, to one portion of the community an advantage over the rest to which they are entitled by no natural superiority of intellect or of virtue. Will the public conscience, then, of the American people tolerate it? Will it sanction privilege? . . .

The American people may be mistaken as to men and measures, but we are confident that in principle they will all assent to the doctrine of equality. We feel confident of their unanimous support when we say that all the members of the community should have, so far as society is concerned, equal chances. But equal chances imply equal starting points. Nobody, it would seem, could pretend that where the points of departure were unequal the chances could be equal. Do the young man inheriting ten thousand pounds and the one whose inheritance is merely the gutter start even? Have they equal chances? It may be said both are free to rise as high as they can—one starting with ten thousand pounds in advance, and the other starting with the gutter. But it might as well be said the chances of the eldest son of the Duke of Newcastle and those of the eldest son of one of the lowest of the Duke's tenants are equal, since both unquestionably are free to rise as high as they can—one starting with a dukedom in advance, and the other with nothing. But to pretend this is mere jesting. . . .

The proposition for the abolition of hereditary property, it follows from these considerations, is merely a logical conclusion from the admitted premises of the American people and, *a fortiori*, of the democratic party. We have merely followed the invincible law of logic in putting it forth. We are compelled either to abandon the American theory of government and society, or else contend for the abolition of hereditary property; and they who censure us as a rash innovator, and call us "infamous" for choosing the latter alternative, are either false in their professions of attachment to American principles, or from two given ideas incapable of inferring a third.

Are we wrong? What in one word is this American system? Is it not the abolition of all artificial distinctions, all social advantages founded on birth or any other accident, and leaving every man to stand on his own feet for precisely what God and nature have made him? Does not this system declare that society should make no distinction between the child of the rich man and the child of the poor man; that she shall neither reward the child for the virtues, nor punish him for the vices of the parent? Is this the American system, yes or no? If it be not, what mean all our boasts of equality, all our Fourth of July oratory, all our patriotic songs and national glorifications? What else is it that we are constantly throwing in the face of the old world? and on what else do we profess to found our claims to admiration and imitation? Everybody knows that this is the system which the American people profess and to which they stand committed before the world. We pray them, then, to tell us how with this system which repudiates all distinctions found on birth they can reconcile hereditary property, which has no other basis than the accident of birth on which to rest? The logic by which they can do it is above, or below, our comprehension. . . .

Theodore Parker

THE TRANSIENT AND PERMANENT IN CHRISTIANITY
(1841)

"HEAVEN AND EARTH SHALL PASS AWAY; BUT MY WORDS SHALL NOT PASS AWAY."—LUKE xxi, 33.

In this sentence we have a very clear indication that Jesus of Nazareth believed the religion he taught would be eternal, that the substance of it would last forever. Yet there are some who are affrighted by the faintest rustle which a heretic makes among the dry leaves of theology; they tremble lest Christianity itself should perish without hope. Ever and anon the cry is raised, "The Philistines be upon us, and Christianity is in danger." The least doubt respecting the popular theology, or the existing machinery of the church; the least sign of distrust in the religion of the pulpit, or the religion of the street, is by some good men supposed to be at enmity with faith in Christ, and capable of shaking Christianity itself. On the other hand, a few bad men, and a few pious men, it is said, on both sides of the water, tell us the day of Christianity is past. The latter, it is alleged, would persuade us that, hereafter, piety must take a new form, the teachings of Jesus are to be passed by, that religion is to wing her way sublime, above the flight of Christianity, far away, toward heaven, as the fledged eaglet leaves forever the nest which sheltered his callow youth. Let us, therefore, devote a few moments to this subject, and consider what is *transient* in Christianity, and what is *permanent* therein. The topic seems not inappropriate to the times in which we live, or the occasion that calls us together. . . .

. . . In actual Christianity—that is, in that portion of Christianity which is preached and believed—there seems to have been, ever since the time of its earthly founder, two elements, the one transient, the other permanent. The one is the thought, the folly, the uncertain wisdom, the theological notions, the impiety of man; the other, the eternal truth of God. These two bear, perhaps, the same relation to each other that the phenomena of outward nature, such as sunshine and cloud, growth, decay, and reproduction, bear to the great law of nature which underlies and supports them all. As in that case more attention is commonly paid to the particular phenomena than to the general law, so in this case more is generally given to the transient in Christianity than to the permanent therein.

It must be confessed, though with sorrow, that transient things form a great part of what is commonly taught as religion. An undue place has often been assigned to forms and doctrines, while too little stress has been laid on the divine life of the soul, love to God and love to man. Religious forms may be useful and beautiful. They are so whenever they speak to the soul and answer a want thereof. In our present state some forms are perhaps necessary. But they are only the accident of Christianity, not its substance. They are the robe, not the angel, who may take another robe quite as becoming and useful. One sect has many forms; another, none. Yet both may be equally Christian, in spite of the redundance or the deficiency. They are a part of the language in which religion speaks, and exist, with few exceptions, wherever man is found. . . . So long as they satisfy or help the pious heart, so long they are good. Looking behind or around us, we see that the forms and rites of the Christians are quite as fluctuating as those of the heathens, from whom some of them have been, not unwisely, adopted by the earlier church.

Again, the doctrines that have been connected with Christianity, and taught in its name, are quite as changeable as the form. This also takes place unavoidably. If observations be made upon nature, which must take place so long as man has senses and understanding, there will be a philosophy of nature and philosophical doctrines. These will differ as the observations are just or inaccurate, and as the deductions from observed facts are true or false. Hence there will be different schools of natural philosophy so long as men have eyes and understandings of different clearness and strength. And if men observe and reflect upon religion—which will be done so long as man is a religious and reflective being —there must also be a philosophy of religion, a theology and

theological doctrines. These will differ, as men have felt much
or little of religion, as they analyze their sentiments cor-
rectly or otherwise, and as they have reasoned right or wrong.
Now the true system of nature, which exists in the outward
facts whether discovered or not, is always the same thing,
though the philosophy of nature, which men invent, change
every month, and be one thing at London and the opposite
at Berlin. Thus there is but one system of nature as it exists
in fact, though many theories of nature, which exist in our
imperfect notions of that system, and by which we may ap-
proximate and at length reach it. Now there can be but one
religion which is absolutely true, existing in the facts of
human nature and the ideas of Infinite God. That, whether
acknowledged or not, is always the same thing, and never
changes. So far as a man has any real religion—either the
principle or the sentiment thereof—so far he has that, by
whatever name he may call it. For, strictly speaking, there
is but one kind of religion, as there is but one kind of love,
though the manifestations of this religion, in forms, doctrines,
and life be never so diverse. . . .

Anyone who traces the history of what is called Christianity
will see that nothing changes more from age to age than the
doctrines taught as Christian and insisted on as essential to
Christianity and personal salvation. What is falsehood in one
province passes for truth in another. The heresy of one age
is the orthodox belief and "only infallible rule" of the next.
Now Arius, and now Athanasius, is lord of the ascendant.
Both were excommunicated in their turn, each for affirming
what the other denied. Men are burned for professing what
men are burned for denying. For centuries the doctrines of the
Christians were no better, to say the least, than those of their
contemporary pagans. The theological doctrines derived from
our fathers seem to have come from Judaism, heathenism, and
the caprice of philosophers, far more than they have come
from the principle and sentiment of Christianity. The doctrine of the Trinity, the very Achilles of theological dogmas,
belongs to philosophy and not religion; its subtleties cannot
even be expressed in our tongue. As old religions became
superannuated and died out, they left to the rising faith, as
to a residuary legatee, their forms and their doctrines; or
rather, as the giant in the fable left his poisoned garment to
work the overthrow of his conqueror. . . . The stream of
Christianity, as men receive it, has caught a stain from every
soil it has filtered through, so that now it is not the pure

water from the well of life which is offered to our lips, but streams troubled and polluted by man with mire and dirt. If Paul and Jesus could read our books of theological doctrines, would they accept as their teaching what men have vented in their name? Never till the letters of Paul had faded out of his memory; never till the words of Jesus had been torn out from the book of life. It is their notions about Christianity men have taught as the only living word of God. They have piled their own rubbish against the temple of truth where piety comes up to worship; what wonder the pile seems unshapely and like to fall? But these theological doctrines are fleeting as the leaves on the trees. They—

> are found
> Now green in youth, now withered on the ground:
> Another race the following spring supplies;
> They fall successive, and successive rise.

Like the clouds of the sky, they are here today; tomorrow, all swept off and vanished, while Christianity itself, like the heaven above, with its sun and moon and uncounted stars, is always over our head, though the cloud sometimes debars us of the needed light. It must of necessity be the case that our reasonings, and therefore our theological doctrines, are imperfect, and so perishing. It is only gradually that we approach to the true system of nature by observation and reasoning, and work out our philosophy and theology by the toil of the brain. But meantime, if we are faithful, the great truths of morality and religion, the deep sentiment of love to man and love to God, are perceived intuitively and by instinct, as it were, though our theology be imperfect and miserable. The theological notions of Abraham, to take the story as it stands, were exceedingly gross, yet a greater than Abraham has told us Abraham desired to see my day, saw it, and was glad. Since these notions are so fleeting, why need we accept the commandment of men as the doctrine of God?

This transitoriness of doctrines appears in many instances, of which two may be selected for a more attentive consideration. First, the doctrine respecting the origin and authority of the Old and New Testament. There has been a time when men were burned for asserting doctrines of natural philosophy which rested on evidence the most incontestable, because those doctrines conflicted with sentences in the Old Testament. Every word of that Jewish record was regarded as

miraculously inspired, and therefore as infallibly true. It was
believed that the Christian religion itself rested thereon, and
must stand or fall with the immaculate Hebrew text. He
was deemed no small sinner who found mistakes in the
manuscripts. On the authority of the written word man was
taught to believe impossible legends, conflicting assertions;
to take fiction for fact, a dream for a miraculous revelation
of God, an Oriental poem for a grave history of miraculous
events, a collection of amatory idyls for a serious discourse
"touching the mutual love of Christ and the church"; they
have been taught to accept a picture sketched by some glowing
eastern imagination, never intended to be taken for a reality,
as a proof that the Infinite God spoke in human words, appeared in the shape of a cloud, a flaming bush, or a man
who ate and drank and vanished into smoke; that he gave
counsels today, and the opposite tomorrow; that he violated
his own laws, was angry, and was only dissuaded by a mortal
man from destroying at once a whole nation—millions of men
who rebelled against their leader in a moment of anguish.
Questions in philosophy, questions in the Christian religion,
have been settled by an appeal to that book. The inspiration
of its authors has been assumed as infallible. Every fact in
the early Jewish history has been taken as a type of some
analogous fact in Christian history. The most distant events,
even such as are still in the arms of time, were supposed to
be clearly foreseen and foretold by pious Hebrews several
centuries before Christ. It is assumed at the outset, with no
shadow of evidence, that those writers held a miraculous
communication with God, such as he has granted to no other
man. What was originally a presumption of bigoted Jews
became an article of faith which Christians were burned for
not believing. This has been for centuries the general opinion
of the Christian church, both Catholic and Protestant, though
the former never accepted the Bible as the *only* source of
religious truth. It has been so. . . .

Now, this idolatry of the Old Testament has not always
existed. Jesus says that none born of a woman is greater
than John the Baptist, yet the least in the kingdom of heaven
was greater than John. Paul tells us the law—the very crown
on the old Hebrew revelation—is a shadow of good things
which have now come; only a schoolmaster to bring us to
Christ, and when faith has come that we are no longer under
the schoolmaster; that it was a law of sin and death from
which we are made free by the law of the spirit of life.

Christian teachers themselves have differed so widely in
their notion of the doctrines and meaning of those books that
it makes one weep to think of the follies deduced therefrom.
But modern criticism is fast breaking to pieces this idol which
men have made out of the scriptures. It has shown that here
are the most different works thrown together; that their authors, wise as they sometimes were, pious as we feel often
their spirit to have been, had only that inspiration which is
common to other men equally pious and wise; that they
were by no means infallible, but were mistaken in facts or in
reasoning—uttered predictions which time has not fulfilled;
men who in some measure partook of the darkness and
limited notions of their age, and were not always above its
mistakes or its corruptions.

The history of opinions on the New Testament is quite
similar. It has been assumed at the outset, it would seem
with no sufficient reason, without the smallest pretense on its
writers' part, that all of its authors were infallibly and miraculously inspired, so that they could commit no error of
doctrine or fact. Men have been bid to close their eyes at the
obvious difference between Luke and John—the serious dis-
agreement between Paul and Peter; to believe, on the smallest
evidence, accounts which shock the moral sense and revolt
the reason, and tend to place Jesus in the same series with
Hercules, and Apollonius of Tyana; accounts which Paul
in the Epistles never mentions, though he also had a vein of
the miraculous running quite through him. Men have been
told that all these things must be taken as part of Christianity,
and if they accepted the religion, they must take all these
accessories along with it; that the living spirit could not be
had without the killing letter. All the books which caprice
or accident had brought together between the lids of the
Bible were declared to be the infallible word of God, the
only certain rule of religious faith and practice. Thus the
Bible was made not a single channel, but the *only* certain
rule of religious faith and practice. . . .

But the current notions respecting the infallible inspiration of the Bible have no foundation in the Bible itself.
Which evangelist, which apostle of the New Testament, what
prophet or psalmist of the Old Testament, ever claims infallible authority for himself or for others? Which of them
does not in his own writings show that he was finite, and,
with all his zeal and piety, possessed but a limited inspiration, the bound whereof we can sometimes discover? Did

Christ ever demand that men should assent to the doctrines of the Old Testament, credit its stories, and take its poems for histories, and believe equally two accounts that contradict one another? Has he ever told you that all the truths of his religion, all the beauty of a Christian life, should be contained in the writings of those men who, even after his resurrection, expected him to be a Jewish king; of men who were sometimes at variance with one another, and misunderstood his divine teachings? Would not those modest writers themselves be confounded at the idolatry we pay them? Opinions may change on these points, as they have often changed —changed greatly and for the worse since the days of Paul. They are changing now, and we may hope for the better; for God makes man's folly as well as his wrath to praise him, and continually brings good out of evil.

Another instance of the transitoriness of doctrines taught as Christian is found in those which relate to the nature and authority of Christ. One ancient party has told us that he is the infinite God; another, that he is both God and man; a third, that he was a man, the son of Joseph and Mary—born as we are, tempted like ourselves, inspired, as we may be, if we will pay the price. Each of the former parties believed its doctrine on this head was infallibly true, and formed the very substance of Christianity, and was one of the essential conditions of salvation, though scarce any two distinguished teachers, of ancient or modern times, agree in their expression of this truth.

Almost every sect that has ever been makes Christianity rest on the personal authority of Jesus, and not the immutable truth of the doctrines themselves, or the authority of God, who sent him into the world. Yet it seems difficult to conceive any reason why moral and religious truths should rest for their support on the personal authority of their revealer, any more than the truths of science on that of him who makes them known first or most clearly. It is hard to see why the great truths of Christianity rest on the personal authority of Jesus, more than the axioms of geometry rest on the personal authority of Euclid or Archimedes. The authority of Jesus, as of all teachers, one would naturally think, must rest on the truth of his words, and not their truth on his authority.

Opinions respecting the nature of Christ seem to be constantly changing. In the three first centuries after Christ, it appears, great latitude of speculation prevailed. Some said he was God, with nothing of human nature, his body only an illusion; others, that he was man, with nothing of the divine nature, his miraculous birth having no foundation in fact. In a few centuries it was decreed by councils that he was God, thus honoring the divine element; next, that he was man also, thus admitting the human side. For some ages the Catholic church seems to have dwelt chiefly on the divine nature that was in him, leaving the human element to mystics and other heretical persons, whose bodies served to flesh the swords of orthodox believers. The stream of Christianity has come to us in two channels—one within the church, the other without the church—and it is not hazarding too much to say that since the fourth century the true Christian life has been out of the established church and not in it, but rather in the ranks of dissenters. From the Reformation till the latter part of the last century, we are told, the Protestant church dwelt chiefly on the human side of Christ, and since that time many works have been written to show how the two —perfect deity and perfect manhood—were united in his character. But all this time scarce any two eminent teachers agree on these points, however orthodox they may be called. What a difference between the Christ of John Gerson and John Calvin—yet were both accepted teachers and pious men. What a difference between the Christ of the Unitarians and the Methodists—yet may men of both sects be true Christians and acceptable with God. What a difference between the Christ of Matthew and John—yet both were disciples, and their influence is wide as Christendom and deep as the heart of man. But on this there is not time to enlarge.

Now it seems clear that the notion men form about the origin and nature of the scriptures respecting the nature and authority of Christ have nothing to do with Christianity except as its aids or its adversaries; they are not the foundation of its truths. These are theological questions, not religious questions. Their connection with Christianity appears accidental: for if Jesus had taught at Athens, and not at Jerusalem; if he had wrought no miracle, and none but the human nature had ever been ascribed to him; if the Old Testament had forever perished at his birth, Christianity would still have been the word of God; it would have lost none of its truths. It would be just as true, just as beautiful, just as lasting, as now it is; though we should have lost

so many a blessed word, and the work of Christianity itself would have been, perhaps, a long time retarded.

To judge the future by the past, the former authority of
the Old Testament can never return. Its present authority cannot stand. It must be taken for what it is worth. The occasional folly and impiety of its authors must pass for no
more than their value; while the religion, the wisdom, the
love which make fragrant its leaves will still speak to the
best hearts as hitherto, and in accents even more divine when
reason is allowed her rights. The ancient belief in the infallible inspiration of each sentence of the New Testament is
fast changing, very fast. One writer, not a sceptic, but a
Christian of unquestioned piety, sweeps off the beginning of
Matthew; another, of a different church and equally religious, the end of John. Numerous critics strike off several
epistles. The Apocalypse itself is not spared, notwithstanding its concluding curse. Who shall tell us the work of re-
trenchment is to stop here; that others will not demonstrate
what some pious hearts have long felt, that errors of doctrine
and errors of fact may be found in many parts of the record,
here and there, from the beginning of Matthew to the end
of Acts? We see how opinions have changed ever since
the apostles' time; and who shall assure us that they were
not sometimes mistaken in historical as well as doctrinal
matters; did not sometimes confound the actual with the
imaginary; and that the fancy of these pious writers never
stood in the place of their recollection?

But what if this should take place? Is Christianity then to
perish out of the heart of the nations, and vanish from
the memory of the world, like the religions that were before
Abraham? It must be so, if it rest on a foundation which a
scoffer may shake, and a score of pious critics shake down.
But this is the foundation of a theology, not of Christianity. . . . Christianity does not rest on the infallible authority
of the New Testament. It depends on this collection of books
for the historical statement of its facts. In this we do not require infallible inspiration on the part of the writers, more
than in the record of other historical facts. To me it seems as
presumptuous, on the one hand, for the believer to claim
this evidence for the truth of Christianity, as it is absurd,
on the other hand, for the sceptic to demand such evidence
to support these historical statements. I cannot see that it
depends on the personal authority of Jesus. He was the organ
through which the infinite spoke. It is God that was mani-

fested in the flesh by him on whom rests the truth which Jesus brought to light and made clear and beautiful in his life; and if Christianity be true, it seems useless to look for any other authority to uphold it, as for someone to support Almighty God. So if it could be proved—as it cannot—in opposition to the greatest amount of historical evidence ever collected on any similar point, that the gospels were the fabrication of designing and artful men, that Jesus of Nazareth had never lived, still Christianity would stand firm, and fear no evil. None of the doctrines of that religion would fall to the ground; for, if true, they stand by themselves. But we should lose—oh, irreparable loss!—the example of that character, so beautiful, so divine, that no human genius could have conceived it, as none, after all the progress and refinement of eighteen centuries, seems fully to have comprehended its lustrous life. If Christianity were true, we should still think it was so, not because its record was written by infallible pens, nor because it was lived out by an infallible teacher; but that it is true, like the axioms of geometry, because it is true, and is to be tried by the oracle God places in the breast. If it rest on the personal authority of Jesus alone, then there is no certainty of its truth if he were ever mistaken in the smallest matter, as some Christians have thought he was in predicting his second coming.

These doctrines respecting the scriptures have often changed, and are but fleeting. Yet men lay much stress on them. Some cling to these notions as if they were Christianity itself. It is about these and similar points that theological battles are fought from age to age. Men sometimes use worst the choicest treasure which God bestows. This is especially true of the use men make of the Bible. Some men have regarded it as the heathen their idol, or the savage his fetish. They have subordinated reason, conscience, and religion to this. Thus have they lost half the treasure it bears in its bosom. No doubt the time will come when its true character shall be felt. Then it will be seen that, amid all the contradictions of the Old Testament its legends, so beautiful as fictions, so appalling as facts; amid its predictions that have never been fulfilled; amid the puerile conceptions of God which sometimes occur and the cruel denunciations that disfigure both psalm and prophecy, there is a reverence for man's nature, a sublime trust in God, and a depth of piety rarely felt in these cold northern hearts of ours. Then the devotion of its authors, the loftiness of their aim,

and the majesty of their life will appear doubly fair, and
prophet and psalmist will warm our hearts as never before. Their voice will cheer the young and sanctify the gray-
headed; will charm us in the toil of life, and sweeten the cup
death gives us when he comes to shake off this mantle of
flesh. Then will it be seen that the words of Jesus are the
music of heaven, sung in an earthly voice, and the echo of
these words in John and Paul owe their efficacy to their truth
and their depth, and to no accidental matter connected there-
with. Then can the word, which was in the beginning and
now is, find access to the innermost heart of man, and speak
there as now it seldom speaks. Then shall the Bible—which
is a whole library of the deepest and most earnest thoughts
and feelings and piety and love ever recorded in human
speech—be read oftener than ever before, not with superstition, but with reason, conscience, and faith fully active.
Then shall it sustain men bowed down with many sorrows;
rebuke sin, encourage virtue, sow the world broadcast and
quick with the seed of love, that man may reap a harvest
for life everlasting. . . .

Doubtless the time will come when men shall see Christ
also as he is. Well might he still say, "Have I been so long
with you, and yet hast thou not known me?" No! we have
made him an idol, have bowed the knee before him, saying,
"Hail, king of the Jews!" called him "Lord, Lord!" but done
not the things which he said. The history of the Christian
world might well be summed up in one word of the evangelist
—"and there they crucified him"; for there has never been
an age when men did not crucify the Son of God afresh. But
if error prevail for a time and grow old in the world, truth
will triumph at the last, and then we shall see the Son of God
as he is. Lifted up, he shall draw all nations unto him. Then
will men understand the word of Jesus, which shall not pass
away. Then we shall see and love the divine life that he
lived. How vast has his influence been! How his spirit
wrought in the hearts of his disciples, rude, selfish, bigoted
as at first they were! How it has wrought in the world!
His words judge the nations. The wisest son of man has not
measured their height. They speak to what is deepest in profound men, what is holiest in good men, what is divinest
in religious men. They kindle anew the flame of devotion in
hearts long cold. They are spirit and life. . . .

But still was he not our brother; the son of man, as we
are; the Son of God, like ourselves? His excellence—was it

not human excellence? His wisdom, love, piety—sweet and celestial as they were—are they not what we also may attain? In him, as in a mirror, we may see the image of God, and go on from glory to glory, till we are changed into the same image, led by the spirit which enlightens the humble. Viewed in this way, how beautiful is the life of Jesus! Heaven has come down to earth, or rather, earth has become heaven. The son of God, come of age, has taken possession of his birthright. The brightest revelation is this— of what is possible for all men, if not now, at least hereafter. How pure is his spirit, and how encouraging its words! "Lowly sufferer," he seems to say, "see how I bore the cross. Patient laborer, be strong; see how I toiled for the unthankful and the merciless. Mistaken sinner, see of what thou art capable. Rise up, and be blessed."

But if, as some early Christians began to do, you take a heathen view, and make him a god, the Son of God in a peculiar and exclusive sense, much of the significance of his character is gone. His virtue has no merit, his love no feeling, his cross no burden, his agony no pain. His death is an illusion, his resurrection but a show. For if he were not a man, but a god, what are all these things? what his words, his life, his excellence of achievement? It is all nothing, weighed against the illimitable greatness of him who created the worlds and fills up all time and space! Then his resignation is no lesson, his life no model, his death no triumph to you or me, who are not gods, but mortal men, that know not what a day shall bring forth, and walk by faith "dim sounding on our perilous way." Alas! we have despaired of man, and so cut off his brightest hope. . . .

To turn away from the disputes of the Catholics and the Protestants, of the Unitarian and the Trinitarian, of old school and new school, and come to the plain words of Jesus of Nazareth, Christianity is a simple thing, very simple. It is absolute, pure morality; absolute, pure religion; the love of man; the love of God acting without let or hindrance. The only creed it lays down is the great truth which springs up spontaneous in the holy heart—there is a God. Its watchword is, Be perfect as your Father in heaven. The only form it demands is a divine life; doing the best thing in the best way, from the highest motives; perfect obedience to the great law of God. Its sanction is the voice of God in your heart; the perpetual presence of Him who made us and the stars over our head; Christ and the Father abiding within us.

All this is very simple—a little child can understand it; very beautiful—the loftiest mind can find nothing so lovely. Try it by reason, conscience, and faith—things highest in man's nature—we see no redundance, we feel no deficiency. Examine the particular duties it enjoins—humility, reverence, sobriety, gentleness, charity, forgiveness, fortitude, resignation, faith, and active love; try the whole extent of Christianity, so well summed up in the command, "Thou shalt love the Lord thy God with all thy heart, and with all thy soul, and with all thy mind—thou shalt love thy neighbor as thyself," and is there anything therein that can perish? No, the very opponents of Christianity have rarely found fault with the teachings of Jesus. The end of Christianity seems to be to make all men one with God as Christ was one with Him; to bring them to such a state of obedience and goodness that we shall think divine thoughts and feel divine sentiments, and so keep the law of God by living a life of truth and love. Its means are purity and prayer; getting strength from God, and using it for our fellow men as well as ourselves. It allows perfect freedom. It does not demand all men to *think* alike, but to think uprightly, and get as near as possible at truth; not all men to *live* alike, but to live holy, and get as near as possible to a life perfectly divine. Christ set up no pillars of Hercules, beyond which men must not sail the sea in quest of truth. He says, "I have many things to say unto you, but ye cannot bear them now. . . . Greater works than these shall ye do." Christianity lays no rude hand on the sacred peculiarity of the individual genius and character. But there is no Christian sect which does not fetter a man. It would make all men think alike, or smother their conviction in silence. Were all men Quakers or Catholics, Unitarians or Baptists, there would be much less diversity of thought, character, and life, less of truth active in the world, than now. But Christianity gives us the largest liberty of the sons of God; and were all men Christians after the fashion of Jesus, this variety would be a thousand times greater than now, for Christianity is not a system of doctrines, but rather a method of attaining oneness with God. It demands, therefore, a good life of piety within, of purity without, and gives the promise that whoso does God's will shall know of God's doctrine. . . .

The form religion takes, the doctrines wherewith she is girded, can never be the same in any two centuries or two men; for since the sum of religious doctrines is both the result and the measure of a man's total growth in wisdom, virtue, and piety, and since men will always differ in these respects, so religious *doctrines* and *forms* will always differ, always be transient, as Christianity goes forth and scatters the seed she bears in her hand. But the *Christianity holy men feel in the heart,* the Christ that is born within us, is always the same thing to each soul that feels it. This differs only in degree, and not in kind, from age to age, and man to man. There is something in Christianity which no sect, from the "Ebionites" to the "Latter-Day Saints," ever entirely overlooked. This is that common Christianity which burns in the hearts of pious men.

Real Christianity gives men new life. It is the growth and perfect action of the holy spirit God puts into the sons of men. It makes us outgrow any form or any system of doctrines we have devised, and approach still closer to the truth. It would lead us to take what help we can find. It would make the Bible our servant, not our master. It would teach us to profit by the wisdom and piety of David and Solomon, but not to sin their sins, nor bow to their idols. It would make us revere the holy words spoken by "godly men of old," but revere still more the word of God spoken through conscience, reason, and faith, as the holiest of all. It would not make Christ the despot of the soul, but the brother of all men. It would not tell us that even he had exhausted the fulness of God, so that he could create none greater; for with him "all things are possible," and neither Old Testament nor New Testament ever hints that creation exhausts the creator. Still less would it tell us the wisdom, the piety, the love, the manly excellence of Jesus was the result of miraculous agency alone, but that it was won, like the excellence of humbler men, by faithful obedience to Him who gave His Son such ample heritage. It would point to him as our brother, who went before, like the good shepherd, to charm us with the music of his words, and with the beauty of his life to tempt us up the steeps of mortal toil, within the gate of heaven. It would have us make the kingdom of God on earth, and enter more fittingly the kingdom on high. It would lead us to form Christ in the heart, on which Paul laid such stress, and work out our salvation by this. For it is not so much by the Christ who lived so blameless and beautiful eighteen centuries ago that we are saved directly, but by the Christ we form in our hearts and live out in our daily life that we save ourselves, God working with us both to will and to do.

Compare the simpleness of Christianity, as Christ sets it forth on the mount, with what is sometimes taught and accepted in that honored name; and what a difference! One is of God; one is of man. There is something in Christianity which sects have not reached; something that will not be won, we fear, by theological battles, or the quarrels of pious men; still we may rejoice that Christ is preached in any way. The Christianity of sects, of the pulpit, of society, is ephemeral—a transitory fly. It will pass off and be forgot. Some new form will take its place, suited to the aspect of the changing times. Each will represent something of truth, but no one the whole. It seems the whole race of man is needed to do justice to the whole of truth, as "the whole church to preach the whole gospel." Truth is intrusted for the time to a perishable ark of human contrivance. Though often shipwrecked, she always comes safe to land, and is not changed by her mishap. That pure ideal religion which Jesus saw on the mount of his vision, and lived out in the lowly life of a Galilean peasant; which transforms his cross into an emblem of all that is holiest on earth; which makes sacred the ground he trod, and is dearest to the best of men, most true to what is truest in them—cannot pass away. Let men improve never so far in civilization, or soar never so high on the wings of religion and love, they can never outgo the flight of truth and Christianity. It will always be above them. It is as if we were to fly toward a star which becomes larger and more bright the nearer we approach, till we enter and are absorbed in its glory. . . .

Let then the transient pass, fleet as it will; and may God send us some new manifestation of the Christian faith that shall stir men's hearts as they were never stirred; some new word ˉwhich shall teach us what we are, and renew us all in the image of God; some better life that shall fulfill the Hebrew prophecy, and pour out the spirit of God on young men and maidens, and old men and children; which shall realize the word of Christ, and give us the Comforter, who shall reveal all needed things! There are Simeons enough in the cottages and churches of New England, plain men and pious women who wait for the consolation, and would die in gladness if their expiring breath could stir quicker the wings that bear him on. There are men enough, sick and "bowed down, in no wise able to lift up themselves," who would be healed could they kiss the hand of their Saviour, or touch but the hem of his garment; men who look up and are not fed, because they ask bread from heaven and water from the rock, not traditions or fancies, Jewish or heathen, or new or old; men enough who, with throbbing hearts, pray for the spirit of healing to come upon the waters which other than angels have long kept in trouble; men enough who have lain a long time sick of theology, nothing bettered by many physicians, and are now dead, too dead to bury their dead, who would come out of their graves at the glad tidings. God send us a real religious life which shall pluck blindness out of the heart, and make us better fathers, mothers, and children! a religious life that shall go with us where we go, and make every home the house of God, every act acceptable as a prayer. We would work for this, and pray for it, though we wept tears of blood while we prayed. . . .

Theodore Parker

*A SERMON OF SLAVERY**

Know ye not that to whom ye yield yourselves servants to obey, his servants ye are whom ye obey; whether of sin unto death, or of obedience unto righteousness?—ROM. vi. 16.

In our version of the New Testament the word *servant* often stands for a word in the original, which means *slave*. Such is the case in this passage just read, and the sense of the whole verse is this:—"If a man yields unconditional service to sin, he is the *slave* of sin, and gets death for his reward." Here, however, by a curious figure of speech, not uncommon in this apostle, he uses the word *slave* in a good sense—*slave* of obedience unto righteousness. I now ask your attention to a short sermon of slavery.

A popular definition has sometimes been given of common bodily slavery, that it is the holding of property in man. In a kindred language it is called body-property. In this case, a man's body becomes the possession, property, chattel, tool, or thing of another person, and not of the man who lives in it. This foreign person, of course, makes use of it to serve his own ends, without regard to the true welfare, or even the wishes, of the man who lives in that body, and to whom it rightfully belongs. Here the relation is necessarily that of force on one side and suffering on the other, though the force is often modified and the suffering sometimes disguised or kept out of sight.

Now man was made to be free, to govern himself, to be his own master, to have no cause stand between him and God, which shall curtail his birthright of freedom. He is never in his

*Excerpt from "A Sermon of Slavery," first delivered in 1841. Reprinted in *The Slave Power* by Theodore Parker, edited by James K. Hosmer, pub. by American Unitarian Association (Boston, 1916), reprinted Arno Press (New York, 1969).

proper element until he attains this condition of freedom; of self-government. Of course, while we are children, not having reached the age of discretion, we must be under the authority of our parents and guardians, teachers, and friends. This is a natural relation. There is no slavery in it; no degradation. The parents, exercising rightful authority over their children, do not represent human caprice, but divine wisdom and love. They assume the direction of the child's actions, not to do themselves a service, but to benefit him. The father restrains his child, that the child may have more freedom, not less. Here the relation is not of force and suffering, but of love on both sides; of ability, which loves to help, and necessity, which loves to be directed. The child that is nurtured by its parent gains more than the parent does. So is it the duty of the wise, the good, the holy, to teach, direct, restrain the foolish, the wicked, the ungodly. If a man is wiser, better, and holier than I am, it is my duty, my privilege, my exaltation to obey him. For him to direct me in wisdom and love, not for his sake but for my own, is for me to be free. He may gain nothing by this, but I gain much.

As slavery was defined to be holding property in man, so freedom may be defined as a state in which the man does, of his own consent, the best things he is capable of doing at that stage of his growth.

By the blessing of Providence, seconding the efforts, prayers, tears of some good men, there is no bodily, personal slavery sanctioned by the law amongst us in New England. But at the South we all know that some millions of our fellow-citizens are held in bondage; that men, women, and children are bought and sold in the shambles of the national Capital; are owned as cattle; reared as cattle; beaten as cattle. We all know that our fathers fought through the War of Independence with these maxims in their mouths and blazoned on their banners: that all men are born free and equal, and that the God of eternal justice will at last avenge the cause of the oppressed, however strong the oppressor may be; yet it is just as well known that the sons of those very fathers now trade in human flesh, separating parent and child, and husband and wife, for the sake of a little gain; that the sons of those fathers eat bread not in the sweat of their own brow, but in that of the slave's face; that they are sustained, educated, rendered rich, and haughty, and luxurious by the labor they extort from men whom they have stolen, or purchased from the stealer, or inherited from the purchaser. It is known to you all, that there are some millions of these forlorn children of Adam, men whom the Declaration

of Independence declares "born free and equal" with their
master before God and the law; men whom the Bible names
"of the same blood" with the prophets and apostles; men "for
whom Christ died," and who are "statues of God in ebony"—
that they are held in this condition and made to feel the full
burden of a corrupt society, and doomed from their birth to
degradation and infamy, their very name a mock-word; their
life a retreat, not a progress,—for the general and natural effect
of slavery is to lessen the qualities of a man in the slave as he
increases in stature or in years,—their children, their wives,
their own bones and sinews at the mercy of a master! That
these things are so, is known to all of us; well known from our
childhood.

Every man who has ever thought at all on any subject, and
has at the same time a particle of manhood in him, knows that
this state of slavery would be to him worse than a thousand
deaths; that set death in one scale, and hopeless slavery for
himself and children in the other, he would not hesitate in his
choice, but would say, "Give me death, though the life be
ground out of me with the most exquisite tortures of lingering
agony that malice can invent or tyranny inflict." To the African
thus made the victim of American cupidity and crime, the state
of slavery, it will be said, may not appear so degrading as to
you and me, for he has never before been civilized, and though
the untaught instinct of man bid him love freedom, yet Christianity has not revealed to him the truth, that all men are
brothers before God, born with equal rights. But this fact is no
excuse or extenuation of our crime. Who would justify a knave
in plundering a little girl out of a fortune that she inherited, on
the ground that she was a little girl "of tender years," and had
never enjoyed or even beheld her birthright? The fact that the
injured party was ignorant and weak, would only enhance and
aggravate the offense, adding new baseness and the suspicion of
cowardice to guilt.

Then, too, it is said, "The slaves are very happy, and it is a
great pity to disturb them," that "the whole mass are better fed
and clothed, and are troubled with fewer cares, than working
men at the North." Suppose this true also, what then? Do you
estimate your welfare in pounds of beef; in yards of cloth; in
exemption from the cares of a man! If so all appeal to you is
vain, your own soul has become servile. The Saviour of the
world was worse fed and clothed, no doubt, than many a
Georgian slave, and had not where to lay his head, wearied
with many cares; but has your Christianity taught you that was

an evil, and the slave's hutch at night, and pottage by day, and exemption from a man's cares by night and day, are a good, a good to be weighed against freedom! Then are you unworthy the soil you stand on; you contaminate the air of New England, which free men died to transmit to their children free!

But there are others, who are willing to countenance the sin and continue it, well knowing that it is a sin. They would not have it abated. They tell you of the stupidity of the African; that he is made for nothing but a slave; is allied to the baboon and the ape, and is as much in his place when fettered, ignorant and savage, in a rice field, to toil under a taskmaster's whip, as a New Englander, free and educated, is in his place, when felling forests, planning railroads, or "conducting" a steam-engine. Hard treatment and poor fare, say they, are the black man's due. Besides, they add, there is a natural antipathy between the black race and the white, which only the love of money, or the love of power, on the part of the white is capable of overcoming; that the blacks are an inferior race, and therefore the white Saxons are justified in making them slaves. They think the strong have a right to the services of the weak, forgetting that the rule of reason, the rule of Christianity, is just the other way; "We that are strong ought to bear the infirmities of the weak." They would have us follow the old rule, that "they should get who have the power, and they should keep who can." Of this class nothing further need be said save this: that they are very numerous, and quote the New Testament in support of slavery, thus contriving to pass for Christians, and have made such a stir in the land that it is scarce safe to open one's mouth and strip the veil from off this sin.

I know some men say, "We have nothing to do with it. Slavery is the affair of the slaveholders and the slaves, not yours and mine. Let them abate it when they will." A most unchristian saying is this. Slavery! we have something to do with it. The sugar and rice we eat, the cotton we wear, are the work of the slave. His wrongs are imported to us in these things. We eat his flesh and drink his blood. I need not speak of our political connection with slavery. You all know what that is, and its effect on us here. But socially, individually, we are brought into contact with it every day. If there is a crime in the land known to us, and we do not protest against it to the extent of our ability, we are partners of that crime. It is not many years since it was said, temperate men had nothing to do with the sin of drunkenness; though they paid for it out of their purse! When they looked they found they had much to do with it, and sought to end it. I have no doubt, to go back to the Hebrew mythical tale, that when God called Cain, "Where is Abel?" he said, "I have nothing to do with it; that is Abel's affair. Am I my brother's keeper?" If the law of Moses made it the duty of a Hebrew to lift up the beast of a public enemy which had stumbled in the street, how much more does the law of God make it a Christian's duty to tell his brother of his sin, and help him out of it; how much more to rescue the oppressed,—"to bind up the broken-hearted; to proclaim liberty to the captives, the opening of the prison to them that are bound."

Such then is slavery at the South; such the action of men at the North to attack or to defend it. But look a moment at the cause of this sin, and of its defense. It comes from the desire to get gain, comfort, or luxury; to have power over matter, without working or paying the honest price of that gain, comfort, luxury, and power; it is the spirit which would knowingly and of set purpose injure another for the sake of gaining some benefit to yourself. Such a spirit would hold slaves everywhere, if it were possible. Now when the question is put to any fair man,—Is not this spirit active at the North as well as the South? there is but one answer. The man who would use his fellow-man as a tool merely, and injure him by that use; who would force another in any way to bend to his caprice; who would take advantage of his ignorance, his credulity, his superstition, or his poverty, to enrich and comfort himself; in a word, who would use his neighbor to his neighbor's hurt,—that man has the spirit of slaveholding, and were circumstances but different, he would chain his brethren with iron bonds. If you, for your own sake, would unjustly put any man in a position which degrades him in your eyes, in his own eyes, in the eyes of his fellow-men, you have the spirit of the slaveholder. There is much of this affair with us still. This is the reason that slavery finds so many supporters amongst us; that we deliver up the fugitives, and "betray him that wandereth," sheltering ourselves under the plea that we keep the law of the land, written by man on parchment half a century ago, while we violate the law of nature, written everlastingly by God on the walls of the world. It was through this spirit,—so genial to our Anglo-Saxon blood,—that our fathers slew the Indians, who would not work, and the Southern planter enslaves the African, who will work. Both acted from the same motives, at North and South; killing or enslaving. That spirit is still with us, and shows itself in many shapes that need not be touched on now. It is not owing so much to our superior goodness, perhaps, as to a fortunate accident, that we have no slaves here at this day. They are not profitable. The shrewd men of our land discerned the fact long ago, and settled the question. Doubtless we have still social institutions which eyes more Christian than ours shall one day look upon as evils only less than that of slavery itself. But it is gradually that we gain light; he that converts it to life as fast as it comes, does well.

3

THE VOICE OF
THE DIAL

R. W. Emerson and Margaret Fuller

THE EDITORS TO THE READER*
(1840)

We invite the attention of our countrymen to a new design. Probably not quite unexpected or unannounced will our journal appear, though small pains have been taken to secure its welcome. Those who have immediately acted in editing the present number cannot accuse themselves of any unbecoming forwardness in their undertaking, but rather of a backwardness, when they remember how often in many private circles the work was projected, how eagerly desired, and only postponed because no individual volunteered to combine and concentrate the free-will offerings of many co-operators. With some reluctance the present conductors of this work have yielded themselves to the wishes of their friends, finding something sacred and not to be withstood in the importunity which urged the production of a journal in a new spirit.

As they have not proposed themselves to the work, neither can they lay any the least claim to an option or determination of the spirit in which it is conceived, or to what is peculiar in the design. In that respect, they have obeyed, though with great joy, the strong current of thought and feeling which for a few years past has led many sincere persons in New England to make new demands on literature, and to reprobate that rigor of our conventions of religion and education which is turning us to stone, which renounces hope, which looks only backward, which asks only such a future as the past, which suspects improvement, and holds nothing so much in horror as new views and the dream of youth.

* From *The Dial*, I (July 1840)

With these terrors the conductors of the present journal have nothing to do—not even so much as a word of reproach to waste. They know that there is a portion of the youth and of the adult population of this country who have not shared them; who have in secret or in public paid their vows to truth and freedom; who love reality too well to care for names, and who live by a faith too earnest and profound to suffer them to doubt the eternity of its object, or to shake themselves free from its authority. Under the fictions and customs which occupied others, these have explored the necessary, the plain, the true, the human—and so gained a vantage ground which commands the history of the past and the present.

No one can converse much with different classes of society in New England without remarking the progress of a revolution. Those who share in it have no external organization, no badge, no creed, no name. They do not vote, or print, or even meet together. They do not know each other's faces or names. They are united only in a common love of truth, and love of its work. They are of all conditions and constitutions. Of these acolytes, if some are happily born and well bred, many are no doubt ill dressed, ill placed, ill made—with as many scars of hereditary vice as other men. Without pomp, without trumpet, in lonely and obscure places, in solitude, in servitude, in compunctions and privations, trudging beside the team in the dusty road, or drudging a hireling in other men's cornfields, schoolmasters who teach a few children rudiments for a pittance, ministers of small parishes of the obscurer sects, lone women in dependent condition, matrons and young maidens, rich and poor, beautiful and hard-favored, without concert or proclamation of any kind, they have silently given in their several adherence to a new hope, and in all companies do signify a greater trust in the nature and resources of man than the laws or the popular opinions will well allow.

This spirit of the time is felt by every individual with some difference, to each one casting its light upon the objects nearest to his temper and habits of thought; to one, coming in the shape of special reforms in the state; to another, in modifications of the various callings of men, and the customs of business; to a third, opening a new scope for literature and art; to a fourth, in philosophical insight; to a fifth, in the vast solitudes of prayer. It is in every form a protest against usage and a search for principles. In all its movements, it is peaceable, and in the very lowest marked with a triumphant success. Of course, it rouses the opposition of all which it judges and condemns, but it is too confident in its tone to comprehend an objection, and so builds no outworks for possible defense against contingent enemies. It has the step of Fate, and goes on existing like an oak or a river, because it must.

In literature, this influence appears not yet in new books so much as in the higher tone of criticism. The antidote to all narrowness is the comparison of the record with nature, which at once shames the record and stimulates to new attempts. Whilst we look at this, we wonder how any book has been thought worthy to be preserved. There is somewhat in all life untranslatable into language. He who keeps his eye on that will write better than others, and think less of his writing, and of all writing. Every thought has a certain imprisoning as well as uplifting quality, and, in proportion to its energy on the will, refuses to become an object of intellectual contemplation. Thus what is great usually slips through our fingers, and it seems wonderful how a lifelike word ever comes to be written. If our journal share the impulses of the time, it cannot now prescribe its own course. It cannot foretell in orderly propositions what it shall attempt. All criticism should be poetic, unpredictable, superseding, as every new thought does, all foregone thoughts, and making a new light on the whole world. Its brow is not wrinkled with circumspection, but serene, cheerful, adoring. It has all things to say, and no less than all the world for its final audience.

Our plan embraces much more than criticism; were it not so, our criticism would be naught. Everything noble is directed on life, and this is. We do not wish to say pretty or curious things, or to reiterate a few propositions in varied forms, but, if we can, to give expression to that spirit which lifts men to a higher platform, restores to them the religious sentiment, brings them worthy aims and pure pleasures, purges the inward eye, makes life less desultory, and, through raising man to the level of nature, takes away its melancholy from the landscape, and reconciles the practical with the speculative powers.

But perhaps we are telling our little story too gravely. There are always great arguments at hand for a true action, even for the writing of a few pages. There is nothing but seems near it and prompts it—the sphere in the ecliptic, the sap in the apple tree—every fact, every appearance seem to persuade to it.

Our means correspond with the ends we have indicated. As we wish not to multiply books but to report life, our resources are therefore not so much the pens of practiced writers as the discourse of the living and the portfolios which friendship has opened to us. From the beautiful recesses of private thought; from the experience and hope of spirits which are withdrawing from all old forms, and seeking in all that is new somewhat to meet their inappeasable longings; from the secret confession of genius afraid to trust itself to aught but sympathy; from the conversation of fervid and mystical pietists; from tear-stained diaries of sorrow and passion; from the manuscripts of young poets; and from the records of youthful taste commenting on old works of art, we hope to draw thoughts and feelings which being alive can impart life.

And so with diligent hands and good intent we set down our Dial on the earth. We wish it may resemble that instrument in its celebrated happiness, that of measuring no hours but those of sunshine. Let it be one cheerful rational voice amidst the din of mourners and polemics. Or to abide by our chosen image, let it be such a Dial, not as the dead face of a clock, hardly even such as the Gnomon in a garden, but rather such a Dial as is the garden itself, in whose leaves and flowers and fruits the suddenly awakened sleeper is instantly apprised not what part of dead time, but what state of life and growth is now arrived and arriving.

Margaret Fuller

A SHORT ESSAY ON CRITICS*
(1840)

An essay on criticism were a serious matter; for, though this age be emphatically critical, the writer would still find it necessary to investigate the laws of criticism as a science, to settle its conditions as an art. Essays entitled critical are epistles addressed to the public through which the mind of the recluse relieves itself of its impressions. Of these the only law is, "Speak the best word that is in thee." Or they are regular articles, got up to order by the literary hack writer for the literary mart, and the only law is to make them plausible. There is not yet deliberate recognition of a standard of criticism, though we hope the always strengthening league of the republic of letters must ere long settle laws on which its Amphictyonic council may act. Meanwhile let us not venture to write on criticism, but by classifying the critics imply our hopes, and thereby our thoughts.

First, there are the subjective class (to make use of a convenient term introduced by our German benefactors). These are persons to whom writing is no sacred, no reverend employment. They are not driven to consider, not forced upon investigation by the fact that they are deliberately giving their thoughts an independent existence, and that it may live to others when dead to them. They know no agonies of conscientious research, no timidities of self-respect. They see no ideal beyond the present hour, which makes its mood an uncertain tenure. How things affect them now they know; let the future, let the whole take care of itself. They state their impressions as they rise of other men's spoken, written, or acted thoughts. They never dream of going out of themselves to seek the motive, to trace the law of another nature. They never dream that there are statures which cannot be measured from their point of view. They love, they like, or they hate; the book is detestable, immoral, absurd, or admirable,

* From *The Dial,* I (July, 1840).

noble, of a most approved scope—these statements they make with authority, as those who bear the evangel of pure taste and accurate judgment, and need be tried before no human synod. To them it seems that their present position commands the universe.

Thus the essays on the works of others which are called criticisms are often, in fact, mere records of impressions. To judge of their value, you must know where the man was brought up, under what influences—his nation, his church, his family even. He himself has never attempted to estimate the value of these circumstances and find a law or raise a standard above all circumstances, permanent against all influence. He is content to be the creature of his place, and to represent it by his spoken and written word. He takes the same ground with the savage, who does not hesitate to say of the product of a civilization on which he could not stand, "It is bad," or "It is good."

The value of such comments is merely reflex. They characterize the critic. They give an idea of certain influences on a certain act of men in a certain time or place. Their absolute, essential value is nothing. The long review, the eloquent article by the man of the nineteenth century are of no value by themselves considered, but only as samples of their kind. The writers were content to tell what they felt, to praise or to denounce without needing to convince us or themselves. They sought not the divine truths of philosophy, and she proffers them not, if unsought.

Then there are the apprehensive. These can go out of themselves and enter fully into a foreign existence. They breathe its life; they live in its law; they tell what it meant, and why it so expressed its meaning. They reproduce the work of which they speak, and make it better known to us in so far as two statements are better than one. There are beautiful specimens in this kind. They are pleasing to us as bearing witness of the genial sympathies of nature. They have the ready grace of love with somewhat of the dignity of disinterested friendship. They sometimes give more pleasure than the original production of which they treat, as melodies will sometimes ring sweetlier in the echo. Besides there is a peculiar pleasure in a true response; it is the assurance of equipoise in the universe. These, if not true critics, come nearer the standard than the subjective class, and the value of their work is ideal as well as historical.

Then there are the comprehensive, who must also be apprehensive. They enter into the nature of another being and judge his work by its own law. But having done so, having ascertained his design and the degree of his success in fulfilling it, thus measuring his judgment, his energy, and skill, they do also know how to put that aim in its place, and how to estimate its relations. And this the critic can only do who perceives the analogies of the universe, and how they are regulated by an absolute, invariable principle. He can see how far that work expresses this principle as well as how far it is excellent in its details. Sustained by a principle, such as can be girt within no rule, no formula, he can walk around the work, he can stand above it, he can uplift it and try its weight. Finally he is worthy to judge it.

Critics are poets cut down, says someone by way of jeer; but in truth they are men with the poetical temperament to apprehend, with the philosophical tendency to investigate. The maker is divine; the critic sees this divine, but brings it down to humanity by the analytic process. The critic is the historian who records the order of creation. In vain for the maker, who knows without learning it, but not in vain for the mind of his race.

The critic is beneath the maker, but is his needed friend. What tongue could speak but to an intelligent ear, and every noble work demands its critic. The richer the work, the more severe would be its critic; the larger its scope, the more comprehensive must be his power of scrutiny. The critic is not a base caviller, but the younger brother of genius. Next to invention is the power of interpreting invention; next to beauty, the power of appreciating beauty.

And of making others appreciate it; for the universe is a scale of infinite gradation, and below the very highest, every step is explanation down to the lowest. Religion, in the two modulations of poetry and music, descends through an infinity of waves to the lowest abysses of human nature. Nature is the literature and art of the divine mind; human literature and art the criticism on that; and they, too, find their criticism within their own sphere.

The critic, then, should be not merely a poet, not merely a philosopher, not merely an observer, but tempered of all three. If he criticize the poem, he must want nothing of what constitutes the poet, except the power of creating forms and speaking in music. He must have as good an eye and as fine a sense; but if he had as fine an organ for expression also, he would make the poem instead of judging it. He must be inspired by the philosopher's spirit of inquiry and need of generalization, but he must not be constrained by the hard cemented masonry of method to which philosophers are prone. And he must have the organic acuteness of the observer, with a love of ideal perfection which forbids him to be content with mere beauty of details in the work or the comment upon the work.

There are persons who maintain that there is no legitimate criticism except the reproductive; that we have only to say what the work is or is to us, never what it is not. But the moment we look for a principle, we feel the need of a criterion, of a standard; and then we say what the work is *not,* as well as what it *is;* and this is as healthy though not as grateful and gracious an operation of the mind as the other. We do not seek to degrade but to classify an object by stating what it is not. We detach the part from the whole, lest it stand between us and the whole. When we have ascertained in what degree it manifests the whole, we may safely restore it to its place and love or admire it there ever after.

The use of criticism in periodical writing is to sift, not to stamp, a work. Yet should they not be "sieves and drainers for the use of luxurious readers," but for the use of earnest inquirers, giving voice and being to their objections, as well as stimulus to their sympathies. But the critic must not be an infallible adviser to his reader. He must not tell him what books are not worth reading, or what must be thought of them when read, but what he read in them. Woe to that coterie where some critic sits despotic, entrenched behind the infallible "We." Woe to that oracle who has infused such soft sleepiness, such a gentle dullness into his atmosphere that when he opes his lips no dog will bark. It is this attempt at dictatorship in the reviewers and the indolent acquiescence of their readers that has brought them into disrepute. With such fairness did they make out their statements, with such dignity did they utter their verdicts that the poor reader grew all too submissive. He learned his lesson with such docility that the greater part of what will be said at any public or private meeting can be foretold by anyone who has read the leading periodical works for twenty years back. Scholars sneer at and would fain dispense with them altogether; and the public, grown lazy and helpless

by this constant use of props and stays, can now scarce
brace itself even to get through a magazine article, but reads
in the daily paper laid beside the breakfast plate a short
notice of the last number of the long established and popular review, and thereupon passes its judgment and is content.

Then the partisan spirit of many of these journals has
made it unsafe to rely upon them as guidebooks and ex-
purgatory indexes. They could not be content merely to stimulate and suggest thought, they have at last become powerless
to supersede it.

From these causes and causes like these, the journals have
lost much of their influence. There is a languid feeling about
them, an inclination to suspect the justice of their verdicts,
the value of their criticisms. But their golden age cannot
be quite passed. They afford too convenient a vehicle for the
transmission of knowledge; they are too natural a feature of
our time to have done all their work yet. Surely they may
be redeemed from their abuses, they may be turned to their
true uses. But how?

It were easy to say what they should *not* do. They should
not have an object to carry or a cause to advocate which
obliges them either to reject all writings which wear the distinctive traits of individual life, or to file away what does not
suit them, till the essay, made true to their design, is made
false to the mind of the writer. An external consistency is
thus produced at the expense of all salient thought, all
genuine emotion of life, in short, and living influences. Their
purpose may be of value, but by such means was no valuable
purpose ever furthered long. There are those who have with
the best intention pursued this system of trimming and adaptation, and thought it well and best to

Deceive their country for their country's good.

But their country cannot long be so governed. It misses
the pure, the full tone of truth; it perceives that the voice
is modulated to coax, to persuade, and it turns from the
judicious man of the world, calculating the effect to be produced by each of his smooth sentences, to some earnest voice
which is uttering thoughts, crude, rash, ill-arranged it may
be, but true to one human breast, and uttered in full faith,
that the God of Truth will guide them aright.

And here, it seems to me, has been the greatest mistake in the conduct of these journals. A smooth monotony has been attained, a uniformity of tone, so that from the title of a journal you can infer the tenor of all its chapters. But nature is ever various, ever new, and so should be her daughters, art and literature. We do not want merely a polite response to what we thought before, but by the freshness of thought in other minds to have new thought awakened in our own. We do not want stores of information only, but to be roused to digest these into knowledge. Able and experienced men write for us, and we would know what they think, as they think it not for us but for themselves. We would live with them, rather than be taught by them how to live; we would catch the contagion of their mental activity, rather than have them direct us how to regulate our own. In books, in reviews, in the senate, in the pulpit, we wish to meet thinking men, not schoolmasters or pleaders. We wish that they should do full justice to their own view, but also that they should be frank with us, and, if now our superiors, treat us as if we might sometime rise to be their equals. It is this true manliness, this firmness in his own position, and this power of appreciating the position of others that alone can make the critic our companion and friend. We would converse with him, secure that he will tell us all his thought and speak as man to man. But if he adapts his work to us, if he stifles what is distinctively his, if he shows himself either arrogant or mean, or, above all, if he wants faith in the healthy action of free thought and the safety of pure motive, we will not talk with him for we cannot confide in him. We will go to the critic who trusts genius and trusts us, who knows that all good writing must be spontaneous, and who will write out the bill of fare for the public as he reads it for himself—

> Forgetting vulgar rules, with spirit free
> To judge each author by his own intent,
> Nor think one standard for all minds is meant.

Such an one will not disturb us with personalities, with sectarian prejudices, or an undue vehemence in favor of petty plans or temporary objects. Neither will he disgust us by smooth obsequious flatteries and an inexpressive, lifeless gentleness. He will be free and make free from the mechanical and distorting influences we hear complained of on every side. He will teach us to love wisely what we before loved well, for he knows the difference between censoriousness and discernment, infatuation and reverence, and, while delighting in the genial melodies of Pan, can perceive, should Apollo bring his lyre into audience, that there may be strains more divine than those of his native groves.

John Sullivan Dwight

THE RELIGION OF BEAUTY*
(1840)

The devout mind is a lover of nature. Where there is
beauty it feels at home. It has not then to shut the windows
of the senses and take refuge from the world within its own
thoughts to find eternal life. Beauty never limits us, never
degrades us. We are free spirits when with nature. The outward scenery of our life, when we feel it to be beautiful,
is always commensurate with the grandeur of our inward
ideal aspiration; it reflects encouragingly the heart's highest,
brightest dreams; it does not contradict the soul's convictions of a higher life; it tells us that we are safe in believing
the thought which to us seems noblest. If we have no sense
of beauty, the world is nothing more than a place to keep
us in. But when the skies and woods reveal their loveliness,
then nature seems a glorious picture of which our own inmost soul is the painter, and our own loves and longings
the subject. It is the apt accompaniment to the silent song
of the beholder's heart.

The greatest blessing which could be bestowed on the
weary multitude would be to give them the sense of beauty,
to open their eyes for them, and let them see how richly we
are here surrounded, what a glorious temple we inhabit,
how every part of it is eloquent of God. The love of nature
grows with the growth of the soul. Religion makes man
sensible to beauty, and beauty in its turn disposes to religion. Beauty is the revelation of the soul to the senses.
In all this outward beauty—these soft swells and curves of
the landscape which seem to be the earth's smile; this inexhaustible variety of form and colors and motion, not
promiscuous, but woven together in as natural a harmony
as the thoughts in a poem; this mysterious hieroglyphic of
the flowers; this running alphabet of tangled vine and bend-

* From *The Dial,* I (July 1840).

ing grass studded with golden paints; this all-embracing perspective of distance rounding altogether into one rainbow-colored sphere, so perfect that the senses and the soul roam abroad over it unsated, feeling the presence and perfection of the whole in each part; this perfect accord of sights, sounds, motions, and fragrance, all tuned to one harmony, out of which run melodies inexhaustible of every mood and measure—in all this, man first feels that God is without him as well as within him, that nature too is holy; and can he bear to find himself the sole exception? . . .

I hold, then, that without a cultivation of the sense of beauty, chiefly to be drunken from the open fountains of nature, there can be no healthy and sound moral development. The man so educated lacks something most essential. He is one-sided, not of a piece with nature; and however correct, however much master of himself, he will be uninteresting, unencouraging, and uninviting. To the student of ancient history, the warm-hearted, graceful Greek, all alive to nature, who made beauty almost his religion, is a more refreshing object than the cold, formal Jew. And here around us, resist it as we may, our hearts are always drawn toward the open, graceful children of impulse, in preference to the stiff, insensible patterns of virtue. The latter may be very unexceptionable, but at the same time very unreal. The former, though purposeless and careless they play through life, yet have trusted themselves to nature and been ravished by her beauty, and nature will not let them become very bad.

Consider a few of the practical effects upon the whole character of a growing love of beauty in the young mind.

It disposes to order. It gives birth in the mind to an instinct of propriety. It suggests imperceptibly, it inclines gently, but irresistibly, to the fit action, to the word in season. The beauty which we see and feel plants its seeds in us. Gazing with delight on nature, our will imperceptibly becomes attuned to the same harmony. The sense of beauty is attended with a certain reverence; we dare not mar what looks so perfect. This sense, too, has a something like conscience contained in it; we feel bound to do and be ourselves something worthy of the beauty we are permitted to admire. This feeling, while it makes alive and quickens, yet is eminently conservative, in the best sense. He who has it is always interested on the side of order, and of all dear and hallowed associations. He who wants it is as destructive as a Goth. The presence of beauty, like that of nature, as soon as we feel it at all, overcomes us with respect and a certain sensitive dread of all violence, mischief, or discord. The beautiful ideal piece of architecture bears no mark of wanton penknife. The handsome schoolroom makes the children neat. The instinct of obedience, of conciliation, of decorum, reverence, and harmony flows into the soul with beauty. The calm spirit of the landscape takes possession of the humble yet soul-exalted admirer. Its harmony compels the jangling chords within himself into smoother undulations. Therefore "walk out," like Isaac, "at even-tide to meditate," and let nature with her divine stillness take possession of thee. She shall give thee back to thyself better, more spiritual, more sensible of thy relationship with all things, and that in wronging any, thou but woundest thyself.

Another grace of character which the sense of beauty gives the mind is freedom—the freedom of fond obedience, not of loose desire. The man whose eyes and soul are open to the beauty there is around him, sees everywhere encouragement. To him the touch of nature's hand is warm and genial. The air does not seem to pinch him, as it does most narrow-minded ones who can see no good in anything but gain, to whose utilitarian vision most that is natural looks hostile. He is not contracted into himself by cautious fear and suspicion, afraid to let his words flow freely, or his face relax in confidence, or his limbs move gracefully, or his actions come out whole and hearty. He trusts nature, for he has kissed her loveliness; he knows that she smiles encouragement to him. Now think what it is that makes virtue so much shunned. Partly, our depravity, if you please. But partly, also, her numerous ungraceful specimens. For it is the instinctive expectation of all minds that what is excellent shall also be beautiful, lovely, natural, and free. Most of the piety we see about us is more or less the product of restraint and fear. It stands there in spectral contrast with nature. Approve it we may, but we cannot love it. It does not bear the divine stamp; it chills, not converts. The love of nature makes in us an ideal of moral beauty, of an elevation of character which shall look free and lovely, something that shall take its place naturally and as matter of course in the center of nature, as the life of Jesus did.

Again, the love of beauty awakens higher aspirations in us. He who has felt the beauty of a summer like this has drunk in an infinite restlessness, a yearning to be perfect, and by obedience free. He can never more rest contented with what he is. And here is the place to attempt some account of the true significance of beauty, and of what is its office to the soul.

Beauty always suggests the thought of the perfect. The smallest beautiful object is as infinite as the whole world of stars above us. So we feel it. Everything beautiful is emblematic of something spiritual. Itself limited, its meanings and suggestions are infinite. In it we seem to see all in one. Each beautiful thing, each dewdrop, each leaf, each true work of painter's, poet's, or musician's art, seems an epitome of the creation. Is it not God revealed through the senses? Is not every beautiful thing a divine hint thrown out to us? Does not the soul begin to dream of its own boundless capacities when it has felt beauty? Does not immortality then, for the first time, cease to be a name, a doctrine, and become a present experience? When the leaves fall in autumn, they turn golden as they drop. The cold winds tell us of coming winter and death, but they tell it in music. All is significant of decay, but the deep, still, harmonious beauty surpasses all felt in summer or spring before. We look on it, and feel that it cannot die. The Eternal speaks to us from the midst of decay. We feel a melancholy, but it is a sweet, religious melancholy, lifting us in imagination above death— since above the grave of the summer so much real beauty lingers.

The beautiful, then, is the spiritual aspect of nature. By cherishing a delicate sensibility to it, we make nature preach us a constant lesson of faith; we find all around an illustration of the life of the spirit. We surround ourselves with a constant cheerful exhortation to duty. We render duty lovely and inviting. We find the soul's deep inexpressible thoughts written around us in the skies, the far blue hills, and swelling waters.

But then to this desirable result one stern condition must be observed. If the sense of beauty disposes to purity of heart, so equally purity of heart is all that can keep the sense of beauty open. All influences work mutually. "One hand must wash the other," said the poet. The world is loveliest to him who looks out on it through pure eyes.

Bronson Alcott

ORPHIC SAYINGS (1840)*

Thou art, my heart, a soul-flower, facing ever and following the motions of thy sun, opening thyself to her vivifying
ray, and pleading thy affinity with the celestial orbs. Thou
dost

the livelong day
Dial on time thine own eternity.

Enthusiasm

Believe, youth, that your heart is an oracle; trust her
instinctive auguries, obey her divine leadings; nor listen too
fondly to the uncertain echoes of your head. The heart is
the prophet of your soul, and ever fulfills her prophecies;
reason is her historian; but for the prophecy the history
would not be. Great is the heart: cherish her; she is big
with the future, she forebodes renovations. Let the flame
of enthusiasm fire always your bosom. Enthusiasm is the
glory and hope of the world. It is the life of sanctity and
genius; it has wrought all miracles since the beginning of
time.

Vocation

Engage in nothing that cripples or degrades you. Your
first duty is self-culture, self-exaltation: you may not violate this high trust. Your self is sacred, profane it not. Forge

* From *The Dial,* I (July 1840).

no chains wherewith to shackle your own members. Either subordinate your vocation to your life, or quit it forever: it is not for you; it is condemnation of your own soul. Your influence on others is commensurate with the strength that you have found in yourself. First cast the demons from your own bosom, and then shall your word exorcise them from the hearts of others.

Spiritualism

Piety is not scientific, yet embosoms the facts that reason develops in scientific order to the understanding. Religion, being a sentiment, is science yet in synthetic relations; truth yet undetached from love; thought not yet several from action. For every fact that eludes the analysis of reason, conscience affirms its root in the supernatural. Every synthetic fact is supernatural and miraculous. Analysis by detecting its law resolves it into science, and renders it a fact of the understanding. Divinely seen, natural facts are symbols of spiritual laws. Miracles are of the heart, not of the head; indigenous to the soul, not freaks of nature, not growths of history. God, man, nature are miracles.

Aspiration

The insatiableness of her desires is an augury of the soul's eternity. Yearning for satisfaction, yet ever balked of it from temporal things, she still prosecutes her search for it, and her faith remains unshaken amidst constant disappointments. She would breathe life, organize light; her hope is eternal, a never-ending, still-beginning quest of the Godhead in her own bosom, a perpetual effort to actualize her divinity in time. Intact, aspirant, she feels the appulses of both spiritual and material things; she would appropriate the realm she inherits by virtue of her incarnation; infinite appetencies direct all her members on finite things; her vague strivings and Cyclopean motions confess an aim beyond the confines of transitory natures; she is quivered with heavenly desires; her quarry is above the stars; her arrows are snatched from the armory of heaven.

Apotheosis

Every soul feels at times her own possibility of becoming a God; she cannot rest in the human, she aspires after the Godlike. This instinctive tendency is an authentic augury of its own fulfillment. Men shall become gods. Every act of admiration, prayer, praise, worship, desire, hope implies and predicts the future apotheosis of the soul.

Discontent

All life is eternal; there is none other; and all unrest is but the struggle of the soul to reassure herself of her inborn immortality, to recover her lost intuition of the same, by reason of her descent amidst the lusts and worship of the idols of flesh and sense. Her discomfort reveals her lapse from innocence, her loss of the divine presence and favor. Fidelity alone shall instaurate the godhead in her bosom.

Temptation

Greater is he who is above temptation than he who, being tempted, overcomes. The latter but regains the state from which the former has not fallen. He who is tempted has sinned; temptation is impossible to the holy.

Choice

Choice implies apostasy. The pure, unfallen soul is above choice. Her life is unbroken, synthetic; she is a law to herself, and finds no lusts in her members warring against the instincts of conscience. Sinners choose; saints act from instinct and intuition: there is no parley of alien forces in their being.

Instinct and Reason

Innocent, the soul is quick with instincts of unerring aim; then she knows by intuition what lapsed reason defines by laborious inference; her appetites and affections are direct and trustworthy. Reason is the left hand of instinct; it is tardy, awkward, but the right is ready and dexterous. By reasoning the soul strives to recover her lost intuitions, groping amidst the obscure darkness of sense, by means of the fingers of logic, for treasures present always and available to the eye of conscience. Sinners must need reason; saints behold.

Identity and Diversity

It is the perpetual effort of conscience to divorce the soul from the dominion of sense; to nullify the dualities of the apparent, and restore the intuition of the real. The soul makes a double statement of all her facts: to conscience and sense; reason mediates between the two. Yet though double to sense, she remains single and one in herself; one in conscience, many in understanding; one in life, diverse in function and number. Sense, in its infirmity, breaks this unity to apprehend in part what it cannot grasp at once. Understanding notes diversity; conscience alone divines unity, and integrates all experience in identity of spirit. Number is predicable of body alone, not of spirit.

Conscience

Ever present, potent, vigilant in the breast of man, there is that which never became a party in his guilt, never consented to a wrong deed nor performed one, but holds itself above all sin, impeccable, immaculate, immutable, the deity of the heart, the conscience of the soul, the oracle and interpreter, the judge and executor of the divine law.

Action

Action translates death into life, fable into verity, speculation into experience, freeing man from the sorceries of tradition and the torpor of habit. The eternal Scripture is thus expurgated of the falsehoods interpolated into it by the supineness of the ages. Action mediates between conscience and sense; it is the gospel of the understanding.

Originality

Most men are on the ebb; but now and then a man comes riding down sublimely in high hope from God on the flood tide of the soul, as she sets into the coasts of time, submerging old landmarks, and laying waste the labors of centuries. A new man wears channels broad and deep into the banks of the ages; he washes away ancient boundaries, and sets afloat institutions, creeds, usages, which clog the everflowing present, stranding them on the shores of the past. Such deluge is the harbinger of a new world, a renovated age. Hope builds an ark; the dove broods over the assuaged waters; the bow of promise gilds the east; the world is again repeopled and replanted. Yet the sons of genius alone venture into the ark, while most pass the rather down the sluggish stream of usage into the turbid pool of oblivion. Thitherward the retreating tide rolls, and wafted by the gales of inglorious ease, or urged by the winds of passion, they glide down the Lethean waters, and are not. Only the noble and heroic outlive in time their exit from it.

Valor

The world, the state, the church, stand in awe of a man of probity and valor. He threatens their order and perpetuity; an unknown might slumbers in him; he is an augury of revolutions. Out of the invisible God, he comes to abide awhile amongst men; yet neither men nor time shall remain as at his advent. He is a creative element, and revises men, times, life itself. A new world pre-exists in his ideal. He overlives, outlives, eternizes the ages, and reports to all men the will of the divinity whom he serves.

Character

Character is the only legitimate institution, the only regal influence. Its power is infinite. Safe in the citadel of his own integrity, principalities, powers, hierarchies, states, capitulate to the man of character at last. It is the temple which the soul builds to herself, within whose fanes genius and sanctity worship, while the kneeling ages bend around them in admiration and love.

Criticism

To just criticism unity of mind is essential. The critic must not esteem difference as real as sameness and as permanent in the facts of nature. This tendency is fatal to all sound and final thinking; it never penetrates to the roots of things. All creative minds have been inspired and guided by the law of unity; their problem is ever to pierce the coarse and superficial rind of diversity, and discover the unity in whose core is the heart and seed of all things.

Calculus

We need what genius is unconsciously seeking and, by some daring generalization of the universe, shall assuredly discover, a spiritual calculus, a novum organon, whereby nature shall be divined in the soul, the soul in God, matter in spirit, polarity resolved into unity; and that power which pulsates in all life, animates and builds all organizations, shall manifest itself as one universal deific energy, present alike at the outskirts and center of the universe whose center and circumference are one; omniscient, omnipotent, self-subsisting, uncontained, yet containing all things in the unbroken synthesis of its being.

Generation and Corruption

The soul decomposes the substances of nature in the reverse order of their composition: read this backward for the natural history of their genesis and growth. Generation and corruption are polar or adverse facts. The tree first dies at the top; to raze the house we first remove the tiling. The decomposition and analysis are from without, according to the order of sense, not of the soul. All investigations of nature must be analytic through the order of decay. Science begins and ends in death; poesy in life; philosophy in organization; art in creation.

Each and All

Life eludes all scientific analysis. Each organ and function is modified in substance and varied in effect by the subtle energy which pulsates throughout the whole economy of things, spiritual and corporeal. The each is instinct with the all; the all unfolds and reappears in each. Spirit is all in all. God, man, nature are a divine synthesis whose parts it is impiety to sunder. Genius must preside devoutly over all investigations, or analysis, with her murderous knife, will seek impiously to probe the vitals of being.

Nature

Nature seems remote and detached because the soul surveys her by means of the extremest senses, imposing on herself the notion of difference and remoteness through their predominance, and thereby losing that of her own oneness with it. Yet nature is not separate from me; she is mine alike with my body; and in moments of true life, I feel my identity with her; I breathe, pulsate, feel, think, will, through her members, and know of no duality of being. It is in such moods of soul that prophetic visions are beheld, and evangels published for the joy and hope of mankind.

Flux

Solidity is an illusion of the senses. To faith, nothing is solid; the nature of the soul renders such fact impossible. Modern chemistry demonstrates that nine-tenths of the human body are fluid, and substances of inferior order in lesser proportion. Matter is ever pervaded and agitated by the omnipresent soul. All things are instinct with spirit.

Embryon

Man is a rudiment and embryon of God: eternity shall develop in him the divine image.

Organization

Possibly organization is no necessary function or mode of spiritual being. The time may come, in the endless career of the soul, when the facts of incarnation, birth, death, descent into matter and ascension from it shall comprise no part of her history; when she herself shall survey this human life with emotions akin to those of the naturalist on examining the relics of extinct races of beings; when mounds, sepulchers, monuments, epitaphs shall serve but as memoirs of a past state of existence, a reminiscence of one metempsychosis of her life in time.

Spirit and Matter

Divined aright, there is nothing purely organic; all things are vital and inorganic. The microscope is developing this sublime fact. Sense looking at the historic surface beholds what it deems matter, yet is but spirit in fusion, fluent, pervaded by her own immanent vitality and trembling to organize itself. Neither matter nor death are possible; what seem matter and death are sensuous impressions which, in our sanest moments, the authentic instincts contradict. The sensible world is spirit in magnitude, outspread before the senses for their analysis, but whose synthesis is the soul herself, whose prothesis is God. Matter is but the confine of spirit limning her to sense.

Life

Life, in its initial state, is synthetic; then feeling, thought, action are one and indivisible; love is its manifestation. Childhood and woman are samples and instances. But thought disintegrates and breaks this unity of soul; action alone restores it. Action is composition; thought decomposition. Deeds executed in love are graceful, harmonious, entire; enacted from thought merely, they are awkward, dissonant, incomplete—a manufacture, not creations, not works of genius.

Beauty

All departures from perfect beauty are degradations of the divine image. God is the one type which the soul strives to incarnate in all organizations. Varieties are historical: the one form embosoms all forms, all having a common likeness at the base of difference. Human heads are images, more or less perfect, of the soul's or God's head. But the divine features do not fix in flesh, in the coarse and brittle clay. Beauty is fluent; art of highest order represents her always in flux, giving fluency and motion to bodies solid and immovable to sense. The line of beauty symbolizes motion.

Prometheus

Know, O man, that your soul is the Prometheus who, receiving the divine fires, builds up this majestic statue of clay, and molds it in the deific image, the pride of gods, the model and analogon of all forms. He chiseled that god-like brow, arched those mystic temples from whose fanes she herself looks forth, formed that miraculous globe above, and planted that sylvan grove below; graved those massive blades yoked in armed powers; carved that heaven-containing bosom; wreathed those puissant thighs, and hewed those stable columns, diffusing over all the grandeur, the grace of his own divine lineaments, and delighting in this cunning work of his hand. Mar not its beauty, spoil not its symmetry by the deforming lines of lust and sin, dethroning the divinity incarnated therein, and transforming yourself into the satyr and the beast.

Frederic Henry Hedge

QUESTIONS* *(1841)*

Hath this world without me wrought,
Other substance than my thought?
Lives it by my sense alone,
Or by essence of its own?
Will its life, with mine begun,
Cease to be when that is done,
Or another consciousness
With the self-same forms impress?

Doth yon fireball, poised in air,
Hang by my permission there?
Are the clouds that wander by,
But the offspring of mine eye,
Born with every glance I cast,
Perishing when that is past?
And those thousand, thousand eyes,
Scattered through the twinkling skies,
Do they draw their life from mine,
Or, of their own beauty shine?

Now I close my eyes, my ears,
And creation disappears;
Yet if I but speak the word,
All creation is restored.
Or—more wonderful—within,
New creations do begin;
Hues more bright and forms more rare,
Than reality doth wear,
Flash across my inward sense,
Born of the mind's omnipotence.

Soul! that all informest, say!

* From *The Dial*, I (Jan. 1841).

Shall these glories pass away?
Will those planets cease to blaze,
When these eyes no longer gaze?
And the life of things be o'er,
When these pulses beat no more?

Thought! that in me works and lives,
Life to all things living gives,
Art thou not thyself, perchance,
But the universe in trance?
A reflection inly flung
By that world thou fanciedst sprung
From thyself—thyself a dream—
Of the world's thinking thou the theme.

Be it thus, or be thy birth
From a source above the earth—
Be thou matter, be thou mind,
In thee alone myself I find,
And through thee alone, for me,
Hath this world reality.
Therefore, in thee will I live,
To thee all myself will give,
Losing still that I may find
This bounded self in boundless Mind.

Theodore Parker

GERMAN LITERATURE* (1841)

Opinions are divided respecting German literature. If we are to believe what is currently reported, and generally credited, there is, somewhere in New England, a faction of discontented men and maidens, who have conspired to love everything Teutonic, from Dutch skates to German infidelity. It is supposed, at least asserted, that these misguided persons would fain banish all other literature clean out of space; or, at the very least, would give it precedence of all other letters, ancient or modern. Whatever is German, they admire; philosophy, dramas, theology, novels, old ballads, and modern sonnets, histories, and dissertations, and sermons; but above all, the immoral and irreligious writings which it is supposed the Germans are chiefly engaged in writing, with the generous intention of corrupting the youth of the world, restoring the worship of Priapus, or Pan, or the Pope—it is not decided which is to receive the honor of universal homage—and thus gradually preparing for the Kingdom of Misrule, and the dominion of chaos and "most ancient night." It is often charitably taken for granted, that the lovers of German works on philosophy and art amongst us are moved thereto either by a disinterested love of whatever is German, or else, which is the more likely, by a disinterested love of evil and the instigation of the devil, who, it is gravely said, has actually inspired several of the most esteemed writers of that nation. This German epidemic, we are told, extends very wide. It has entered the boarding schools for young misses of either sex, and committed the most frightful ravages therein. We have been apprised that it has sometimes seized upon a college, nay, on universities,

* From *The Dial*, I (Jan. 1841).

and both the faculty and the corporation have exhibited symptoms of the fatal disease. Colleges, did we say?

No place is sacred, not the Church is free.

It has attacked clergymen, in silk and in lawn. The doctors of divinity fall before it. It is thought, that

> Fever and ague, jaundice and catarrh,
> The grim-looked tyrant's heavy horse of war;
> And apoplexies, those light troops of death,
> That use small ceremony with our breath,

are all nothing to the German epidemic. We meet men with umbrellas and overshoes, men "shawled to the teeth," and suppose they are prudent persons who have put on armor against this subtle foe. Histories of this plague, as of the cholera, have been written; the public has often been called to defend itself from the enemy, and quarantine regulations are put in force against all suspected of the infection. In short, the prudent men of the land, men wise to foresee, and curious to prevent evil, have not failed to advise the public from time to time of the danger that is imminent, and to recommend certain talismans as effectual safeguards. We think a copy of the "Westminster Catechism," or the "Confessions of Faith adopted by the Council of Trent," or the "Athanasian Creed," perhaps, if hung about the neck, and worn next the skin, might save little children, and perhaps girls nearly grown up, especially if they read these amulets every morning, fasting. . . .

But there is one peculiar charm in this literature, quite unequaled, we think, in modern days, that is, the *religious* character of German works. We know it is often said the Germans are licentious, immoral in all ways, and above all men—not the old giants excepted—are haters of religion. One would fancy Mezentius or Goliath was the archetype of the nation. We say it advisedly that this is, in our opinion, the most religious literature the world has seen since the palmy days of Greek writing, when the religious spirit seemed fresh and warm, coming into life, and playing grateful with the bland celestial light reflected from each flower cup and passing cloud, and received direct and straightway from the source of all. It stands an unconscious witness to

the profound piety of the German heart. We had almost
said it was the only Christian national literature the world
has ever seen. Certainly, to our judgment, the literature of
Old England in her best days was less religious in thought
and feeling as it was less beautiful in its form, and less
simple in its quiet, loving holiness than this spontaneous
and multiform expression of the German soul. But we speak
not for others; let each drink of "that spiritual rock" where
the water is most salubrious to him. But we do not say that
German literature comprises no works decidedly immoral
and irreligious. Certainly we have read such, but they are
rare, while almost every book not entirely scientific and
technical breathes a religious spirit. You meet this coming
unobtrusively upon you where you least of all expect it. We
do not say that the idea of a Christian literature is realized
in Germany, or likely to be realized. No, the farthest from
it possible. No nation has yet dreamed of realizing it. Nor
can this be done, until Christianity penetrates the heart of
the nations, and brings all into subjection to the spirit of
life. The Christianity of the world is yet but a baptized
heathenism, so literature is yet heathen and profane. We
dare not think, lest we think against our faith. As if truth
were hostile to faith, and God's house were divided against
itself. The Greek literature represents the Greek religion; its
ideal and its practical side. But all the literature of all Christian nations taken together does not represent the true Christian religion, only that fraction of it these nations could
translate into their experience. Hence, we have as yet only
the cradle song of Christianity, and its nursery rhymes. The
same holds true in art—painting, sculpture, and architecture.
Hitherto it is only the church militant, not the church triumphant, that has been represented. A Gothic cathedral gives
you the aspiration, not the attainment, the resting in the fulness of God, which is the end of Christianity. We have
Magdalens, Madonnas, saints, emaciated almost to anatomies,
with most rueful visage, and traditional faces of the Saviour.
These, however, express the penitence, the wailing of the
world lying in darkness, rather than the light of the nations.
The *Son of Man* risen from the grave is yet lacking in art.
The Christian Prometheus, or Apollo, is not yet; still less
the triple graces, and the Olympian Jove of Christianity.
What is Saint Peter's to the Parthenon, considered as symbols of the two religions? The same deficiency prevails in
literature. We have inherited much from the heathen, and

so Christianity, becoming the residuary legatee of deceased religions, has earned but little for itself. History has not yet been written in the spirit of the Christian scheme; as a friend says, hitherto it has been the "history of elder brothers." Christianity would write of the whole family. The great Christian poem, the tragedy of mankind, has not yet been conceived. A Christian philosophy founded on an exhaustive analysis of man is among the things that are distant. The true religion has not yet done its work in the heart of the nations. How, then, can it reach their literature, their arts, their society, which come from the nation's heart? Christianity is still in the manger, wrapped in swaddling bands and unable to move its limbs. Its Jewish parent watches fearful, with a pondering heart. The shepherds that honor the newborn are Jewish still, dripping as yet with the dews of ancient night. The heathen magicians have come up to worship, guided by the star of truth which goes before all simple hearts and lighteth every man that cometh into the world. But they are heathen even now. They can only offer "gold, and frankincense, and myrrh." They do not give their mind, and still less their heart. The celestial child is still surrounded by the oxen that slumber in their stalls, or wake to blame the light that prevents their animal repose. The Herod of superstition is troubled, and his city with him. Alarmed at the new tidings, he gathers together his mighty men, his chief priests and scribes, to take counsel of his twin prophets, the Flesh and the Devil, and while he pretends to seek only to worship, he would gladly slay the young child that is born King of the world. But Christianity will yet grow up to manhood and escape the guardianship of traditions to do the work God has chosen. Then, and not till then, will the gospel of beautiful souls, fair as the light and "terrible as an army with banners," be written in the literature, arts, society, and life of the world. Now when we say that German literature is religious above all others, we mean that it comes nearer than any other to the Christian ideal of literary art. Certainly it by no means reaches the mark. . . .

Christopher Pearse Cranch

GLIMMERINGS* (1841)

What is there in the full moon that it should disturb the soul with these thousand old dim recollections? Why should her long shadows point ever to the past? Why should they waken melancholy? Childhood and youth, romance and love, sad and merry hours—ye are all out there in the moonlight! Ye have gone out from my soul, and hang all around me in this silvered darkness. Mysterious power of association! How strangely nature mirrors the soul! How her phases reflect back, and give us again our long-lost dreams! He who has never hung with fond sadness on the wondrous moon has never loved.

All human knowledge is but approximation. Man can never compass the infinite, any more than he can inhale the whole atmosphere. Yet what he does know mirrors the infinite. Every drop of night-dew reflects the whole star-firmament; every pure night-thought hath a glimmer of the all-true within its bosom. All is prophesied in each. Every part is an evangel inspired by the whole. Each opening flower is a Messiah of the uncontained dispensation of beauty; each visitation of high thought a herald who proclaims the coming of the kingdom of truth; and each virtuous deed a voice crying in the wilderness, "Make straight the pathway of our God."

What should we be but for the gentle teachings of this green summertime? I feel that I am at God's school when I sit on the grass under these elms and look about me and think upon Nature's impersonality. Man has not broken into the charmed circle in any way. Least of all does Nature imitate the obtrusiveness of our moral codes. She reads her mysterious fables, but we are not pestered by the word

* From *The Dial*, I (Jan. 1841).

"application" at the bottom of the picture. What lesson, before another, shall she point us to, who is thus infinitely wealthy? Generously she lets the soul feed its own instincts, grazing where it will in her green pastures, knowing that if we love her wisely, we cannot be poisoned or starved in her company. Thus she feeds us as she does the bee and butterfly, with many flowers and odors, trusting that like theirs, our appropriative instincts will be unfolded harmoniously, and that we shall come evermore to *her* law by coming to ourselves.

And here come the bee and the butterfly themselves to tell us about it. But, as I said, they obtrude not their precepts upon us. Nay, they seem rather shy than not. And yet these two insects have been, unconsciously to themselves and to man, preachers and parable-bringers since thought began.

So come here, thou little citizen of this green republic, and tell us more than the dull books, which prate as if they knew all about thee. We may fling aside Kirby and Spence, now *thou* art here. Come, leave that clover-blossom awhile, where thou art rolling thyself about and packing away thy nectar; cease that monotonous talking to thyself, that hurried merchant-like air; leave dunning the poor, drooping, insolvent field-flowers, for they will pay thee one day; come out of the sunshine, thou hot, petulant, systematic little worker, and tell us why thou hast ever been a stirrer of deep thoughts and resolves to the earnest soul! And thou, my lady butterfly—gay dancer in the breeze, living air-flower, silent ever, but not from thought, making thy demure morning calls on the very flowers at whose doors the disappointed bee has been grumbling—who made thee a proverb and a perpetual homily in the courts of kings, or saw thee flitting along in thy relations of the street or the ballroom? Did some poet invent these correspondences, or stand they not as they have ever stood, written in the double-leaved book of the Most High?

For indeed God writes all his decrees dually. They are simultaneously proclaimed at the two open gates of His city to the inhabitants of the suburbs—which open gates are nature and the soul. They who hear one proclamation rejoice, but feebly. But they who hear both mingle faith and wisdom with their joy. The gliding river tells me of this fleeting time; the sunrise, of the appearing of God's truth; the fragrance of the fields, going forever silently up to heaven, teaches me how to pray without ceasing; the young green spring says more to me of the new birth than libraries of sermons—and so all the world over, and from the beginning of time, has nature been a scroll whose letters and pages are nought till the soul's language, in which it is written, be mastered.

I am no Swedenborgian, nor must the following lines be bound down to a dogmatic meaning; yet I will confess that they were written after rising from an hour or two spent over the attractive writings of the great seer of Sweden.

CORRESPONDENCES

All things in Nature are beautiful types to the soul that will read them;
    Nothing exists upon earth but for unspeakable ends.
Every object that speaks to the senses was meant for the spirit:
    Nature is but a scroll—God's hand-writing thereon.
Ages ago, when man was pure, ere the flood overwhelmed him,
    While in the image of God every soul yet lived,
Everything stood as a letter or word of a language familiar,
    Telling of truths which *now* only the angels can read.
Lost to man was the key of those sacred hieroglyphics—
    Stolen away by sin—till with Jesus restored.
Now with infinite pains we here and there spell out a letter;
    Now and then will the sense feebly shine through the dark.
When we perceive the light which breaks through the visible symbol,
    What exultation is ours! *we* the discovery have made!
Yet is the meaning the same as when Adam lived sinless in Eden,
    Only long-hidden it slept and now again is restored.
Man unconsciously uses figures of speech every moment,
    Little dreaming the cause why to such terms he is prone—
Little dreaming that everything has its own correspondence
    Folded within it of old, as in the body the soul.
Gleams of the mystery fall on us still, though much is forgotten,
    And through our commonest speech illumines the path of our thoughts.

Thus does the lordly sun shine out a type of the Godhead;
  Wisdom and Love the beams that stream on a darkened
  world.
Thus do the sparkling waters flow, giving joy to the desert,
  And the great Fountain of Life opens itself to the thirst.
Thus does the word of God distil like the rain and the
  dewdrops,
  Thus does the warm wind breathe like to the Spirit of God,
And the green grass and the flowers are signs of the re-
  generation.

O thou Spirit of Truth! visit our minds once more!
Give us to read, in letters of light, the language celestial
  Written all over the earth—written all over the sky:
Thus may we bring our hearts at length to know our Creator,
  Seeing in all things around types of the Infinite Mind.

Margaret Fuller

A DIALOGUE: POET, CRITIC*
(1841)

POET: Approach me not, man of cold, steadfast eye and compressed lips. At thy coming nature shrouds herself in dull mist; fain would she hide her sighs and smiles, her buds and fruits even in a veil of snow. For thy unkindly breath, as it pierces her mystery, destroys its creative power. The birds draw back into their nests, the sunset hues into their clouds, when you are seen in the distance with your tablets all ready to write them into prose.

CRITIC: O my brother, my benefactor, do not thus repel me. Interpret me rather to our common mother; let her not avert her eyes from a younger child. I know I can never be dear to her as thou art, yet I am her child, nor would the fated revolutions of existence be fulfilled without my aid.

POET: How meanest thou? What have thy measurements, thy artificial divisions and classifications to do with the natural revolutions? In all real growths there is a "give and take" of unerring accuracy; in all the acts of thy life there is falsity, for all are negative. Why do you not receive and produce in your kind, like the sunbeam and the rose? Then new life would be brought out, were it but the life of a weed, to bear witness to the healthful beatings of the divine heart. But this perpetual analysis, comparison, and classification never add one atom to the sum of existence.

CRITIC: I understand you.

POET: Yes, that is always the way. You understand me, who never have the arrogance to pretend that I understand myself.

CRITIC: Why should you? That is my province. I am the rock which gives you back the echo. I am the tuning-key

* From *The Dial*, I (April 1841).

which harmonizes your instruments, the regulator to your watch. Who would speak, if no ear heard? nay, if no mind knew what the ear heard?

POET: I do not wish to be heard in thought but in love, to be recognized in judgment but in life. I would pour forth my melodies to the rejoicing winds. I would scatter my seed to the tender earth. I do not wish to hear in prose the meaning of my melody. I do not wish to see my seed neatly put away beneath a paper label. Answer in new paeans to the soul of our souls. Wake me to sweeter childhood by a fresher growth. At present you are but an excrescence produced by my life; depart, self-conscious egotist, I know you not.

CRITIC: Dost thou so adore nature, and yet deny me? Is not art the child of nature, civilization of man? As religion into philosophy, poetry into criticism, life into science, love into law, so did thy lyric in natural order transmute itself into my review.

POET: Review! Science! the very etymology speaks. What is gained by looking again at what has already been seen? What by giving a technical classification to what is already assimilated with the mental life?

CRITIC: What is gained by living at all?

POET: Beauty loving itself—happiness!

CRITIC: Does not this involve consciousness?

POET: Yes! consciousness of truth manifested in the individual form.

CRITIC: Since consciousness is tolerated, how will you limit it?

POET: By the instincts of my nature, which rejects yours as arrogant and superfluous.

CRITIC: And the dictate of my nature compels me to the processes which you despise, as essential to my peace. My brother (for I will not be rejected), I claim my place in the order of nature. The word descended and became flesh for two purposes: to organize itself, and to take cognizance of its organization. When the first poet worked alone, he paused between the cantos to proclaim, "It is very good." Dividing himself among men, he made some to create, and others to proclaim the merits of what is created.

POET: Well! if you were content with saying, "It is very good"; but you are always crying, "It is very bad," or ignorantly prescribing how it might be better. What do you know of it? Whatever is good could not be otherwise than it is.

Why will you not take what suits you, and leave the rest? True communion of thought is worship, not criticism. Spirit will not flow through the sluices nor endure the locks of canals.

CRITIC: There is perpetual need of Protestantism in every church. If the church be Catholic, yet the priest is not infallible. Like yourself, I sigh for a perfectly natural state, in which the only criticism shall be tacit rejection, even as Venus glides not into the orbit of Jupiter, nor do the fishes seek to dwell in fire. But as you soar toward this as a maker, so do I toil toward the same aim as a seeker. Your pinions will not upbear you toward it in steady flight. I must often stop to cut away the brambles from my path. The law of my being is on me, and the ideal standard seeking to be realized in my mind bids me demand perfection from all I see. To say how far each object answers this demand is my criticism.

POET: If one object does not satisfy you, pass on to another, and say nothing.

CRITIC: It is not so that it would be well with me. I must penetrate the secret of my wishes, verify the justice of my reasonings. I must examine, compare, sift, and winnow; what can bear this ordeal remains to me as pure gold. I cannot pass on till I know what I feel and why. An object that defies my utmost rigor of scrutiny is a new step on the stair I am making to the Olympian tables.

POET: I think you will not know the gods when you get there, if I may judge from the cold presumption I feel in your version of the great facts of literature.

CRITIC: Statement of a part always looks like ignorance, when compared with the whole, yet may promise the whole. Consider that a part implies the whole, as the everlasting No the everlasting Yes, and permit to exist the shadow of your light, the register of your inspiration.

As he spake the word he paused, for with it his companion vanished, and floating on the cloud left a starry banner with the inscription AFFLATUR NUMINE. The critic unfolded one on whose flagstaff he had been leaning. Its heavy folds of pearly gray satin slowly unfolding, gave to view the word NOTITIA, and *Causarum* would have followed, when a sudden breeze from the west caught it, those heavy folds fell back round the poor man, and stifled him probably —at least he has never since been heard of.

Theodore Parker

THOUGHTS ON LABOR* (1841)

. . . In a rational and natural state of society—that is, one in which every man went forward toward the true end he was designed to reach, toward perfection in the use of all his senses, toward perfection in wisdom, virtue, affection, and religion—labor would never interfere with the culture of what was best in each man. His daily business would be a school to aid in developing the whole man, body and spirit, because he would then do what nature fitted him to do. Thus his business would be really his calling. The diversity of gifts is quite equal to the diversity of work to be done. There is some one thing which each man can do with pleasure, and better than any other man, because he was born to do it. Then all men would labor, each at his proper vocation, and an excellent farmer would not be spoiled to make a poor lawyer, a blundering physician, or a preacher who puts the world asleep. Then a small body of men would not be pampered in indolence, to grow up into gouty worthlessness, and die of inertia; nor would the large part of men be worn down as now by excessive toil before half their life is spent. They would not be so severely tasked as to have no time to read, think, and converse. When he walked abroad, the laboring man would not be forced to catch mere transient glimpses of the flowers by the wayside, or the stars over his head, as the dogs, it is said, drink the waters of the Nile, running while they drink, afraid the crocodiles should seize them if they stop. When he looked from his window at the landscape, distress need not stare at him from every bush. He would then have leisure to cultivate his mind and heart no less than to do the world's work. . . .

* From *The Dial*, I (April 1841).

There are remedies at hand. It is true a certain amount of labor must be performed, in order that society be fed and clothed, warmed and comforted, relieved when sick, and buried when dead. If this is wisely distributed, if each performs his just portion, the burden is slight, and crushes no one. Here, as elsewhere, the closer we keep to nature, the safer we are. It is not under the burdens of nature that society groans, but the work of caprice, of ostentation, of contemptible vanity, of luxury which is never satisfied, these oppress the world. If these latter are given up, and each performs what is due from him, and strives to diminish the general burden and not add to it, then no man is oppressed, there is time enough for each man to cultivate what is noblest in him, and be all that his nature allows. . . .

Another remedy is this: the mind does the body's work. The head saves the hands. It invents machines, which, doing the work of many hands, will at last set free a large portion of leisure time from slavery to the elements. The brute forces of nature lie waiting man's command, and ready to serve him. At the voice of Genius, the river consents to turn his wheel, and weave and spin for the antipodes. The mine sends him iron vassals to toil in cold and heat. Fire and water embrace at his bidding, and a new servant is born, which will fetch and carry at his command, will face down all the storms of the Atlantic, will forge anchors, and spin gossamer threads, and run of errands up and down the continent with men and women on his back. This last child of science, though yet a stripling and in leading strings, is already a stout giant. The Fable of Orpheus is a true story in our times. There are four stages of progress in regard to labor, which are observable in the history of man. First, he does his own work by his hands. Adam tills the ground in the sweat of his own face, and Noah builds an ark in many years of toil. Next he forces his fellow mortal to work for him, and Canaan becomes a servant to his brother, and Job is made rich by the sweat of his great household of slaves. Then he seizes on the beasts, and the Bull and the Horse drag the plow of Castor and Pollux. At last he sets free his brother, works with his own hands, commands the beasts, and makes the brute force of the elements also toil for him. Then he has dominion over the earth and enjoys his birthright.

Man, however, is still in bondage to the elements; and since the beastly maxim is even now prevalent that the strong

should take care of themselves, and use the weak as their
tools, though to the manifest injury of the weak, the use of
machinery has hitherto been but a trifling boon in comparison with what it may be. In the village of Humdrum, its
thousand able-bodied men and women, without machinery,
and having no intercourse with the rest of the world, must
work fourteen hours out of the twenty-four that they may
all be housed, fed, and clothed, warmed, instructed, and
made happy. Some ingenious hands invent water mills, which
saw, plane, thrash, grind, spin, weave, and do many other
things, so that these thousand people need work but five hours
in the day to obtain the result of fourteen by the old process.
Here then a vast amount of time—nine hours in the day—
is set free from toil. It may be spent in study, social improvement, the pursuit of a favorite art, and leave room
for amusement also. But the longest heads at Humdrum have
not Christian but only selfish hearts beating in their bosoms,
and sending life into the brain. So these calculators think
the men of Humdrum shall work fourteen hours a day as
before. "It would be dangerous," say they, "to set free so
much time. The deluded creatures would soon learn to lie
and steal, and would speedily end by eating one another up.
It would not be Christian to leave them to this fate. Leisure
is very good for us, but would be ruinous to them." So
the wise men of Humdrum persuade their neighbors to work
the old fourteen hours. More is produced than is consumed.
So they send off the superfluities of the village, and in return bring back tea and porcelain, rich wines, and showy
gewgaws, and contemptible fashions that change every month.
The strong-headed men grow rich; live in palaces; their
daughters do not work, nor their sons dirty their hands.
They fare sumptuously every day; are clothed in purple and
fine linen. Meanwhile the common people of Humdrum work
as long as before the machines were invented, and a little
harder. They also are blessed by the "improvement." The
young women have red ribbons on their bonnets, French
gloves on their hands, and shawls of India on their shoulders, and "tinkling ornaments" in their ears. The young man
of Humdrum is better off than his father who fought through
the Revolution, for he wears a beaver hat and a coat of
English cloth, and has a Birmingham whittle and a watch
in his pocket. When he marries he will buy red curtains to
his windows, and a showy mirror to hang on his wall. For
these valuable considerations he parts with the nine hours

a day which machinery has saved, but has no more bread than before. For these blessings he will make his body a slave, and leave his mind all uncultivated. He is content to grow up a body—nothing but a body. So that if you look therein for his understanding, imagination, reason, you will find them like three grains of wheat in three bushels of chaff. You shall seek them all day before you find them, and at last they are not worth your search. At Humdrum, nature begins to revolt at the factitious inequality of condition, and thinks it scarce right for bread to come fastest into hands that add nothing to the general stock. So many grow restless and a few pilfer. In a ruder state crimes are few—the result of violent passions. At Humdrum they are numerous—the result of want, indolence, or neglected education; they are in great measure crimes against property. To remedy this new and unnatural evil, there rises a courthouse and a jail which must be paid for in work; then judges and lawyers and jailers are needed likewise in this artificial state, and add to the common burden. The old Athenians sent yearly seven beautiful youths and virgins—a tribute to the Minotaur. The wise men of Humdrum shut up in jail a larger number—a sacrifice to the spirit of modern cupidity, unfortunate wretches who were the victims not the foes of society, men so weak in head or heart that their bad character was formed *for* them through circumstances, far more than it was formed *by* them through their own free will. Still farther, the men who violate the law of the body, using the mouth much and the hand little, or in the opposite way, soon find nature taking vengeance for the offense. Then unnatural remedies must oppose the artificial disease. In the old time, every sickly dunce was cured "with motherwort and tansey" which grew by the roadside, suited all complaints, and was administered by each mother in the village. Now Humdrum has its "medical faculty," with their conflicting systems, homoeopathic and allopathic, but no more health than before. Thus the burden is increased to little purpose. The strong men of Humdrum have grown rich and become educated. If one of the laboring men is stronger than his fellows, he also will become rich and educate his children. He becomes rich, not by his own work, but by using the hands of others whom his cunning overreaches. Yet he is not more avaricious than they. He has perhaps the average share of selfishness, but superior adroitness to gratify that selfishness. So he gets and saves and takes care of himself, a part of their duty which the strong have always known how to perform, though the more difficult part, how to take care of others, to think for them, and help them to think for themselves, they have yet to learn, at least to practice. Alas, we are still in bondage to the elements, and so long as two of the "enlightened" nations of the earth, England and America, insist on weaving the garments for all the rest of the world, not because they would clothe the naked, but that their strong men might live in fine houses, wear gay apparel, dine on costly food, and their mouths be served by other men's hands, we must expect that seven-tenths of mankind will be degraded, and will hug their chains, and count machinery an evil. Is not the only remedy for all the evils at Humdrum in the Christian idea of wealth and the Christian idea of work?

Elizabeth Palmer Peabody

CHRIST'S IDEA OF SOCIETY*
(1841)

There are men and women . . . who have dared to say to one another, "Why not have our daily life organized on Christ's own idea? Why not begin to move the mountain of custom and convention? Perhaps Jesus' method of thought and life is the Saviour—is Christianity! For each man to think and live on this method is perhaps the second coming of Christ; to do unto the little ones as we would do unto *him* would be perhaps the reign of the saints—the kingdom of heaven. We have hitherto heard of Christ by the hearing of the ear; now let us see him, let us be him, and see what will come of that. Let us communicate with each other, and live."

Such a resolution has often been made under the light of the Christian idea; but the light has shone amidst darkness, and the darkness comprehended it not. Religious communities have ever but partially entered into the idea of Christ. They have all been churches, *ex parte* society, in some degree. They have been tied up and narrowed by creeds and tests. Yet the temporary success of the Hernhutters, the Moravians, the Shakers, even the Rappites, have cleared away difficulties and solved problems of social science. It has been made plain that the material goods of life, "the life that now is," are not to be sacrificed (as by the anchorite) in doing fuller justice to the social principle. It has been proved that, with the same degree of labor, there is no way to compare with that of working in a community banded by some sufficient idea to animate the will of the laborers. A greater quantity of wealth is procured with fewer hours of toil and without any degradation of any laborer. All these communities have dem-

* From *The Dial*, II (Oct. 1841)

onstrated what the practical Dr. Franklin said, that if everyone worked bodily three hours daily, there would be no necessity of anyone's working more than three hours.

But one rock upon which communities have split is that this very ease of procuring wealth has developed the desire of wealth, and so the hours redeemed by community of labor have been reapplied to sordid objects too much. This is especially the case with the Shakers, whose fanaticism is made quite subservient to the passion for wealth engendered by their triumphant success. The missionary objects of the Moravians have kept them purer.

The great evil of community, however, has been a spiritual one. The sacredness of the family and personal individuality have been sacrificed. Each man became the slave of the organization of the whole. In becoming a Moravian, a Shaker, or whatever, men have ceased to be men in some degree. Now a man must be religious, or he is not a man. But neither is a *Religieux* a *man*. That there are other principles in human nature to be cultivated beside the religious must be said, though we are in danger, by saying it, of being cried out upon as of old, "Behold a gluttonous man and a wine-bibber, a friend of publicans and sinners." The liberal principle always exposes a man to this outcry, no less than the religious principle, passionately acted out, has ever exposed the enthusiast to the charge, "He hath a Devil." *Inanes voces!* ...

The final cause of human society is the unfolding of the individual man into every form of perfection, without let or hindrance, according to the inward nature of each. In strict correspondence to this, the ground idea of the little communities which are the embryo of the kingdom to come must be Education. When we consider that each generation of men is thrown, helpless and ignorant even of the light within itself, into the arms of a full-grown generation which has a power to do it harm all but unlimited, we acknowledge that no object it can propose to itself is to be compared with that of educating its children truly. Yet every passion has its ideal having its temple in society, while the schools and universities in all Christendom struggle for existence, how much more than the banks, the East India companies, and other institutions for the accumulation of a doubtful external good! how much more than even the gambling houses and other temples of acknowledged vice!

The difficulty on this subject lies very deep in the present constitution of things. As long as education is made the object of an institution in society, rather than is the generating idea of society itself, it must be apart from life. It is really too general an interest to suffer being a particular one. Moral and religious education is the indispensable condition and foundation of a true development. But an apparatus for this of a mechanical character, in any degree, is in the nature of things an absurdity. Morals and religion are not something induced upon the human being, but an opening out of the inner life. What is now called moral and religious education in the best institutions is only a part of the intellectual exercises, as likely to act against as for the end. Those laws which should be lived before they are intellectually apprehended are introduced to the mind in the form of propositions, and assented to by the reason in direct opposition to the life which the constitution of society makes irresistible. Hence is perpetually reproduced that internal disorganization of the human being which was described of old in the fable of man's eating of the tree of knowledge to the blinding of his eyes to the tree of life—the whole apparatus of education being the tempting serpent. Moral and religious life should be the atmosphere in which the human being unfolds, it being freely lived in the community in which the child is born. Thus only may he be permitted to freely act out what is within him, and have no temptations but necessary ones, and the intellectual apprehensions follow rather than precede his virtue. This is not to take captive the will, but to educate it. If there were no wrong action in the world organized in institutions, children could be allowed a little more moral experimenting than is now convenient for others or safe for themselves. As the case now is, our children receive, as an inheritance, the punishment and anguish due to the crimes that have gone before them, and the paradise of youth is curtailed of its fair proportions cruelly and unjustly, and to the detriment of the future man.

In the true society, then, education is the ground Idea. The highest work of man is to call forth man in his fellow and child. This was the work of the Christ in Jesus and in his Apostles; and not only in them, but in poets and philosophers of olden time; in all who have had immortal aims, in *all* time, whether manifested in act or word, builded in temples, painted on canvas, or chiseled in stone. All action addressed to the immortal nature of man in a self-forgetting spirit is of the same nature—the divine life. The organization which shall give freedom to this loving creative spirit, glimpses of which were severally called the law in Rome, the ideal in Greece, freedom and manliness in northern Europe, and Christ by the earnest disciples of Jesus of Nazareth, is at once the true human society and the only university of education worthy the name.

R. W. Emerson and
Albert Brisbane

FOURIERISM AND THE
SOCIALISTS* (1842)

The increasing zeal and numbers of the disciples of
Fourier, in America and in Europe, entitle them to an attention which their theory and practical projects will justify and
reward. . . .

We had lately an opportunity of learning something of
these Socialists and their theory from the indefatigable
apostle of the sect in New York, Albert Brisbane. Mr. Brisbane pushes his doctrine with all the force of memory,
talent, honest faith, and importunacy. As we listened to his
exposition, it appeared to us the sublime of mechanical
philosophy; for the system was the perfection of arrangement
and contrivance. The force of arrangement could no farther
go. The merit of the plan was that it was a system; that it
had not the partiality and hint-and-fragment character of
most popular schemes, but was coherent and comprehensive
of facts to a wonderful degree. It was not daunted by distance or magnitude or remoteness of any sort, but strode
about nature with a giant's step and skipped no fact, but
wove its large Ptolemaic web of cycle and epicycle, of
phalanx and phalanstery, with laudable assiduity. Mechanics
were pushed so far as fairly to meet spiritualism. One could
not but be struck with strange coincidences betwixt Fourier
and Swedenborg. Genius hitherto has been shamefully mis-
applied, a mere trifler. It must now set itself to raise the
social condition of man, and to redress the disorders of the
planet he inhabits. The Desert of Sahara, the Campagna di
Roma, the frozen polar circles, which by their pestilential or

* From *The Dial*, III (July 1842).

hot or cold airs poison the temperate regions, accuse man. Society, concert, cooperation, is the secret of the coming paradise. By reason of the isolation of men at the present day, all work is drudgery. By concert, and the allowing each laborer to choose his own work, it becomes pleasure. "Attractive Industry" would speedily subdue, by adventurous, scientific, and persistent tillage, the pestilential tracts; would equalize temperature; give health to the globe, and cause the earth to yield "healthy imponderable fluids" to the solar system, as now it yields noxious fluids. The hyena, the jackal, the gnat, the bug, the flea were all beneficent parts of the system; the good Fourier knew what those creatures should have been, had not the mold slipped, through the bad state of the atmosphere, caused, no doubt, by these same vicious imponderable fluids. All these shall be redressed by human culture, and the useful goat and dog and innocent poetical moth, or the wood-tick to consume decomposing wood, shall take their place. It takes 1680 men to make one Man, complete in all the faculties; that is, to be sure that you have got a good joiner, a good cook, and a barber, a poet, a judge, an umbrella-maker, a mayor and aldermen, and so on. Your community should consist of 2000 persons, to prevent accidents of omission; and each community should take up 6000 acres of land. Now fancy the earth planted with fifties and hundreds of these phalanxes side by side—what tillage, what architecture, what refectories, what dormitories, what reading rooms, what concerts, what lectures, what gardens, what baths! What is not in one, will be in another, and many will be within easy distance. Then know you and all, that Constantinople is the natural capital of the globe. There, in the golden horn, will be the arch-phalanx established, there will the omniarch reside. Aladdin and his magician, or the beautiful Scheherazade, can alone in these prosaic times, before the sight, describe the material splendors collected there. Poverty shall be abolished; deformity, stupidity, and crime shall be no more. Genius, grace, art shall abound, and it is not to be doubted but that, in the reign of "Attractive Industry," all men will speak in blank verse.

Certainly we listened with great pleasure to such gay and magnificent pictures. The ability and earnestness of the advocate and his friends, the comprehensiveness of their theory, its apparent directness of proceeding to the end they would secure, the indignation they felt and uttered at all other speculation in the presence of so much social misery, commanded our attention and respect. It contained so much truth, and promised in the attempts that shall be made to realize it so much valuable instruction, that we are engaged to observe every step of its progress. Yet in spite of the assurances of its friends that it was new and widely discriminated from all other plans for the regeneration of society, we could not exempt it from the criticism which we apply to so many projects for reform with which the brain of the age teems. Our feeling was that Fourier had skipped no fact but one, namely, life. He treats man as a plastic thing, something that may be put up or down, ripened or retarded, molded, polished, made into solid, or fluid, or gas, at the will of the leader; or, perhaps, as a vegetable, from which, though now a poor crab, a very good peach can by manure and exposure be in time produced, but skips the faculty of life which spawns and scorns system and system-makers, which eludes all conditions, which makes or supplants a thousand phalanxes and New-Harmonies with each pulsation. There is an order in which in a sound mind the faculties always appear, and which, according to the strength of the individual, they seek to realize in the surrounding world. The value of Fourier's system is that it is a statement of such an order externalized, or carried outward into its correspondence in facts. The mistake is that this particular order and series is to be imposed by force of preaching and votes on all men, and carried into rigid execution. But what is true and good must not only be begun by life, but must be conducted to its issues by life. Could not the conceiver of this design have also believed that a similar model lay in every mind, and that the method of each associate might be trusted, as well as that of his particular committee and general office, No. 200 Broadway? nay, that it would be better to say, Let us be lovers and servants of that which is just; and straightway every man becomes a center of a holy and beneficent republic, which he sees to include all men in its law, like that of Plato, and of Christ. Before such a man the whole world becomes Fourierized or Christized or humanized, and in the obedience to his most private being, he finds himself, according to his presentiment, though against all sensuous probability, acting in strict concert with all others who followed their private light.

Yet in a day of small, sour, and fierce schemes, one is admonished and cheered by a project of such friendly aims, and of such bold and generous proportion; there is an intellectual courage and strength in it which is superior and commanding; it certifies the presence of so much truth in the theory, and insofar is destined to be fact.

But now, whilst we write these sentences, comes to us a paper from Mr. Brisbane himself. We are glad of the opportunity of letting him speak for himself. He has much more to say than we have hinted, and here has treated a general topic. We have not room for quite all the matter which he has sent us, but persuade ourselves that we have retained every material statement, in spite of the omissions which we find it necessary to make, to contract his paper to so much room as we offered him.

Mr. Brisbane, in a prefatory note to his article, announces himself as an advocate of the social laws discovered by Charles Fourier, and intimates that he wishes to connect whatever value attaches to any statement of his with the work in which he is exclusively engaged, that of social reform. He adds the following broad and generous declaration:

It seems to me that, with the spectacle of the present misery and degradation of the human race before us, all scientific researches and speculations, to be of any real value, should have a bearing upon the means of their social elevation and happiness. The mass of scientific speculations, which are every day offered to the world by men who are not animated by a deep interest in the elevation of their race, and who exercise their talents merely to build up systems or to satisfy a spirit of controversy or personal ambition, are perfectly valueless. What is more futile than barren philosophical speculation that leads to no great practical results?

MEANS OF EFFECTING A FINAL RECONCILIATION BETWEEN RELIGION AND SCIENCE

by Albert Brisbane

The intellectual history of humanity has been one series of combats, one ceaseless war. Religion has warred with religion, sect with sect, philosophy with philosophy, and system with system. Doubt, uncertainty, and contradiction have bewildered the human mind, and the human race have been wandering blindly amidst fragments of doctrines and systems which have choked up and hidden the road of truth and led them innumerable times astray upon false routes.

The most unfortunate contest, however, which has taken place is that between religion and science, or faith and reason. These two means or powers by which man obtains knowledge have been completely divided and arrayed in hostile opposition to each other. They have undermined reciprocally each other's labors; they have combatted with and tyrannized by turns over each other. I call this combat of faith and reason the most unfortunate, because had they been united—had they combined their powers—had they aided each other, they would have discovered, centuries since, enough of universal truth to have put an end to the war of religions, sects, and philosophies which has bewildered human judgment, dispelled the deep spiritual gloom in which humanity is sunk, and put it on the true road of progress to universal knowledge. . . .

To have two concise designations of the two sources of knowledge, I will call the first source reason, and the second faith. Faith is first active in the human mind; we find that in the savage state, long before the reason begins to search for first principles, faith reveals to man the existence of a God, his immortality, and other great truths. Reason follows later, and only exercises its power when it is developed and cultivated. Its function is to elucidate, define, and explain clearly the nature of the spontaneous conceptions of the soul and to discover the exact sciences. . . .

The ideas of God and immortality, which have their source in the spontaneous conceptions of the Soul, become with time so blended with the images and symbols under which they are represented that the original ideas can no longer be conceived separate from them. Hence to destroy the image or symbol appears to the believer to be the destruction of the idea itself, and hence his tenacious adherence to external forms and symbols, and the accusation of impiety and irreligion which he casts upon reason when it criticizes and attacks them.

Reason, on the other hand, generally carries its criticisms to an extreme; it does not separate the forms or dress in which the ideas of the divinity and immortality are clothed from those grand ideas themselves; it does not separate the symbols from the truths which they cover, but, confounding the two, wanders so far astray as to deny often the existence of a God and the immortality of the soul. It then falls into irreligion and atheism, and a complete breach takes place between faith and reason. The two means of knowledge in man then clash with instead of lending to each other their aid. Faith denounces reason as impious, and reason accuses faith of a puerile credulity. . . .

To produce a reconciliation and union between faith and reason, the latter must discover the nature of the soul, and its origin and learn that its spontaneous conceptions are absolutely true, however false the images and symbols may be in which they are clothed. It must then study and discover the nature of the truths which the soul conceives, and explain them scientifically to faith, so that the strong aspiration which exists in man to believe may be fully gratified. Thus will faith which clings to its instinctive conceptions and Reason which clings to its scientific deductions be satisfied, and the contest, which has been so long going on between them, be terminated, and a union effected.

Science must progress so far as to understand fully the nature of the soul and the elements composing it.* When it discovers that the intellectual, active principle in man is good, when it discovers its divine origin, then it will believe in the truths which the soul spontaneously conceives, take them as the basis of its researches, and study them with profound respect. When enlightened faith sees this, it will be satisfied; it will recognize reason with joy as a sister-partner in the search of truth, and will accept the full and scientific explanations furnished by reason of the great problems which it had previously conceived but only in a general or abstract manner. It will then see that the function of Reason is to explain and demonstrate clearly what it conceives vaguely and in general terms; and it will then lean upon it and seek cordially its aid. . . .

Thus faith conceives spontaneously, while reason analyzes and proves scientifically—these are the two sources of knowl-

---

* Up to the time of Charles Fourier, this had not been done. Science had always condemned human nature as imperfect or degraded, and it could not, under the influence of such a belief, respect and confide in the instinctive conceptions which go forth from the soul. Fourier has proved human nature to be good, true, and holy, although he recognizes that it is now prevented and degraded by our false systems of society. [Brisbane's note.]

edge in man. There should be union and concert of action between them—between the two means which the soul possesses of obtaining knowledge. The intellectual nature of man is ONE, and all its powers should be directed to the same ends. First come the spontaneous conceptions of the soul; they precede the investigations of reason, and on the light which should guide it on in the great work of discovering universal truth. Reason follows, and with study and investigation explains the true and full nature of the problems which before were only indistinctly conceived. . . .

I have pointed out the principle which should be proceeded upon to effect a final accord of faith and reason, or of religion and science. I will now explain briefly the practical means which must be employed to realize this great object, an object second in importance to no other.

1. The social condition of the mass of mankind must be vastly improved; their minds must be cultivated and developed, and their feelings ennobled and elevated. When poverty and harassing cares deaden the sympathies and noble impulses of the soul, and ignorance and groveling pursuits degrade or pervert the intelligence, how can the one feel with purity, and the other understand scientifically the great truths of the universe? So absorbed or degraded are the feelings and faculties of the vast majority by the miseries, conflicts, discords, wrongs, and prosaic occupations of our false societies, that the desire and aspirations for universal truth are smothered, and the power of comprehending it destroyed.

So long as the great body of the human race are sunk in ignorance and degradation, religion must present its great truths to them in the simplest manner, and clothe them in material images and symbols. So long as this is the case, science will disregard and criticize the simple explanations and symbols of religion, and the contest between them will be continued. They cannot be reconciled until the dogmas of religion are taught with scientific purity, and there is an intelligent humanity capable of comprehending them.

The minds of the mass cannot be developed, their social condition cannot be greatly elevated in our present false societies. The present repugnant system of industry, the poverty, discords, conflicts of interest, and the miserable methods of education which exist are insurmountable obstacles in the way. The first practical condition, consequently, of an accord of religion and science is the establishment of a true social order which will lead to the moral and intellectual elevation of mankind.

2. A great genius must arise who, piercing the veil that covers the mysteries of the universe, will discover, or prepare the way to the discovery of, the nature and essence of God, the true theory of the immortality of the soul, the laws of order and harmony which govern creation, and solve the great problems on which religion and science are based. This will be declared impossible by the world, for men have abandoned all hope of comprehending God and the system of nature; but the human mind can arrive at this knowledge, and a genius equal to the task has arisen, and in our age, and has accomplished it. That Genius is CHARLES FOURIER.

An age never believes in the discoveries of its great minds, and the achievements of Fourier—the discovery of the theory of *universal unity* in its five cardinal branches—will not be understood by the great body even of the educated of the present day. But the few who have studied thoroughly his discoveries know that the principles of a true universal science are now in the possession of mankind. He has opened the book of beauties in which humanity henceforth can read; he has explained the nature of man and pointed out how, from this and other knowledge, he can attain to a comprehension of the nature and essence of God; he has proved scientifically the immortality of the soul, shown the destiny of the human race upon the earth, and explained in detail the organization of a true system of society which will secure the moral, intellectual, and physical elevation of mankind, and give to all a higher degree of mental culture and development than the most favored have yet attained.

I will repeat briefly, in concluding, the conditions which must be fulfilled to effect a reconciliation and union of religion and science, as it is important to have them clearly before the mind. The first condition contains properly two within itself, and I will separate them for the sake of greater clearness.

1. A true social order must be discovered and established which will give education, or intellectual development, and abundance of pecuniary independence to man, and which will direct and develop properly his passions.

2. The condition of mankind must be morally and intellectually elevated, so that they can feel purely and comprehend scientifically universal truth, the exaltation and explanation of which are the aims of religion and science.

3. Genius must discover the system of the universe, and give a full and scientific elucidation of its laws. Such an elucidation will open to man views of God, a future state, and the scheme of creation, infinitely more sublime than his faith or the spontaneous conceptions of the soul have yet conceived. It will in consequence exalt his faith, while it satisfies his reason, and will unite and harmonize them fully....

The age is ready for a great movement; the human mind has, during the last three centuries, broken the chains of intellectual despotism and run through an epoch of doubting, criticizing, and inconclusive philosophy, and is now prepared for a work of reconstruction, both in a scientific and religious sense.

The world has nearly thrown off also another despotism, that of the warrior interest, and it is planting the peaceful standard of production and industry in its place. Human intelligence has matured beyond all precedent during the last hundred years, and must now be capable of comprehending the grand idea of a social reform and the elevation of the human race. The disciples of Fourier hope and trust that it is so, and that the dawn of universal truth and human happiness is now breaking upon this earth, so long sunk in ignorance, and so long the abode of tyranny and misery.

R. W. Emerson

ON STUDENT REBELLIONS
AT HARVARD* (1842)

On the subject of the University we cannot help wishing that a change will one day be adopted which will put an end to the foolish bickering between the government and the students which almost every year breaks out into those uncomfortable fracases which are called "Rebellions." Cambridge is so well endowed, and offers such large means of education, that it can easily assume the position of an university, and leave to the numerous younger colleges the charge of pupils too young to be trusted from home. This is instantly effected by the faculty's confining itself to the office of instruction, and omitting to assume the office of parietal government. Let the college provide the best teachers in each department, and for a stipulated price receive the pupil to its lecture-rooms and libraries; but in the matter of morals and manners, leave the student to his own conscience, and if he is a bad subject to the ordinary police. This course would have the effect of keeping back pupils from College a year or two or, in some cases, of bringing the parents or guardians of the pupil to reside in Cambridge; but it would instantly destroy the root of endless grievances between the student and teacher, put both parties on the best footing—indispensable,

* From *The Dial*, III (July 1842).

one would say, to good teaching—and relieve the professors of an odious guardianship, always degenerating into espionage, which must naturally indispose men of genius and honorable mind from accepting the professor's chair.

H. D. Thoreau

ANACREON* (1843)

Nor has he ceased his charming song, but still that lyre,
Though he is dead, sleeps not in Hades.
Simonides' Epigram on Anacreon.

We lately met with an old volume from a London bookshop, containing the Greek minor poets, and it was a pleasure
to read once more only the words—Orpheus—Linus—
Musæus—those faint poetic sounds and echoes of a name
dying away on the ears of us modern men, and those hardly
more substantial sounds, Mimnermus—Ibycus—Alcæus—
Stesichorus—Menander. They lived not in vain. We can converse with these bodiless fames without reserve or personality.

We know of no studies so composing as those of the classical scholar. When we have sat down to them, life seems as
still and serene as if it were very far off, and we believe it
is not habitually seen from any common platform so truly
and unexaggerated as in the light of literature. In serene
hours we contemplate the tour of the Greek and Latin authors with more pleasure than the traveler does the fairest
scenery of Greece or Italy. Where shall we find a more refined society? That highway down from Homer and Hesiod
to Horace and Juvenal is more attractive than the Appian.
Reading the classics, or conversing with those old Greeks and
Latins in their surviving works, is like walking amid the stars
and constellations, a high and byway serene to travel. Indeed,
the true scholar will be not a little of an astronomer in his
habits. Distracting cares will not be allowed to obstruct the
field of his vision, for the higher regions of literature, like
astronomy, are above storm and darkness.

But passing by these rumors of bards, we have chosen to

* From *The Dial*, III (April 1843).

pause for a moment at Anacreon, the Teian poet, and present some specimens of him to our readers.

There is something strangely modern about him. He is very easily turned into English. Is it that our lyric poets have resounded only that lyre which would sound only light subjects, and which Simonides tells us does not sleep in Hades? His odes are like gems of pure ivory. They possess an ethereal and evanescent beauty like summer evenings, δ χρή σε νοεῖν νόου ἄνθει, *which you must understand with the flower of the mind*, and show how slight a beauty could be expressed. You have to consider them, as the stars of lesser magnitude, with the side of the eye, and look aside from them to behold them. They charm us by their serenity and freedom from exaggeration and passion, and by a certain flower-like beauty, which does not propose itself, but must be approached and studied like a natural object. But, perhaps, their chief merit consists in the lightness and yet security of their tread,

> The young and tender stalk
> Ne'er bends when *they* do walk.

True, our nerves are never strung by them; it is too constantly the sound of the lyre, and never the note of the trumpet; but they are not gross, as has been presumed, but always elevated above the sensual.

ON HIS LYRE

> I wish to sing the Atridæ,
> And Cadmus I wish to sing;
> But my lyre sounds
> Only love with its chords.
> Lately I changed the strings
> And all the lyre;
> And I began to sing the labors
> Of Hercules; but my lyre
> Resounded loves.
> Farewell, henceforth, for me,
> Heroes! for my lyre
> Sings only loves.

ON A SILVER CUP

Turning the silver,
Vulcan, make for me,
Not indeed a panoply,
For what are battles to me?
But a hollow cup,
As deep as thou canst.
And make for me in it
Neither stars, nor wagons,
Nor sad Orion;
What are the Pleiades to me?
What the shining Bootes?
Make vines for me,
And clusters of grapes in it,
And of gold Love and Bathyllus
Treading the grapes
With the fair Lyæus.

ON HIMSELF

Thou sing'st the affairs of Thebes,
And he the battles of Troy,
But I of my own defeats.
No horse have wasted me,
Nor foot, nor ships;
But a new and different host,
From eyes smiting me.

TO A DOVE

Lovely dove,
Whence, whence dost thou fly?
Whence, running on air,
Dost thou waft and diffuse
So many sweet ointments?
Who art? What thy errand?

Anacreon sent me
To a boy, to Bathyllus,
Who lately is ruler and tyrant of all.
Cythere has sold me
For one little song,
And I'm doing this service
For Anacreon.
And now, as you see,
I bear letters from him.
And he says that directly
He'll make me free,
But though he release me,
His slave I will tarry with him.
For why should I fly
Over mountains and fields,
And perch upon trees,
Eating some wild thing?
Now indeed I eat bread,
Plucking it from the hands
Of Anacreon himself;
And he gives me to drink
The wine which he tastes,
And drinking, I dance,
And shadow my master's
Face with my wings;
And, going to rest,
On the lyre itself do I sleep.
That is all; get thee gone.
Thou hast made me more talkative,
Man, than a crow.

ON LOVE

Love walking swiftly
With hyacinthine staff,
Bade me to take a run with him;
And hastening through swift torrents,
 And woody places, and over precipices,
A water-snake stung me.
And my heart leaped up to
My mouth, and I should have fainted;
But Love fanning my brows

With his soft wings, said,
Surely, thou art not able to love.

ON WOMEN

Nature has given horns
To bulls, and hoofs to horses,
Swiftness to hares,
To lions yawning teeth,
To fishes swimming,
To birds flight,
To men wisdom.
For woman she had nothing beside;
What then does she give? Beauty—
Instead of all shields,
Instead of all spears;
And she conquers even iron
And fire, who is beautiful.

ON LOVERS

Horses have the mark
Of fire on their sides,
And some have distinguished
The Parthian men by their crests;
So I, seeing lovers,
Know them at once,
For they have a certain slight
Brand on their hearts.

TO A SWALLOW

What dost thou wish me to do to thee—
What, thou loquacious swallow?
Dost thou wish me taking thee
Thy light pinions to clip?
Or rather to pluck out
Thy tongue from within,
As that Tereus did?
Why with thy notes in the dawn

Hast thou plundered Bathyllus
From my beautiful dreams?

TO A COLT

Thracian colt, why at me
Looking aslant with thy eyes,
Dost thou cruelly flee,
And think that I know nothing wise?
Know I could well
Put the bridle on thee,
And holding the reins, turn
Round the bounds of the course.
But now thou browsest the meads,
And gamboling lightly dost play,
For thou hast no skillful horseman
Mounted upon thy back.

CUPID WOUNDED

Love once among roses
Saw not
A sleeping bee, but was stung;
And being wounded in the finger
Of his hand cried for pain.
Running as well as flying
To the beautiful Venus,
I am killed, mother, said he,
I am killed, and I die.
A little serpent has stung me,
Winged, which they call
A bee—the husbandmen.
And she said, If the sting
Of a bee afflicts you,
How, think you, are they afflicted,
Love, whom you smite?

H. D. T.

Margaret Fuller

THE GREAT LAWSUIT: MAN VS. MEN, WOMAN VS. WOMEN* (1843)

. . . It is worthy of remark that, as the principle of liberty is better understood and more nobly interpreted, a broader protest is made in behalf of woman. As men become aware that all men have not had their fair chance, they are inclined to say that no women have had a fair chance. The French Revolution, that strangely disguised angel, bore witness in favor of woman, but interpreted her claims no less ignorantly than those of man. Its idea of happiness did not rise beyond outward enjoyment, unobstructed by the tyranny of others. The title it gave was *citoyen, citoyenne,* and it is not unimportant to woman that even this species of equality was awarded her. Before, she could be condemned to perish on the scaffold for treason, but not as a citizen, but a subject. The right with which this title then invested a human being was that of bloodshed and license. The goddess of liberty was impure. Yet truth was prophesied in the ravings of that hideous fever induced by long ignorance and abuse. Europe is conning a valued lesson from the bloodstained page. The same tendencies, farther unfolded, will bear good fruit in this country. . . .

Here, as elsewhere, the gain of creation consists always in the growth of individual minds which live and aspire, as flowers bloom and birds sing, in the midst of morasses; and in the continual development of that thought, the thought of human destiny, which is given to eternity to fulfill, and which ages of failure only seemingly impede. Only seemingly, and whatever seems to the contrary, this country is as

*From *The Dial,* IV (July 1843).

surely destined to elucidate a great moral law as Europe
was to promote the mental culture of man.

Though the national independence be blurred by the servility of individuals; though freedom and equality have been
proclaimed only to leave room for a monstrous display of
slave dealing and slave keeping; though the free American so
often feels himself free, like the Roman, only to pamper his
appetites and his indolence through the misery of his fellow
beings, still it is not in vain that the verbal statement has
been made, "All men are born free and equal." There it
stands, a golden certainty, wherewith to encourage the
good, to shame the bad. The new world may be called clearly
to perceive that it incurs the utmost penalty if it reject the
sorrowful brother. And if men are deaf, the angels hear. But
men cannot be deaf. It is inevitable that an external freedom,
such as has been achieved for the nation, should be so also
for every member of it. That which has once been clearly
conceived in the intelligence must be acted out. . . .

As to men's representing women fairly at present, while
we hear from men who owe to their wives not only all that is
comfortable and graceful, but all that is wise in the arrangement of their lives, the frequent remark, "You cannot reason
with a woman," when from those of delicacy, nobleness,
and poetic culture, the contemptuous phrase, "Women and
children," and that in no light sally of the hour, but in works
intended to give a permanent statement of the best experiences, when not one man in the million, shall I say, no,
not in the hundred million, can rise above the view that
woman was made *for man*, when such traits as these are daily
forced upon the attention, can we feel that man will always
do justice to the interests of woman? Can we think that he
takes a sufficiently discerning and religious view of her office
and destiny, ever to do her justice, except when prompted by
sentiment; accidentally or transiently, that is, for his sentiment will vary according to the relations in which he is
placed. The lover, the poet, the artist are likely to view her
nobly. The father and the philosopher have some chance of
liberality; the man of the world, the legislator for expediency,
none.

Under these circumstances, without attaching importance
in themselves to the changes demanded by the champions of
woman, we hail them as signs of the times. We would have
every arbitrary barrier thrown down. We would have every
path laid open to woman as freely as to man. Were this

done, and a slight temporary fermentation allowed to subside, we believe that the divine would ascend into nature to a height unknown in the history of past ages, and nature, thus instructed, would regulate the spheres not only so as to avoid collision, but to bring forth ravishing harmony.

Yet then, and only then, will human beings be ripe for this, when inward and outward freedom for woman, as much as for man, shall be acknowledged as a right, not yielded as a concession. As the friend of the Negro assumes that one man cannot, by right, hold another in bondage, so should the friend of woman assume that man cannot, by right, lay even well-meant restrictions on woman. If the Negro be a soul, if the woman be a soul, appareled in flesh, to one master only are they accountable. There is but one law for all souls, and, if there is to be an interpreter of it, he comes not as man, or son of man, but as Son of God.

Were thought and feeling once so far elevated that man should esteem himself the brother and friend, but nowise the lord and tutor of woman, were he really bound with her in equal worship, arrangements as to function and employment would be of no consequence. What woman needs is not as a woman to act or rule, but as a nature to grow, as an intellect to discern, as a soul to live freely, and unimpeded to unfold such powers as were given her when we left our common home. If fewer talents were given her, yet, if allowed the free and full employment of these so that she may render back to the giver his own with usury, she will not complain, nay, I dare to say she will bless and rejoice in her earthly birthplace, her earthly lot.

Let us consider what obstructions impede this good era, and what signs give reason to hope that it draws near.

I was talking on this subject with Miranda, a woman who, if any in the world, might speak without heat or bitterness of the position of her sex. Her father was a man who cherished no sentimental reverence for woman, but a firm belief in the equality of the sexes. She was his eldest child, and came to him at an age when he needed a companion. From the time she could speak and go alone, he addressed her not as a plaything but as a living mind. Among the few verses he ever wrote were a copy addressed to this child, when the first locks were cut from her head, and the reverence expressed on this occasion for that cherished head he never belied. It was to him the temple of immortal intellect. He respected his child, however, too much to be an indulgent parent. He called on her for clear judgment, for courage, for honor and fidelity, in short, for such virtues as he knew. Insofar as he possessed the keys to the wonders of this universe, he allowed free use of them to her, and by the incentive of a high expectation he forbade, as far as possible, that she should let the privilege lie idle.

Thus this child was early led to feel herself a child of the spirit. She took her place easily, not only in the world of organized being, but in the world of mind. A dignified sense of self-dependence was given as all her portion, and she found it a sure anchor. Herself securely anchored, her relations with others were established with equal security. She was fortunate in a total absence of those charms which might have drawn to her bewildering flatteries, and of a strong electric nature, which repelled those who did not belong to her and attracted those who did. With men and women her relations were noble, affectionate without passion, intellectual without coldness. The world was free to her, and she lived freely in it. Outward adversity came, and inward conflict, but that faith and self-respect had early been awakened which must always lead at last to an outward serenity and an inward peace.

Of Miranda, I had always thought as an example that the restraints upon the sex were insuperable only to those who think them so, or who noisily strive to break them. She had taken a course of her own, and no man stood in her way. Many of her acts had been unusual, but excited no uproar. Few helped, but none checked her; and the many men who knew her mind and her life showed to her confidence as to a brother, gentleness as to a sister. And not only refined, but very coarse men approved one in whom they saw resolution and clearness of design. Her mind was often the leading one, always effective.

When I talked with her upon these matters, and had said very much what I have written, she smilingly replied, "And yet we must admit that I have been fortunate, and this should not be. My good father's early trust gave the first bias, and the rest followed of course. It is true that I have had less outward aid, in after years, than most women, but that is of little consequence. Religion was early awakened in my soul, a sense that what the soul is capable to ask it must attain, and that, though I might be aided by others, I must depend on myself as the only constant friend. This self-dependence, which was honored in me, is deprecated as a fault in most women. They are taught to learn their rule from without, not to unfold it from within.

"This is the fault of man, who is still vain, and wishes to be more important to woman than by right he should be."

"Men have not shown this disposition toward you," I said.

"No, because the position I early was enabled to take was one of self-reliance. And were all women as sure of their wants as I was, the result would be the same. The difficulty is to get them to the point where they shall naturally develop self-respect, the question how it is to be done.

"Once I thought that men would help on this state of things more than I do now. I saw so many of them wretched in the connections they had formed in weakness and vanity. They seemed so glad to esteem women whenever they could!

"But early I perceived that men never, in any extreme of despair, wished to be women. Where they admired any woman they were inclined to speak of her as above her sex. Silently I observed this, and feared it argued a rooted skepticism which for ages had been fastening on the heart, and which only an age of miracles could eradicate.

"Ever I have been treated with great sincerity; and I look upon it as a most signal instance of this that an intimate friend of the other sex said in a fervent moment that I deserved in some star to be a man. Another used as highest praise, in speaking of a character in literature, the words 'a manly woman.'

"It is well known that of every strong woman they say she has a masculine mind.

"This by no means argues a willing want of generosity toward woman. Man is as generous toward her as he knows how to be.

"Wherever she has herself arisen in national or private history, and nobly shone forth in any ideal of excellence, men have received her, not only willingly, but with triumph. Their encomiums indeed are always in some sense mortifying; they show too much surprise.

"In everyday life the feelings of the many are stained with vanity. Each wishes to be lord in a little world, to be superior at least over one; and he does not feel strong enough to retain a lifelong ascendant over a strong nature. Only a Brutus would rejoice in a Portia. Only Theseus could conquer before he wed the Amazonian Queen. Hercules wished rather to rest from his labors with Dejanira, and received the poisoned robe as a fit guerdon. The tale should be interpreted to all those who seek repose with the weak.

"But not only is man vain and fond of power, but the same want of development which thus affects him morally in the intellect prevents his discerning the destiny of woman. The boy wants no woman, but only a girl to play ball with him, and mark his pocket handkerchief. . . ."

It is not the transient breath of poetic incense that women want; each can receive that from a lover. It is not lifelong sway; it needs but to become a coquette, a shrew, or a good cook to be sure of that. It is not money, nor notoriety, nor the badges of authority that men have appropriated to themselves. If demands made in their behalf lay stress on any of these particulars, those who make them have not searched deeply into the need. It is for that which at once includes all these and precludes them; which would not be forbidden power, lest there be temptation to steal and misuse it; which would not have the mind perverted by flattery from a worthiness of esteem. It is for that which is the birthright of every being capable to receive it—the freedom, the religious, the intelligent freedom of the universe, to use its means, to learn its secret as far as nature has enabled them, with God alone for their guide and their judge.

Ye cannot believe it, men, but the only reason why women ever assume what is more appropriate to you is because you prevent them from finding out what is fit for themselves. Were they free, were they wise fully to develop the strength and beauty of woman, they would never wish to be men or manlike. . . .

Mary Wollstonecraft, like Madame Dudevant (commonly known as George Sand) in our day, was a woman whose existence better proved the need of some new interpretation of woman's rights than anything she wrote. Such women as these, rich in genius, of most tender sympathies, and capable of high virtue and a chastened harmony, ought not to find themselves by birth in a place so narrow that in breaking bonds they become outlaws. Were there as much room in the world for such as in Spenser's poem for Britomart, they would not run their heads so wildly against its laws. They find their way at last to purer air, but the world will not take off the brand it has set upon them. The champion of the rights of woman found in Godwin one who pleaded her own cause like a brother. George Sand smokes, wears male attire, wishes to be addressed as *mon frère;* perhaps if she found those who

were as brothers indeed, she would not care whether she
were brother or sister. . . .

Women like Sand will speak now, and cannot be silenced;
their characters and their eloquence alike foretell an era
when such as they shall easier learn to lead true lives. But
though such forebode, not such shall be the parents of it.
Those who would reform the world must show that they do
not speak in the heat of wild impulse; their lives must be
unstained by passionate error; they must be severe lawgivers
to themselves. As to their transgressions and opinions, it
may be observed that the resolve of Eloise to be only the
mistress of Abelard was that of one who saw the contract of
marriage a seal of degradation. Wherever abuses of this sort
are seen, the timid will suffer, the bold protest. But society
is in the right to outlaw them till she has revised her law,
and she must be taught to do so by one who speaks with
authority, not in anger and haste. . . .

The especial genius of woman I believe to be electrical in
movement, intuitive in function, spiritual in tendency. She is
great not so easily in classification, or re-creation, as in an
instinctive seizure of causes, and a simple breathing out of
what she receives that has the singleness of life, rather than
the selecting or energizing of art.

More native to her is it to be the living model of the
artist than to set apart from herself any one form in objective reality; more native to inspire and receive the poem
than to create it. Insofar as soul is in her completely developed, all soul is the same; but as far as it is modified in
her as woman, it flows, it breathes, it sings, rather than de-
posits soil, or finishes work, and that which is especially
feminine flushes in blossom the face of earth, and pervades
like air and water all this seeming solid globe, daily renewing and purifying its life. Such may be the especially
feminine element spoken of as femality. But it is no more
the order of nature that it should be incarnated pure in any
form than that the masculine energy should exist unmingled
with it in any form.

Male and female represent the two sides of the great
radical dualism. But, in fact, they are perpetually passing into
one another. Fluid hardens to solid, solid rushes to fluid.
There is no wholly masculine man, no purely feminine
woman.

History jeers at the attempts of physiologists to bind great
original laws by the forms which flow from them. They make

a rule; they say from observation what can and cannot be. In vain! Nature provides exceptions to every rule. She sends women to battle, and sets Hercules spinning; she enables women to bear immense burdens, cold, and frost; she enables the man who feels maternal love to nourish his infant like a mother. Of late she plays still gayer pranks. Not only she deprives organizations, but organs, of a necessary end. She enables people to read with the top of the head, and see with the pit of the stomach. Presently she will make a female Newton, and a male Siren.

Man partakes of the feminine in the Apollo, woman of the masculine as Minerva.

Let us be wise and not impede the soul. Let her work as she will. Let us have one creative energy, one incessant revelation. Let it take what form it will, and let us not bind it by the past to man or woman, black or white. Jove sprang from Rhea, Pallas from Jove. So let it be.

If it has been the tendency of the past remarks to call woman rather to the Minerva side—if I, unlike the more generous writer, have spoken from society no less than the soul—let it be pardoned. It is love that has caused this, love for many incarcerated souls that might be freed could the idea of religious self-dependence be established in them, could the weakening habit of dependence on others be broken up.

Every relation, every gradation of nature, is incalculably precious, but only to the soul which is poised upon itself, and to whom no loss, no change, can bring dull discord, for it is in harmony with the central soul.

If any individual live too much in relations, so that he becomes a stranger to the resources of his own nature, he falls after a while into a distraction, or imbecility, from which he can only be cured by a time of isolation, which gives the renovating fountains time to rise up. With a society it is the same. Many minds, deprived of the traditionary or instinctive means of passing a cheerful existence, must find help in self-impulse or perish. It is therefore that while any elevation, in the view of union, is to be hailed with joy, we shall not decline celibacy as the great fact of the time. It is one from which no vow, no arrangement, can at present save a thinking mind. For now the rowers are pausing on their oars, they wait a change before they can pull together. All tends to illustrate the thought of a wise contemporary. Union is only possible to those who are units. To be fit for relations in time, souls, whether of man or woman, must be able to do without them in the spirit.

It is therefore that I would have woman lay aside all thought such as she habitually cherishes of being taught and led by men. I would have her, like the Indian girl, dedicate herself to the sun, the sun of truth, and go nowhere if his beams did not make clear the path. I would have her free from compromise, from complaisance, from helplessness, because I would have her good enough and strong enough to love one and all beings from the fullness, not the poverty, of being.

Men, as at present instructed, will not help this work, because they also are under the slavery of habit. I have seen with delight their poetic impulses. A sister is the fairest ideal, and how nobly Wordsworth, and even Byron, have written of a sister.

There is no sweeter sight than to see a father with his little daughter. Very vulgar men become refined to the eye when leading a little girl by the hand. At that moment the right relation between the sexes seems established, and you feel as if the man would aid in the noblest purpose, if you ask him in behalf of his little daughter. Once two fine figures stood before me thus. The father of very intellectual aspect, his falcon eye softened by affection as he looked down on his fair child, she the image of himself, only more graceful and brilliant in expression. I was reminded of Southey's Kehama, when lo, the dream was rudely broken. They were talking of education, and he said,

"I shall not have Maria brought too forward. If she knows too much, she will never find a husband; superior women hardly ever can."

"Surely," said his wife, with a blush, "you wish Maria to be as good and wise as she can, whether it will help her to marriage or not."

"No," he persisted, "I want her to have a sphere and a home, and someone to protect her when I am gone."

It was a trifling incident, but made a deep impression. I felt that the holiest relations fail to instruct the unprepared and perverted mind. If this man, indeed, would have looked at it on the other side, he was the last that would have been willing to have been taken himself for the home and protection he could give, but would have been much more likely to repeat the tale of Alcibiades with his phials.

But men do *not* look at both sides, and women must leave

off asking them and being influenced by them, but retire within themselves and explore the groundwork of being till they find their peculiar secret. Then when they come forth again, renovated and baptized, they will know how to turn all dross to gold, and will be rich and free though they live in a hut, tranquil, if in a crowd. Then their sweet singing shall not be from passionate impulse, but the lyrical overflow of a divine rapture, and a new music shall be elucidated from this many-chorded world.

Grant her then for a while the armor and the javelin. Let her put from her the press of other minds and meditate in virgin loneliness. The same idea shall reappear in due time as Muse, or Ceres, the all-kindly, patient earth-spirit. . . .

A profound thinker has said, "No married woman can represent the female world, for she belongs to her husband. The idea of woman must be represented by a virgin."

But that is the very fault of marriage, and of the present relation between the sexes, that the woman does belong to the man instead of forming a whole with him. Were it otherwise there would be no such limitation to the thought.

Woman, self-centered, would never be absorbed by any relation; it would be only an experience to her as to man. It is a vulgar error that love, *a* love to woman is her whole existence; she also is born for truth and love in their universal energy. Would she but assume her inheritance, Mary would not be the only Virgin Mother. Not Manzoni alone would celebrate in his wife the virgin mind with the maternal wisdom and conjugal affections. The soul is ever young, ever virgin.

And will not she soon appear? The woman who shall vindicate their birthright for all women; who shall teach them what to claim, and how to use what they obtain? Shall not her name be for her era Victoria, for her country and her life Virginia? Yet predictions are rash; she herself must teach us to give her the fitting name.

Samuel Gray Ward

NOTES ON ART AND ARCHITECTURE* (1843)

. . . What architecture must a nation situated as we are adopt? It has no indigenous architecture; it is not therefore a matter of religion with us, but a matter of taste. We may and must have all the architectures of the world, but we may ennoble them all by an attention to truth and a contempt of littleness. Nay, is not our position, if we will use our advantages properly, the more fortunate, inasmuch as we are not by the force of circumstance or example bound to be or to build in this or that particular way, but all ways are before us to choose. If our position is unfavorable to a speedy development of national taste, it is most adapted to give fair play to individual.

The crowning and damning sin of architecture with us, nay, that of bad taste everywhere, is the doing of unmeaning, needless things. A Friends' meeting sits silent till one has something to say; so should a man always—so should the building man never presume to do aught without reason. To *adorn the needful,* to add a frieze to life, this is Art.

Rightly does the uninstructed caviller ask, when he sees a *fine* house, for what purpose is this balustrade or that screen, these windows blocked up, and so on. Let any man of good sense say to himself what sort of a house he would have for convenience, supposing him to have the space to build it on; then let him frame and roof these rooms, and if he has made his house truly convenient, its appearance cannot be absurd. Well, but he says, my house is plain, I want it to be beautiful—I will spend what you choose upon it, but it shall be the most beautiful in the country. Very

* From *The Dial,* IV (July 1843).

good, my friend. We will not change a single line, but we will ornament these lines. We will not conceal but adorn your house's nakedness; delicate moldings shall ornament every joint; whatever is built for convenience or use shall seem to have been built for beautiful details; your very doorlatch and hinges shall be beautiful. For house, say church; for the purposes of daily life, say the worship of God, and behold we have the history of architecture.

There is nothing arbitrary in true architecture, even to the lowest detail. The man who should for the first time see a Greek temple of marble would indeed ask and with reason what meaning there was in triglyph and metope and frieze; but when he is told that this is a marble imitation of a wooden building, a reproduction in a more costly material of a sacred historical form, he then sees in the triglyph the end of the wooden beam, with the marks of the trickling water drops, in the metope the flat panel between. But, says our modern builder, there is no reason that I should use triglyphs and metopes. I have no historical recollection to beautify them; what shall I use for ornaments? My friend, what form has ever struck you as beautiful? He answers, Why, the form of every living thing, of every tree and flower and herb. And can you ask then what ornaments you shall use? If your cornice were a wreath of thistles and burdocks curiously carved or cast, can you not see how a hundred mouths would proclaim its superiority over yonder unmeaning layer of plaster?

A mistaken plainness has usurped the place of true simplicity, which is the same mistake as an affected plainness in manners or appearance, lest one should be suspected of foppery. All houses, all churches are finished within side by the plane (or mold-plane) and plaster-smoother. Has a man made a fortune, he moves from his plain house which cost ten thousand, to one which cost an hundred thousand. Now perhaps his poor friend shall see something beautiful. Alas, it is but the old house three times as large, the walls and the woodwork three times as smooth; a little warmer house in winter, than the old one, a little airier in summer. Verily, friend, thou hast done little with thy hundred thousand, beyond enriching thy carpenter.

To see materials used skillfully and in accordance with their peculiar qualities is a great source of beauty in architecture. The vice of many of our would-be pretty buildings is that the material is entirely disguised, so that for aught we know they may be marble or wood or pasteboard; all we see is a plain white surface. Have done with this paltry concealment; let us see how the thing is built. . . .

4

THE BROOK FARM EXPERIMENT

George Ripley

*LETTER TO R. W. EMERSON**
(1840)

My dear Sir: Our conversation in Concord was of such a general nature that I do not feel as if you were in complete possession of the idea of the association which I wish to see established. As we have now a prospect of carrying it into effect, at an early period, I wish to submit the plan more distinctly to your judgment, that you may decide whether it is one that can have the benefit of your aid and co-operation.

Our objects, as you know, are to insure a more natural union between intellectual and manual labor than now exists; to combine the thinker and the worker, as far as possible, in the same individual; to guarantee the highest mental freedom by providing all with labor adapted to their tastes and talents, and securing to them the fruits of their industry; to do away with the necessity of menial services by opening the benefits of education and the profits of labor to all; and thus to prepare a society of liberal, intelligent, and cultivated persons whose relations with each other would permit a more simple and wholesome life than can be led amidst the pressure of our competitive institutions.

To accomplish these objects, we propose to take a small tract of land, which, under skillful husbandry, uniting the garden and the farm, will be adequate to the subsistence of the families, and to connect with this a school or college in which the most complete instruction shall be given, from the first rudiments to the highest culture. Our farm would be a place for improving the race of men that lived on it; thought would preside over the operations of labor, and labor would contribute to the expansion of thought; we

* From Octavius B. Frothingham, *George Ripley* (Boston, 1882).

379

should have industry without drudgery, and true equality without its vulgarity.

An offer has been made to us of a beautiful estate, on very reasonable terms, on the borders of Newton, West Roxbury, and Dedham. I am very familiar with the premises, having resided on them a part of last summer, and we might search the country in vain for anything more eligible. Our proposal now is for three or four families to take possession on the first of April next, to attend to the cultivation of the farm and the erection of buildings, to prepare for the coming of as many more in the autumn, and thus to commence the institution in the simplest manner, and with the smallest number with which it can go into operation at all. It would thus be not less than two or three years before we should be joined by all who mean to be with us; we should not fall to pieces by our own weight; we should grow up slowly and strong; and the attractiveness of our experiment would win to us all whose society we should want.

The step now to be taken at once is the procuring of funds for the necessary capital. According to the present modification of our plan, a much less sum will be required than that spoken of in our discussions at Concord. We thought then $50,000 would be needed; I find now, after a careful estimate, that $30,000 will purchase the estate and buildings for ten families, and give the required surplus for carrying on the operations for one year.

We propose to raise this sum by a subscription to a joint stock company among the friends of the institution, the payment of a fixed interest being guaranteed to the subscribers, and the subscription itself secured by the real estate. No man then will be in danger of losing; he will receive as fair an interest as he would from any investment, while at the same time he is contributing toward an institution in which, while the true use of money is retained, its abuses are done away. The sum required cannot come from rich capitalists; their instinct would protest against such an application of their coins; it must be obtained from those who sympathize with our ideas, and who are willing to aid their realization with their money, if not by their personal cooperation. There are some of this description on whom I think we can rely; among ourselves we can produce perhaps $10,000; the remainder must be subscribed for by those who wish us well, whether they mean to unite with us or not.

I can imagine no plan which is suited to carry into effect so many divine ideas as this. If wisely executed, it will be a light over this country and this age. If not the sunrise, it will be the morning star. As a practical man, I see clearly that we must have some such arrangement, or all changes less radical will be nugatory. I believe in the divinity of labor; I wish to "harvest my flesh and blood from the land"; but to do this, I must either be insulated and work to disadvantage, or avail myself of the services of hirelings who are not of my order and whom I can scarce make friends, for I must have another to drive the plow which I hold. I cannot empty a cask of lime upon my grass alone. I wish to see a society of educated friends, working, thinking, and living together, with no strife except that of each to contribute the most to the benefit of all.

Personally, my tastes and habits would lead me in another direction. I have a passion for being independent of the world and of every man in it. This I could do easily on the estate which is now offered, and which I could rent at a rate that, with my other resources, would place me in a very agreeable condition as far as my personal interests were involved. I should have a city of God on a small scale of my own; and please God, I should hope one day to drive my own cart to market and sell greens. But I feel bound to sacrifice this private feeling in the hope of a great social good. I shall be anxious to hear from you. Your decision will do much toward settling the question with me, whether the time has come for the fulfillment of a high hope or whether the work belongs to a future generation. All omens now are favorable; a singular union of diverse talents is ready for the enterprise; everything indicates that we ought to arise and build; and if we let slip this occasion, the unsleeping Nemesis will deprive us of the boon we seek. For myself, I am sure that I can never give so much thought to it again; my mind must act on other objects, and I shall acquiesce in the course of fate, with grief that so fair a light is put out. A small pittance of the wealth which has been thrown away on ignoble objects during this wild contest for political supremacy would lay the cornerstone of a house which would ere long become the desire of nations. . . .

GEORGE RIPLEY.

P. S. I ought to add that in the present stage of the enterprise no proposal is considered as binding. We wish only to know what can probably be relied on, provided always that no pledge will be accepted until the articles of association are agreed on by all parties.

I recollect you said that if you were sure of compeers of the right stamp, you might embark yourself in the adventure: as to this, let me suggest the inquiry, whether our association should not be composed of various classes of men? If we have friends whom we love and who love us, I think we should be content to join with others with whom our personal sympathy is not strong, but whose general ideas coincide with ours, and whose gifts and abilities would make their services important. For instance, I should like to have a good washerwoman in my parish admitted into the plot. She is certainly not a Minerva or a Venus, but we might educate her two children to wisdom and varied accomplishments, who otherwise will be doomed to drudge through life. The same is true of some farmers and mechanics whom we should like with us.

R. W. Emerson

REPLY TO GEORGE RIPLEY*

My dear Sir: It is quite time I made an answer to your proposition that I should venture into your new community. The design appears to me noble and generous, proceeding, as I plainly see, from nothing covert or selfish or ambitious, but from a manly and expanding heart and mind. So it makes all men its friends and debtors. It becomes a matter of conscience to entertain it in a friendly spirit and examine what it has for us.

I have decided not to join it, and yet very slowly and I may almost say with penitence. I am greatly relieved by learning that your coadjutors are now so many that you will no longer attach that importance to the defection of individuals which, you hinted in your letter to me, I or others might possess—the painful power, I mean, of preventing the execution of the plan.

My feeling is that the community is not good for me, that it has little to offer me which, with resolution, I cannot procure for myself; that it would not be worth my while to make the difficult exchange of my property in Concord for a share in the new household. I am in many respects placed as I wish to be, in an agreeable neighborhood, in a town which I have some reason to love, and which has respected my freedom so far that I have reason to hope it will indulge me further when I demand it. I cannot accuse my townsmen or my neighbors of my domestic grievances, only my own sloth and conformity. It seems to me a circuitous and operose way of relieving myself to put upon your community the emancipation which I ought to take on myself. I must assume my own vows.

The institution of domestic hired service is to me very disagreeable. I should like to come one step nearer to

* From Octavius B. Frothingham, *George Ripley* (Boston, 1882).

nature than this usage permits. But surely I need not sell my house and remove my family to Newton in order to make the experiment of labor and self help. I am already in the act of trying some domestic and social experiments which would gain nothing.

I ought to say that I do not put much trust in any arrangements or combinations, only in the spirit which dictates them. Is that benevolent and divine, they will answer their end. Is there any alloy in that, it will certainly appear in the result.

I have the same answer to make to the proposition of the school. According to my ability and according to yours, you and I do now keep school for all comers, and the energy of our thought and of our will measures our influence.

I do not think I should gain anything, I, who have little skill to converse with people, by a plan of so many parts, and which I comprehend so slowly and bluntly.

I almost shudder to make any statement of my objections to our ways of living, because I see how slowly I shall mend them. My own health and habits of living and those of my wife and my mother are not of that robustness that should give any pledge of enterprise and ability in reform. Nor can I insist with any heat on new methods when I am at work in my study on any literary composition. Yet I think that all I shall solidly do, I must do alone, and I am so ignorant and uncertain in my improvements that I would fain hide my attempts and failures in solitude where they shall perplex none or very few beside myself. The result of our secretest attempts will certainly have as much renown as shall be due to it.

I do not look on myself as a valuable member to any community which is not either very large or very small and select. I fear that yours would not find me as profitable and pleasant an associate as I should wish to be, and as so important a project seems imperatively to require in all its constituents. . . .

LETTER FROM A MINISTER*
(1843)

***

Dear Sir: I have an earnest and well-matured desire to join your community with my family, if I can do it under satisfactory circumstances—I mean satisfactory to all parties. I am pastor of the First Congregational Church in this town. My congregation is quiet, and in many respects very pleasant; but I have felt that my views of late are not sufficiently in accordance with the forms under which I have undertaken to conduct the ministry of Christian truth. This want of accordance increases, and I feel that a crisis is at hand. I must follow the light that guides me, or renounce it to become false and dead. The latter I cannot do. I have thought of joining your association ever since its commencement. Is it possible for me to do so under satisfactory circumstances?

I have deep, and I believe intelligent, sympathy with your idea. I have a wife and four children, the oldest ten, the youngest seven years old. Our habits of life are very simple, very independent of slavery to the common forms of "gigmanity," and our bodies have not been made to waste and pine by the fashionable follies of this generation. It is our creed that life is greater than all forms, and that the soul's life is diviner than the *conveniences* of fashion.

As to property we can bring you little more than ourselves. But we can bring a hearty good will to work, and in work we have some skill. I have unimpaired health, and an amount of muscular strength beyond what ordinarily falls to the lot of mortals. In the early part of my life I labored on a farm, filling up my leisure time with study, until I entered my present profession. My *hands* have some skill for many things; and if I join you I wish to live a true life. My selfish aims are two: first, I wish to be under circum-

* From Octavius B. Frothingham, *George Ripley* (Boston, 1882).

stances where I may live truly; and second and chiefly, I wish to do the best thing for my children.

Be so good as to reply to this at your earliest convenience. Yours, sincerely.

George Ripley

*REPLY TO AN INQUIRY**

Dear Sir: It gives me the most sincere pleasure to reply to the inquiries proposed in your favor of the 31st instant. I welcome the extended and increasing interest which is manifested in our apparently humble enterprise, as a proof that it is founded in nature and truth, and as a cheering omen of its ultimate success. Like yourself, we are seekers of universal truth. We worship only reality. We are striving to establish a mode of life which shall combine the enchantments of poetry with the facts of daily experience. This we believe can be done by a rigid adherence to justice, by fidelity to human rights, by loving and honoring man as man, by rejecting all arbitrary, factitius distinctions. We are not in the interest of any sect, party, or coterie; we have faith in the soul of man, in the universal soul of things. Trusting to the might of benignant Providence which is over all, we are here sowing in weakness a seed which will be raised in power. But I need not dwell on these general considerations with which you are doubtless familiar.

In regard to the *connection* of a family with us, our arrangements are liberal and comprehensive. We are not bound by fixed rules which apply to all cases. One general principle we are obliged to adhere to rigidly: not to receive any person who would increase the expenses more than the revenue of the establishment. Within the limits of this principle we can make any arrangement which shall suit particular cases.

A family with resources sufficient for self-support, independent of the exertion of its members, would find a favorable situation with us for the education of its children and for social enjoyment. An annual payment of $1,000 would probably cover the expenses of board and instruction, supposing that no services were rendered to diminish the ex-

---

*From Octavius B. Frothingham, *George Ripley* (Boston, 1882).

pense. An investment of $5,000 would more than meet the original outlay required for a family of eight persons, but in that case an additional appropriation would be needed, either of productive labor or of cash to meet the current expenditures. I forward you herewith a copy of our prospectus, from which you will perceive that the whole expense of a pupil with us, including board in vacations, is $250 per annum; but in case of one or more pupils remaining with us for a term of years, and assisting in the labors of the establishment, a deduction of one or two dollars per week would be made, according to the services rendered, until such time as, their education being so far completed, they might defray all their expenses by their labor. In the case of your son fifteen years of age, it would be necessary for him to reside with us for three months, at least, on the usual terms, and if, at the end of that time, his services should be found useful, he might continue by paying $150 or $200 per annum, according to the value of his labors; and if he should prove to have a gift for active industry, in process of time he might defray his whole expenses, complete his education, and be fitted for practical life. With the intelligent zeal which you manifest in our enterprise, I need not say that we highly value your sympathy, and should rejoice in any arrangement which might bring us into closer relations. It is only from the faith and love of those whose hearts are filled with the hopes of a better future for humanity that we look for the building up of our "city of God." So far we have been prospered in our highest expectations. We are more and more convinced of the beauty and justice of our mode of life. We love to breathe this pure, healthy atmosphere; we feel that we are living in the bosom of Nature, and all things seem to expand under the freedom and truth which we worship in our hearts. . . .

Sincerely your friend,
GEO. RIPLEY.

George Ripley

LETTER ON ASSOCIATION*

. . . Although my present strong convictions are in favor
of cooperative association rather than of community of
property, I look with an indescribable interest on every attempt to redeem society from its corruptions. The evils arising from trade and money, it appears to me, grow out
of the defects of our social organization, not from an intrinsic vice in the things themselves; and the abolition of
private property, I fear, would so far destroy the independence of the individual as to interfere with the great object of all social reforms, namely, the development of humanity, the substitution of a race of free, noble, holy men
and women, instead of the dwarfish and mutilated specimens which now cover the earth. The great problem is to
guarantee individualism against the masses on the one hand,
and the masses against the individual on the other.

In society as now organized the many are slaves to a
few favored individuals in a community. I should dread the
bondage of the individual to the power of the masses; while
association, by identifying the interests of the many and
the few, the less gifted and the highly gifted, secures the
sacred personality of all, gives to each individual the largest
liberty of the children of God. Such are my present views,
subject to any modification which farther light may produce. Still, I consider the great question of the means of
human regeneration yet open, indeed hardly touched as yet,
and Heaven forbid that I should not at least give you my
best wishes for the success of your important enterprise. In
our own little association we practically adopt many community elements. We are eclectics and learners; but day by
day increases our faith and joy in the principle of combined
industry, and of bearing each other's burdens instead of seek-

* From Octavius B. Frothingham, *George Ripley* (Boston, 1882).

ing every man his own. It will give me great pleasure to hear from you whenever you may have anything to communicate interesting to the general movement. I feel that all who are seeking the emancipation of man are brothers, though differing in the measures which they may adopt for that purpose. And from our different points of view it is not perhaps presumption to hope that we may aid each other by faithfully reporting the aspects of earth and sky as they pass before our field of vision. One danger, of which no doubt you are aware, proceeds from the growing interest in the subject, and that is, the crowd of converts who desire to help themselves rather than to help the movement. It is as true now as it was of old, that he who would follow this new Messiah must deny himself and take up his cross daily, or he cannot enter the promised kingdom. The path of transition is always covered with thorns and marked with the bleeding feet of the faithful. This truth must not be covered up in describing the paradise for which we hope. We must drink the water of Marah in the desert, that others may feed on the grapes of Eshcol. We must depend on the power of self-sacrifice in man, not on appeals to his selfish nature, for the success of our efforts. We should hardly be willing to accept of men or money unless called for by earnest convictions that they are summoned by a divine voice. I wish to hear less said to capitalists about a profitable investment of their funds, as if the holy cause of humanity was to be speeded onward by the same force which constructs railroads and ships of war. Rather preach to the rich, "Sell all that you have and give to the poor, and you shall have treasure in heaven."

Elizabeth Palmer Peabody

PLAN OF THE WEST ROXBURY COMMUNITY* (1841)

In the last number of the *Dial* were some remarks under the perhaps ambitious title of "A Glimpse of Christ's Idea of Society," in a note to which it was intimated that in this number would be given an account of an attempt to realize in some degree this great ideal by a little company in the midst of us as yet without name or visible existence. The attempt is made on a very small scale. A few individuals, who, unknown to each other, under different disciplines of life, reacting from different social evils, but aiming at the same object—of being wholly true to their natures as men and women—have been made acquainted with one another, and have determined to become the faculty of the embryo university.

In order to live a religious and moral life worthy the name, they feel it is necessary to come out in some degree from the world, and to form themselves into a community of property so far as to exclude competition and the ordinary rules of trade—while they reserve sufficient private property, or the means of obtaining it, for all purposes of independence and isolation at will. They have bought a farm, in order to make agriculture the basis of their life, it being the most direct and simple in relation to nature.

A true life, although it aims beyond the highest star, is redolent of the healthy earth. The perfume of clover lingers about it. The lowing of cattle is the natural bass to the melody of human voices.

On the other hand, what absurdity can be imagined greater than the institution of cities? They originated not in love, but in war. It was war that drove men together in multitudes,

* From *The Dial*, II (Jan. 1842).

and compelled them to stand so close, and build walls around them. This crowded condition produces wants of an unnatural character, which resulted in occupations that regenerated the evil by creating artificial wants. Even when that thought of grief,

> I know, where'er I go
> That there hath passed away a glory from the Earth,

came to our first parents as they saw the angel with the flaming sword of self-consciousness standing between them and the recovery of spontaneous life and joy, we cannot believe they could have anticipated a time would come when the sensuous apprehension of creation—the great symbol of God—would be taken away from their unfortunate children, crowded together in such a manner as to shut out the free breath and the universal dome of Heaven, some opening their eyes in the dark cellars of the narrow, crowded streets of walled cities. How could they have believed in such a conspiracy against the soul as to deprive it of the sun and sky and glorious appareled Earth! The growth of cities, which were the embryo of nations hostile to each other, is a subject worthy the thoughts and pen of the philosophic historian. Perhaps nothing would stimulate courage to seek, and hope to attain social good so much as a profound history of the origin, in the mixed nature of man and the exasperation by society, of the various organized evils under which humanity groans. Is there anything which exists in social or political life contrary to the soul's ideal? That thing is not eternal, but finite, saith the pure reason. It had a beginning, and so a history. What man has done, man may *undo*. "By man came death; by man also cometh the resurrection from the dead."

The plan of the community, as an economy, is in brief this: for all who have property to take stock, and receive a fixed interest thereon; then to keep house or board in commons, as they shall severally desire, at the cost of provisions purchased at wholesale or raised on the farm; and for all to labor in community and be paid at a certain rate an hour, choosing their own number of hours and their own kind of work. With the results of this labor, and their interest, they are to pay their board, and also purchase whatever else they require at cost at the warehouses of the community, which are to be filled by the community as such. To perfect this economy, in the course of time they must have all trades and all modes of business carried on among themselves, from the lowest mechanical trade which contributes to the health and comfort of life, to the finest art which adorns it with food or drapery for the mind.

All labor, whether bodily or intellectual, is to be paid at the same rate of wages, on the principle that as the labor becomes merely bodily, it is a greater sacrifice to the individual laborer to give his time to it because time is desirable for the cultivation of the intellect in exact proportion to ignorance. Besides, intellectual labor involves in itself higher pleasures, and is more its own reward, than bodily labor.

Another reason for setting the same pecuniary value on every kind of labor is to give outward expression to the great truth that all labor is sacred when done for a common interest. Saints and philosophers already know this, but the childish world does not; and very decided measures must be taken to equalize labors in the eyes of the young of the community, who are not beyond the moral influences of the world without them. The community will have nothing done within its precincts but what is done by its own members, who stand all in social equality, that the children may not "learn to expect one kind of service from love and good will, and another from the obligation of others to render it"—a grievance of the common society stated by one of the associated mothers as destructive of the soul's simplicity. Consequently, as the universal education will involve all kinds of operation necessary to the comforts and elegances of life, every associate, even if he be the digger of a ditch as his highest accomplishment, will be an instructor in that to the young members. Nor will this elevation of bodily labor be liable to lower the tone of manners and refinement in the community. The "children of light" are not altogether unwise in their generation. They have an invisible but all-powerful guard of principles. Minds incapable of refinement will not be attracted into this association. It is an ideal community, and only to the ideally inclined will it be attractive; but these are to be found in every rank of life, under every shadow of circumstance. Even among the diggers in the ditch are to be found some who through religious cultivation can look down, in meek superiority, upon the outwardly refined and the book-learned.

Besides, after becoming members of this community, none

will be engaged merely in bodily labor. The hours of labor for the association will be limited by a general law, and can be curtailed at the will of the individual still more; and means will be given to all for intellectual improvement and for social intercourse calculated to refine and expand. The hours redeemed from labor by community will not be reapplied to the acquisition of wealth but to the production of intellectual goods. This community aims to be rich, not in the metallic representative of wealth, but in the wealth itself which money should represent, namely, *leisure to live in all the faculties of the soul.* As a community, it will traffic with the world at large, in the products of agricultural labor; and it will sell education to as many young persons as can be domesticated in the families, and enter into the common life with their own children. In the end, it hopes to be enabled to provide not only all the necessaries, but all the elegances desirable for bodily and for spiritual health: books, apparatus, collections for science, works of art, means of beautiful amusement. These things are to be common to all, and thus that object which alone gilds and refines the passion for individual accumulation will no longer exist for desire, and whenever the sordid passion appears, it will be seen in its naked selfishness. In its ultimate success, the community will realize all the ends which selfishness seeks, but involved in spiritual blessings which only greatness of soul can aspire after.

And the requisitions on the individuals, it is believed, will make this the order forever. The spiritual good will always be the condition of the temporal. Everyone must labor for the community in a reasonable degree, or not taste its benefits. The principles of the organization, therefore, and not its probable results in future time, will determine its members. These principles are cooperation in social matters instead of competition or balance of interests, and individual self-unfolding, in the faith that the whole soul of humanity is in each man and woman. The former is the application of the love of man, the latter of the love of God, to life. Whoever is satisfied with society as it is, whose sense of justice is not wounded by its common action, institutions, spirit of commerce has no business with this community; neither has anyone who is willing to have other men (needing more time for intellectual cultivation than himself) give their best hours and strength to bodily labor to secure himself immunity therefrom. And whoever does not measure what society owes to its members of cherishing and instruction, by the needs of the individuals that compose it, has no lot in this new society. Whoever is willing to receive from his fellow men that for which he gives no equivalent will stay away from its precincts forever.

But whoever shall surrender himself to its principles shall find that its yoke is easy and its burden light. Everything can be said of it, in a degree, which Christ said of his kingdom, and therefore it is believed that in some measure it does embody his idea. For its gate of entrance is straight and narrow. It is literally a pearl *hidden in a field.* Those only who are willing to lose their life for its sake shall find it. Its voice is that which sent the young man sorrowing away. "Go sell all thy goods and give to the poor, and then come and follow me." "Seek first the kingdom of Heaven, and its righteousness, and all other things shall be added to you."

This principle, with regard to labor, lies at the root of moral and religious life; for it is not more true that "money is the root of all evil" than that *labor is the germ of all good....*

This plan of letting all persons choose their own departments of action will immediately place the genius of instruction on its throne. Communication is the life of spiritual life. Knowledge pours itself out upon ignorance by a native impulse. All the arts crave response. "Wisdom cries." If every man and woman taught only what they loved, and so many hours as they could naturally communicate, instruction would cease to be a drudgery and, we may add, learning would be no longer a task. The known accomplishments of many of the members of this association have already secured it an interest in the public mind as a school of literary advantages quite superior. Most of the associates have had long practical experience in the details of teaching and have groaned under the necessity of taking their method and law from custom or caprice when they would rather have found it in the nature of the thing taught and the condition of the pupil to be instructed. Each instructor appoints his hours of study or recitation, and the scholars, or the parents of the children, or the educational committee, choose the studies for the time, and the pupils submit, as long as they pursue their studies with any teacher, to his regulations....

It seems impossible that the little organization can be looked on with any unkindness by the world without it.

Those who have not the faith that the principles of Christ's kingdom are applicable to real life in the world will smile at it as a visionary attempt. But even they must acknowledge it can do no harm, in any event. If it realizes the hope of its founders, it will immediately become a manifold blessing. Its moral *aura* must be salutary. As long as it lasts, it will be an example of the beauty of brotherly love. If it succeeds in uniting successful labor with improvement in mind and manners, it will teach a noble lesson to the agricultural population, and do something to check that rush from the country to the city which is now stimulated by ambition, and by something better, even a desire for learning. Many a young man leaves the farmer's life because only by so doing can he have intellectual companionship and opportunity; and yet, did he but know it, professional life is ordinarily more unfavorable to the perfection of the mind than the farmer's life, if the latter is lived with wisdom and moderation and the labor mingled as it might be with study. This community will be a school for young agriculturalists, who may learn within its precincts not only the skillful practice, but the scientific reasons of their work, and be enabled afterward to improve their art continuously. It will also prove the best of normal schools, and as such may claim the interest of those who mourn over the inefficiency of our common school system with its present ill-instructed teachers.

It should be understood also that after all the working and teaching which individuals of the community may do, they will still have leisure, and in that leisure can employ themselves in connection with the world around them. Some will not teach at all, and those especially can write books, pursue the fine arts, for private emolument if they will, and exercise various functions of men. From this community might go forth preachers of the gospel of Christ who would not have upon them the odium, or the burden, that now diminishes the power of the clergy. And even if *pastors* were to go from this community to reside among congregations as now, for a salary given, the fact that they would have something to retreat upon at any moment would save them from that virtual dependence on their congregations which now corrupts the relation. There are doubtless beautiful instances of the old true relation of pastor and people, even of teacher and taught, in the decaying churches around us, but it is in vain to attempt to conceal the ghastly fact that many a taper is burning dimly in the candlestick, no longer silver or golden, because compassion forbids to put it quite out. But let the spirit again blow "where it listeth" and not circumscribe itself by salary and other commodity and the preached word might reassume the awful dignity which is its appropriate garment, and though it sit down with publicans and sinners, again speak "with authority and not as the scribes." . . .

INTRODUCTORY STATEMENT TO THE REVISED CONSTITUTION OF BROOK FARM* (1844)

The Association at Brook Farm has now been in existence upward of two years. Originating in the thought and experience of a few individuals, it has hitherto worn for the most part the character of a private experiment, and has avoided rather than sought the notice of the public. It has, until the present time, seemed fittest to those engaged in this enterprise to publish no statements of their purposes or methods, to make no promises or declarations, but quietly and sincerely to realize, as far as might be possible, the great ideas which gave the central impulse to their movement. It has been thought that a steady endeavor to embody these ideas more and more perfectly in life would give the best answer, both to the hopes of the friendly and the cavils of the skeptical, and furnish in its results the surest grounds for any larger efforts.

Meanwhile, every step has strengthened the faith with which we set out; our belief in a divine order of human society has in our own minds become an absolute certainty; and considering the present state of humanity and of social science, we do not hesitate to affirm that the world is much nearer the attainment of such a condition than is generally supposed.

The deep interest in the doctrine of association, which now fills the minds of intelligent persons everywhere, indicates plainly that the time has passed when even initiative movements ought to be prosecuted in silence, and makes it imperative on all who have either a theoretical or practical

* From Octavius B. Frothingham, *George Ripley* (Boston, 1882).

knowledge of the subject to give their share to the stock of public information.

Accordingly we have taken occasion, at several public meetings recently held in Boston, to state some of the results of our studies and experience, and we desire here to say emphatically that, while, on the one hand, we yield an unqualified assent to that doctrine of universal unity which Fourier teaches, so, on the other, our whole observation has shown us the truth of the practical arrangements which he deduces therefrom. The law of groups and series is, we are convinced, the law of human nature, and when men are in true social relations, their industrial organization will necessarily assume those forms.

But beside the demand for information respecting the principles of association, there is a deeper call for action in the matter. We wish, therefore, to bring Brook Farm before the public as a location offering at least as great advantages for a thorough experiment as can be found in the vicinity of Boston. It is situated in West Roxbury, three miles from the depot of the Dedham Branch Railroad, and about eight miles from Boston, and combines a convenient nearness to the city with a degree of retirement and freedom from unfavorable influences, unusual even in the country. The place is one of great natural beauty, and, indeed, the whole landscape is so rich and various as to attract the notice even of casual visitors. The farm now owned by the Association contains two hundred and eight acres of as good quality as any land in the neighborhood of Boston, and can be enlarged by the purchase of land adjoining to any necessary extent. The property now in the hands of the Association is worth nearly or quite thirty thousand dollars, of which about twenty-two thousand dollars is invested either in the stock of the company or in permanent loans to it at six per cent, which can remain as long as the Association may wish.

The fact that so large an amount of capital is already invested and at our service as the basis of more extensive operations, furnishes a reason why Brook Farm should be chosen as the scene of that practical trial of association which the public feeling calls for in this immediate vicinity, instead of forming an entirely new organization for that purpose.

The completeness of our educational department is also not to be overlooked. This has hitherto received our greatest care, and in forming it we have been particularly successful. In any new association it must be many years before so many accomplished and skillful teachers in the various branches of intellectual culture could be enlisted. Another strong reason is to be found in the degree of order our organization has already attained, by the help of which a large association might be formed without the losses and inconveniences which would otherwise necessarily occur. The experience of nearly three years in all the misfortunes and mistakes incident to an undertaking so new and so little understood carried on throughout by persons not entirely fitted for the duties they have been compelled to perform, has, as we think, prepared us to assist in the safe conduct of an extensive and complete association.

Such an institution, as will be plain to all, cannot, by any sure means, be brought at once and full grown into existence. It must, at least in the present state of society, begin with a comparatively small number of select and devoted persons, and increase by natural and gradual aggregations. With a view to an ultimate expansion into a perfect phalanx, we desire without any delay to organize the three primary departments of labor, namely, agriculture, domestic industry, and the mechanic arts.

For this purpose, additional capital will be needed, which it is most desirable should be invested by those who propose to connect themselves personally with the institution. These should be men and women accustomed to labor, skillful, careful, in good health, and, more than all, imbued with the idea of association, and ready to consecrate themselves without reserve to its realization. For it ought to be known that the work we propose is a difficult one, and, except to the most entire faith and resolution, will offer insurmountable obstacles and discouragements. Neither will it be possible to find in association, at the outset, the great outward advantages it ultimately promises. The first few years must be passed in constant and unwearied labor, lightened chiefly by the consciousness of high aims and the inward content that devotion to a universal object cannot fail to bring. Still there are certain tangible compensations which association guarantees immediately. These are freedom from pecuniary anxiety and the evils of competitive industry, free and friendly society, and the education of children. How great these are, those who have felt the terrible burdens which the present civilized society imposes in these respects will not need to be informed.

Those who may wish to further this cause by investments of money only will readily perceive that their end is not likely to be lost in an association whose means are devoted mainly to productive industry, and where nothing will ever be risked in uncertain speculations.

The following constitution is the same as that under which we have hitherto acted, with such alterations as, on a careful revision, seemed needful. All persons who are not familiar with the purposes of association will understand from this document that we propose a radical and universal reform, rather than to redress any particular wrong, or to remove the sufferings of any single class of human beings. We do this in the light of universal principles, in which all differences, whether of religion, or politics, or philosophy, are reconciled, and the dearest and most private hope of every man has the promise of fulfillment. Herein, let it be understood, we would remove nothing that is truly beautiful or venerable; we reverence the religious sentiment in all its forms, the family, and whatever else has its foundation either in human nature or the Divine Providence. The work we are engaged in is not destruction, but true conservation; it is not a mere revolution, but, as we are assured, a necessary step in the course of social progress which no one can be blind enough to think has yet reached its limit. We believe that humanity, trained by these long centuries of suffering and struggle, led onward by so many saints and heroes and sages, is at length prepared to enter into that universal order toward which it has perpetually moved. Thus we recognize the worth of the whole past, and of every doctrine and institution it has bequeathed us; thus, also, we perceive that the present has its own high mission, and we shall only say what is beginning to be seen by all sincere thinkers, when we declare that the imperative duty of this time and this country—nay more, that its only salvation, and the salvation of all civilized countries—lies in the reorganization of society according to the unchanging laws of human nature and of universal harmony.

We look, then, to the generous and hopeful of all classes for sympathy, for encouragement, and for actual aid, not to ourselves only, but to all those who are engaged in this great work. And, whatever may be the result of any special efforts, we can never doubt that the object we have in view will finally be attained; that human life shall yet be developed, not in discord and misery, but in harmony and joy, and the perfected earth shall at last bear on her bosom a race of men worthy of the name.

GEORGE RIPLEY,
MINOT PRATT,   } *Directors*
CHARLES A. DANA,

BROOK FARM, WEST ROXBURY,
        January 18, 1844.

5

FULL CIRCLE

Orestes A. Brownson

TRANSCENDENTALISM* (1846)

. . . Transcendentalism is virtually the ground on which the enemies of the church, generally, are rallying and endeavoring to make a stand, and the ground on which they are to be met and vanquished. Protestantism, as set forth by the early reformers, is virtually no more. It yielded to the well-directed blows of Bossuet and other Catholic divines in the seventeenth century. But its spirit was not extinguished. It survived, and in the beginning of the eighteenth century reappeared in England under the form of infidelity, or the denial of all supernatural revelation from God to men; and, by the aid of Voltaire, Rousseau, and other French *philosophes,* soon passed into France and Germany and, to no inconsiderable extent, penetrated even into Italy and Spain. Forced to abandon the form with which it had been clothed by Luther and Calvin and their associates, it found it could subsist and maintain its influence only by falling back on natural religion, and finally on no religion. But this did not long avail it. The world protested against incredulity, and the human race would not consent to regard itself as a "child without a sire" condemned to eternal orphanage. Either Protestantism must assume the semblance at least of religion, or yield up the race once more to Catholicity. But the latter alternative was more than could be expected of human pride and human weakness. The reform party could not willingly forego all their dreams of human perfectibility, "the march of mind," "the progress of the species," the realization of what they had emblazoned on their banners, and in the name of which they had established the Reign of Terror, and drenched Europe in her noblest and richest blood. To abandon these glorious dreams, these sublime hopes, to bow down their lofty heads before priests

* From *The Works of Orestes A. Brownson,* VI, 1-113.

and monks, to sheathe the sword and embrace the cross, to give up the Age of Reason, and readmit the Age of Faith was a sacrifice too great for poor human nature. Yet what other alternative was left? The race demanded a religion— would have some kind of faith and worship. To stand on open, avowed infidel ground was impossible. To return to the elder Protestantism was also impossible, for that had ceased to exist; and if it had not, a return to it would have been only subjecting itself anew to the necessity of going further and reuniting with Rome, or of falling back once more on deism, and then on atheism. It must, then, either vanish in thin air or invent some new form of error which, in appearance at least, should be neither the Protestantism of the sixteenth century nor the unbelief of the eighteenth. The last hope of the party was in the invention of this new form. Germany, mother of the Reformation, saw the extremities to which it was reduced, and charged herself with conceiving and bringing it forth, as sin conceives and brings forth death. The period of gestation was brief; the child was forthwith ushered into the world. France applauded, young America hurrahed, and even old England pricked up her ears, and calculated the practical advantages she might derive from adopting the bantling.

The bantling is named Transcendentalism . . . that is, a doctrine founded on that which transcends or surpasses sense and understanding.

According to Mr. Parker, this transcendental faculty is a sort of pipe, or conduit, through which the Divinity flows naturally into the human soul. The soul has a double set of faculties, one set on each side. Each at the terminus is furnished with a valve which the soul opens and shuts at will. If it opens one set, the external world flows in and it lives a purely material or animal life; if the other, the Divinity flows in, it becomes filled to its capacity with God, and lives a divine life. As the pipe or conduit through which the Divinity is let in as a natural endowment essential to the soul, and as we open or close its valve and let in or shut out God at will, the "supply of God" obtained is said to be obtained *naturally,* and as it is really God who runs in and fills the soul, the influx is said to be *divine,* or *divine* inspiration. As it is of God, and received through a natural inlet in a natural manner, it is *natural* inspiration and distinguishable, on the one hand, from the mere light of nature, and on the other, from *supernatural* inspiration, and may be termed, if you will, natural supernaturalism, natural spiritualism, or "the natural *religious* view."

Religious institutions are constructed by the human intellect and passions on the ideas of God furnished the soul through this natural channel. They are the more or less successful efforts of men to realize outwardly as well as inwardly the ideas and sentiments of God, of spirit, of the true, permanent, eternal, and absolute, which are supplied by this natural influx of God. Considered in their idea and sentiment, all religious institutions are true, sacred, divine, immutable, and eternal; but considered solely as institutions, they are human, partial, incomplete, variable, and transitory. . . .

As all religious institutions have a common origin in the soul, and do, in their degree and after their manner, shadow forth the same idea and sentiment, they are all, as to their idea and sentiment, identical. Mumbo-Jumbo of the African, or Manitou of the North American savage, is, at bottom, the true God as much as the Zeus of the Greeks, the Jupiter of the Romans—and either of these as much as the Jehovah of the Jews, or God the Father of the Christians. One or another is nothing but the form with which, in different ages and in different nations, men clothe the eternal and immutable idea of the highest and best, which is the same in all ages and nations and in all individuals. The difference is all in the form; there is none in the idea. . . .

Weak and ignorant men naturally imagine that the idea and sentiment must be inoperative and inefficacious unless clothed with positive institutions. . . . But the race has now advanced far enough to correct this mistake. Jesus saw the mistake, and his superiority lies in his having risen superior to all forms and asserted the sufficiency of the idea and sentiment alone, that is, of *absolute religion*. He discarded all forms, all institutions, all contrivances of men, and fell back on absolute religion, on the naked idea and sentiment, and taught his followers to do the same. Here was his transcendent merit. Here he proved himself in advance of his age—nay, in advance of all ages since. Unhappily, the world knew him not. His immediate disciples did not comprehend his divine work. They foolishly imagined that he came to introduce a new form, or to found a new religious institution which, like Aaron's rod, should swallow up all the rest; and even to this day the great mass of his professed followers have supposed that to be Christians they must sustain some formal institution, believe certain formal dogmas, and observe certain prescribed rites and ceremonies. Nevertheless, in all ages a bold few branded as heretics by the orthodox of their time have had some glimpses of the real significance of the Christian movement, and have stood forth the prophets and harbingers of the glory hereafter to be revealed. . . . The mighty *Welt-Geist,* the world-spirit, is on their side, moves in them, and fights and conquers for them; and we may trust that the time draws near when, in this country at least, we can dispense with all religious forms and institutions and carry out the sublime thought of Jesus, for proclaiming which a corrupt and formal age crucified him between two thieves. Then men will be satisfied with absolute religion; then the noble spirit of man will be emancipated, and the godlike mind that would explore all things and rise to its primal source, will spurn all formal dogmas, all contracting and debasing forms, and scorn to seek the living word of God in the dead petrifactions of crafty priests and besotted monks. Then God himself will be our teacher, and the soul nestle in the bosom of the All-Father; then man will be man, dare act out himself, and bow to no authority but that of the invisible Spirit, to whom gravitation and purity of heart, a man, a maggot, a mountain, a moss, are all the same; and then the human race will—what?

A peculiar excellence of Transcendentalism is that it permits its advocates to use the consecrated words of faith and piety in impious and infidel senses, and with so much speciousness as to deceive men and women not contemptible either for their intelligence or their motives. All religious institutions are symbolical and shadow forth, or *conceal,* real facts. Every rite, every ceremony, every dogma of religion has its root in the soul and conceals some truth of the soul. This truth *is* a truth, and therefore not to be rejected; but this truth, or fact, is all that in the symbol is valuable, or that it is essential to retain. Penetrate the symbol, then, ascertain this fact, and you have its real meaning, all that it has ever *meant,* even for the race. Thus, the human race believes in divine inspiration. Very well. Then divine inspiration is a fact. But the human race believes that divine inspiration is the supernatural communication, through chosen individuals, of truths pertaining to the supernatural order. But this is not the fact; it is only the form with which, through craft, ignorance, or credulity, the fact has been clothed, not the fact itself but its symbol. The real fact is

that every man's soul is furnished with a pipe through which
God runs into it as it wills, in any quantity not exceeding
its capacity. The church asserts the Incarnation—that the
human nature and the divine nature were united in Jesus
in one person. Very true. She also asserts that the two
natures were so united in him and in no other. There she is
wrong, for there she gives not the fact but its symbol. The
real fact is the union of the human and divine in all men,
or that no man need look out of his own nature to find
God, who is one with the nature of each man. I and my
Father are one. The Christian life is a combat, a warfare;
we must take up the cross, and fight constantly against the
world, the flesh, and the devil. All very true. But *the* world,
flesh, and devil against which we are to fight are not what
stupid ascetics dream, but low and debasing views of religion, attachment to obsolete forms, and unwillingness to
receive new light. The real devil is the conservative spirit. At
one time it is the church; at another, civil government;
among Protestants, it is the Bible; among Christians generally, the authority of Jesus. In a word, the devil is always
that particular thing, institution, or party which restrains the
free action of the soul and confines it to a prescribed
formula, whether of religion, politics, or morals, or whatever
would subject the soul to any law or authority distinguishable
from itself. Against this, in our own time and country, be it
what it may, we must take up arms, fight the good fight,
regardless of what may be the consequences to ourselves.
In this way, Transcendentalists appropriate to their own
use all the sacred language of religion and utter the foulest
blasphemy in the terms of faith and piety. . . .

The primal error of Transcendentalism, as must be obvious
to the philosophic reader, is in the denial of substantial
forms or distinct natures, and the assertion of the unity and
identity of all natures in one and the same universal nature.
Granting this denial and assertion, the greater part of their
system follows as a necessary logical consequence. But the
absurdity of the consequence is the refutation of the principle. Any principle which compels us to assert that there is
no difference between gravitation and purity of heart, between the nature of a stone and the nature of man, and between the nature of man and the nature of God, thus making
God the nature of the stone, and therefore stone itself, is
refuted by that figure of logic termed *reductio ad absurdum,*
and may be dismissed without further comment.

Transcendentalists have probably been led *philosophically* to the adoption of this error by attempting to reduce the categories of reason to the single category of being and phenomenon. Aristotle gave us ten categories which he made forms of the object, or at least forms of the reason, with their foundation in reality; Kant has given us fifteen, which he makes purely forms of the subject; Transcendentalists, following Schelling, Hegel, and Cousin, attempt to identify the subject and object, and to resolve all the categories into one. . . .

Transcendentalists have been led also into the same error by misapprehending the true doctrine of God's immanence in creation. God, say they, is not merely *causa transiens* but also *causa immanens,* and therefore must be immanent in all his works, which is true. He must be immanent in his essential character. True again. He is essentially being; then he must be immanent as being; then immanent as the being of all and of each. He is essentially cause; then he must be immanent as cause; then he is the causativeness of all and of each. But the conclusions do not follow. He is, indeed, immanent in all as being, not as the being *of* all and of each, but as *that which creates and sustains* the being of all and of each. He is immanent as cause, not as the causativeness of all and of each; but as *that which creates and sustains* the causativeness of all and of each. He is immanent not as the subject, but as that which creates and sustains the subject, and distinguishable from it as the cause from the effect. . . .

Assuming the reality of distinct natures—that God has made and sustains all beings, each after its kind—that there are real genera and species, substantial forms—and that each race of beings has its specific nature, then what comes within the scope of that nature is *natural,* pertains to the natural order, and what transcends it is *super*natural, pertains to the supernatural order. Each specific nature, by the fact that it is specific, is limited, finite; and then an infinite distance between it and God, who is infinite. Then necessarily an infinite order above the highest specific or created nature, that is to say, an infinite supernatural order, of which the highest conceivable created nature knows and can conceive nothing by virtue of its natural powers. If there is a God, then there is and must be a supernatural order. The Transcendentalists profess to believe in God. Then they must admit that there is a supernatural order of which they neither have nor can have any knowledge by any natural means. Nothing, then, hinders God, if he chooses, from revealing supernaturally more or less of this supernatural order to such of his creatures as he has made naturally intelligent. It may be that the end for which he intended man, when he made him, lies not in the plane of his natural powers but in this very supernatural order. If so, our true end is attainable by no natural means, and is, and must be, unattainable without supernatural aid. Then either God has made us for an unattainable end, which would implicate his power, his wisdom, or his justice; or he furnishes us the supernatural aid by which it is attainable, and without which it is not attainable. If he furnishes this aid, he may, if he chooses, furnish it through positive institutions, to the observance of which he attaches the grace needed. But whether he has made us for a supernatural destiny, for an end which transcends the natural order and pertains to the supernatural order, whether he has furnished us the supernatural means of attaining it, and whether he has furnished these means through positive institutions, and, if so, through what or which institutions, are all questions of fact, and must be decided as questions of fact, not of reason. The human race believes that he has made us for a supernatural end, and that he furnishes us the necessary aid through positive institutions, and Catholics believe through the positive institutions which we call the Catholic Church. Transcendentalists believe, or at least assert, the contrary. Here are the parties, and here is the issue. . . .

But, after all, what is the real sum and substance of Transcendentalism, this latest and noblest birth of time, as its friends regard it, and from which we are promised the universal *palingenesia* of man and nature—what is it when reduced to its simple, positive teachings? We have been led through tomes of metaphysical lore; we have been allured by brilliant promises of a recovered Eden; we have been flattered by glowing descriptions of our godlike powers, affinities, and tendencies; we have been transported by the assurance that we may dispense with priests, prophets, intercessors, and mediators, and of ourselves approach the Infinite One face to face, and drink our supply at the primal fountain of truth itself; but now, having lingered till the ascending sun has exhaled the dewdrops and exhausted the gems and precious stones which sparkled in rich profusion at our feet, what is the real and positive value of what has so long detained and charmed us? Things are what they are; man is what he is, and by a right use of his faculties may be, do, and know all he can be, do, and know. So far as we are wise, good, and loving, so far we have and know wisdom, goodness, love; and so far as we have and know wisdom, goodness, love, we have and know God, insofar as he is wisdom, goodness, love. He who knows more of these knows more than he who knows less. If the possession of wisdom, goodness, love be inspiration, then he who has the most wisdom, goodness, love is the most inspired—and to be more inspired, he must get more wisdom, goodness, love. To be more inspired, he must be more inspired. If white be white, then white is white; if black be black, then what is black is black; if two be two, then two are two. Or, in two grand formulas from Mr. Parker, "Goodness is goodness," and "Be good and do good," and—you will be good and do good! If this is not the whole of Transcendentalism when divested of its denials, its blasphemy, and its impiety, and reduced to its simple dogmatic teaching, then we have given days, weeks, months, and years to its study to no purpose. Stated in plain and simple terms, it is the veriest commonplace imaginable. It is merely "much ado about nothing," or "a tempest in a teapot." Dressed up in the glittering robes of a tawdry rhetoric, or wrapped in the mystic folds of an unusual and unintelligible dialect, it may impose on the simple and credulous; but to attempt to satisfy one's spiritual wants with it is as vain as to attempt to fill one's self with the east wind, or to warm one's freezing hands on a cold winter's night by holding them up to the moon. Yet its teachers are the great lights of this age of light, before whom all the great lights of past times pale as the stars before the sun. Men and women, through some mistake not in a lunatic hospital, run after them with eagerness, hang with delight on their words, and smack their lips as if feeding on honey. Our Protestant populations, on whom the sun of the Reformation shines in its effulgence, are moved, run toward their teaching, and are about to hail it as the Tenth Avatar come to redeem the world. Wonderful teachers! Wonderful populations! Wonderful age!

In conclusion, while surveying the mass of absurdities and impieties heaped together under the name of Transcendentalism, and which attract so many, and even some of our own friends, whose kindness of heart, whose simple manners, and whose soundness of judgment on all other subjects command our love and esteem, we have been forcibly struck with the utter impotence of human reason to devise a scheme which reason herself shall not laugh to scorn. As often as man has attempted of himself alone to build a tower which should reach to heaven, or to connect by his own skill and labor the earthly with the celestial and make a free and easy passage from one to the other, the Lord has derided his impotent efforts, confounded his language, and made confusion more confused. Uniform failure should teach us the folly of the attempt, and lead us to ask if it be not the highest reason to bow to the divine reason, and the most perfect freedom to have no will but the will of God. "O Israel! thou destroyest thyself; in *me* is thy help."

Theodore Parker

THEODORE PARKER'S
EXPERIENCE AS A MINISTER
(1859)

. . . In due time I entered the Theological School at Cambridge, then under the charge of the Unitarians, or "Liberal Christians." I found excellent opportunities for study: there were able and earnest professors who laid no yoke on any neck but left each man free to think for himself and come to such conclusions as he must. Telling what they thought they knew, they never pretended they had learned all that may be known, or winnowed out all error from their creed. They were honest guides, with no more sophistry than is perhaps almost universal in that calling, and did not pretend to be masters. There, too, was a large library containing much valuable ancient lore, though, alas! almost none of the new theologic thought of the German masters. Besides, there was leisure and unbounded freedom of research, and I could work as many hours in the study as a mechanic in his shop, or a farmer in his field. The pulpits of Boston were within an easy walk, and Dr. Channing drew near the zenith of his power.

Here, under these influences, I pursued the usual routine of theological reading, but yet, of course, had my own private studies, suited to my special wants. It is now easy to tell what I then attempted without always being conscious of my aim, and what results I gradually reached before I settled in the ministry.

I. I studied the Bible with much care. First, I wished to learn, What is the Bible—what books and words compose it? this is the question of criticism; next, What does the Bible mean—what sentiments and ideas do its words contain? this is the question of interpretation. I read the Bible critically,

414

in its original tongues, the most important parts of it also in the early versions, and sought for the meaning early attributed to its words, and so studied the works of Jewish rabbis on the Old Testament, and of the early Christian Fathers on both New and Old; besides, I studied carefully the latest critics and interpreters, especially the German.

I soon found that the Bible is a collection of quite heterogeneous books, most of them anonymous or bearing names of doubtful authors, collected none knows how, or when, or by whom, united more by caprice than any philosophic or historic method, so that it is not easy to see why one ancient book is kept in the canon and another kept out. I found no unity of doctrine in the several parts; the Old Testament "reveals" one form of religion, and the New Testament one directly its opposite; and in the New Testament itself, I found each writer had his own individuality, which appears not only in the style, the form of thought, but quite as much in the doctrines, the substance of thought, where no two are well agreed.

Connected with this Biblical study, came the question of inspiration and of miracles. I still inconsistently believed, or half believed, in the direct miraculous interposition of God, from time to time, to set things right which else went wrong, though I found no historic or philosophic reason for limiting it to the affairs of Jews and Christians, or the early ages of the Church. The whole matter of miracles was still a puzzle to me, and for a long time a source of anxiety; for I had not studied the principles of historic evidence, nor learned to identify and scrutinize the witnesses. But the problem of inspiration got sooner solved. I believed in the immanence of God in man as well as matter, His activity in both; hence, that all men are inspired in proportion to their actual powers, and their normal use thereof; that truth is the test of intellectual inspiration, justice of moral, and so on. I did not find the Bible inspired except in this general way, and in proportion to the truth and justice therein. It seemed to me that no part of the Old Testament or New could be called the "Word of God," save in the sense that all truth is God's word.

II. I studied the historical development of religion and theology amongst Jews and Christians, and saw the gradual formation of the great ecclesiastical doctrines which so domineered over the world. As I found the Bible was the work of men, so I also found that the Christian Church was no more divine than the British State, a Dutchman's shop, or an Austrian's farm. The miraculous, infallible Bible, and the miraculous, infallible Church, disappeared when they were closely looked at; and I found the fact of history quite different from the pretension of theology.

III. I studied the historical development of religion and theology amongst the nations not Jewish or Christian, and attended as well as I then could to the four other great religious sects—the Brahmanic, the Buddhistic, the Classic, and the Mahometan. As far as possible at that time, I studied the sacred books of mankind in their original tongues, and with the help of the most faithful interpreters. Here the Greek and Roman poets and philosophers came in for their place, there being no sacred books of the classic nations. I attended pretty carefully to the religion of savages and barbarians, and was thereby helped to the solution of many a difficult problem. I found no tribe of men destitute of religion who had attained power of articulate speech.

IV. I studied assiduously the metaphysics and psychology of religion. Religious consciousness was universal in human history. Was it then natural to man, inseparable from his essence, and so from his development? In my own consciousness I found it automatic and indispensable; was it really so likewise in the human race? The authority of bibles and churches was no answer to that question. I tried to make an analysis of humanity, and see if by psychologic science I could detect the special element which produced religious consciousness in me and religious phenomena in mankind— seeking a cause adequate to the facts of experience and observation. The common books of philosophy seemed quite insufficient; the sensational system so ably presented by Locke in his masterly Essay, developed into various forms by Hobbes, Berkeley, Hume, Paley, and the French Materialists, and modified, but not much mended, by Reid and Stewart, gave little help; it could not legitimate my own religious instincts, nor explain the religious history of mankind, or even of the British people, to whom that philosophy is still so manifold a hindrance. Ecclesiastical writers, though able as Clarke and Butler, and learned also as Cudworth and Barrow, could not solve the difficulty; for the principle of authority, though more or less concealed, yet lay there, and, like buried iron, disturbed the free action of their magnetic genius, affecting its dip and inclination. The brilliant mosaic which Cousin set before the world was of great service, but not satisfactory. I found most help in the works of Immanuel Kant, one of the profoundest thinkers in the world, though one of the worst writers, even of Germany; if he did not always furnish conclusions I could rest in, he yet gave me the true method, and put me on the right road.

I found certain great primal intuitions of human nature which depend on no logical process of demonstration but are rather facts of consciousness given by the instinctive action of human nature itself. I will mention only the three most important which pertain to religion:

1. The instinctive intuition of the divine, the consciousness that there is a God;

2. The instinctive intuition of the just and right, a consciousness that there is a moral law, independent of our will, which we ought to keep;

3. The instinctive intuition of the immortal, a consciousness that the essential element of man, the principle of individuality, never dies.

Here, then, was the foundation of religion, laid in human nature itself, which neither the atheist nor the more pernicious bigot, with their sophisms of denial or affirmation, could move, or even shake. I had gone through the great spiritual trial of my life, telling no one of its hopes or fears; and I thought it a triumph that I had psychologically established these three things to my own satisfaction, and devised a scheme which to the scholar's mind, I thought, could legitimate what was spontaneously given to all by the great primal instincts of mankind.

Then I proceeded to develop the contents of these instinctive intuitions of the divine, the just, and the immortal, and see what God actually is, what morality is, and what eternal life has to offer. In each case I pursued two methods—the inductive and deductive.

First, from the history of mankind—savage, barbarous, civilized, enlightened—I gathered the most significant facts I could find relating to men's opinions about God, morality, heaven, and hell, and thence made such generalizations as the facts would warrant, which, however, were seldom satisfactory, for they did not represent facts of the universe, the actual God, justice, and eternal life, but only what men had thought or felt thereof; yet this comparative and inductive theology was of great value to me.

Next, from the primitive facts of consciousness, given by the power of instinctive intuition, I endeavored to deduce the true notion of God, of justice, and futurity. Here I could draw from human nature and not be hindered by the limitations of human history; but I know now better than it was possible then, how difficult is this work, and how often the inquirer mistakes his own subjective imagination for a fact of the universe. It is for others to decide whether I have sometimes mistaken a little grain of brilliant dust in my telescope for a fixed star in heaven. . . .

Many circumstances favored both studious pursuits and the formation of an independent character. The years of my preliminary theological study and of my early ministry fell in the most interesting period of New England's spiritual history, when a great revolution went on—so silent that few men knew it was taking place, and none then understood its whither or its whence.

The Unitarians, after a long and bitter controversy, in which they were often shamelessly ill-treated by the "orthodox," had conquered, and secured their ecclesiastical right to deny the Trinity, "the Achilles of dogmas"; they had won the respect of the New England public; had absorbed most of the religious talent of Massachusetts, founded many churches, and possessed and liberally administered the oldest and richest college in America. Not yet petrified into a sect, they rejoiced in the large liberty of "the children of God," and, owning neither racks nor dungeons, did not covet any of those things that were their neighbors'. With less education and literary skill, the Universalists had fought manfully against eternal damnation—the foulest doctrine which defiles the pages of man's theologic history—secured their ecclesiastical position, wiping malignant statutes from the law books, and, though in a poor and vulgar way, were popularizing the great truth that God's chief attribute is *love,* which is extended to all men. Alone of all Christian sects, they professedly taught the immortality of man in such a form that it is no curse to the race to find it true. But, though departing from those doctrines which are essential to the Christian ecclesiastic scheme, neither Universalist nor Unitarian had broken with the authority of revelation, the word of the Bible, but still professed a willingness to believe both Trinity and damnation, could they be found in the miraculous and infallible Scripture.

Mr. Garrison, with his friends, inheriting what was best in the Puritan founders of New England, fired with the zeal of the Hebrew prophets and Christian martyrs, while they were animated with a spirit of humanity rarely found in any of the three, was beginning his noble work, but in a style so humble that, after much search, the police of Boston discovered there was nothing dangerous in it, for "his only visible auxiliary was a Negro boy." Dr. Channing was in the full maturity of his powers, and after long preaching the dignity of man as an abstraction, and piety as a purely inward life, with rare and winsome eloquence and ever progressive humanity, began to apply his sublime doctrines to actual life in the individual, the state, and the church. In the name of Christianity, the great American Unitarian called for the reform of the drunkard, the elevation of the poor, the instruction of the ignorant, and above all, for the liberation of the American slave. A remarkable man, his instinct of progress grew stronger the more he traveled and the further he went, for he surrounded himself with young life. Horace Mann, with his coadjutors, began a great movement to improve the public education of the people. Pierpont, single-handed, was fighting a grand and twofold battle—against drunkenness in the street, and for righteousness in the pulpit —against fearful ecclesiastic odds maintaining a minister's right and duty to oppose actual wickedness, however popular and destructive. The brilliant genius of Emerson rose in the winter nights and hung over Boston, drawing the eyes of ingenuous young people to look up to that great, new star, a beauty and a mystery, which charmed for the moment, while it gave also perennial inspiration, as it led them forward along new paths and toward new hopes. America had seen no such sight before; it is not less a blessed wonder now.

Besides, the phrenologists, so ably represented by Spurzheim and Combe, were weakening the power of the old supernaturalism, leading men to study the constitution of man more wisely than before, and laying the foundation on which many a beneficent structure was soon to rise. The writings of Wordsworth were becoming familiar to the thoughtful lovers of nature and of man and drawing men to natural piety. Carlyle's works got reprinted at Boston, diffusing a strong, and then, also, a healthy influence on old and young. The writings of Coleridge were reprinted in America, all of them "Aids to Reflection" and brilliant with the scattered sparks of genius; they incited many to think, more especially young Trinitarian ministers; and, spite of the lack of both historic and philosophic accuracy, and the utter

absence of all proportion in his writings; spite of his haste,
his vanity, prejudice, sophistry, confusion, and opium—he
yet did great service in New England, helping to emancipate
enthralled minds. The works of Cousin, more systematic, and
more profound as a whole, and far more catholic and comprehensive, continental, not insular in his range, also became
familiar to the Americans—reviews and translation going
where the eloquent original was not heard—and helped to
free the young mind from the gross sensationalism of the
academic philosophy on one side, and the grosser supernaturalism of the ecclesiastic theology on the other.

The German language, hitherto the priceless treasure of a
few, was becoming well known, and many were thereby
made acquainted with the most original, deep, bold, comprehensive, and wealthy literature in the world, full of theologic and philosophic thought. Thus, a great storehouse was
opened to such as were earnestly in quest of truth. Young
Mr. Strauss, in whom genius for criticism was united with
extraordinary learning and rare facility of philosophic
speech, wrote his *Life of Jesus* where he rigidly scrutinized
the genuineness of the Gospels and the authenticity of their
contents, and, with scientific calmness, brought every statement to his steady scales, weighing it, not always justly, as I
think, but impartially always, with philosophic coolness and
deliberation. The most formidable assailant of the ecclesiastical theology of Christendom, he roused a host of foes,
whose writings—mainly ill-tempered, insolent, and sophisti-
cal—it was yet profitable for a young man to read.

The value of Christian miracles, not the question of fact,
was discussed at Boston as never before in America. Prophecy
had been thought the Jachin, and miracles the Boaz, whereon
alone Christianity could rest; but, said some, if both be
shaken down, the Lord's house will not fall. The claims of
ecclesiastical tradition came up to be settled anew; and young
men, walking solitary through the moonlight, asked, Which
is to be permanent master, a single accident in human history, nay, perchance only the whim of some anonymous
dreamer, or the substance of human nature, greatening with
continual development. . . .

The question was also its answer.

The rights of labor were discussed with deep philanthropic
feeling, and sometimes with profound thought, metaphysic
and economic both. The works of Charles Fourier—a
strange, fantastic, visionary man, no doubt, but gifted also

with amazing insight of the truths of social science—shed some light in these dark places of speculation. Mr. Ripley, a born democrat in the high sense of that abused word, and one of the best cultured and most enlightened men in America, made an attempt at Brook Farm in West Roxbury so to organize society that the results of labor should remain in the workman's hand and not slip thence to the trader's till; that there should be "no exploitation of man by man," but toil and thought, hard work and high culture, should be united in the same person.

The natural rights of women began to be inquired into, and publicly discussed; while in private, great pains were taken in the chief towns of New England, to furnish a thorough and comprehensive education to such young maidens as were born with two talents, mind and money.

Of course, a strong reaction followed. At the Cambridge Divinity School, Professor Henry Ware, Jr., told the young men, if there appeared to them any contradiction between the reason of man and the letter of the Bible, they "must follow the written word," "for you can never be so certain of the correctness of what takes place in your own mind, as of what is written in the Bible." In an ordination sermon, he told the young minister not to preach himself, but Christ, and not to appeal to human nature for proof of doctrines, but to the authority of revelation. Other Unitarian ministers declared, "There are limits to free inquiry," and preached, "Reason must be put down, or she will soon ask terrible questions"; protested against the union of philosophy and religion, and assumed to "prohibit the banns" of marriage between the two. Mr. Norton—then a great name at Cambridge, a scholar of rare but contracted merit, a careful and exact writer born for controversy, really learned and able in his special department, the interpretation of the New Testament—opened his mouth and spoke: the mass of men must accept the doctrines of religion solely on the authority of the learned, as they do the doctrines of mathematical astronomy; the miracles of Jesus—he made merry at those of the Old Testament—are the only evidence of the truth of Christianity; in the popular religion of the Greeks and Romans there was no conception of God; the new philosophic attempts to explain the facts of religious consciousness were "the latest form of infidelity"; the great philosophical and theological thinkers of Germany were "all atheists"; "Schleiermacher was an atheist," as was also Spinoza, his master, before him; and Cousin, who was only "that Frenchman," was no better; the study of philosophy, and the neglect of "Biblical criticism," were leading mankind to ruin; everywhere was instability and insecurity! . . .

The movement party established a new quarterly, the *Dial*, wherein their wisdom and their folly rode together on the same saddle, to the amazement of lookers-on. The short-lived journal had a narrow circulation, but its most significant papers were scattered wide by newspapers which copied them. A *Quarterly Review* was also established by Mr. Brownson, then a Unitarian minister and "skeptical democrat" of the most extravagant class, but now a Catholic, a powerful advocate of material and spiritual despotism, and perhaps the ablest writer in America against the rights of man and the welfare of his race. In this he diffused important philosophic ideas, displayed and disciplined his own extraordinary talents for philosophic thought and popular writings, and directed them toward Democracy, Transcendentalism, "New Views," and the "Progress of the Species."

I count it a piece of good fortune that I was a young man when these things were taking place, when great questions were discussed, and the public had not yet taken sides. . . .

Let me arrange, under three heads, some of the most important doctrines I have aimed to set forth.

I. THE INFINITE PERFECTION OF GOD—This doctrine is the cornerstone of all my theological and religious teaching —the foundation, perhaps, of all that is peculiar in my system. It is not known to the Old Testament or the New; it has never been accepted by any sect in the Christian world, for though it be equally claimed by all, from the Catholic to the Mormon, none has ever consistently developed it, even in theory, but all continually limit God in power, in wisdom, and still more eminently in justice and in love. . . .

The infinitely perfect God is immanent in the world of matter and in the world of spirit, the two hemispheres which to us make up the universe; each particle thereof is inseparable from Him, while He yet transcends both, is limited by neither, but in Himself is complete and perfect. . . .

He is a perfect Creator, making all from a perfect motive, for a perfect purpose, of perfect substance, and as a perfect means; none other are conceivable with a perfect God. The motive must be love, the purpose welfare, the means the constitution of the universe itself, as a whole and in parts—

for each great or little thing coming from Him must be perfectly adapted to secure the purpose it was intended for, and
achieve the end it was meant to serve, and represent the
causal motive which brought it forth. So there must be a
complete solidarity between God and the twofold universe
which He creates. The perfect Creator is thus also a perfect
Providence; indeed, creation and Providence are not objective accidents of Deity, nor subjective caprices, but the development of the perfect motive to its perfect purpose, love becoming a universe of perfect welfare. . . .

II. The Adequacy of Man for All His Functions—
From the infinite perfection of God there follows unavoidably the relative perfection of all that He creates. So the nature of man, tending to a progressive development of all
his manifold powers, must be the best possible nature, most
fit for the perfect accomplishment of the perfect purpose,
and the attainment of the perfect end which God designs for
the race and the individual. It is not difficult in this general
way to show the relative perfection of human nature, deducing this from the infinite perfection of God; but I think it
impossible to prove it by the inductive process of reasoning
from concrete facts of external observation, of which we
know not yet the entire sum, nor any one, perhaps, completely. Yet I have traveled also this inductive road as far
as it reaches, and tried to show the constitution of man's
body, with its adaptation to the surrounding world of matter,
and the constitution of his spirit, with its intellectual, moral,
affectional, and religious powers, and its harmonious relation
with the world of matter, which affords them a playground,
a school, and a workshop. So I have continually taught that
man has in himself all the faculties he needs to accomplish
his high destination, and in the world of matter finds, one by
one, all the material helps he requires. . . .

III. Absolute or Natural Religion—In its complete and
perfect form, this is the normal development, use, discipline,
and enjoyment of every part of the body and every faculty
of the spirit, the direction of all natural powers to their natural purposes. I have taught that there were three parts
which make up the sum of true religion: the emotional part,
of right feelings, where religion at first begins in the automatic, primal instinct; the intellectual part, of true ideas
which either directly represent the primitive, instinctive feelings of whoso holds them, or else produce a kindred, secondary, and derivative feeling in whoso receives them; and

the practical part, of just actions which correspond to the feelings and the ideas, and make the mere thought or emotion into a concrete deed. So, the true religion which comes from the nature of man consists of normal feelings toward God and man, of correct thoughts about God, man, and the relation between them, and of actions corresponding to the natural conscience when developed in harmony with the entire constitution of man. . . .

The absolute religion which belongs to man's nature, and is gradually unfolded thence, like the high achievements of art, science, literature, and politics is only distinctly conceived of in an advanced stage of man's growth; to make its idea a fact is the highest triumph of the human race. This is the idea of humanity, dimly seen but clearly felt, which has flitted before the pious eyes of men in all lands and many an age, and been prayed for as the "kingdom of heaven." The religious history of the race is the record of man's continual but unconscious efforts to attain this "desire of all nations"; poetic stories of the "golden age," or of man in the Garden of Eden, are but this natural wish looking back and fondly dreaming that "the former days were better than these." But while all the other forms of religion must ultimately fail before this, fading as it flowers, each one of them has yet been a help toward it, probably indispensable to the development of mankind. . . .

For these three great doctrines—of God, of man, of religion—I have depended on no church and no scripture; yet have I found things to serve me in all scriptures and every church. I have sought my authority in the nature of man—in facts of consciousness with me, and facts of observation in the human world without. To me the material world and the outward history of man do not supply a sufficient revelation of God, nor warrant me to speak of infinite perfection. It is only from the nature of man, from facts of intuition that I can gather this greatest of all truths, as I find it in my consciousness reflected back from Deity itself. . . .

ABOUT THE AUTHORS

William Ellery Channing (1780–1842). Channing was born and brought up in Newport, Rhode Island, where his family was prominent in Federalist politics. After graduating from Harvard in 1798, he lived in Richmond, Virginia, for a year and a half, employed as a tutor. He returned to Harvard in 1801 to continue his studies in divinity, and in 1803 became pastor of the Federal Street Church in Boston, where he remained till the end of his life. After the publication of his sermon on "Unitarian Christianity," Channing came more and more to be regarded as the leading spokesman for liberal religion in the United States, and his reputation extended to England and the Continent. He was never a Transcendentalist, but his work, especially "Likeness to God," exhibits clearly all the tendencies in Unitarianism which encouraged the independent growth of younger Unitarian ministers like Emerson, Ripley, and Parker. In later life, despite a shy and reclusive temper, he became increasingly involved in movements for social reform, especially the agitation against slavery.

Andrews Norton (1786–1853). Born in Hingham, Massachusetts, Norton spent most of his life at Harvard, where, from 1819 to 1830, he ruled the Divinity School as Dexter Professor of Sacred Literature. He was the preeminent theologian of Boston Unitarianism; his *magnum opus, The Evidence of the Genuineness of the Four Gospels* (1838), is an exhaustive statement of the kind of rationalistic, "historical" Christianity against which the Transcendentalists rebelled. His most famous piece, however, is the "Discourse" reprinted (in part) in this volume. It was delivered to a gathering of alumni of the Harvard Divinity School almost exactly a year after Emerson's notorious "Divinity School Address."

James Marsh (1794–1842). Marsh was a Vermonter who graduated from Dartmouth and studied at Andover Theological Seminary. An orthodox minister, he was president of the University of Vermont from 1826 to 1833 and professor of philosophy until his death. As a Calvinist, his intention in publishing Coleridge had nothing to do with Unitarianism or Transcendentalism; rather, he hoped to counteract the influence of Locke in the orthodox churches. But with his edition of *Aids to Reflection*, "he put," Perry Miller has said, "into the hands of Emerson, Parker, Alcott, and their group the book that was of the greatest single importance in the formation of their minds."

Bronson Alcott (1799–1888). Alcott was born in Wolcott, Connecticut, and in his youth was a traveling peddler before he tried his hand at schoolteaching. From 1823 to 1828 he conducted schools near his home in Bristol and Cheshire, Connecticut, deriving much inspiration from works by and about the Swiss educator J. H. Pestalozzi. In 1828 he opened his first school in Boston, but left after two years to teach in Germantown, Pennsylvania, returning in 1834 to found the Temple School, his most famous educational venture. *Record of a School* and *Conversations with Children on the Gospels* (1836–1837)—both written by Elizabeth Peabody —describe very fully the novel methods and purposes of this school. The notoriety of the latter work almost wrecked Alcott's undertaking, and the admission of a Negro child to his classes in 1839 was the final blow to his teaching career. For much of the rest of his life Alcott supported himself by giving "conversations" and by accepting the bounty of his friends and admirers. In 1843 he attempted, with Charles Lane, to found an ideal community at "Fruitlands" near Harvard, Massachusetts; more successfully, he served as school superintendent in Concord from 1859 to 1865, and helped organize the Concord School of Philosophy, which met every summer from 1879 to the year of his death.

Sampson Reed (1800–1880). Born in Bridgewater, Massachusetts, the son of a minister, Reed went to Harvard, graduating in 1818, and then attended the Divinity School for three years. During that time he became a Swedenborgian, and finding no career open to him in the tiny New Jerusalem Church, he apprenticed himself to a druggist. Ultimately he grew rich in trade, remaining an ardent supporter of the Swedenborgian movement, and serving as editor of some of its periodicals. In 1838 he denounced Transcendentalism as a parasite of Lockian sensualism; but in the 1820's his two short works, "On Genius" and "Observation on the Growth of the Mind," had a powerful effect on members of the emerging "new school."

George Ripley (1802–1880). Ripley was born in Greenfield, Massachusetts, attended Harvard and the Divinity School, and after his graduation in 1826, became minister of the Purchase Street Church in Boston, where he remained until 1840. An unusually able and energetic man, his articles, translations, and editions of contemporary European authors in translation, made him one of the most effective spokesmen of the Transcendentalist movement during the 1830's. Feeling that his ministry had outlived its usefulness, he resigned, and in 1841 became one of the founders of Brook Farm. After the collapse of this venture in 1847, he moved to New York where he lived for the rest of his life, working as a freelance writer and as literary editor for the New York *Tribune.* By the time of his death, he was widely acknowledged to be the best literary journalist then at work in the United States.

Ralph Waldo Emerson (1803–1882). A native Bostonian, Emerson went to Harvard from 1817 to 1821, taught school for a while, returned to the Divinity School in 1825, and was ordained at the Second Church of Boston in 1829. Three years later he resigned from the ministry and began a new career as writer and lecturer. His writings of the mid-thirties were landmarks in the evolution of the Transcendentalist movement in America: especially to be mentioned are *Nature* (1836), "The American Scholar" (1837), and the "Divinity School Address" (1838). Emerson's literary genius was quickly recognized by most of his colleagues, but he was never regarded as the authoritative voice of the "new school." In fact, his lifelong insistence on the priority of "self-culture," his distaste for organizations or associations of whatever stripe, might be regarded as the source of the deepest division in the ranks of American Transcendentalism.

Orestes A. Brownson (1803–1876). Brownson's was one of the most erratic and brilliant intellectual careers of the nineteenth century. He was born in Stockbridge, Vermont, and never acquired much formal education, though he ultimately became one of the most learned men of his time. Beginning as a Presbyterian, he passed through Universalism and skepticism before arriving at Unitarianism in about 1831. For a while he served as minister in Canton, Massachusetts, but inevitably he was drawn to Boston where he organized, in 1836, an independent church called the Society for Christian Union and Progress. From 1838 to 1842 Brownson also edited, and wrote almost single-handedly, the *Boston Quarterly Review,* in which his strongly democratic political views were aired along with his philosophic and religious opinions. In 1843–44 Brownson underwent a conversion to Catholicism, which effectively cut him off from his former sympathies and associations. He revived his periodical as *Brownson's Quarterly Review,* and for many years continued writing as the liveliest and most contentious Catholic propagandist in the country.

Elizabeth Palmer Peabody (1804–1894). Miss Peabody was probably one of the most energetic women of the nineteenth century. Born in Billerica, Massachusetts, she spent most of her life in Salem and Boston. She began to teach in 1820, and the chief business of her career remained education in one form or another. For a while she was a protégée of Dr. Channing, and she served as Alcott's assistant at the Temple School. In 1839 she opened a bookshop in Boston, the only one in which foreign books were sold; it was long a meeting place for Transcendentalist intellectuals. She also published various works, among them the first (and only) volume of *Aesthetic Papers,* in which Thoreau's essay on "Civil Disobedience" was first printed. Earlier, in 1833, she began giving what she called "conferences" on history and literature for women; these conferences set the pattern for the later "conversations" of Alcott and Margaret Fuller. Among her many activities of subsequent years, Miss Peabody's promotion of the kindergarten movement in America was most successful. She opened the first kindergarten in Boston in 1860, and for many years she lectured and wrote on the methods of Friedrich Froebel, which she had studied in Germany at first hand. James Freeman Clarke, one of the Transcendentalist ministers, is reported to have said of her that "she was always engaged in supplying some want that had first to be created," and it was T. W. Higginson's opinion that "she always preached the need, but never accomplished the supply until she advocated the kindergarten; there she caught up with her mission and came to identify herself with its history."

Frederic Henry Hedge (1805–1890). Hedge was the son of a Harvard professor; he studied in Germany from 1818 to 1821 and brought back a firsthand acquaintance with recent

German philosophy. He graduated from Harvard in 1825, spent four years in the Divinity School, and was minister in West Cambridge and then in Bangor, Maine. The Transcendental Club was often convened on his visits to Boston, which is why it was sometimes called the "Hedge Club." After 1857 he returned to Harvard, serving as professor both of ecclesiastical history and German literature.

Theodore Parker (1810–1860). The youngest of eleven children born to poor parents in Lexington, Massachusetts, Parker was a phenomenally precocious, and largely self-taught, student. He took examinations at Harvard without enrolling in classes for want of funds, and in 1834 he entered the Divinity School. In 1837 he was ordained at West Roxbury and soon became embroiled in the controversy over miracles. His sermon on "The Transient and Permanent in Christianity" caused a storm when it was delivered, and Parker found himself ostracized by the main body of the Unitarian ministry of Boston. Four years later he was invited to that city to head the Twenty-Eighth Congregational Society, which met, from 1852 on, in the Music Hall, where Parker's audiences often numbered two or three thousand. In Boston he turned more and more to social and political matters and to reform movements of all kinds; his contribution to the cause of abolition was enormous. His reputation grew steadily until his death, and in the long run he has probably had a greater impact on modern Unitarianism than any other single individual.

(Sarah) Margaret Fuller (1810–1850). Margaret Fuller embodied more strains of romanticism than any of her American contemporaries. She was born in Cambridgeport, Massachusetts, and her early education was administered by her father, who had her learn Latin at six and read Shakespeare, Cervantes, and Molière before her teens. She taught school for a while; conducted highly successful "conversations" for the bluestockings of Boston from 1839 to 1844; and was chief editor of *The Dial* from 1840 to 1842. Brilliant, homely, demanding, a virtuoso of lofty and rhapsodic emotion, she lived intensely within herself, in her letters, and in her relations with a whole range of distinguished persons, from Emerson to Mazzini and the Brownings. After leaving Boston, she wrote criticism for the New York *Tribune* and published

her best-known book, *Woman in the Nineteenth Century* (1845), an expansion of her earlier *Dial* article, "The Great Lawsuit." In 1846 she went to Europe, became involved as a nurse in the Roman republican uprising, and married the Marchese Angelo Ossoli, a man younger and considerably less intellectual than herself. She, her husband, and their child were drowned in a shipwreck off Fire Island as they were returning to America.

Jones Very (1810–1888). Very was not really a Transcendentalist, but his work was read, published, and admired by the Transcendentalists, for whom his intense mysticism provided an illustration of their poetic theories. Except for his early years, his life was without incident. He was born in Salem, graduated from Harvard in 1836, and served as tutor there for a while until his eccentricities made it impossible for him to continue. He was possessed by a sort of beneficent religious mania, which made him impatient with secular concerns and convinced him that his poems were dictated by God. After 1840 Very subsided into relative normalcy and passed the rest of his years in quiet and seclusion at his ancestral home in Salem.

James Freeman Clarke (1810–1888). Clarke was one of the most active of the group of Unitarian-Transcendentalist ministers. He was born in Hanover, New Hampshire, but was brought up in Boston and went to Harvard, where he finished his studies at the Divinity School in 1833. He went to Louisville, Kentucky, to serve in the Unitarian pulpit there, and he edited the *Western Messenger* from 1836 to 1839. This periodical was a valiant attempt to import eastern Unitarian culture into the hinterland; it was also the first to come under marked Transcendentalist influence. Clarke returned to Boston in 1840, began a new ministry there, and played a leading part in educational and reform activities. He was a prolific writer on religious subjects, a member of the State Board of Education and the Harvard Board of Overseers, and for several years a professor in the Divinity School.
Christopher Pearse Cranch (1813–1892). Cranch had the most varied talents—for painting, music, poetry, and society —of any of the Unitarian ministers belonging to the Transcendentalist party. He was born in Alexandria, then part of

the District of Columbia, attended Columbian College, and entered the Harvard Divinity School in 1831. He preached in various places in New England and the Midwest, settling for a while in Louisville, where he helped edit the *Western Messenger*. In the 1840's Cranch decided to cultivate his interest in painting and took it up professionally, though with only moderate success. He spent three years in Rome where he knew Browning, and from 1853 to 1863 lived in Paris. The rest of his life was spent chiefly in New York and Cambridge, Massachusetts.

John Sullivan Dwight (1813–1893). Born in Boston, Dwight was educated at Harvard, where he graduated in 1832, and at the Divinity School. Apparently destined for the usual ministerial career, he served at Northampton for about a year in 1840–41, and then gave it up for good. He spent the next several years at Brook Farm, where his first love, music, became his vocation. He organized and conducted choral groups, taught the children of Brook Farm, and wrote many reviews and articles for *The Dial* and *The Harbinger*, Brook Farm's socialist organ. In 1851 he founded *Dwight's Journal of Music,* which continued for nearly thirty years as the leading American periodical concerned with music and one of the most influential of our history.

Henry David Thoreau (1817–1862). Thoreau's major work, of course, was *Walden* (1854), but the impulse to write poetry, to reduce and compress his expression to a quintessential form, was early and constant with him. Most of his own work, however, is labored and awkward. In the translations from Anacreon included in this volume, he exhibits a quite unexpected charm and the capacity to respond to quite unexpected feelings: the refined sensuality and offhand irony of his classic author. The translations are his best poetic work. Thoreau passed most of his life in and around Concord. He graduated from Harvard in 1837, served an apprenticeship to Emerson in the early forties, and then struck out on his own. Outwardly his career was desultory: surveyor, lecturer, saunterer, pencil maker, writer. Inwardly he was gripped by one consuming ambition: to wrest from nature the moments of visionary unity which were life's redemption. He pushed the Emersonian Transcendental ideal as far toward practical realization as seems humanly possible.

SELECTED BIBLIOGRAPHY

ANTHOLOGIES OF TRANSCENDENTALIST WRITINGS

Miller, Perry, ed. *The Transcendentalists: An Anthology.* Cambridge, Mass., 1950.
———. *The American Transcendentalists, Their Prose and Poetry.* New York, 1957.
Myerson, Joel, ed. *Transcendentalism, A Reader.* New York, 2000.

CRITICAL AND HISTORICAL WORKS RELATED TO TRANSCENDENTALISM

Albanese, Catherine. *Corresponding Motion: Transcendental Religion and the New America.* Philadelphia, 1977.
Asselineau, Roger. *The Transcendentalist Constant in American Literature.* New York, 1980.
Barbour, Brian M., ed. *American Transcendentalism: An Anthology of Criticism.* Notre Dame, 1973.
Boller, Paul F. *American Transcendentalism, 1830–1860: An Intellectual Inquiry.* New York, 1974.
Brooks, Van Wyck. *The Flowering of New England, 1815–1865.* New York, 1941.
Buell, Lawrence. *Literary Transcendentalism: Style and Vision in the American Renaissance.* Ithaca, N.Y., 1973.
Capper, Charles, and Conrad Edick Wright, eds. *Transient and Permanent: The Transcendentalist Moment and Its Contexts.* Boston, 1999.
Chai, Leon. *The Romantic Foundations of the American Renaissance.* Ithaca, N.Y., 1987.

Francis, Richard. *Transcendental Utopias: Individual and Community at Brook Farm, Fruitlands, and Walden.* Ithaca, N.Y., 1997.

Frothingham, Octavius Brooks. *Transcendentalism in America: A History.* New York, 1876.

Haraszti, Zoltan. *The Idyll of Brook Farm.* Boston, 1937.

Howe, Daniel Walker. *The Unitarian Conscience: Harvard Moral Philosophy, 1805–1861.* Cambridge, Mass., 1970.

Hutchison, William R. *The Transcendentalist Ministers.* New Haven, 1959.

Koster, Donald N. *Transcendentalism in America.* Boston, 1975.

Matthiessen, F. O. *American Renaissance.* New York, 1941.

Miller, Perry. *Nature's Nation.* Cambridge, Mass., 1967.

Mott, Wesley T., ed. *Biographical Dictionary of Transcendentalism.* Westport, Conn., 1996.

———. *Encyclopedia of Transcendentalism.* Westport, Conn., 1996.

Mumford, Lewis. *The Golden Day.* New York, 1926.

Rose, Anne C. *Transcendentalism as a Social Movement, 1830–1850.* New Haven, 1981.

Stoehr, Taylor. *Nay-saying in Concord: Emerson, Alcott, and Thoreau.* Hamden, Conn., 1979.

Versluis, Arthur. *American Transcendentalism and Asian Religions.* New York, 1993.

Vogel, Stanley M. *German Literary Influence on the American Transcendentalists.* New Haven, 1955.

Wright, Conrad. *The Beginnings of Unitarianism in America.* Boston, 1955.

Wright, Conrad, ed. *American Unitarianism, 1805–1865.* Boston, 1989.

Ziff, Larzer. *Literary Democracy: The Declaration of Cultural Independence in America.* New York, 1981.

THE INTERNET

American Transcendentalism Web: www.transcendentalism.org